New millennium, new perspectives

UNU Millennium Series

Series editors: Hans van Ginkel and Ramesh Thakur

The *UNU Millennium Series* examines key international trends for peace, governance, human development, and the environment into the twenty-first century, with particular emphasis upon policy relevant recommendations for the United Nations. The series also contributes to broader academic and policy debate concerning the challenges that are faced at the international level at the turn of the Millennium, and envisions potential for partnerships among states, international organizations, and civil society actors in collectively addressing these challenges.

New millennium, new perspectives: The United Nations, security, and governance

Edited by Ramesh Thakur and Edward Newman

United Nations University Press
TOKYO • NEW YORK • PARIS

© The United Nations University, 2000

The views expressed in this publication are those of the authors and do not necessarily reflect the views of the United Nations University.

The United Nations University
53-70, Jingumae 5-chome,
Shibuya-ku, Tokyo, 150-8925, Japan
Tel: +81-3-3499-2811   Fax: +81-3-3406-7345
E-mail: sales@hq.unu.edu
http://www.unu.edu

United Nations University Office in North America
2 United Nations Plaza, Room DC2-1462-70, New York, NY 10017, USA
Tel: +1-212-963-6387   Fax: +1-212-371-9454
E-mail: unuona@igc.apc.org

Cover design by Joyce C. Weston

Printed in the United States of America

UNUP-1054
ISBN 92-808-1054-5

Contents

Tables and figures vii

1 Introduction 1
   Ramesh Thakur

2 Security and governance in the new millennium:
   Observations and syntheses 7
   Edward Newman

Security

3 The Security Council in the 1990s: Inconsistent,
   improvisational, indispensable? 21
   David M. Malone

4 Intervention: Trends and challenges 46
   Chantal de Jonge Oudraat

5 Trends in military expenditure and arms transfers ... 77
   Elisabeth Sköns

6 "Alliances" and regional security developments: The role
   of regional arrangements in the United Nations' promotion
   of peace and stability 108
   Brian Job

7 Weapons of mass destruction 131
    Trevor Findlay

8 "New" and "non-traditional" security challenges 150
    Paul Stares

Governance

9 Recasting global governance 163
    Samuel Makinda

10 Democracy and regression 182
    Sakuntala Kadirgamar-Rajasingham

11 Civil society and global governance 205
    Michael Edwards

12 The United Nations and human rights 220
    David Forsythe

13 Gender and international society: Law and policy 242
    Christine Chinkin

14 Decentralized governance for human development 261
    G. Shabbir Cheema and Mounir Tabet

15 Governing global public goods in a multi-actor world:
    The role of the United Nations 296
    Inge Kaul

Contributors 317

Index 319

Tables and figures

Tables

4.1 UN Security Council sanctions imposed under Chapter VII of the UN Charter, 1945–2000 48
4.2 Uses of military force authorized by the UN Security Council under Chapter VII of the UN Charter, 1945–2000 50
5.1 World military expenditure, 1949–85 81
5.2 World military expenditure, 1989–98 82
5.3 Regional military expenditure estimates, 1989–98 83
5.4 Volume of imports of major conventional weapons, 1988–98 85
5.5 Leading suppliers of major conventional weapons, 1994–98 86
5.6 Military expenditures as a percentage of GDP, selected countries, 1990–98 87
5.7 Largest arms-producing countries, 1996 93
6.1 Forms of multilateral security management 112
6.2 Regional, subregional, and interregional organizations: Peace-keeping and peace-related activities 119
6.3 Budget estimates of organizations and their peace-related programmes, 1997 126
14.1 Political decentralization in selected countries, 1999 269

14.2 Extent of fiscal decentralization in selected countries,
1990–97 272
14.3 Sustainable human development objectives in the case
studies 279
14.4 Good governance principles in the case studies 283
15.1 Global concerns as global public goods:
A selective typology 300

Figures
14.1 Decentralization and good governance 278
14.2 Service delivery and institutional structures 282
14.3 Participation 285
14.4 Initiative and leadership 289

1

Introduction

Ramesh Thakur

The business of the world has changed almost beyond recognition over the course of the last hundred years. At the turn of the last century, Japan was the first country outside Europe to break into the ranks of the great powers. Yet even until the Second World War, international affairs were largely Eurocentric in composition, concern, and agenda.

There are many more actors today, and their patterns of interaction are far more complex. In 1950, the soldier and the diplomat could still be said to symbolize the two lead actors on the world stage. In 2000, the international peace-keeper, financier, and NGO activist have noisily clambered aboard as well—not to mention the terrorist, the drug smuggler, and the currency speculator. The national bureaucrat must work alongside the international civil servant.

The United Nations

International organizations touch our daily lives in myriad ways. They are an essential means of conducting world affairs more satisfactorily than would be possible under conditions of international anarchy or total self-help. The United Nations lies at their legislative and normative centre.

One hundred years ago, although a considerable body of discourse and proposals had been advanced, the first large general international organization had not yet been established. Although the League of Nations died under the weight of the Second World War in the middle of the twentieth century, the *idea* of a universal organization dedicated to protecting peace and promoting welfare—of achieving a better life in a safer world, for all—survived the death, destruction, and disillusionment of the war.

The threshold of the new millennium is also the cusp of a new era in world affairs. In this period of transition, the United Nations is the focus of hopes and aspirations for a future where men and women live at peace with themselves and in harmony with nature.

The Charter of the United Nations, which codifies best-practice state behaviour, was a triumph of hope and idealism over the experience of two world wars. The flame flickered in the chill winds of the Cold War, but did not, and must not, die out. The global public goods of peace, prosperity, sustainable development, and good governance cannot be achieved by any country acting on its own. The United Nations is still the symbol of our dreams for a better world, where weakness can be compensated by justice and fairness, and the law of the jungle replaced by the rule of law.

The sad reality is that the twentieth century was the most murderous on record. The need for international assistance in many continents is an unhappy reminder of man's inhumanity against fellow man and his rapaciousness against nature. Furthermore, almost three billion people living in abject poverty will have had neither the spirit nor the means to cheer the arrival of the new millennium.

In consolidating gains and mitigating setbacks, sustained success requires us all to make a greater commitment to the vision and values of the United Nations, and to make systematic use of the UN forum and modalities for international collaboration.

UNU mission and roles

The United Nations University is an institution, based in Japan but with a global reach and network, that is engaged with the world of problem-solving scholarship through the United Nations system and beyond. Its mission is to contribute, through research and capacity-building, to efforts to resolve the pressing global problems that now concern the United Nations, its Member States, and their peoples.

The forward-looking, problem-solving orientation of the United Nations University distinguishes its work from that of traditional universities. It eschews basic research for its own sake, focusing instead on education and research for the United Nations, the international scientific community, and the people of the world. It tries to bring the state of scientific scholarship to bear on problems of international public policy.

Knowledge and information are said to be power. Over the course of the millennium, there has occurred the progressive democratization, secularization, and universalization of knowledge. Previously it was restricted to a narrow circle of courtiers and/or members of the religious hierarchy and served to reinforce the social status and authority of the elite. Today it is a basic right, an entitlement owed to everyone as a human being. Literacy in the industrialized world is universal. Among developing countries, it is increasingly seen as a prerequisite for, as well as an indicator of, development.

Scientists emphasize complexity and nuance and eschew simplistic solutions based on simple-minded analyses. The scholar is more comfortable with the subtle footnote than with the soundbite. Policy-makers demand instant prescriptions within the urgency of real-time constraints and incomplete information. They abhor jargon. The taxpayer supports university research—in many countries directly, through publicly funded educational institutions, and in some cases indirectly, through the provision of public goods without which the private sector could not run universities at a reasonable cost.

The millennium conference

The United Nations University is all about bridging the gap: between theory and practice, scholarship and diplomacy, and the United Nations and the world community of scholars; between governments, non-governmental organizations (NGOs), and people. The landmark millennium conference of January 2000—where the papers in this volume were initially presented—was an important demonstration of how the United Nations University can implement its mandate with respect to its many constituencies. The conference had three integral and complementary elements that were organized to create new ideas and fresh thinking relevant to the United Nations and, in a wider sense, to the challenges faced by humanity.

First, the plenary session at the opening, including the keynote speech of Deputy Secretary-General Louise Fréchette, served as a high profile "kick-off" event to lay out the challenges and the agenda that confront the United Nations. Secondly, four parallel working groups—for human development, security, governance, and the environment—took stock of key international trends and considered their implications in these areas as we move into the twenty-first century. The groups were a focused and interdisciplinary exercise aimed at producing substantive policy-orientated ideas. The themes and topics were selected in consultation with the Strategic Planning Unit of the Executive Office of the Secretary-General.

Most of the position papers were forwarded to New York in advance of the Tokyo conference and were used in the preparations for the Secretary-General's Millennium Assembly report. The results of the discussions at the time of the conference were also forwarded to the Executive Office of the Secretary-General.

During the working sessions—where the real scientific work took place—the authors of all papers were asked to address the following:

- The major trends and policy implications/recommendations;
- The impact of globalization;
- The key challenges in the short and medium terms (up to the year 2005);
- How national governments and the international community might more broadly address the challenges;
- What comparative advantage the United Nations has, or might have, in working with and in the name of the international community in addressing the challenges;
- The potential for partnerships among states, international organizations, the private sector, and civil society actors in collectively addressing these challenges;
- The element of "surprise" or unpredictability—whether it is possible to identify critical triggers of unforeseeable potential developments.

Thirdly, the public plenary on the final day (21 January) concluded, synthesized, and projected the key issues and challenges of the conference into the new millennium. During the plenary, a number of prominent authorities delivered keynote speeches that considered the key subjects of the conference with reference to the following themes. Firstly, vision: looking ahead to where, from their point of view, they would like the world to be at the turn of the *next* century. Then, they considered what is realistic and feasible: what practical steps will need to be taken over the next hundred years for the world to achieve this state by the turn of the next century?

Confronting the challenge

As we stand on the threshold of the new millennium, the locus of power and influence is shifting. The demands and expectations made on governments and international organizations by the people of the world can no longer be satisfied through isolated and self-contained efforts.

The salience of territorial frontiers is steadily declining in today's seamless world. The partial erosion of the once sacrosanct principle of national sovereignty is rooted today in the reality of global interdependence: no country is an island unto itself any more. The international policy-making stage is increasingly congested as private and public non-state actors jostle alongside national governments in setting and implementing the agenda of the new century. The multitude of new actors adds depth and texture to the increasingly rich tapestry of international civil society.

Diplomacy is undergoing revolutionary change as a consequence. In Seattle, for example, an odd alliance of opponents including environmental and human rights activists, organized labour, and cultural and economic nationalists helped to defeat efforts to begin a new round of world trade talks. Trade may be global but politics is still local, and the alliances of convenience forged to frustrate the World Trade Organization (WTO) proved more effective than the standard model of diplomatic negotiation among governments.

The old order of the pursuit of national interests and formal alliances through state-to-state relations is giving way to ad hoc "coalitions of the willing" in pursuit of agreed-upon international goals. Attention to child soldiers, children as war victims, and child poverty represent another element in the shift from "national security" to "human security." This shift presents a great challenge to national diplomats, NGOs, and the United Nations to work in partnership with one another. They are required to reinterpret and use the UN Charter in pursuit of security for the peoples of the world, as well as that of member governments.

New diplomacy has been driven by a growing intensity of public impatience with the settled pace and contours of traditional diplomacy. On environmental and human rights issues in particular, the people of the world, in whose name the United Nations was founded, have grown tired of years of negotiations leading to a final product that may be accepted or rejected by countries. They look instead for a rolling process of self-adjusting agreements that can respond quickly to growing scientific understanding. This also means that new diplomacy has a feel of improvisation about it as officials scramble to cope with the rapidly changing diplomatic terrain from one issue and region to the next.

In this vastly more complex, interlinked, and mutually dependent world, an enduring basis for a stable world order lies not in the threat or use of military force but in the patient building of institutions which embody norms and behaviour that ordinary people and countries value and seek—backed if necessary by properly authorized force. Changes are under way. Change offers new opportunities to move beyond the bloody nationalisms of the past century, to a new century of peace based on the welfare of all people everywhere.

Universities are the marketplace of ideas. The United Nations University lies at the interface of the interaction between ideas, international organizations, and international public policy. The United Nations has the responsibility to maintain international peace and security and promote human development. Scientists have a duty to make their knowledge available for the betterment of humanity. The United Nations University has the mandate to link the two normally isolated worlds of scholarship and policy-making. This volume is an effort, however modest, to fulfill our mandate.

2
Security and governance in the new millennium: Observations and syntheses

Edward Newman

New thinking in governance and security

The bases and modalities of security and governance—both within and between societies—are evolving. In parallel, the interconnectedness, and sometimes interdependencies, between security and governance are increasingly understood. It follows, as we consider collective responses to the challenges of security and governance at the international level, that these two subjects should be considered together, in an integrated manner.

"Security" lies at the heart of our individual and communal existence. It is the public good from which all other individual and societal values and goods can flourish. Whilst our basic human needs have changed little, our conceptualization of security, and our approaches to achieving and maintaining security, have undergone a rapid evolution. Progressive models of security—"human security"—are based upon a comprehensive security from fear, conflict, ignorance, poverty, social and cultural deprivation, and hunger, which are built on positive and negative freedoms. Human security is thus a paradigm; a broad, comprehensive, and integrated matrix of all the tenets of life that give meaning to, and support, human existence.

Governance is the means through which we collectively provide security in all its forms. Governance describes the modalities, values, and institutions that we employ to organize human life at all levels, within and between societies. Governance is a vehicle for optimizing certain goods—peace, prosperity, health—and responding to challenges or problems, such as conflict, environmental degradation, poverty, and underdevelopment. Traditionally, a sharp distinction was made between governance within states and between them. However, transnational forces are conditioning and transforming norms of governance at all levels. In the "domestic" context, the growing consensus within and between states is that certain standards of governance—based upon participation, transparency, equality, and accountability—are conducive to sound development, and that stable, plural societies are more likely to ensure peace within and between societies. They can also play a particularly important role in post-conflict and divided societies. Thus, issues of governance *within* states are of direct relevance to peace and security *between* states, and are therefore a legitimate issue of contemporary international relations.

In parallel, expectations of governance in international organizations are evolving; transparency, accountability, and representation—in a word, legitimacy—are increasingly demanded of international forms of governance. This is not just a matter of ethics; legitimacy also comes from efficiency. Globalization and the broadening and deepening activities of international organizations are also placing severe strain upon narrow intergovernmental approaches. Partnership between different types of actors—intergovernmental organizations (IGOs), states, NGOs, commercial entities—is therefore increasingly recognized as an essential approach to problem-solving. Yet evolving theoretical frameworks do not necessarily translate into enlightened policies. While the means and knowledge for addressing most challenges exists, the political will and consensus required for collective action often does not. Bridging the gap between new ways of thinking—indeed, new paradigms—and policy is the most daunting remaining challenge. This volume seeks to make a contribution to the bridging of this gap.

Changing context

A number of systemic international changes have underscored these developments in governance and security. First, the end of the Cold War eroded the bipolar model of international relations that had provided the context—but sometimes a pretext—for the extremes of the national security paradigm in theory and practice. The traditional model of international relations—based on the need for states to survive and increase power in an anarchical system of deterrence and counterbalances—was losing both intellectual currency and policy utility. The end of the Cold War coincided with—and, to an extent, was intertwined with—a challenge to the state-centric, power-based concept of international politics that prioritised "high politics" above all else. The "changing context" appeared to have brought an increased opportunity to address "global" problems—among them ethnic strife, the management of weapons of mass destruction, environmental and population problems, illegal narcotics, and HIV/AIDS—at the international level, and a growing acceptance of a wider conception of peace and security. There has simultaneously been a broadening of attitudes regarding the unit of analysis in international politics and a growing recognition of the key role of non-state actors.

The second factor, globalization, is fundamental to this changing context. The breaking down of national economic boundaries, the internationalization of production, and the general deregulation and marketization of national economies in the context of networks of international rules and standards are having a huge impact upon governance and security. These rules and standards are increasingly codified and upheld—and even enforced—by regional and global institutions and international agreements, building networks of regulation and authority that transcend national bases. Moreover, these economic trends are paralleled and facilitated by a broader globalization in many other areas, such as culture and political ideas. The state enclosure is being undermined as national economic tools are less and less effective in the face of a globalized finance and commodities market and current advances in information technology. The socio-economic impact of the processes of globalization has often been a severe challenge to security and governance.

In this context, power is becoming increasingly diffuse; globalizing forces in economics, information, and culture, and various fragmentary forces, are imposing pressures upon the state from above and below. The utility of traditional power political tools is increasingly in question. Years ago, Keohane and Nye popularized the concept of "complex interdependence" which argued that the nature of international politics was changing: states were increasingly entrenched in transnational economic interdependencies that were altering the nature of national interest and national security and reducing the utility of military power.[1] This process has since accelerated. Within this already complicated environment there are paradoxical forces at work: localization and globalization, fragmentation and integration. Many issues and processes have an ever-wider sphere of influence, but—in a seemingly contradictory manner—some societies are reverting to narrower identities, perhaps in a reaction against globalizing or homogenizing forces, in favour of reasserting culture, religion, and diversity. Sometimes this is manifested in conflict. In the realm of international politics, the traditional key characteristic, state sovereignty, has likewise undergone change. Kofi Annan stated that:

. . . the State is now widely understood to be the servant of its people, and *notice versa*. At the same time, individual sovereignty—and by this I mean the human rights and fundamental freedoms of each and every individual as enshrined in our Charter—has been enhanced by a renewed consciousness of the right of every individual to control his or her own destiny.[2]

Thirdly, normative changes have underpinned, and resulted from, these developments, and taken on a momentum of their own. This has conditioned expectations and standards of governance within and between communities. There has been an internationalization of standards of political morality and governance—international law, regimes, political norms—that have increasingly impinged upon "national" laws and norms. Forms of government, human rights and gender equality, rights to development, and education have all become "international" issues.

The cumulative effect is that the human needs and rights that form the matrix of human security—in the areas of economics, education, health, culture, and civil and political rights—take on an increasingly central role in political decision-making at all levels. People's awareness and expectations of rights—in the context of the neighbourhood, national communities, and global regimes—are raised as a result of this. Forms of governance that do not respond to this are seen increasingly as inefficient and illegitimate. Similarly, people's expectations and attitudes towards governance and authority have evolved. Transparency, accountability, representation, and justice—the central tenets of democracy—now form the benchmark from which all forms of governance are judged, at all levels. In parallel with this rising awareness of rights and expectations, legitimate governance is increasingly judged not as an end in itself but as a means to an end, to be judged by its ability to serve the people from whose name it derives and is given authority. In the parlance of political science, the balance of legitimacy is shifting from the procedural dimensions of governance to substantive outputs of governance, measured in human welfare terms.

Thus, in recent years, the individual has been accorded greater prominence in international governance and codes of conduct. Shifts in attitudes—and, at a slower rate, shifts in policy—are placing increasing emphasis upon human rights and human needs in a model of "human security." This model goes beyond traditional military and state-centric concepts of security, and increasingly blurs the distinction between the international and domestic realms, embracing a far wider agenda than is traditionally accepted. In line with this, the visible processes and agendas of international politics are clearly changing. New actors are likewise making their presence known. If one considers the "Jubilee 2000" movement that has been working for debt relief, the movement that culminated in the convention banning landmines, the opposition that saw the derailing of the Multilateral Agreement on Investments, and the demonstrations that challenged the 1999 WTO forum in Seattle, we see a whole new range of alliances, actors, and agendas at work that has taken us beyond the traditional scope of international politics and diplomacy. At the same time, certain institutions or values—such as national security and state sovereignty—appear increasingly in tension with others, such as human rights and human security. This is the new international politics.

The theme that underlies, and is common to, the changing meaning of security and governance is the focus upon the human as the level of analysis. Further to this, a number of overarching themes present themselves:

- The interconnectedness of issues—and therefore solutions—relating to security and governance;
- The growing multiplicity of actors that must be brought together in synergetic partnerships;
- The importance of having the right balance between subsidiarity—whereby problems and solutions are orientated around the people that are affected by them, at the local level—and intersocietal approaches, whether international or global, on matters of governance and security;
- The growing importance of legitimacy within governance and security mechanisms; the efficacy of "legitimate" politics over "power politics" in the forging of institutions and consensus around problem-solving endeavours.

The chapters that comprise this volume present a number of issues and challenges relating to security and governance in a policy-orientated, forward-looking manner. They address a number of overarching questions that highlight points of commonality in problem-solving ethos and methodology, and demonstrate the extent to which security and governance are integrated. These themes are:

- The impact of globalization: how these economic, political, and cultural processes condition the challenges of governance and security, and how they must therefore be embraced in the international community's responses, as well as how new challenges can be used as new opportunities and in turn as new tools for dealing with challenges;
- Key challenges in the short and medium terms that suggest areas of prioritization;
- The manner in which national governments and the international community might more broadly address the issues involved in the light of evolving understanding of the challenges—and interconnectedness—of governance and security;

- The comparative advantage the United Nations might have in working with the international community in addressing the challenges: its diplomatic and political resources; its legitimacy as a broad-based, "universal" organization; its capacity for bringing together disparate interests; and its record as an agent of peaceful change;
- The potential for partnerships among states, international organizations, commercial organizations, and civil society actors, in collectively addressing challenges of security and governance;
- The element of "surprise" or unpredictability; potential critical developments in governance and security issues.

Security

David Malone's chapter, "The Security Council in the 1990s: Inconsistent, improvisational, indispensable?", examines the structure and impact of the UN organ with primacy in areas of peace and security. He argues that the decisions of the Security Council over the last decade have eroded the foundations of absolute state sovereignty and fundamentally altered the way in which many of us perceive the relationship between state and citizen all over the world. The Security Council has redefined what constitutes a threat to international peace and security and stimulated several radical legal developments at the international level; notably, the creation of the International Criminal Tribunals that in turn greatly intensified pressure for a more universal International Criminal Court. The Security Council is a focus of the continuing struggle to address questions relating to the nature of the post–Cold War security environment and an appropriate role within it for the UN organization. Throughout the 1990s, the United Nations became more deeply engaged in the process of democratization and with issues relating to human rights and humanitarianism. The organization has demonstrated a number of strengths, including the successful monitoring and support of large-scale refugee movements, as well as a number of weaknesses, including an inability to conduct effective Chapter VII military operations. One of the most striking developments has been the recognition of a broadening and multi-faceted agenda of security, embracing human rights and needs, socio-economic issues, and justice in political problem-solving. NGOs are also being increasingly embraced within this widening agenda of peace and security.

Paradoxically, perhaps, a measure of the Security Council's success—its improved decision-making ability and informality—has raised tensions within the rest of the organization. There has been a perceived marginalization of weaker voices within the United Nations that suggests that, amongst the discussion on reform of the Security Council, any new formula must contain a greater emphasis upon consensus and creative diplomacy, and less on power politics in the traditional sense. Middle powers, such as Canada, have been instrumental in demonstrating the practical utility of such an approach.

Chantal de Jonge Oudraat's chapter on "Intervention: Trends and challenges" deals with intervention in internal conflicts. It focuses on three questions—whether to intervene, who intervenes, how to intervene—and identifies the patterns and challenges that this growing phenomenon involves. In the 1990s, the UN Security Council has increasingly intervened to stop communal violence. The Council has considered that the gross violation of human rights represents a threat to international peace and security and, in several cases, has authorized the use of force to put a stop to such violence. In other cases, the UN Security Council has failed to equate gross human rights abuses with threats to international peace and security and has failed to authorize the use of force to end them. It is this failure to act, along with the intervention by the United States and its NATO allies in Kosovo and the former Yugoslavia in March 1999, that has reinvigorated the debate over the appropriateness of humanitarian intervention.[3] With respect to the instruments of intervention, Oudraat argues that six conditions need to be fulfilled for the effective use of these instruments: outside powers need to have a clear political objective; they need to correctly identify and assess the political, economic, and military characteristics of the group they seek to coerce; one party needs to take the lead in the intervention; whoever takes the lead must build widespread international support; sufficient resources need to be made available; and outside powers need to develop an appropriate strategy, including escalation, exit, and post-intervention strategies.

Elisabeth Sköns' contribution examines trends in military expenditure and arms transfers and identifies a number of patterns, globally and regionally, that are both expected and unexpected. The end of the Cold War brought a reduction in military expenditures and international arms transfers in global, regional, and national terms. The level of arms transfers decreased at the beginning of the post–Cold War period, yet recent figures indicate a possible shift towards an upward trend; world military expenditure may be experiencing a similar shift, towards a slightly upward trend. In addition, hopes for a "peace dividend"—a diversion of resources to peaceful uses after the Cold War—have been largely unrealized. The amount of global economic resources spent on military activities remains staggering. In 1998, world military expenditure corresponded to 2.6 percent of aggregate world GNP. The challenges are to reduce world military spending and redirect the released resources to more economically and socially beneficial uses; to improve security regimes and security in all its aspects; to promote non-military policies and measures for providing security; and to ensure that there is an appropriate match between existing security requirements and the nature of the perceived threat. Sköns also observes the need to address the growing phenomenon of private security forces and "vested interests" that fuel arms expenditure.

Brian Job's chapter, "Alliances and regional security developments: The role of regional arrangements in the United Nations' promotion of peace and security," surveys the nature of multilateral regional arrangements, reviewing the rationale for their different forms and functions and then looking at the shifts in the patterns of regional security arrangements and activities in the post–Cold War decade. He demonstrates where and how regional security mechanisms have been effective in Europe and the Asia-Pacific region and observes that conflict prevention through confidence-building, good offices, monitoring, inclusive dialogue, and consultation appears to be the key. Finally, Job considers how predominant patterns of conflict—namely intra-state, communal warfare in weak, failing, or predatory state environments—can be managed by arrangements (both regional and global) that are basically designed to preserve and protect the prerogatives of states. This fundamental dilemma will continue; the tension between human needs/security and the structure of international political life is an issue that is unavoidable at whatever level we consider security arrangements. The evolution of patterns of conflict also leads one to consider the development of new institutional forms for security and peace management that include non-state actors such as NGOs, and directly facilitate alternate strategies of preventive diplomacy and peacebuilding.

Trevor Findlay's contribution discusses trends and projections regarding weapons of mass destruction. His paper assesses the short- and medium-term outlook in the twenty-first century for weapons of mass destruction, examines the contradictory effects of globalization, and attempts to identify the major challenges ahead as well as the actors and measures that hold the most promise of tackling them. The recent past has been somewhat encouraging in the sense that most states are committed, through their membership in the Non-Preliferation Treaty (NPT), the Comprehensive Test Ban Treaty (CTBT), the Chemical Weapons Convention (CWC), and the Biological Weapons Convention (BWC), not to acquire weapons of mass destruction. Nevertheless, large numbers of nuclear weapons are still deployed on hair-trigger alert. Globalization has been simultaneously beneficial and harmful in relation to the spread of weapons of mass destruction. In making it harder to control knowledge, technology, and expertise, globalization makes it harder to control the spread of these weapons. Yet developments in information technology are permitting wider, faster dissemination of information to all parts of the globe, enhancing transparency. Further, the inability of governments to control the flow of information makes "societal verification" more likely. Findlay concludes that whilst there are multiple challenges—such as containing "nuclear leakage" from the former Soviet Union—the greatest need is for an initiative to break the gridlock that has developed between nuclear disarmament, ballistic missile defences, and nuclear non-proliferation. Only the United States, the predominant world power, is in a position to take a unilateral leap or propose a package deal to move the process forward.

Paul Stares focuses on the growing salience of so called "new" or "non-traditional" security challenges. This issue highlights a key question of contemporary politics, both within and between states: what should be the unit of analysis, or focus, of security? The state, the globe, or individuals? This chapter considers a normative reconceptualization of security that puts primary emphasis on protecting the well-being of people and the planet in general, rather than the survival of the state. By doing so, the range of conceivable security concerns broadens dramatically to include a host of economic, social, political, environmental, and epidemiological problems. This could be interpreted as evidence that a "paradigm shift" is underway and already well advanced. Yet the considerable resilience of the nation state along with traditional security practices should caution against oversimplification or drawing too much of a distinction between traditional and non-traditional security. The two are not necessarily mutually exclusive. The defence of the state as a policy goal can coexist alongside a desire to improve the human condition regardless of geographical location or citizenship. The comparative advantages that the United Nations has, according to Stares, comprise its leadership, legitimacy, labour, and logistics.

"Recasting global governance," by Samuel M. Makinda, demonstrates that global governance can be understood from several (value-based) perspectives that involve formal and informal regulatory mechanisms embracing many different types of actors. This chapter focuses on three themes: state sovereignty, globalization, and Western hegemony. Makinda argues that "global" governance in fact facilitates and reflects Western hegemony, and that a global "interpretive community" has sought to influence perceptions of international power structures as "global governance." He cautions against being too hasty in seeing changes in state sovereignty, although he admits the impact of globalization on the international system. His overriding point is that globalization is not value-free, and the main instruments of international governance—including the United Nations—are dominated by Western industrialized interests. Nevertheless, he concludes that the United Nations can help to shape global governance; but it must rethink its norms, structure, and procedures to reflect the multiplicity of actors that now impact upon international challenges and responses, and the emerging normative agenda.

Democracy has proliferated globally and broadened in terms of the issues that are considered to legitimately fall within its scope. Sakuntala Kadirgamar-Rajasingham's chapter, "Democracy and regression," identifies the uneven trends of democracy and the prospects for promoting democracy from "outside." There is a global trend towards democracy, although regression to authoritarian tendencies cannot be excluded, and whilst the procedural tenets of democracy are clearly proliferating, the substance of democracy does not necessarily always follow. This raises the issue of how the international community can effectively and efficiently support countries to establish and consolidate democratic regimes, building local capacity and institutions. Moreover, there is also the question of which model of democracy to embrace for a particular country, and the implications of adopting mixed democratic models. To a large degree, democracy and human rights are indivisible. However, democracy and human rights do not necessarily or automatically always develop in parallel, both theoretically and in practice. Indeed, according to the tradition of liberal democracy, some human rights exist to actually counteract or restrain majoritarian democracy, by indicating that certain issues—such as personal privacy and minority protection—should not be subject to majority legislation. Finally, by focusing on market efficiency rather than on the welfare of all the people, globalization brings new challenges as well as opportunities.

Analyses of democracy—and in fact governance in the broad sense, both within and between states—must embrace the multiplicity of, and relationships between, different types of actors. Internationally, non-governmental actors have made a systemically significant impact upon decision-making and agenda-setting. Michael Edwards' chapter, "Civil society and global governance," considers the rise of international NGOs against a number of backgrounds: changing ideas about international development, new conceptions of governance, and international commercial issues. The rhetoric of partnership and participation in promoting sustainable development has come to stay, definitely placing civil society at the centre of decision-making and problem-solving at the global level. Accompanying this transformation is a range of new challenges facing both the United Nations and non-state actors in global governance. Edwards identifies a number of challenges, including ensuring that NGOs and community-based organizations become legitimate, accountable, and representative; connecting the local and the global—linking, coherently, different levels of local, national, regional, and global activity; avoiding the tendency by some NGOs to focus on global advocacy to the exclusion of national-level processes; and supporting civic groups to move from "conversion strategies" (the traditional view of advocacy) to "engagement strategies" (aiming to support a process of dialogue).

Human rights—or human security or human needs—are clearly the focus and objective of governance and security. David Forsythe's chapter on human rights takes an expressly problem-solving approach. He argues that economics and human rights should be integrated, bringing the international financial institutions and transnational corporations into the human rights movement and paying more attention to socio-economic rights. In multilateral terms, he observes that the United States tendency towards exceptionalism, unilateralism, and neo-isolationism presents a major challenge. Similarly, correcting a tendency in the Security Council to rely too heavily on paper solutions rather than appropriately robust measures is essential. One institutional recommendation is to consider merging the human rights, humanitarian, and refugee regimes into one meta-regime—a "human dignity regime"—so as to improve protection and assistance *sur place*, thus coordinating the activities of United Nations High Commission for Refugees (UNHCR), UNICEF, the World Food Programme (WFP), the International Committee of the Red Cross (ICRC), and others, while not losing the ability to seek criminal prosecutions under existing treaties. Forsythe also demonstrates how improving the treatment of civilians in conflicts, promoting and strengthening procedures, and support of international criminal and humanitarian law are priority areas.

Christine Chinkin's chapter, "Gender and international society: Law and policy," demonstrates that women's rights and status have undergone changes over the last decade and that these have not been entirely positive. The formal articulation of the norm of non-discrimination on the grounds of sex, the inclusion of women within the discourse of development, and the shift towards the recognition of women's rights as human rights represent great leaps in the promotion of women's rights. The World Conference on Human Rights in Vienna in 1993 and the Beijing Platform for Action agreed upon at the Fourth World Conference on Women in 1995 were in many ways the culmination of these developments. An increasing awareness of women's rights, formal equality, and education have occurred at the same time as globalization and free market economics have in some cases marginalized the position of women. The challenge of mainstreaming gender is central to building upon the codification of gender rights and making them a reality.

In addition to the issues of "unit of analysis" and types of actors involved in governance, there is growing recognition given to the optimum geographical focus of governance. Globalizing trends may suggest the logic of ever-wider forms of organization. Yet this is sometimes contrary to the reality that needs are usually addressed most effectively and fairly by the people who themselves face the consequences of collective decision-making. The chapter by Shabbir Cheema and Mounir Tabet, "Decentralized governance for human development," demonstrates that decentralized governance can play an essential role in promoting and sustaining human development at the local and sub-national level, if properly planned and carefully implemented. Many countries in the world are beginning to acknowledge the importance of the role of local government, NGOs, and firms in meeting developmental challenges at the local and national levels. The chapter introduces the concepts of human development and decentralized governance and establishes the relationship between them, presenting five recent experiences in decentralization based upon original research.

Inge Kaul's chapter, "Governing global public goods in a multi-actor world: The role of the United Nations," presents a "public goods" paradigm for providing services and managing challenges within and between states. The chapter examines the role of the United Nations in ensuring an enhanced provision of global public goods (GPGs) and explores how the United Nations could help the international community to better manage—and govern—the provision of GPGs. The overall conclusion is that there is an urgent need for a custodian of GPG concerns. Today, GPG concerns are typically addressed one by one, and often managed in a technocratic way, by representatives of the executive branches of government and other sector specialists. Political governance of *global* issues is sorely lacking. The United Nations could help fill that vacuum. However, in order to do so, it would have to undergo a major transformation. It would have to turn from an intergovernmental technocratic organization into an intergovernmental parliamentary body. In a broader sense, her work also highlights the need to achieve greater complementarity between the activities of private and public actors in the transnational management of public goods.

Notes

1. Robert O. Keohane and J. S. Nye, *Power and Interdependence* (Boston: Little Brown, 1977).
2. Speech of the UN Secretary-General to the General Assembly, 20 September 1999.
3. See Albrecht Schnabel and Ramesh Thakur (eds.), *Kosovo and the challenge of humanitarian intervention: Selective indignation, collective action, and international citizenship* (Tokyo: United Nations University Press, 2000).

Security

3
The Security Council in the 1990s: Inconsistent, improvisational, indispensable?

David M. Malone

In discussing the United Nations' role in global governance in the new millennium, it may be useful to look back on the record of the UN Security Council during the 1990s. The question mark is the most important item in the title of this chapter, which seeks to address the Council's performance in recent years. The central thesis is this: through its decisions over the past ten years, largely improvised and inconsistent though they may be, the Security Council has, for good or ill, eroded the foundations of absolute conceptions of state sovereignty and fundamentally altered the ways in which many of us see the relationship between state and citizen the world over.

Introduction

One important signal of the thaw in the Cold War was a noticeable improvement in the climate among the Permanent Five (P5) members of the United Nations Security Council. The first evidence of the relaxation in East–West tensions within the Council was the cooperative manner in which these countries discussed options for the position of UN Secretary-General as Javier Pérez de Cuéllar's first term drew to a close in 1986. As it turned out, the P5 agreed without much difficulty to a second term for the incumbent who, in January 1987, challenged them publicly to tackle resolution of the murderous Iran–Iraq war.[1] As of mid-1987, Security

Council proposals for a cease-fire, monitored by a small UN observer mission, were making serious headway. The post–Cold War era, initially such a hopeful one, had started at the United Nations.

The ability and disposition of the five Permanent Members—those holding veto power—to cooperate with each other seriously diminished the margin for manoeuvre of the other Council members. Some of them had in earlier times developed skills and occupied political space as "helpful fixers" or, in the case of some developing nations, had learned how to play the Permanent Members off against one another, greatly amplifying the voice and enhancing the apparent influence of the Non-Aligned Movement (NAM) within the Council. Now non-permanent members were grumbling that they were systematically marginalized, a complaint lent more weight by a tendency of the Secretariat to consult privately with some or all of the P5 before advancing recommendations to the Council as a whole. This tacit collusion between the P5 and the Secretariat was aggravated, from the perspective of other members, by the growing tendency to resort to "informal consultations" for decision-making purposes, rather than the open Council meetings which had served as the principal forum for Council decision-making in earlier decades. Non-permanent members of the Council made little impression on the whole and rarely sought to challenge the P5's cosy new arrangements.[2] However, where a non-permanent member has an activist, coherent, and compelling agenda to pursue—as is, for example, the case with Canadian Foreign Minister Lloyd Axworthy's human security agenda—and when it is also well represented in New York—as is the case with the current Canadian Permanent Representative, Robert Fowler—new ideas can be introduced into the Council and advanced incrementally.[3] However, such efforts are never easy and rarely progress fast.

The 1990s were marked by the Council's disposition to tackle many more conflicts than it had been able to earlier, when it was stymied by Cold War animosities and the plethora of vetoes (cast and threatened) by the Permanent Members. The 1990s witnessed a sharp drop in the use of the veto, accompanying the introduction of a culture of accommodation among the Permanent Five, and momentous shifts in the Council's approach to conflicts and their resolution. Factors held by the Council as constituting a threat to international peace expanded to include a range of humanitarian catastrophes, particularly those generating large exoduses of displaced persons and refugees, internally and internationally.[4] This, in turn, allowed the Council to address a range of conflicts, mostly internal in nature, which it most likely would have avoided in the past when the Cold War antagonists often played out their hostility through regional proxies and were prepared to frustrate Council involvement. The Council's decisions in the 1990s proved highly innovative in shaping the normative framework for international relations and stimulated several radical legal developments at the international level, notably the creation of International Criminal Tribunals for the former Yugoslavia in 1993 and Rwanda in 1994. This in turn greatly intensified pressure for a more universal International Criminal Court, a Statute for which was adopted at a diplomatic conference in Rome in 1998.

Nevertheless, late in the decade, serious tensions resurfaced in the Council over issues relating to state sovereignty, legitimation of the use of force, and the growing incidence of unilateralism by some major UN members. Differences crystallized in 1998 and 1999 over conflicting objectives and approaches among the P5 to Iraq and Kosovo.

A number of characteristics mark the Council's record in the 1990s, under several broad headings.

The nature of the conflicts addressed by the Council, and of its decisions

The Council's willingness to involve itself in a broad range of internal conflicts forced it to confront hostilities of a much more complex nature than the inter-state disputes with which it had greater experience. These internal conflicts typically encompassed intercommunal strife, crises of democracy, fighting caused by a fierce struggle for control of national resources and wealth, and several other precipitating causes or incentives for continuation of war. International efforts to mitigate and resolve these conflicts required complex mandates significantly more ambitious than those which the modalities of "classic" peace-keeping were designed to meet.[5] The most striking features of the "new generation" peace-keeping operations (PKOs) launched by the Council in the 1990s were not so much the large numbers of military personnel involved—several earlier PKOs, such as in the Sinai, Congo, and even Cyprus had featured large deployments of Blue Helmets—but rather the important role and substantive diversity of their civilian and police components.[6] Civilian functions discharged by PKOs or otherwise mandated by the Council included civil administration (most notably in Namibia, Cambodia, and the former Yugoslavia); humanitarian assistance; human rights monitoring and training; police and judicial support, training, and reform; and even a degree of leadership on economic revival and development.[7] The ambitious objectives served by these activities proved significantly more difficult to attain in many circumstances than the Council seems to have anticipated. Even Council-mandated military activities encountered significant resistance by frequently shadowy belligerents, leading to incidents involving heavy loss of life amongst peace-keepers (in Rwanda, Somalia, and the former Yugoslavia). The UN Security Council's inability to induce compliance with its decisions fuelled two apparently contradictory but all too frequently complementary responses: on the one hand, it moved to enforce decisions which had failed to generate consent in the field, notably in the former Yugoslavia,[8] Somalia,[9] and Haiti;[10] on the other, in the face of significant casualties, it cut and ran, as in Somalia and at the outset of genocide in Rwanda.[11]

Resort to the provisions of Chapter VII of the UN charter and to enforcement of Council decisions was not new: Council decisions were enforced in Korea and to a much lesser extent in the Congo during the UN's early years. Nevertheless, the extent to which the Council adopted decisions under Chapter VII during the 1990s was wholly unprecedented. At first, it was hoped that the United Nations would prove capable of launching and managing enforcement operations. In the face of disappointing, occasionally catastrophic results in the former Yugoslavia and Somalia, it became clear to Member States—as many within the Secretariat, notably Under-Secretary General Marrack Goulding, had argued all along—that transition from peace-keeping to peace enforcement represented more than "mission creep." The two types of operations were, in fact, fundamentally different. One required consent and impartiality, the other required international personnel to confront one or several belligerent groups, albeit in defence of a Council mandate which was supposedly neutral relative to the parties in conflict. UN Secretary-General Boutros Boutros-Ghali concluded by 1994 that the UN should not itself seek to conduct large-scale enforcement activities. Consequently, the Security Council increasingly resorted for enforcement of its decisions to "coalitions of the willing" such as Operation Uphold Democracy (in Haiti, 1994–95); International Force and then Stabilization Force in Bosnia since 1995; MISAB in the Central African Republic, 1997; and International Force in East Timor in 1999.[12] It also alternately both worried about and supported in qualified terms enforcement activities by regional bodies, notably ECOMOG, the military arm of the West African economic cooperation arrangement ECOWAS (Economic Community of West African States), in Liberia and Sierra Leone. One enforcement technique, employed only once previously by the Council, against Rhodesia, was the resort to naval blockades to control access of prohibited goods to regions of conflict. Such blockades were mandated and occurred with varying success against Iraq in the Persian Gulf and the Gulf of Aqaba, against various parties in the former Yugoslavia on the Danube and in the Adriatic Sea, and against Haiti.[13]

More common than military enforcement decisions by the Council was the resort to mandatory economic (and, increasingly, diplomatic) sanctions under Chapter VII of the Charter.[14] While arms embargoes remained in vogue, imposition of comprehensive trade and other economic sanctions, seen as more gentle than the resort to force, faded noticeably once the humanitarian costs of sanctions regimes against Haiti and Iraq became widely known late in the decade. The ability of government regimes in countries struck by sanctions to enrich themselves greatly by controlling black markets in prohibited products also took some time to sink in. By then, more targeted sanctions—such as the ban on air flights to and from Libya, aimed at inducing Libyan cooperation with Council efforts to address several terrorist aircraft bombings, and diplomatic sanctions, such as the reduction in the level of diplomatic representation mandated by the Council against the Sudan following an assassination attempt in Addis Ababa against Egyptian President Hosni Mubarak—were more in favour.[15] Another example of targeted sanctions (addressing financial transactions and air links) went into effect on 14 November 1999 against the Taleban in Afghanistan over the protection they have provided to the alleged terrorist Osama Bin Laden.[16] Some advantages—but also the difficulty—of designing and implementing effective financial sanctions were brought to light by a useful research and dialogue initiative, the Interlaken process, sponsored by the Swiss Government in 1998–99. The German Government launched a similar project on arms embargoes and other forms of targeted sanctions in 1999,[17] while Canada, that same year, focused attention within the Security Council more broadly on the need for more effective, less counter-productive sanctions regimes.[18] Canada also provided creative and energetic leadership to the Council's Sanctions Committee for Angola, pressing for more rigorous application of its mandate to suffocate UNITA's ability to fund its war effort through the sale of diamonds.[19] This has resulted, *inter alia*, in the decision of the De Beers corporation to close down its operations in Angola.[20] A commission of experts on sanctions in Angola, chaired by Ambassador Anders Mollander of Sweden, will doubtless articulate further recommendations.[21]

Beyond issues of enforcement, the Council in the 1990s increasingly confronted, shaped and adapted to the role of regional organizations in seeking to prevent and resolve conflict. The Council initially did not seek a lead role on crises in the western hemisphere, such as those of Central America and of Haiti, preferring to leave the Organization of American States (OAS) in the driver's seat.[22] Nevertheless, in circumstances in which the OAS proved incapable of achieving a negotiated settlement alone or in which parties to conflict and affected regional powers displayed greater confidence in the United Nations, the Council, sometimes reluctantly, did move to centre stage, generally continuing to reserve some place for the OAS in its strategies.[23]

The Organization of African Unity (OAU) experienced a disappointing decade, sometimes claiming the lead role in addressing the many conflicts plaguing the continent, but being unable to deliver any major settlements. The weakness of the organization was due not so much to its secretariat, led by the widely respected Salim Salim, but rather to the difficulty its member states had in agreeing on political strategies which favoured conflict resolution, in spite of the creation of OAU conflict prevention "mechanisms" mid-decade.[24] Its relations with the United Nations were characterized by resentment over its own lack of resources and political support from Member States, and by justifiable demands that the world body should not slough off responsibility for some of the worst conflicts of the decade in an under-resourced and divided regional body.

In a rather different vein, the Council and UN staff found themselves contending with an array of regional actors in the former Yugoslavia. These included European Community monitors (and some from further afield, such as Canada) within the European monitoring mission, European Union civil administrators in Mostar, Organization of Security and Cooperation in Europe negotiators and NATO enforcement units in the skies and subsequently on the ground. The United Nations, with Council support and jointly with the European Community, led negotiations with various parties to the conflicts in the former Yugoslavia (most memorably in the Vance–Owen configuration). In other conflicts, such as those in Georgia[25] and several in West Africa,[26] UN Missions mandated by the Council monitored the activities of regional organizations purportedly keeping or promoting the peace. This proved particularly delicate in Georgia, where peace-keeping forces of the Commonwealth of Independent States (CIS) were seen by a number of Western powers neither as markedly impartial nor as deserving treatment which might imply or confer recognition on the CIS as a respectable regional organization.

Late in the decade, with the Council stymied by several conflicts and disunited in facing major international challenges, regional organizations came to be seen by some as a possible if not particularly desirable substitute for the United Nations. However, with the exception of NATO, regional bodies generally commanded even scarcer resources and offered even more limited capacities than the United Nations. Furthermore, a system of international security founded on regional organizations begged the question of who would arbitrate differences between them and how this would be done. The UN Charter, for all the many failures of UN Member States to live up to it, continued to serve as a beacon from this perspective, and the Council's authority, even if respected too often in the breach, remained indispensable.

The shifts in the nature and scope of Council decisions, many setting precedents even where the Council asserted that they did not, arose from evolving interpretations of the Charter and had a deep effect on the understanding of sovereignty at the international level, both shaped by, and influencing, the Council.

Considerations driving Council decision-making

An innovative feature of the Council's decisions on a number of crises was its concern over the humanitarian plight of civilian victims of conflicts, particularly refugees. Refugees were hardly a new topic of concern for the Council.[27] The miserable fate of Palestinian refugees proved a spur (at least nominally) to the Arab–Israeli dispute following Israel's war of independence in 1947–48, leading also to the creation of a UN agency, the United Nations Relief and Works Agency for Palestine Refugees in the Near East (UNRWA), exclusively dedicated to the welfare of refugees. Those displaced by war, particularly where mass exoduses of the population had occurred, had long been seen as deserving the care of the international community and were among the primary "clients" of both the Red Cross system (ICRC and the Federation of World Red Cross and Red Crescent Societies) and the UN High Commissioner for Refugees. Nevertheless, in the 1990s as never before, the Security Council invoked the plight of refugees and their implied destabilizing effect on neighbouring states as grounds for its own involvement in conflict. Early Council resolutions on the former Yugoslavia[28] and on Somalia[29] illustrate this development. Any threat that the Haitian crisis of democracy in 1991–94 may actually have posed to international peace and security could only have arisen from the outflow of Haitian boat-people, which might have threatened to engulf a number of Caribbean countries had the shores of Florida not been their preferred destination. (As it was, the burden on several Caribbean countries and dependencies arising from inflows of Haitians should not be minimized.) The widespread acceptance that refugee flows could actually be a major catalyst to conflict, rather than merely an outcome of it, was new.

Furthermore, the intense, if highly selective, media scrutiny (the so-called "CNN effect") of horrendous conditions endured by victims of war impelled populations worldwide to press their governments to alleviate extreme suffering arising from a variety of conflicts. Several factors conspired to focus attention on the United Nations to act on behalf of the international community: the limited impact of most bilateral assistance in these dramatic circumstances; the existence of several UN specialized agencies with the skills and "critical mass" required; and the possibility for the UN to deploy peace missions of various types and sizes with mandates focused on humanitarian objectives or at least including them. The most important consideration for many governments was that in delegating the responsibility to act to the United Nations, mostly in situations where few vital national interests were at stake, the costs and risks of response nationally were usefully curtailed. In the early 1990s, at the peak of media and public fervour for humanitarian initiatives, a lively debate unfolded over not only the international right to intervene in the internal affairs of countries to save civilian lives, but also a purported duty to do so.[30] By the bleaker end of the decade, with millions suffering untold horrors unassisted, mainly in Africa, this debate rang hollow in the absence of any actual desire to intervene on the part of those governments with the capacities to do so. Indeed, efforts by the United Nations to administer Kosovo (alongside the NATO-dominated military deployment of KFOR, the United Nations force in Kosovo) were proving once again, by late 1999, how difficult ambitious humanitarian action can be.

Canada chose the plight of civilians in war as the theme of its Security Council presidency in February 1999.[31] The Netherlands has also focused heavily on this question during its 1999–2000 terms on the Council. Practical measures to protect civilian populations, particularly women and children, from the ravages of war are all the more urgent and difficult in the conflicts of the 1990s, where civilians are frequently targeted rather than simply absorbing collateral damage from military operations. Dutch and Canadian advocacy on this front is paying off: UN Secretary-General Kofi Annan and many others have been increasingly calling for action in this area, not least by instituting effective accountability for those violating humanitarian norms pertaining to civilians.[32] My predecessor at the International Peace Academy (IPA), Olara Otunnu, has succeeded brilliantly in directing international attention to the plight of children in armed conflict, not least those pressed into service as combatants.[33] In September 1999, the Carnegie Corporation, led by Vartan Gregorian, in partnership with the IPA, began working on ways to move beyond the normative framework developed since the first Hague Peace Conference in 1899 on the regulation of war, to the actual protection of civilians today in actual theatres of war.[34] Given the types of weaponry widely available and traded today, and the nature of the belligerents of the 1990s, who are rarely knowledgeable about or interested in multilateral treaties in this field, this task will not be easy.

Human rights, long cloistered within intergovernmental machinery and Secretariat bureaucracy (in part to keep the topic at a safe distance from those responsible for international peace and security at the United Nations), burst onto the Security Council's agenda with the realization that civil strife was not amenable to negotiated solutions as long as human rights continued to be massively violated. For this reason, the protection, promotion, and monitoring of human rights formed an important and uncontroversial part of the mandates of several UN peace-keeping operations, notably in El Salvador and Guatemala.[35] Where this was not the case, as in Rwanda and Haiti, the UN General Assembly, as part of the broader UN strategy, often deployed parallel human rights missions. This tendency to address human rights objectives in Security Council debates and decisions was reinforced by the appointment of a UN High Commissioner for Human Rights as of 1994.[36] Although the first incumbent, an accomplished Ecuadorian politician and diplomat, proved lack-lustre in this role, his successor, Mary Robinson, a former President of Eire, adopted a more assertive approach to her responsibilities, putting pressure on the Council (even while underscoring a frequent lack of coordination and identity of view within the UN system). The quandaries faced by the Council in factoring human rights considerations into its decisions were highlighted when the parties to Sierra Leone's civil war reached a peace agreement in mid-1999, including sweeping amnesty provisions against which Mrs Robinson sharply protested (and over which the UN Secretary-General's representative at the peace pact's signing ceremony had registered a formal reservation). On the one hand, Sierra Leone's population was clearly eager for peace on virtually any terms; on the other, the agreement's amnesty provisions patently ran against long-standing and emerging human rights norms. The trade-off seemed to be that those requiring and benefiting from the amnesty need not expect to do so unimpeded beyond Sierra Leone's borders.

The Council also appeared to be increasingly engaged in the promotion of democracy, by mandating the organization and monitoring of elections *inter alia*. This was a trend which would have been as unlikely during the Cold War as the driving force of humanitarian considerations and the Council's role on human rights in the 1990s.[37] Nevertheless, the Council favored electoral processes not so much as an end in themselves, but rather as a means of effecting a "new deal" in countries emerging from civil war, in which power could, in some cases, be shared with former combatants in rough proportion to electoral results. Such elections proved an unreliable indicator of the extent to which genuinely democratic cultures would take root. The stilted, power-driven, and unstable coalition arrangements resulting from Cambodia's UN-monitored elections of 1993 and 1998 contrast with the more natural, relaxed electoral rhythms apparently achieved in El Salvador, where an alternation of power between rival parties seems more likely in the long run.

The United Nations' mushrooming electoral activities, very much driven by demand rather than supply of the personnel and other resources required for effectiveness in this field, presented multiple dangers for the organization. Countries having once required electoral assistance were likely to require it again, due to the high level of political tension and the limited degree of administrative and security capacity. In addition, many of the elections observed by UN teams were conducted in adverse circumstances, often contributing to results which could barely be described as having been attained freely and fairly. In most cases, short of occurrences of massive fraud, UN electoral missions were loath to risk igniting or reigniting civil strife by contesting the results of polling and, consequently, were seen as willing to compromise on principle and to be less than the impartial arbiters local parties had a right to expect. Losers were rarely gracious and the United Nations was little thanked for its prominent role in such electoral processes, which it frequently carried out alongside regional organizations and non-governmental teams of eminent persons, such as those associated with former US President Jimmy Carter.[38]

Institutional developments

Member States not serving on the Council, particularly the "Troop-Contributing Nations" (TCNs), which provide personnel and matériel to the United Nations for peace-keeping operations, have been intensely irritated by the UNSC's working methods. Subsequently, and quite reluctantly, the Council allowed some light to shine on its autocratic and opaque proceedings in the early 1990s.[39] The origins of the problem were quite recent. Council members, and the P5 in particular, had always needed to consult privately among themselves. However, with active cooperation among the Permanent Members increasingly the norm by 1990, the P5 saw little value in continuing to conduct much of the Council's business in open, public meetings. "Informal consultations," or "informals," closed to all non-Council members and most Secretariat staff and leaving no formal record, became the norm. Non-members were in the dark on the agenda of upcoming informals, and had to scramble for information, feeding off scraps provided in the antechamber by those emerging from the consultations—a humiliating experience for the supplicants. By 1992, leading non-Council TCNs, such as Canada, the Netherlands, Malaysia, India, Argentina, Pakistan, and some Scandinavian countries, were making it clear that if the Council expected them to provide national assets in support of Council decisions, often in risky circumstances, they at least expected to be consulted, if only in some formal, face-saving sense. As a result, a number of measures were adopted to introduce greater clarity in the Council's program of work, and meetings between the Council and TCNs (long resisted by the P5, which preferred TCNs to meet merely with the Secretariat) started occurring in 1994.[40]

A somewhat related development was the emergence of groups of friends, composed of countries which were influential in a given crisis.[41] Some of these groups, such as that on Haiti, were convened at the invitation of the Secretary-General, while others constituted themselves, with several hybrid varieties emerging. They generally featured one or several Permanent Members, either formally or in the wings (as was the case with the USA on El Salvador). Their purpose was not only to advise the Secretary-General and Council on strategies to promote settlement of the conflict and implementation of a peace agreement, but also to serve as a potent lobby group *vis-à-vis* parties to the conflict, regional actors, and the General Assembly (from which decisions relating to Council strategies were sometimes required, in areas such as human rights monitoring, and always on the financing of its initiatives). Often, representatives in the field of such groups, or of Security Council members, helped support locally the efforts of the Secretary-General's Special Representatives (SRSGs), as was the case in Cambodia, Mozambique, and Haiti.[42] Complaints were sometimes heard that such groups usurped the role of the Council as a whole, and the Secretariat occasionally voiced concern that the Secretary-General was sometimes unhelpfully constrained by them; but given the vastly increased pressure for action within this body, most members saw groups of friends as a useful clearing house for consideration of options by the Council.

The relationship of the three Secretary-Generals of the 1990s with the Council varied. Javier Pérez de Cuéllar of Peru completed his distinguished, quietly creative, but somewhat understated stewardship at the end of 1991. He had done much to encourage the Council to play a more active role and was highly regarded by most of its members. Boutros Boutros-Ghali of Egypt, who took office in early 1992, proved himself a passionate and well-reasoned advocate of a stronger UN role in conflict resolution and post-conflict peace-building, launching his seminal *An Agenda for Peace* in mid-1992, following the only Security Council Summit of leaders in the body's history. However, he was damaged by the United Nations' reverses in the former Yugoslavia and Somalia. His brittle personality and tone-deafness relative to the US domestic political scene brought him into conflict with the Washington administration. The latter, in spite of superficially strong support for Boutros-Ghali by the rest of the UN membership, vetoed his re-election and ensured the re-election of Kofi Annan of Ghana in late 1995. On assuming his new responsibilities in 1996, Annan, the first career UN official to hold the position, staked out new ground in championing human rights and concern for civilians in war as key themes. His advocacy of humanitarian intervention was articulated most unambiguously in a speech to the UN General Assembly on 20 September 1999.[43] In spite of his commitment to these and other values held dear in Washington, the United States clashed with him over his handling of the Iraqi regime and sought to limit his role in addressing the Kosovo crisis. Nevertheless, at the decade's end the quietly charismatic Annan remained, in the view of many seasoned observers of the UN scene, the only other Secretary-General to enjoy the esteem accorded the legendary Dag Hammarskjöld (admired most fully after his untimely demise in 1961).[44]

The Council's expanding role in the early 1990s, and both the number and sweeping scope of its resolutions, gave rise to growing calls for judicial review of its decisions by the World Court.[45] Libya contested the Council's decisions targeting it, clearly embarrassing the Court, which prudently awaited the 1999 diplomatic solution to the impasse that pitted the Council against Tripoli throughout most of the decade before addressing the merits of the case (over which it did accept jurisdiction, much to the annoyance of some of the P5).[46] Pressure for judicial review, as well as for access to advisory opinions from the Court on peace and security issues by the Secretary-General (a proposal advanced by Boutros Boutros-Ghali in *An Agenda for Peace* in 1992) was resisted by the P5, but a sense of inevitability developed over growing involvement of the Court in the Council's institutional life.

The Council in the 1990s may be remembered in part for its contribution to radical innovation in international criminal law, notably through its creation of ad hoc International Criminal Tribunals for the former Yugoslavia in 1993 and Rwanda in 1994, to bring to justice those responsible for war crimes, crimes against humanity, and genocide.[47] The foremost champion of these tribunals was the United States (possibly because of frustration over its own inability at the time to influence the course of events on the ground in the former Yugoslavia, due to sharp policy differences with European allies and guilt over its refusal to confront genocide in Rwanda). The creation of the tribunals greatly intensified pressures for a permanent International Criminal Court with universal jurisdiction; but when a Statute for this Court was adopted in Rome in 1998, the USA, along with six other countries of varying respectability, voted against the text out of concern over its potential implications for US citizens, particularly US troops serving abroad. Negotiations continued throughout 1999 on operational modalities for the Court and efforts were quietly made to frame understandings of the Statute which would allow the United States, some day, to sign on.

The role and interaction of non-governmental organizations (NGOs) with respect to the Security Council both grew significantly and evolved in nature during the 1990s. NGOs have for many years been accredited by the UN Economic and Social Council (ECOSOC) to monitor and contribute to UN activity in a broad range of fields. The accrediting body itself suggests the extent to which NGOs were traditionally viewed as focusing on economic and social issues such as the environment, human rights, humanitarian, health, labour, education, and population issues. In the 1990s, conflicts, particularly of an internal nature, were increasingly seen as featuring economic and social causes as well as effects. For this reason, *inter alia*, relevant NGOs clamoured for access to the Council, for which the Charter and the Council's long-established working methods made no provision. The role of NGOs as major partners for the United Nations in humanitarian operations, the success of many NGO programs in the field, the mandate for the Secretariat's Department of Humanitarian Affairs to offer coordination services to NGOs as well as official agencies, the mediagenic nature of some NGO activity, and a rapidly spreading fad late in the decade in favour of interaction with "civil society" (a term never satisfactorily defined) all conspired to encourage the Council to display greater openness to NGO views and more generous recognition of NGO achievements.[48] Within the Council, a number of governments, including Sweden, the Netherlands, Germany, and Canada, advocated greater access for NGOs (while the Secretary-General lavishly praised them). This was achieved in two ways. First, in a breakthrough of sorts, the Council met informally with a small group of NGOs in 1998. More meaningfully, although less visibly, Council members increasingly met with NGOs on their own and in groups, not only to brief them on recent developments and upcoming debates in the informals, but also to seek their input for Council decision-making.[49] While the sincerity of some Council members in engaging in these exchanges might be questioned, the achievement of genuine access, and the growing recognition of NGOs as significant and mostly constructive contributors to international peace and security, marked a new departure for the Council in its relations with the "outside" world.

Cumulative impact of Council decisions

Arguably the most important, although one of the least noticed, of the consequences of Council decisions in the 1990s as a whole, has been the erosion and shift at the international level of understanding of national sovereignty. By 1999, it was widely but not universally accepted that tyrants could no longer seek refuge behind the walls of sovereignty to shield themselves from international concern, and even action, over massive human rights violations and humanitarian catastrophes. The Council has not so much overridden Article 2.7 of the Charter (which exempts Chapter VII decisions from its non-intervention provisions), but rather sharply redefined in practice our conception of what can constitute a threat to international peace and security and a proper subject for international intervention. This has been spearheaded by repeated intervention to address the humanitarian consequences of mostly civil wars, often authorizing coercive measures, and by designing increasingly complex and intrusive mandates for international actors within member countries, sometimes without their consent. The degree of intrusiveness the Council was prepared to mandate throughout the 1990s was striking, even though its own members were not always helpful in implementing decisions involving risks to their nationals, for example in the arrest of those indicted by the International Criminal Tribunals.

The path ahead

The major challenge facing the Council by the end of the decade was the poor state of relations between the United States and the United Nations.[50] The Clinton Administration's instinctive penchant for UN-bashing whenever they found themselves in a tight spot from which blame might be delegated, first seen following the Mogadishu fiasco of 4 October 1993, was displayed repeatedly in subsequent years. This was most tellingly the case when leaks from Washington in early 1999 suggested that the United States had used UNSCOM, the UN expert body charged with overseeing and monitoring Iraq's compliance with Security Council decisions on its weapons programmes, as a cover to spy on Iraq for its own purposes rather than those of the United Nations.[51] Seeming to decide that the best defence was a strong offence, the Clinton Administration roundly attacked Kofi Annan through the US media for purported "appeasement" of the Iraqi regime.[52] Legislative strictures introduced in the mid-1990s had required the Administration to consult Congress prior to the launch or significant expansion of any UN peace-keeping operations, which, with both the House of Representatives and the Senate in the hands of the Republican majorities, produced a deadening effect on the Administration's willingness to advocate or countenance large new UN peace missions. (The Administration was less explicitly constrained on its leadership of, or participation in, multinational coalitions not under the UN flag.) Indeed, so nervous was the Administration of an engagement with Congress on this front that it fretted endlessly in 1998 and 1999 over the approval of tiny UN missions in the Central African Republic and Sierra Leone involving little US staff or money. (Oddly enough, the approval by Washington in October 1999 of a large-scale peace-keeping operation in Sierra Leone, succeeding the United Nations' earlier small monitoring missions there, proved less problematic because a formal settlement, however troubling in nature, had been reached by the parties to the conflict, and because the need for a large international presence to nurture peace was by then so clear.)

In areas where American interests were perceived to be more centrally engaged in 1999, such as East Timor and Kosovo, the Clinton Administration did work to authorize and support sizeable UN civilian and police efforts on the ground, but its commitment to strong international action to counter Africa's slide into widespread civil conflict remained, at the UN, more rhetoric than reality. Furthermore, approval by the United States in 1999 of large UN deployments in Kosovo, East Timor, and Sierra Leone did not guarantee payment of their dues for these missions. The repayment of a significant portion of US arrears to the United Nations, amounting to roughly US $1.7 billion in late 1999 according to the United Nations, was conditionally authorized by Congress in November 1999, but the range and scope of Congressional demands needing to be met before much of the repayment could be disbursed represented a major challenge for the United States in its relations with other Member States.[53] The new US Permanent Representative to the United Nations, the controversial but energetic Richard Holbrooke, confirmed only after a prolonged struggle with the US Senate, touted the tired theme of UN reform as his top priority, seemingly with an eye to domestic political advantage, but mounted an impressive campaign on repayment of arrears in the halls of Congress and elsewhere. His decision to devote the US presidency of the UN Security Council in January 2000 to issues of conflict in Africa, aiming particularly to turn the Council into the locus for meaningful negotiations among the relevant African heads of state and government on the fighting in the Democratic Republic of Congo, seemed promising.[54]

Implementation of Security Council resolutions on Iraq remains the most contentious issue today between the United Nations and the United States. After its criticism of Kofi Annan's attempt in February 1998 to negotiate a return by Iraq to compliance with these resolutions, noted above, it failed to gain the support of most UN Member States for its policy (with the United Kingdom) of punitive bombing of Iraq since December 1998. Its insistence on maintaining a sanctions regime to encourage Iraqi compliance with UN efforts to prevent further development of weapons of mass destruction has also enjoyed decreasing support at the United Nations. Efforts by the United Kingdom to broker a compromise between the US position and that of countries no longer willing to support the sanctions regime (although, in some cases, still prepared to adopt other measures to contain Iraq) led to a pyrrhic modification of the sanctions regime in December 1999, but there was a sense at the United Nations and in US political circles that the policy now lacked momentum and credibility.[55]

The United Nations featured in the US presidential election campaign of 2000, although only tangentially compared to the attacks of Senator Robert Dole on UN Secretary-General Boutros Boutros-Ghali in 1996. Republican party foreign policy advisors suggested that Washington should use the United Nations only in support of narrowly defined US interests.[56] (This stance is at some variance with the practice of the last Republican president, George Bush, and his secretary of state, Jim Baker, who, during the years 1989–1993, worked extensively through the United Nations on a broad range of topics, exhibiting considerable altruism on crises such as Somalia.) A serious Democratic party challenger, Senator Bill Bradley, on the other hand, suggested greater US reliance on the United Nations in addressing humanitarian and other global security crises.[57] From the debate among candidates, it was hard to discern, in mid-January 2000, where any of them would actually seek to move US–UN relations if elected.

The role of the remaining P5 members was less clear by the end of the decade. On and off throughout the 1990s, the United Kingdom had largely dominated Council deliberations due to the skill of its representatives and its close alliance with the United States. It was not clear that this advantage could be sustained with Richard Holbrooke newly on the scene. As had been the case throughout the post–Second World War period, France single-mindedly and with great finesse pursued its own interests in the Council. Although its foreign minister, Hubert Védrine, decried the emergence of an excessively dominant United States as an "*hyper-puissance*" in early 1999, France continued to work closely with the United States and United Kingdom on many issues. While this was the case on such issues as Libya and Kosovo, France's position on Iraq, by 1999, was much closer to that of Moscow than Washington.[58] China remained mostly passive within the Council. Even after NATO bombers struck its embassy in Belgrade during their campaign to relieve oppression in Kosovo, China did not seek to block Security Council approval of a settlement crafted there by the G8 countries. The only occasions on which China did display initiative related to diplomatic manoeuvring by Taiwan for greater recognition. China threatened to veto a Security Council decision on Haiti in 1996, briefly vetoed Council action on Guatemala in 1997 and, in early 1999, forced the withdrawal of the UN's preventive deployment of peace-keepers in Macedonia,[59] each time in order to contain or reverse diplomatic advances by Taipei. Given their own pursuit of narrow national interests within the Council, criticism of China's actions in this regard by several of its other members sounded unconvincing.

The most significant question mark over the Council, beyond the US stance, related to the Russian Federation. Moscow had earlier viewed cooperation with other major powers in the Council as a means of ending, without excessive loss of face, so-called "regional" conflicts the world over which had been fuelled by the Cold War. By 1998, however, it was displaying a more jaundiced appreciation of its Western partners' policies on both Iraq and Kosovo. Russia was powerless to stop the US and UK bombing of Iraq as of late 1998, but its furious attacks on UNSCOM Executive Chairman Richard Butler in early 1999 helped seal the fate of the Commission.[60] Equally, it proved powerless to halt the NATO air campaign over Kosovo in the spring of 1999 (most humiliatingly highlighted by its failure to secure much support within the Security Council for a resolution to halt the bombing); but it was potentially too disruptive to be ignored by NATO countries, and was brought into the decision-making loop on Kosovo through the G8 channel.[61] It subsequently staged a minor and somewhat farcical military offensive to seize control of Pristina Airport before NATO forces did so. These shenanigans on the ground expressed both the depth of Russian frustration over its limited margin for manoeuvre, even in its former strategic backyard, and Moscow's need to demonstrate to the Russian population that it could still play a relevant role on the ground. The Russian Federation's unhappiness over Western use of force against Iraq and the former Yugoslavia without recourse to the Council for specific authorization (nullifying the impact of the Russian veto) did not immediately induce much reflection in Russia on what alternative, more positive approaches might work better for Moscow than threatening the use of the veto. Rather, the mood appeared to be one of sullen defiance regarding Iraq and Kosovo, somewhat mitigated by the genuine effort of Russian peace-keepers associated with KFOR to carry out their responsibilities in the face of overwhelming hostility from the Kosovar population of Albanian extraction. Furthermore, Russia worked closely with other Council members to address the crises of East Timor, Sierra Leone, the African Great Lakes region, and Angola, although its role in all of these was circumscribed by its severe resource constraints. Renewal of its military campaign against Chechnyan separatists in mid-1999 elicited widespread condemnation for its indiscriminate attacks on civilian targets, including from the UN Secretary-General. However, the issue was not placed on the Security Council agenda, reinforcing cynicism that double standards within the body strongly favour the P5. While sympathy existed internationally for Russia's need to contain terrorist attacks on its own civilian population, the campaign smacked of domestic political opportunism by the faction in power in the Kremlin, and did little to enhance Russia's stature at the United Nations.

Russia's performance within the Security Council was anchored to its highly regarded and singularly accomplished Ambassador to the United Nations, Sergey Lavrov, but the degree of future Russian partnership with other Permanent Members in the conduct of Council business hung very much in the balance in late 1999. Key factors included pressure from domestic quarters to demonstrate Russian foreign policy independence, and the issue of whether Moscow could afford to accommodate such pressures meaningfully, given its precarious financial position and reliance on Western sources of funding to remain solvent. The resignation of Boris Yeltsin as President of Russia as the century turned, and the electoral climate it spawned in Russia, did nothing to dissipate this uncertainty.

Africa remained the sore point on the Council's agenda. The United Nations' failing peace-keeping operation in Angola was withdrawn in February 1999.[62] The UN Security Council did little to solve the acute problems of tiny Guinea–Bissau.[63] The conflict in Eastern Congo continued to draw in numerous neighbouring countries and the settlement reached mid-year appeared so fragile as to militate against deployment of a UN peace-keeping operation.[64] This conflict split SADCC, the subregional organization of Southern Africa, with Zimbabwe and South Africa, its two most powerful members, placing them at loggerheads. Negotiations towards a settlement in Sierra Leone culminated in a mid-year agreement that looked more like a division of the spoils (with the lion's share going to the murderous rebel RUF) than a recipe for future national concord.[65] Its amnesty provisions were particularly sweeping and controversial. A largely pointless but deadly war raged between Ethiopia and Eritrea, two of the world's poorest countries, during much of the year, defying the efforts of the OAU and the United States to bring the belligerents to their senses. In spite of efforts by France, the United Kingdom, and the United States to equip and train a number of African armed forces to lead regional peace-keeping efforts, the United Nations' active involvement continued to be sought by the Africans, and response from the countries of the northern hemisphere was at best ambivalent. With approval by the Security Council of the 6,000-strong UN peace-keeping operation for Sierra Leone in October 1999,[66] Western countries appeared to be facing up to their responsibilities, but few volunteered personnel and equipment in significant numbers. The prospect of a future peace-keeping operation in the Congo—Kofi Annan has mentioned a requirement of as many as 15,000 troops—produces hyperventilation among many Western delegations, whose armed forces are already spread thin in Bosnia, Kosovo, and East Timor. The industrialized countries need to think hard about their attitudes towards Africa and offer more assistance in conflict prevention, peace implementation, and post-war reconstruction in the years ahead. African leaders and societies need to provide stronger support to the OAU and subregional organizations and move from rhetoric to action on improved governance, as Nigeria is currently trying to do.

Reform of the Security Council remained a live issue at the decade's end. Pressure for reform had sprung from several sources.[67] The Council's activism in the early 1990s made it a more desirable place to sit. The hermetic nature of its working methods excited greater attention at a time when its decisions were proving genuinely important. In an era marked by P5 cooperation and a P5 tendency to impose decisions on the remainder of the Council, resentment of the Permanent Members grew. This resentment focused largely on their possession of the veto, a paradoxical trend since the veto was so little used during the 1990s. Indeed, only nine vetoes have been cast since January 1990, compared to 192 previous ones in the years 1946–1989.

In 1993, consultations hosted by Singapore were launched by key Member States on how to proceed with a reform agenda encompassing working methods, the veto and composition of the Council, it being recognized that any modification in the latter could only lead to expansion of its membership. Under intense pressure from TCNs, the Council's working methods became more transparent and the Council itself somewhat more accessible to non-member states (and NGOs), but its reliance on informal consultations as the locus for decision-making rather than open meetings remained marked. Discussion of the veto revealed a broad understanding of why it had been necessary during the Cold War, but also confirmed that it was now widely seen by most delegations as undesirable. It was clear, however, that the existing P5 members would not willingly give up their vetoes and could not be compelled to do so under Charter provisions. For this reason, debate focused more on whether any new Permanent Members should be granted vetoes rather than on veto suppression. The proposal that vetoes only stand when two or more permanent members had cast them seemed highly unlikely to be accepted by the United States and the other P5 members. Voluntary agreement among Permanent Members to use the veto only in relation to decisions under Chapter VII of the Charter (which would, for example, eliminate vetoes on the selection of the UN Secretary-General) seemed only slightly less unrealistic.

Expansion of the Security Council proved by far the most difficult element of the package. Germany and Japan expressed their wish to be allocated permanent seats early in the proceedings. They alternately demanded and waffled on their wish for a veto, emphasizing at times that the Council should not feature "second-class" Permanent Members. (This proved sufficiently unpopular among small Member States to encourage the fudging of this demand in hopes of securing greater support for their candidacy to a permanent seat.) Developing countries made clear that any expansion of the permanent membership of the Council would have to include the allocation of several new permanent seats to the developing world; notionally, a new seat each for developing countries in Asia, Africa, and Latin America. However, there was little agreement among them on which countries should be granted these permanent seats. While Brazil seemed an obvious candidate for Latin America, the issue generated a squall in Brazilian bilateral relations with Argentina mid-decade. In Africa, neither Egypt (more Arab than African), South Africa (under new and very busy management), nor Nigeria (oppressed by a highly reprehensible military regime for most of the 1990s) seemed entirely satisfactory candidates. In Asia, the obvious contender, India, was violently opposed by Pakistan, while Indonesia quietly registered a claim of its own. Meanwhile, a range of "middle powers" strongly opposed any allocation of new permanent seats, instead proposing a variety of schemes including the rotation of several countries through new non-permanent seats. At times, the only likely outcome seemed a limited expansion of the Council's non-permanent seats, weighted to accommodate the developing countries so clearly underrepresented in existing seat distribution arrangements.[68]

By decade's end, seven years after serious discussion of Council reform had been initiated, no progress had been registered, except for limited gains in transparency in the Council's *modus operandi*. Nevertheless, the issue continued to arouse bitter resentments and promised to remain controversial well into the new millennium.

Conclusion

The early 1990s showed the Council at its most optimistic and activist, leading to some notable successes, as in El Salvador and Mozambique. Wishful thinking on resources, increasing risk, poor planning, the dilution of responsibility inevitable in committee decision-making, and the absence of a powerful and consistently engaged leader among its members all contributed to the Council's subsequent decline into recrimination, risk-aversion, and flight from reality. Its pretense of activity, underscored by myriad resolutions and presidential statements of barely passing interest, fails to disguise its disorientation by the end of 1999. Nevertheless, often *faute de mieux*, particularly given the limited capacities of most regional organizations, the United Nations was again called upon in 1999 to deploy large peace operations in Kosovo, East Timor, and Sierra Leone. After several years during which US domestic political factors seriously constrained its capacity to act, the role of the Security Council not only in conferring legitimacy on certain forms of international intervention but also in providing a mechanism for burden-sharing of expenses and risk, in an era averse to both, is once again proving indispensable.

Even in its darkest hours mid-decade, no alternative international institution was mooted to supplant the Council. Indeed, the degree of consensus which would be required to create a different multilateral structure to promote collective security is inconceivable in the absence of a global cataclysm. Thus, the Council is fated to struggle on. Stronger, more sympathetic US leadership in the Council is urgently required (and perhaps not precluded forever, as the cycle of US politics moves inexorably forward). While all is not for the best in the best of all possible councils, its Permanent Members are stuck with each other, and the rest of the Member States with them. In years ahead, through decisions taken on a case-by-case basis, they will continue to chart the course of international relations on such sensitive and important issues as humanitarian intervention. Study of the Security Council has never been more interesting.

Notes

1. SG/SM/3956 of 13 January 1987.
2. For an account of the evolving dynamics within the Security Council, see Cameron Hume, *The United Nations, Iran and Iraq: How Peacemaking Changed* (Bloomington: University of Indiana Press, 1994) and C. S. R. Murphy, "Change and continuity in the functioning of the Security Council since the end of the Cold War," *International Studies* 32/4 (1995): 423.
3. For documents relating to the Canadian Human Security Initiative, see Canadian Foreign Affairs and International Trade Department, "Human security: Safety for people in a changing world," April 1999, on website: <http://www.dfait-maeci.gc.ca/foreignp/humansecurity/secur-e.htm>.
4. How far the Council's agenda has opened up to non-traditional issues can be gauged from its refusal, in 1989, to accede to UK pressure for discussion of international drug trafficking and environmental issues as potential threats to peace, while on 10 January 2000, under a US presidency (that of Vice-President Al Gore), it engaged in a debate on the implications of the AIDS pandemic in Africa for stability and peace in that continent in the twenty-first century. This development struck some observers as ironic, given long-standing US scepticism of Security Council debates on "thematic" issues. To the irritation of some Security Council members, who were used to (and comfortable with) an increasingly stodgy and defensive US stance in the Council, the new US Permanent Representative to the UN, Richard Holbrooke, was seizing on the opportunities the Council can present for debates of wide public interest, with more imagination than some of his predecessors.
5. For discussion of the evolution of peace-keeping, see in particular Thomas G. Weiss, David P. Forsythe, and Roger A. Coate, *The United Nations and a Changing World Politics*, 2nd ed. (Boulder: Westview Press, 1997).
6. See in particular Michael C. Williams, *Civil–Military Relations and Peacekeeping* (London and New York: Oxford University Press, 1998).
7. See Steven R. Ratner, *The New UN Peace-keeping: Building Peace in Lands of Conflict After the Cold War* (New York: St Martins Press and Council on Foreign Relations, 1996).

8. There is a plethora of literature regarding the former Yugoslavia and the constraints and obstacles encountered in the field, including: Adam Roberts, "Communal conflict as a challenge to international organization: The case of former Yugoslavia," *Review of International Studies* 21 (1995): 389–410; International Crisis Group, "Kosovo: Let's learn from Bosnia—models and methods of international administration," Sarajevo, 17 May 1999, on website: <http://www.crisisweb.org/projects/kosovo/reports/kos21maina.htm>.
9. See John L. Hirsch and Robert Oakley, *Somalia and Operation Restore Hope: Reflections on Peacemaking and Peacekeeping* (Washington, DC: United States Institute for Peace Press, 1995) and more recently Mark Bowden, *Black Hawk Down: A Story of Modern War* (New York: Atlantic Monthly Press, 1999).
10. David M. Malone, *Decision-Making in the UN Security Council: The Case of Haiti* (Oxford: Clarendon Press, 1998); James F. Dobbins, "Haiti: A case study in post-Cold War peacekeeping," *ISD Reports* II.1 (Washington, DC: Institute for the Study of Diplomacy, Georgetown University, October 1995); on Haiti and Somalia, see David Bentley and Robert Oakley, "Peace operations: A comparison of Somalia and Haiti," *Strategic Forum* 30 (Washington, DC: Institute for National Strategic Studies, National Defense University, May 1995).
11. See in particular Gérard Prunier, *The Rwanda Crisis: History of a genocide* (New York: Columbia University Press, 1995); Michael Barnett, "The UN Security Council, indifference and genocide in Rwanda," *Cultural Anthropology*, 12/4 (1997): 551; and J. Matthew Vaccaro, "The politics of genocide: Peacekeeping and disaster relief in Rwanda," in William J. Durch (ed.) *The UN, Peacekeeping, American Policy and the Uncivil Wars of the 1990s* (New York: St Martins Press, 1996).
12. For an excellent reference work covering UN peace-keeping operations from 1947 to the present, see Oliver Ramsbotham and Tom Woodhouse, *Encyclopedia of International Peacekeeping Operations* (Santa Barbara: ABC-CLIO, 1999).
13. UN Department of Political Affairs, "A brief overview of Security Council applied sanctions," *Interlaken* 2 (1998).
14. For an in-depth discussion of the Council's experience with sanctions regimes since 1990, see David Cortright and George Lopez, *The Sanctions Decade*, An IPA Project (Boulder: Lynne Rienner, 2000).
15. For a recent discussion of sanctions and the increasing use of targeted sanctions, see Daniel W. Drezner, *The Sanctions Paradox: Economic Statecraft and International Relations* (Cambridge: Cambridge University Press, 1999).
16. See Security Council Res. 1267 of 15 October 1999.
17. See the German Permanent Mission to the UN website for details on this: <http://www.undp.org/missions/germany/state.htm>.
18. See Canada on the UN Security Council 1999–2000: <http://www.un.int/canada/english.html>.
19. For a recent articulation of the Canadian initiative on Angola, see Ambassador Robert R. Fowler, "Notes for an intervention by H. E. Robert R. Fowler, Ambassador and Permanent Representative of Canada, to the United Nations Security Council on the Humanitarian Situation in Angola," Canada on the UN Security Council 1999–2000, 23 August 1999 (see note 18, above).
20. "Le négociant De Beers arrête tout achat de diamants d'Angola," *AFP*, 6 October 1999.
21. The Sanctions Committee on Angola was established by UN Res. 864 in 1993. For a report regarding recent developments in the committee, see UN Doc. S/1999/147.
22. David M. Malone, "Haiti and the international community: A case study," *Survival* 39/2 (1997): 126–45.

23. William G. O'Neil, "Human rights monitoring vs. political expediency: The experience of the OAS/U mission in Haiti," *Harvard Human Rights Journal* VIII (1995): 101–28; and United Nations/OAS, *Haiti—Learning the Hard Way: The UN/OAS Human Rights Monitoring Operation in Haiti, 1993–94* (New York: United Nations, 1995).
24. For a first-hand account of this, see Salim Ahmed Salim, "The OAU role in conflict management," in Olara A. Otunnu and Michael W. Doyle (eds.), *Peacemaking and Peacekeeping for the New Century* (Lanham: Rowman and Littlefield, 1996): 245–53. See also Ali A. Mazrui, "The failed state and political collapse in Africa," in Otunnu and Doyle, *op. cit.*: 233–43.
25. UN Observer Mission in Georgia (UNOMIG) was established by UN Security Council Resolution 853 in 1993 with the task of observing the operation of the peace-keeping force of the Commonwealth of Independent States (CIS), among others.
26. The UN Observer Mission in Liberia (UNOMIL) is a pertinent example of the UN working closely with regional organizations: established in September 1993 under UN Security Council Resolution 866, its mandate was to exercise its "good offices" to support the efforts of ECOWAS and the Liberian Transitional Government.
27. Weiss, Forsythe, and Coate, *The United Nations and Changing World Politics* (see note 5, above); Francis Kofi Abiew, *The Evolution of the Doctrine and Practice of Humanitarian Intervention* (The Hague and Boston: Kluwer Law International, 1999); and Stephen A. Garrett, *Doing Good and Doing Well: An Examination of Humanitarian Intervention* (Westport: Praeger, 1999).
28. See the Secretary-General's report (S/23069, 1991) and Security Council Res. 713 of 25 September 1991, declaring that the "rapid loss of human life and widespread material damage" were a threat to international peace and security, largely due to the spillover of refugees into neighbouring countries.
29. See the Secretary-General's report requesting the Security Council to take up the case of Somalia (S/23445, 1991) and Security Council Resolution 733 of 23 January 1992, similarly concerned with the spillover of refugees and its effect on the safety and security of bordering countries.
30. Jonathan Moore (ed.), *Hard Choices: Moral Dilemmas in Humanitarian Intervention* (Lanham: Rowman and Littlefield, 1998) is a good collection of works broaching this debate.
31. For a concise statement of the Canadian Human Security policy, see Canadian Department of Foreign Affairs and International Trade, "Human Security: Safety for people in a changing world," April 1999 (see note 3 above); see also Canada on the UN Security Council 1999–2000 on website: <http://www.un.int/canada/english.html>.
32. See S/PRST/1999/6 of 12 February 1999.
33. Ambassador Otunnu is currently serving as Under-Secretary-General to the UN for Children and Armed Conflict.
34. Charles Cater, Elizabeth Cousens, and Bruce Jones (eds.), *Civilians In War: 100 Years After The Hague Conference*, An International Peace Academy Project, (Boulder: Lynne Rienner, forthcoming).
35. On El Salvador, see in particular Michael W. Doyle, Ian Johnstone, and Robert C. Orr (eds.), *Keeping the Peace: Multidimensional UN Operations in Cambodia and El Salvador* (Cambridge: Cambridge University Press, 1997).
36. Mr. José Ayala-Lasso of Ecuador assumed the post of the first United Nations High Commissioner for Human Rights on 5 April 1994.
37. Ratner, *The New UN Peacekeeping* (see note 7, above).
38. For an excellent work dealing with elections in post-conflict situations, see Krishna Kumar (ed.), *Postconflict Elections, Democratization and International Assistance* (Boulder: Lynne Rienner Publishers, 1998).

39. Sydney D. Bailey and Sam Daws, *The Procedure of the UN Security Council*, 3rd ed. (Oxford: Clarendon Press, 1998) is the benchmark volume on the working methods of the Security Council, and a splendid achievement. To gauge how these working methods have changed over time, see Michael Wood, "Security Council working method and procedure: Recent developments," *The International and Comparative Law Quarterly* 45 (1996): 150–61.
40. Previously, the Security Council considered TCN interests to be confined to the implementation of mandates by the Secretariat, rather than the formulation of mandates by the Council. Subsequently, TCN meetings came to be co-chaired in many instances by the Secretariat and the Council presidency. See S/PRST/1994/22 of 3 May 1994 and S/PRST/1994/62 of 4 November 1994. In March of 1996, the Council established a more structured approach to consultations with TCNs (S/PRST/1996/13 of 28 March 1996).
41. An interesting first-person account of a Group of Friends can be found in Diego Arria, "Diplomacy and the four friends of Haiti," in Georges Fauriol (ed.), *Haitian Frustrations: Dilemmas for US Policy* (Washington, DC: Center for Strategic and International Studies, 1995): 96–7.
42. For an illustration of the workings of the 'groups of friends' mechanism, see Diego Arria, "Diplomacy and the four friends of Haiti," in Georges Fauriol, (ed.), *Haitian Frustration, Dilemmas for US Foreign Policy* (see note 41, above).
43. This speech was published as "Two Concepts of Sovereignty," *The Economist*, 18 September 1999.
44. Kofi Annan's willingness to accept unreserved personal responsibility for his role (while UN Under-Secretary-General for Peace-keeping Operations) in the slaughter of civilians at Srebrenica in 1995, and in the United Nations' hideously inadequate response to genocide in Rwanda in 1994, in the wake of detailed reports on the United Nations' lamentable performance on these two occasions during Autumn 1999, seemed to have enhanced his standing with some observers while undermining it with others. See Barbara Crossette, "Kofi Annan unsettles people, as he believes he should," *The New York Times*, 31 December 1999, p. 1.
45. See Dapo Akande, "The International Court of Justice and the Security Council: Is there room for judicial control of decisions of the political organs of the United Nations?," *The International and Comparative law Quarterly* 46/2 (1997): 309; and Mohammed Bedjaoui, *Nouvel Ordre Mondial et Contrôle de la Légalité des Actes du Conseil de Sécurité* (Brussels: Bruylant, 1994).
46. See "Libya, the ICJ and the Security Council," *Middle East International* 50 (1998): 18.
47. See Security Council Res. 808 (22 February 1993) and 827 (25 May 1993) on the former Yugoslavia tribunal, and Security Council Res. 955 (8 November 1994) on Rwanda.
48. See Francis Kofi Abiew and Tom Keating, "NGOs and UN peacekeeping operations: Strange Bedfellows," *International Peacekeeping* 6/2 (1999): 89–111.
49. These consultations, arranged by the Global Policy Forum and involving approximately 30 NGOs (in the fields of humanitarian relief, human rights, disarmament, faith, global governance, and development) are conducted through a Working Group founded in 1995. This group receives remarkably frank off-the-record briefings from the Security Council presidency, and other individual delegations, on Council deliberations.
50. For a first-hand, if self-pitying, account of this, see Boutros Boutros-Ghali, *Unvanquished: a US-UN Saga* (New York: Random House, 1999). See also David M. Malone, "Goodbye UNSCOM: A tale in UN-US relations," *Security Dialogue*, 30/4, 1999: 393–411.
51. See Philip Shenon, "Ex-inspector cites early role of CIA on UN arms team," *The New York Times*, 23 February 1999.

52. See Philip Shenon, "Former arms inspector is criticized by state department," *The New York Times*, 24 February 1999.
53. For Secretary-General Kofi Annan's positive but cautious reaction to this development, see SG/SM7229 of 19 November 1999.
54. See editorial, "US leadership at the UN," *The New York Times*, 4 January 2000.
55. See Security Council Res. 1284 of 17 December 1999, which created a new UN monitoring operation, UNMOVIC, to replace a discredited and paralysed UNSCOM.
56. See Condolezza Rice, "Promoting the national interest," *Foreign Affairs*, January/February 2000; and Robert B. Zoellick, "A republican foreign policy," *Foreign Affairs*, January/February 2000.
57. Transcript of remarks made by Senator Bill Bradley at the Fletcher School of Law and Diplomacy, Tufts University (29 November 1999), at a Foreign Policy Town Meeting.
58. For an official statement of French policy relating to Iraq, see "La France et la crise des sites présidentiels" at website: <http://www.diplomatie.fr/cominfo/dossiers/iraq.html>.
59. See Press Release SC/6648 on this question and the draft resolution S/199/201 of 25 February 1999.
60. For a recent letter from the Secretary-General to the Director of the IAEA detailing the past and current stalemate on this question, see S/1999/393 of 7 April 1999.
61. A resolution advanced in the Security Council on 26 March 1999 by Russia and some others, seeking to condemn and halt NATO bombing against the Belgrade regime, was defeated 12 to 3, thus seriously undermining Moscow's position on Kosovo at the United Nations. For text of the resolution and an account of the related Security Council debate, see UN Press Release SC/6659 of 26 March 1999.
62. See Security Council Res. 1229 of 26 February 1999.
63. Security Council Res. 1233 of 6 April 1999 weakly emphasizes that "the primary responsibility for achieving lasting peace in Guinea-Bissau rests with the parties and strongly calls upon them to implement fully all the provisions of the Abuja Agreement and subsequent undertakings."
64. See Security Council Res. 1258 of 6 August 1999 on this question.
65. See Security Council Res. 1260 of 20 August 1999.
66. See Security Council Res. 1270 of 22 October 1999 mandating the UN Mission in Sierra Leone (UNAMISIL).
67. For a review of the options that have been suggested regarding the reform of the Security Council, see "The United Nations and the twenty-first century: The imperative for Change" (Gleneden Beach, Oregon: The Stanley Foundation, Report of the thirty-first United Nations of the Next Decade Conference, 16–21 June 1996).
68. For an eclectic discussion of reform and issues facing the UN today, see James P. Muldoon, (ed.), *Multilateral Diplomacy and the UN Today* (Boulder: Westview Press, 1999).

4
Intervention: Trends and challenges
Chantal de Jonge Oudraat

This chapter deals with intervention in internal conflicts. It focuses on three questions: whether to intervene, who intervenes, and how to intervene. For each of these three questions the chapter will examine recent trends, identify policy challenges for the future, and formulate policy recommendations. Particular attention will be given to the role of the United Nations.

In this chapter, "intervention" is defined as a coercive action intended to change the behaviour of a party in the country in question. This may involve both the threat or use of economic sanctions and the threat or use of force.[1]

Since the end of the Cold War, the most pervasive form of violent conflict in the world has been internal. These conflicts cause great suffering to civilian populations. They often involve direct and deliberate attacks on civilians. Intimidation, mutilation, forced expulsion, and systematic slaughter are common. The numbers of people displaced, maimed, or killed in such conflicts are counted in tens and hundreds of thousands, even in millions.[2] Moreover, these conflicts almost always produce huge flows of refugees. They also give rise to cross-border military activities, and often involve international criminal elements. In sum, these conflicts pose grave moral questions and almost always pose threats to regional and international peace and security.

The United Nations Security Council has increasingly intervened to stop internal conflicts. At various occasions in the 1990s, it has considered gross violations of human rights and civil strife to be "threats to international peace and security," and decided on the imposition of economic sanctions or authorized the use of force. Since 1989, the Council has imposed economic sanctions fourteen times—compared to twice in the period 1945–1988 (see table 4.1). In nine of these fourteen cases, sanctions were imposed to contain or stop internal conflicts.[3] The use of force other than for self-defence was authorized in eleven cases as opposed to three in the period 1945–1988 (see table 4.2). Ten of these cases concerned internal conflicts.[4] Despite this increase in coercive action, the results have been limited; in some cases coercive actions have led to outright failures.[5]

Moreover, the international consensus that seemed to emerge in the beginning of the 1990s is crumbling. The new globalized world order of the late 1990s appeared to many states as a very unequal order; an order that favored one state—the United States—far more than others.[6] Many states resented the "bullish" behaviour exhibited by the United States, as well as their willingness to push multilateral organizations aside when such organizations could not agree on a course of action that was to their liking. Consequently, articulating and organizing collective responses to peace and security threats was becoming increasingly difficult within the confines of the UN Security Council at the end of the 1990s.

The debate surrounding possible US–NATO air strikes in Kosovo and Serbia epitomized the tensions amongst members of the United Nations.[7] Throughout the summer and autumn of 1998, China and Russia strongly opposed the possibility of a NATO intervention and threatened to cast their veto.[8] In March 1999, the United States and its NATO allies nonetheless went ahead and without consulting the Council or the UN General Assembly launched a 78-day air war against Belgrade.

The Kosovo crisis reignited the debate over humanitarian intervention. Unlike the early 1990s, the question was not whether humanitarian considerations could be characterized as "threats to international peace and security" and thus justify intervention in the domestic affairs of the states, but rather whether such interventions needed the authorization of the UN Security Council.

I believe that this debate will intensify in the near- and mid-term future. The March 1999 intervention by the United States and its NATO allies in Kosovo and Serbia highlights the dilemmas faced today. On the one hand, in an increasingly interdependent and globalized world, communal strife is difficult to ignore. Images of gross human rights abuses will frequently create pressures on outside powers to intervene. On the other hand, allowing for the use of force in humanitarian emergencies without UN Security Council authorization could easily lead to erosion of the general rule on the prohibition of the use of force and efforts to restrict its use in relations

Table 4.1 UN Security Council sanctions imposed under Chapter VII of the UN Charter, 1945–2000

Country	Date imposed	Arms embargo	Targeted financial sanctions	Partial economic sanctions	Comprehensive economic sanctions	Date lifted	Enabling UNSC Res.
Southern Rhodesia	16 Dec 1966				✓	21 Dec 1979	232 (1966) 460 (1979)
South Africa	4 Nov 1977	✓				25 May 1994	418 (1977) 919 (1994)
Iraq	6 Aug 1990				✓		661 (1990)[1]
Rep. Former Yugoslavia	25 Sept 1991	✓				18 June 1996	713 (1991)[2] 1021 (1995)
Fed. Rep. Yugoslavia	30 May 1992				✓	22 Nov 1995	757 (1992)[3] 1022 (1995)[4]
	31 March 1998	✓					1160 (1998)
Bosnian Serbs	23 Sept 1994				✓	1 Oct 1996	942 (1994) 1074 (1996)
Somalia	23 Jan 1992	✓					733 (1992)
Libya	31 March 1992	✓		✓		5 April 1999	748 (1992)[5] 788 (1992)
Liberia	19 Nov 1992	✓					
	16 June 1993	✓		✓		27 Aug 1993	841 (1993) 861 (1993)
Haiti	18 Oct 1993	✓		✓			873 (1993)
	21 May 1994				✓	16 Oct 1994	917 (1994) 944 (1994)
UNITA/Angola	15 Sept 1993	✓		✓			864 (1993)[6]
	12 June 1998		✓				1173 (1998)
Rwanda	17 May 1994	✓				16 Aug 1995	918 (1994)[7]

INTERVENTION: TRENDS AND CHALLENGES   49

Sudan	10 May 1996	✓			1011 (1995)[8]
Sierra Leone	8 Oct 1997	✓			1054 (1996)[9]
					1132 (1997)
Taliban/Afghanistan	15 Nov 1999		✓	5 June 1998	1171 (1998)[10]
					1267 (1999)
Eritrea/Ethiopia	17 May 2000	✓			1298 (2000)

Source: United Nations, Office of the Spokesman for the Secretary-General, "Use of Sanctions Under Chapter VII of the UN Charter," 31 March 2000. <http://www.un.org/News/ossg/sanction.htm>

Note: Economic sanctions are non-military measures that restrict or arrest normal international economic exchanges with a state or a non-governmental group, with the purpose of changing the political or military behaviour of the government or group in question. Economic sanctions can be comprehensive or partial. Targeted financial sanctions consist of freezing designated individual or corporate assets and prohibiting international financial transactions with such designated corporations or individuals.

[1] For subsequent resolutions see Office of the Spokesman for The Secretary-General (OSSG), "Use of Sanctions Under Chapter VII of the UN Charter," at <http://www.un.org/News/ossg/sanction.htm>

[2] See also UNSC Res. 727 (1992) of January 8, 1992, which reaffirms that the arms embargo applies to all republics of the Former Yugoslavia.

[3] See also UNSC Res. 787 (1992) of November 16, 1992 and UNSC Res. 820 (1993) of April, 17 1993, which strengthened the sanction regime. UNSC 943 (1994) of September 23, 1994 suspended certain sanctions on the Federal Republic of Yugoslavia.

[4] Sanctions were suspended in November 1995. They were lifted on 1 October 1996. See UNSC Res. 1074 of October 1, 1996.

[5] See also UNSC Res. 883 (1993) of 11 November 1993, which tightened sanctions on Libya. Sanctions were suspended on 5 April 1999. See UN Security Council Presidential Statement, S/PRST/1999/10.

[6] See also UNSC Res. 1127 (1997) of 28 August 1997, and UNSC Res. 1130 (1997) of 29 September 1997, which strengthened the sanction regime.

[7] See also UNSC Res. 997 (1995) of 9 June, 1995, which affirmed that the prohibition on the sale and supplies of arms for use in Rwanda also applied to persons in the states neighbouring Rwanda.

[8] The sale and supply of arms to non-governmental forces for use in Rwanda remained prohibited.

[9] See also UNSC Res. 1070 (1996) of 16 August, 1996, which foreshadowed an air embargo on Sudan. This embargo never went into effect because of the expected humanitarian consequences.

[10] The arms embargo remained in place for members of the former military junta and RUF.

Table 4.2 Uses of military force authorized by the UN Security Council under Chapter VII of the UN Charter, 1945–2000

Country	Year	Name of operation	Command	Enabling UNSC Res.
Korea	1950–1953	Multinational Force	US	83 (1950), 27 June 1950
Congo	1960–1964	UNOC	UN	161 (1961), 21 Feb. 1961
Rhodesia	1965	"Tanker Operation"*	UK	217 (1990), 12 Nov. 1965
Iraq	1991	Operation Desert Storm	US	678 (1990), 29 Nov. 1990
Bosnia	1992–1996	Operation Sharp Guard*	WEU/NATO	787 (1992), 16 Nov. 1992
	1992–1995	UNPROFOR	UN	816 (1993), 31 March 1993
				836 (1993), 4 June 1993
	1993–1996	WEU Danube Mission*	WEU	787 (1992), 16 Nov. 1992
	1995–1996	IFOR	NATO	1031 (1995), 15 Dec. 1995
	1996–1998	SFOR	NATO	1088 (1996), 12 Dec. 1996
Somalia	1992–1993	UNITAF	US	794 (1992), 3 Dec. 1992
	1993–1995	UNOSOM II	UN	814 (1993), 26 March 1993
Rwanda	1994	Operation Turquoise	French	929 (1994), 22 June 1994
Haiti	1994	Multinational Force	US	940 (1994), 31 July 1994
Zaire	Never deployed	Multinational Force	Canadian	1080 (1996), 15 Nov. 1996
Albania	1997	Multinational Force	Italian	1101 (1997), 28 March 1997
Fed. Rep. Yugoslavia (Serbia and Montenegro)/Kosovo	1999	KFOR	NATO	No UNSC Res. 1244 (1999), 10 June 1999, authorizes presence of international forces
East Timor	1999	INTERFET	Australia	1264 (1999), 15 Sept. 1999
	1999	UNTAET	UN	1272 (1999), 25 Oct. 1999
Sierra Leone	1999	UNAMSIL	UN	1270 (1999), 22 Oct. 1999
				1289 (2000), 7 Feb. 2000
Democratic Republic of Congo	1999	MONUC	UN	1279 (1999), 30 Nov. 1999
				1291 (2000), 24 Feb. 2000

* Economic sanctions enforcement operations. In the case of Rhodesia, the Council authorized the UK to use military force against a specific oil tanker which was headed for the port of Beira (Mozambique) with a full cargo of oil destined for Rhodesia, which at that time was subjected to mandatory comprehensive economic sanctions. See UNSC Res. 217 of 12 November 1965.

between states. It would also contribute to a weakening of the United Nations.

The UN Secretary-General, Kofi Annan, is acutely aware of the dilemmas and dangers involved. In September 1999, he took the debate to the UN General Assembly and urged states to develop criteria to permit humanitarian interventions in the absence of a consensus in the UN Security Council.[9] Algeria, China, and India—countries which had vehemently opposed the US–NATO intervention in Kosovo and Serbia in March 1999 and spoken against the idea of humanitarian intervention in the 1999 General Assembly debate—were asked by Annan what they would have done if, in the case of Rwanda, a coalition of states had been prepared to act in defence of the Tutsi population, but did not receive prompt UN Security Council authorization. "Should such a coalition have stood aside and allowed the horror to unfold?" Similarly, those who heralded the Kosovo operation were asked what type of precedent their actions had set, and to consider how their actions had undermined the prohibition on the use of force and the system created after World War II to deal with such security threats.[10]

This chapter will first address issues associated with the legal framework of intervention—whether to intervene. It will sketch the contours of the debate on a new doctrine and legal framework for humanitarian intervention. A doctrine that allows for humanitarian intervention without UN Security Council authorization is sorely needed. Such a doctrine should integrate the legal, political, and operational aspects of humanitarian interventions.

The chapter then turns to the agent issue—who intervenes. I argue that state actors will continue to dominate the scene. These actors may subcontract some activities to international organizations or private organizations, but subcontractors will rarely have much latitude for independent actions. Non-state actors, including international organizations, will often be important implementers of decisions by states. Heads of international organizations should be aware that the type of buck-passing that occurred in the 1990s in Somalia and Bosnia—when the United Nations was blamed for the failures of these operations—will continue. The success or failure of operations carried out by international organizations is in great part dependent on the support they receive from states. International organizations will want to adopt strategies that show where responsibility lies for the outcomes of interventionary operations. Such strategies should enable them to minimize the possibilities for buck-passing.

Thirdly, the chapter addresses questions related to the instruments of intervention—how to intervene. I argue that six conditions need to be fulfilled for the effective multilateral use of coercive instruments. First, outside powers need to have a clear political objective. Second, they need to correctly identify and assess the political, economic, and military characteristics of the group they seek to coerce. Third, someone needs to take the lead and guide and coordinate the coercive action. Fourth, whoever takes the lead of such an action needs to build widespread international support. Fifth, sufficient resources need to be made available; otherwise, policy pronouncements will not be followed by effective policy implementation. Sixth, outside powers need to develop an appropriate strategy, including escalation, exit, and post-intervention strategies.

Finally, the chapter will outline some policy recommendations, particularly as they relate to the United Nations.

The legal framework for intervention

Under Chapter VII of the UN Charter, the UN Security Council can impose coercive measures and disregard the general principle of non-intervention in the domestic affairs of states if it determines that a particular problem poses a "threat to international peace and security."[11] In the 1990s, the UN Security Council has shown great creativity in defining such threats. It has increasingly deemed internal conflicts and gross violations of human rights to be legitimate reasons for international action. At the end of the 1990s, the idea that states should not be allowed to hide behind the shield of sovereignty when gross violations of human rights take place on their territory has firmly taken root.[12] That said, many states remain hesitant to accept a right of humanitarian intervention outside the UN framework. They believe that the current system, whereby the UN Security Council determines whether a situation merits the imposition of economic sanctions or military intervention by qualifying such a situation as a "threat to international peace and security," is the best guarantee yet, and that economic embargoes and military interventions are not launched for self-serving political reasons.[13]

At the heart of the humanitarian intervention debate lies the question of whether force can lawfully be used in situations other than those foreseen by the UN Charter. This debate sets different legal schools of thought, as well as declaratory policies and practices of states in opposition.

Most legal scholars and governments argue that the UN Charter contains a general prohibition on the use of force. This prohibition is embodied in Article 2 (4):

All Members shall refrain in their international relations from the threat or use of force against the territorial integrity or political independence of any state, or in any other manner inconsistent with the Purposes of the United Nations.

Scholars and governments generally maintain that the Charter allows for only two exceptions to this rule. One is in response to an armed attack (Article 51). The other is when the use of force is authorized by the UN Security Council in order to maintain or restore international peace and security (Article 42).[14]

That said, some legal scholars maintain that Article 2 (4) does not contain a general and comprehensive prohibition on the use of force. They argue that it merely regulates the conditions under which force is prohibited, but leaves room for exceptions—only two of which are mentioned in the Charter (Articles 51 and 42). They defend the notion that the Charter permits the use of force in other circumstances. State practice, despite declaratory policies to the contrary, seems to concur with this view. Over the years, governments and legal scholars have argued that force can be lawfully used to protect and rescue one's nationals abroad; free people from colonial domination; fight terrorism; and protect people from gross violations of human rights.

The idea that force can be used to protect one's nationals abroad (or even nationals of another country) whose lives are in immediate danger, or who are in a hostage situation, has not formally been accepted as an exception to Article 2 (4) of the Charter. Yet a growing number of states have failed to actively oppose such actions, while not openly condoning them.

Interventions to free people from colonial domination received widespread political support in the UN General Assembly in the 1960s and 1970s, but legal scholars disagreed over the legality of the use of force in such cases.[16] While many scholars thought that with decolonization this issue had become irrelevant, the larger question of self-determination and the liberation of "oppressed people" remained on the agenda. Indeed, throughout the Cold War, socialist states supported military interventions in support of liberation movements and to preserve "Marxist gains" within the eastern bloc. The United States defended military interventions to counter communism and to further democracy during this period. These justifications for the use of force were repudiated by the International Court of Justice in 1986 in its decision on the Nicaragua case, and were abandoned with the end of the Cold War.[17] The self-determination debate nonetheless resurfaced in the 1990s with the dissolutions of Yugoslavia and the Soviet Union, and the increased focus on ethnic conflicts. Groups in Bosnia, Chechnya, Kosovo, Sri Lanka, and East Timor have all claimed a right to self-determination, and justified their use of force and requests for outside help on these grounds. Most legal scholars assert that there is no right of outside military intervention in those types of situations. Moreover, the UN Security Council has almost always called on outside powers to show restraint and imposed arms embargoes in these situations. That said, state practice is often at odds with legal rules or UN Security Council injunctions.

Claims regarding the legality of coercive action to combat terrorism, other than in hostage situations, are similarly shaky, but are gaining some ground. The strikes by the United States in August 1998, when it destroyed a pharmaceutical plant in Sudan and training facilities in Afghanistan believed to be associated with Osama bin Laden—the man accused of being responsible for the terrorist attacks on the US embassies in Kenya and Tanzania—were widely criticized throughout the world. Yet, UN Security Council resolutions on terrorism in the 1990s testify to greater international concern with terrorism; they acknowledge that terrorism can endanger "the lives and well-being of individuals worldwide as well as the peace and security of all states"; they also call for greater international cooperation.[18] Moreover, in 1992, the UN Security Council adopted, for the first time, economic sanctions on a state—Libya—because of its alleged support of international terrorists.[19] In 1996, it imposed economic sanctions on Sudan and, in 1999, on the Taliban (Afghanistan).[20] The United States has also increasingly resorted to the unilateral adoption of economic sanctions.[21] These unilateral sanctions are generally not followed by US allies.[22]

The most divisive question, and the question which has received most attention in the 1990s, is that of military intervention to protect people from gross violations of human rights. The 1999 UN General Assembly debate showed that the majority of states clearly reject a unilateral right to intervene for humanitarian purposes. China, Russia, and most developing states claim that such a right would allow meddling in their internal affairs. They fear abuse from the United States in particular, and strongly condemned NATO's unauthorized intervention in Kosovo.

Armed intervention for humanitarian purposes received a bad name during the nineteenth century, when military interventions by European powers were frequently justified in terms of humanitarian purposes. Since the adoption of the UN Charter, states have generally avoided referring to humanitarian purposes when justifying their military interventions, relying instead on broad interpretations of self-defence and "assistance" to "legitimate" governments.

The end of the Cold War resuscitated the question of military intervention for humanitarian purposes, and this notion has steadily received more supporters. Indeed, compared to the early 1990s, the idea that the UN Security Council can order interventions for humanitarian purposes seems to be commonly accepted in 1999. It did so, for example, in Bosnia, Somalia, Haiti, and Rwanda. It is the non-authorized intervention that poses a problem for most states. Genocide and gross violations of human rights are universally considered morally unacceptable acts. Many analysts and governments agree that, in such cases, economic sanctions or the threat of criminal prosecution are weak deterrents and even weaker instruments of compellence. Yet, few have accepted the idea that in such cases military intervention has to become a duty. The absence of a legal framework within which such interventions can take place contributes to the unease that states feel when considering such interventions.[24] The current system, whereby the UN Security Council determines whether a situation merits military intervention by qualifying such a situation as a "threat to international peace and security," is an insufficient warranty that the Council will indeed intervene when the next Rwanda comes around, and legally prevents others from doing so.

Developing a legal framework which would regulate unilateral interventions for humanitarian purposes would not ensure action. However, it is a necessary measure to help deter humanitarian disasters in the future. Those who fear that the formulation of a doctrine of humanitarian intervention would lead to abuse—particularly Western abuse—should be reassured by Western behavior in Chechnya, East Timor, Sierra Leone, or the Democratic Republic of Congo. In Chechnya, Russia was permitted to muck around with impunity. In East Timor, the Australians intervened only after having received the consent of the Indonesian government. In Sierra Leone, Western governments' reaction to the taking of 500 UN peace-keepers in May 2000 consisted of evacuating their nationals abroad. The United Kingdom sent in 800 well-trained troops in May 2000, but the defence minister repeatedly told the press and others that their mission would be terminated in June 2000, and that their primary mandate was to evacuate and protect UK nationals abroad. The US government responsible for the negotiation of the peace deal which provided amnesty to Foday Sankoh—a man worthy of the epithet "war criminal" and responsible for the May 2000 crisis—wrung its hands and sent the Reverend Jesse Jackson to neighbouring Liberia! Finally, in the Democratic Republic of Congo, only a fraction of the available troops had been committed in May 2000. None of them were of US origin.

A new doctrine and legal framework for humanitarian intervention

Several analysts and scholars have put forward proposals that would regulate recent state practice and make humanitarian intervention legal under specific sets of circumstances. Two different approaches can be identified. The first elaborates on the framework laid down in the UN Charter; proponents of this school advocate new interpretations of certain Charter articles. The second elaborates on the law outside the UN Charter and draws on the inherent rights of states. Advocates of this school of thought argue that states have a unilateral right to humanitarian intervention.

Amongst the analysts who advocate a new look at the Charter, those who suggest an extended reading of Chapter VIII—the Chapter that deals with regional arrangements—are the most convincing.[25] In essence, they propose to broaden the mandate of regional organizations and to give them the right, under certain conditions, to authorize the use of force.[26] Like the "Uniting for Peace" resolution, which gives the UN General Assembly the right to recommend military action in case the Council is paralyzed, most of these proposals maintain the central role of the UN Security Council and allow for the activation of other loci of authority only in case of the Council's incapacity to act.

For example, Winrich Kühne, a German analyst of the Stiftung Wissenschaft und Politik, has proposed to invest regional organizations with the authority to use force under three conditions: when the UN Security Council is unwilling or unable to act; when the UN Security Council has not explicitly denied the existence of a humanitarian crisis; and when the regional institution in question can act within the confines of a predetermined institutional structure that could authorize such action. Kühne proposes that the UN Security Council adopt a declaration that would invite regional organizations to develop such mechanisms and which would interpret Article 53 of the Charter as giving regional organizations a right of humanitarian intervention when the Council is unwilling or unable to act.[27] The question of whether NATO is a regional organization under the terms of Chapter VIII notwithstanding, under Kühne's proposal, NATO's action in Kosovo would have been lawful.

There are three problems with the Kühne proposal and similar proposals. First, regional organizations might not always be the best choice to intervene in internal conflicts. Members of regional organizations are neighbours, and neighbours are the international actors most prone to having ulterior political motives for intervention. Indeed, they often meddle in unhelpful ways in such conflicts.[28] Second, these proposals merely shift the problem from the global level to the regional level. Indeed, the decisions of these regional authorities would be based on political considerations and not on a set of agreed-upon principles—law. The fact that such decisions are being made collectively in and of itself does not make such decisions more lawful. More consensus means greater might, but not necessarily greater right. Finally, the Kühne proposal would give the great powers a key role in deciding on interventions. Great powers could block small powers from intervening by adopting declarations in the Council that would nullify the existence of a humanitarian crisis. But an attempt to block intervention by any of the great powers could be opposed through the veto. In practice, this would mean that only the regional organizations in Africa or Asia would be subjected to international scrutiny. Of course, Kühne's proposal was designed to redress insufficient enthusiasm for intervention, rather than possible abuse. Yet, this feature of his proposal might make it unattractive to many developing countries.

Other analysts have argued that states have an inherent right to use force.[29] This right, they say, is restricted by the UN Charter, but not prohibited by it. Several scholars have outlined conditions under which military intervention would be lawful.[30] Many draw on "just war" theories of the nineteenth century. These theories established criteria by which war could be considered just and legitimate. They include:

- Right authority—which actor has the authority to decide on war?
- Just cause—is the cause legitimate?
- Right intention—what are the motives behind the launching of the war?
- Last resort—have other actions been considered?
- Open declaration—did the war start with a declaration?
- Proportionality—is the act of war proportionate to the harm inflicted?
- Reasonable hope—is there a reasonable chance for a successful outcome?[31]

These criteria provide a useful framework when considering the conditions under which intervention should be allowed. They point to the essential role of actors, objectives, strategies, and outcomes.

Serge Sur, Professor of International Law at the University of Paris, incorporates these elements in his proposal for a new doctrine and legal framework for humanitarian intervention. He suggests that humanitarian intervention should be considered lawful under the following conditions. First, states would publicly declare in which cases they would reserve the right to intervene. They would do so in advance and not on the spur of the moment. For example, they could stipulate in a unilateral or collective declaration that they would intervene in cases covered by Article 3 of the Geneva Conventions or in such cases as covered by the statutes of the International Criminal Tribunals set up for the former Yugoslavia and Rwanda, or those of the International Criminal Court.[32] This right of intervention would be a discretionary right. States would not be obliged to intervene, neither could third parties hold them responsible for not intervening. Second, states would outline in advance how they would intervene. They would specify the military means they would consider employing. In view of the controversy over the use of air power in Kosovo and a military doctrine which allows for zero death on the side of the intervenor, one should force states to envisage the deployment of ground troops if the situation so demands. Moreover, states would want to make it clear that the military intervention would not itself become a violation of humanitarian law.[33] States would also have to clarify the timing of the intervention. In sum, states would outline both entry and exit strategies. Third, states would outline how they would coordinate and harmonize their military intervention with efforts for national and international criminal prosecution of those responsible for the humanitarian crisis. Such prosecution is foreseen in the Geneva Conventions and is an integral part of international humanitarian law.[34]

By emphasizing that a just doctrine of humanitarian intervention is not just about legal authority but also about ensuring that such interventions have strong political support and sufficient military resources, Sur comes full circle and integrates two other problems that have plagued coercive actions in the 1990s—political commitment and material resources. Moreover, his approach also focuses on the long-term problems of intervention. Indeed, military action is often but the beginning of intervention. The success or failure of a military intervention ultimately depends on the success or failure of the post-intervention phase. Those who contemplate military intervention should have a game plan ready for that phase. Reintroducing the United Nations (including the UN Security Council) at this stage would allow the full legitimization or disavowal of unilateral or collective unauthorized interventions after the event. Involving regional organizations at this stage should ensure integration of the conflict-stricken territories in their natural geographic space, and might give such organizations a stake in making the post-intervention phase succeed. In Kosovo, *ex post facto* involvement of the UN Security Council helped to legitimize the unauthorized US–NATO intervention. The involvement of the European Union helps to ensure that resources will be made available to the post-conflict operation.

Every approach contains possibilities for abuse, and none provides a guarantee to future victims of genocide or gross violations of human rights. Yet forcing states to define the parameters under which they would consider military intervention for humanitarian purposes might introduce a measure of predictability, and thus have a deterrent effect. It would also constitute a start at undercutting arguments about double standards, and serve as a shield against accusations that interventions are carried out solely in a state's own self-interest and are mainly of a self-serving nature.

Some measure of international consensus on when, why, and whether to intervene for humanitarian purposes is sorely needed.[35] The United Nations has an important role in this regard. It will be crucial in creating a new consensus. Devising a framework under which military intervention for humanitarian purposes can lawfully be undertaken should go hand in hand with an effort to mobilize public support for such interventions. Indeed, humanitarian interventions are long-term operations. As such, they are not sustainable without large public support. All actors within society have an important role to play in supporting and forging a consensus for humanitarian interventions. Research institutes and universities have a particularly important role to play: they should lay out the intellectual and moral dilemmas of such endeavours.

The agents of intervention

Under the rules of the UN Charter, military intervention was to be carried out by armed forces put at the disposal of the Council. These forces were supposed to be commanded by the UN Military Staff Committee.[36] However, because of the East–West conflict, such an international army was never established. Although the Cold War is over, it seems unlikely that the United Nations will be endowed with its own troops in the near future.

Proposals in the early 1990s calling for the establishment of a UN volunteer military force or the creation of UN peace enforcement units remained extremely controversial.[37] In 1993, the United Nations introduced a stand-by programme that called on Member States to earmark their forces for UN operations. The limits of this programme were soon highlighted. Indeed, during the genocide in Rwanda, the UN Secretary-General was unable to find 5,000 soldiers—despite the pledge of 19 governments to keep 31,000 troops available on a stand-by basis.[38] By 1995, the idea of stand-by forces was limited to a stand-by arrangements system whereby states made conditional pledges to contribute troops to future UN peace-keeping operations. In May 2000, 88 states had pledged a total of some 147,900 troops.[39] Yet, few of these states had volunteered troops for the missions in Sierra Leone and the Democratic Republic of Congo.[40] Ideas for a rapid reaction force have been tabled since 1992, but such forces remain very much in a conceptual stage at the end of 1999. The UN Secretariat now talks less ambitiously about a core headquarters unit that could be quickly deployed.

In sum, as Brian Urquhart put it, the idea of a UN force is "further than ever from becoming a reality."[41] Troops are put at the disposal of the United Nations on an ad hoc basis. At times they are put under UN command, at other times under national command, or that of a regional organization. Most peace-keeping operations—that is, operations where local parties have agreed to the deployment of international forces—are under UN command. Military interventions, including UN enforcement operations, are generally under national command or that of a regional organization because of the risk of casualties. In the latter case, there is often a lead state that drives and controls the operation. In Europe it is NATO, and within NATO it is the United States; in Western Africa it is the Military Observer Group (ECOMOG) of the Economic Community of West African States, and within ECOMOG it is Nigeria; in East Timor it is Australia.

Whether a country will intervene or lead a "coalition of the willing" is a function of the international environment (including the legal environment) and national interests (including national military capabilities and domestic political considerations). For large-scale operations, the United States has to take the lead, if only because it alone possesses the capabilities to carry out such operations.[42] Moreover, involvement—even limited involvement—of the United States will signal the seriousness of the effort.

Unfortunately, the United States has a mixed track record in this regard.[43] In many cases, the United States failed to take any meaningful action; Rwanda, Zaire/Congo, and East Timor are notable examples. The United States took the lead in Bosnia after agonizing for three years about whether and how to get involved in the conflict.[44] In Somalia, it took the lead for four months, but it then distanced itself from the operation and eventually pulled out altogether.[45] In Haiti, the United States decided and acted only in 1994, three years after Jean Bertrand Aristide, the democratically elected president, was deposed in a military coup.[46] Similarly, in 1998 and 1999, the United States was hesitant to intervene in Kosovo.[47]

Other countries have also taken up leadership roles, but these interventions have succeeded only if they have been supported by a regional or global power. Italy, because of its interests in Albania and because it was directly affected by the crisis there in 1997, took the lead for Operation Alba. It managed to secure both UN Security Council authorization and NATO support, and it successfully completed its mission. In 1999, Australia took the lead in East Timor. Given the lukewarm support for intervention given by the great powers, the success of the Australian mission was dependent on Indonesian cooperation; indeed, Australia intervened only after it had secured approval from the Indonesian government.

Inversely, the multinational force authorized by the UN Security Council in November 1996 to stave off the starvation of hundreds of thousands of Hutu refugees in Zaire and to create humanitarian corridors to lead them back into Rwanda failed; Washington and Paris were unwilling to lead and provide support for this operation. Canada, which had been given lead responsibility for the mission, was unable to pull off the operation on its own. Similarly, the UN force in Sierra Leone failed miserably to uphold its authority when attacked in May 2000. Only after the United Kingdom had introduced some 800 well-trained troops did tension start to subside in Sierra Leone.

In the absence of agreement within the UN Security Council, regional organizations are an attractive alternative to states contemplating military interventions. They add political legitimacy to such operations. This happened in Liberia and Sierra Leone, where Nigeria used ECOMOG, and in Kosovo, where the United States used NATO. However, as noted above, the legal justifications for intervention by these organizations were dubious.

Many scholars and policy-makers emphasize the importance of developing and sustaining domestic support for international actions. They argue that a country will only take the lead if it can obtain domestic support for such an action.[49] Domestic politics and domestic public opinion can thus be seen as separate agents that influence decisions on intervention.

Domestic support is often believed to be dependent on keeping combat casualties to a minimum. The conventional wisdom is that the riskier an operation the weaker the domestic support for action. This explains why US policy-makers in particular were wary of intervening in Bosnia, Somalia, Rwanda, and Haiti. However, a series of public opinion polls conducted at the University of Maryland, as well as a series of studies by the Triangle Institute for Security Studies, show that the American public will support military interventions that are morally and politically compelling.[50] For example, in a 1999 poll, people were asked to identify the highest number of American military deaths that would be acceptable to stabilize a democratic government in Congo; a figure as high as 6,861 casualties was given. Similarly, the public was willing to tolerate 29,853 deaths to prevent Iraq from obtaining weapons of mass destruction.[51]

European politicians, for their part, are not immune to domestic concerns about casualties, but they believe that the casualty-tolerance index is higher in Europe—particularly France and the United Kingdom—than in the United States.

Given the reluctance of many Western powers to engage peace-keepers in far away lands and their fear of combat casualties, some authors have advocated hiring private military corporations.[52] In the 1990s, private military forces have increasingly been hired for logistical support, to dispense military advice, to provide security services (protection of property and personnel), and for combat. In the former Yugoslavia, for example, the United States has hired an NGO run by retired US military personnel—Military Professional Resources Incorporated (MPRI)—to dispense military advice and train the Croat military. In other cases, private military companies were hired by states to fight rebels on their territory. For example, Executive Outcomes (EO)—a company run by former members of the South African military—was hired by Sierra Leone and Angola to fight rebels on their territory.[53]

Some authors have pointed out that, in certain cases, these private military forces have helped to stop internal strife. David Shearer, for example, credits EO with bringing the warring parties in Sierra Leone to the negotiating table in 1996.[54] Some believe that they may be a solution to the United Nations' chronic lack of military personnel in messy and risky situations. Others, however, believe that the activities of these companies should be more closely monitored and regulated.

Indeed, many of these companies operate in a legal vacuum. They do business predominantly in Africa. Often, countries or rebel groups pay these companies not in hard currency but in mining rights. At times, mining companies themselves have agreed to pay for the services of these private military companies in return for mining rights. In many instances, there are close links between mining companies and military companies.

The diamond-mining business in Africa is very profitable. According to estimates, the African diamond trade represents US $5–7 billion a year. A country such as Sierra Leone, ripped apart by an extremely bloody war that has lasted over eight years and killed tens of thousands of people, and mutilated many more, still produces between US $300–450 million worth of diamonds each year. Not surprisingly, the stakes in this conflict are high, not only for the warring factions but also for the mining companies and their military sister organizations.[55] Of course, this also makes these private military corporations more than simple hirelings; it makes them active actors in the conflicts in question. Ominously, they may actually profit from dragging out and escalating such conflicts.

David Shearer has suggested that the international community should engage these companies, instead of banning them or pretending that they do not exist. Yet, it seems that that is exactly what is happening. Increasingly, these companies perform tasks that governments cannot or will not carry out. Moreover, many of these activities are initiated without any consideration of the longer-term consequences involved. Finally, these activities often take place in both a domestic and international legal vacuum; here, again, an internationally agreed-upon legal framework is sorely needed.

International organizations also increasingly engage private firms, but thus far the role of these firms has been limited to the protection of property and civilian personnel. Some believe that success in this domain may lead to the employment of such firms for combat purposes or enforcement operations. That, however, would amount to giving the United Nations its own standing forces. Given the reluctance of Member States to do so and the lack of UN financial resources, this seems an unlikely prospect.

In this respect, it is important to make a clear distinction between hiring the services of such firms and entering into partnerships with them. The United Nations might wish to do the former; it should not, however, be allowed to do the latter. The current enthusiasm of the United Nations to enter into business partnerships may be innocent and even mutually profitable in certain areas. However, questions of war and peace and life and death should not be governed by profit motives; it is contrary to everything the United Nations stands for.

The instruments of intervention

States have two main coercive instruments available when considering intervention: the use of force and economic sanctions.[56] Six conditions need to be fulfilled for the effective use of coercive instruments.[57]

First, outside powers need to have a clear idea of the political objectives they hope to achieve. They should try to pursue one objective at a time. Multiple objectives muddy the waters. The imposition of sanctions or the use of military force should not be intended to punish troublemakers. These instruments should be used to change behaviour, or to bring those responsible to justice.

Second, outside powers need to correctly assess the economic, political, and military characteristics of the target. It should be noted that the targets of intervention will often be non-state actors.[58] Our knowledge of how coercive actions affect targets—particularly non-state targets—is limited. This cripples the development of a coherent and effective strategy. The imposition of economic sanctions on some targets is ineffective and can even be counterproductive. For example, imposing economic sanctions on parties in very poor states (Burundi) or failed states (Somalia) is at best futile. Similarly, the effectiveness of the use of force is dependent on the characteristics of the target. Aiming the use of force at "the conflict," as was done in the early 1990s in Bosnia and Somalia, instead of at the belligerent parties, has led to dramatic policy failures.

Third, one country or international organization has to take the lead in interventions. Leadership gives direction to interventions and is one of the keys to building strong coalitions. Moreover, in the absence of a leader, sanctions regimes will quickly be crippled because of interpretation problems, and multiple and conflicting purposes may be proposed for military interventions. This frequently leads to failure. In theory, international leadership should come from the UN Security Council. In practice, it comes from individual states. A leader has to be able to chart an effective course of action and articulate its position to others. A lot depends on the political and military strength of the country in question. That said, being a leader does not mean bullying others around. True leaders know how to translate national interests into global and international interests, and persuade other states to get on board.

Fourth, leaders need to build strong international coalitions of support for proposed coercive undertakings. Whether international support for these interventions is obtained depends on a function of the threat that has been posed to regional and international security and human life. It is also dependent on national interests and leadership. The more countries see an internal conflict as a threat to their own security and a threat to higher values, the easier it will be to build a coalition to support international intervention. The participation of many states is necessary for the success of sanctions regimes. It may also be preferable when it comes to the use of military force; indeed, it may help to ensure that sufficient troops are available for coercive actions. Moreover, it may help to bring down costs. The United Nations has an important role to play in building and organizing international support for coercive actions, and it can provide legitimacy to these actions.

Fifth, outside powers need to ensure that enough resources are available. As far as economic sanctions regimes are concerned, resources may be needed to implement and enforce a regime. Sanctions regimes often experience implementation problems. Resources may also be needed to compensate some states for losses associated with the implementation of sanctions. Similarly, military interventions need to be endowed with sufficient resources. This is not to say that such operations need to have overwhelming military capabilities to be successful, but they need enough firepower and the right mix of forces—air power and ground troops—to get the job done.

Sixth, outside powers need to adopt appropriate strategies. Intervention strategies are the subject of wide debate within the scholarly and analytical communities. Two main schools of thought exist on the imposition of sanctions and the use of force. The first school of thought believes that coercive instruments are most effective when imposed immediately and comprehensively. The second believes that coercive instruments can—and often should—be imposed gradually. Both schools of thought are right some of the time. Some cases warrant swift and comprehensive coercive actions; others call for gradual approaches.

The use of economic sanctions and military force should be proportionate to the goal. Limited goals do not warrant the massive imposition of sanctions or the massive use of force. If goals are more ambitious, stronger coercive actions are generally called for. If the threat to international peace and security or human life is both significant and immediate, strong sanctions and military operations might be needed. Less urgent situations call for the use of more incremental approaches.

The political, economic, and military characteristics of the target should also guide strategy selection. For example, authoritarian regimes are less vulnerable to economic sanctions than democratic regimes; when dealing with an authoritarian regime, it may be advisable to forgo economic sanctions altogether and threaten the use of force immediately.

Similarly, small guerrilla groups are mostly immune to economic sanctions. Many sanctions regimes stay in place for a long time and often start producing adverse social and humanitarian effects. Contrary to what many people think, such effects rarely lead to the overthrow of the politicians in place or a change in behaviour of the political elites. On the contrary, empirical evidence in the former Yugoslavia, Haiti, and Iraq tends to confirm that prolonged sanctions strengthen—rather than weaken—the political regimes in place. The existence and level of development of political opposition in the target country is very important in this respect. If the opposition is weak, the imposition of comprehensive sanctions may ruin their chances to develop into a real opposition. This happened in the Federal Republic of Yugoslavia (Serbia and Montenegro), for example. Economic and military characteristics of the target regime should also guide coercive strategies. For example, weak economies should be hit with gradual and partial sanctions. Conversely, robust economies, as well as centrally planned economies, should be hit swiftly and comprehensively; because of their ability to shift resources around, they are better able to withstand sanctions. In the same vein, the limited use of force may be sufficient in conventional wars. Indeed, traditional military organizations may be more vulnerable to the coercive uses of force than guerrilla or insurgent fighters. Much has been written about the use of air power, particularly after Kosovo. Air power remains an extremely problematic tool in internal conflict situations and in situations where gross violations of human rights are taking place. It is often forgotten that Bosnia showed the limited utility of air power in these types of situations; it demonstrated that air strikes cannot serve as a substitute for ground forces. The use of air power in the Balkans in 1999 also raises very important questions about NATO's targeting policy and its utilization of cluster bombs.

Coercive strategies should also be flexible. As time goes by, the economic, military, and political characteristics of a target can change. The coercer's objectives and means may also change over time. A strategy that was sound early on in a conflict, therefore, may no longer be effective later in the conflict. Finally, all good strategies should contain exit strategies. Exit strategies should not be confused with exit schedules. Exits need to be based on local political and strategic conditions, not arbitrary and rigid timetables. They should also encompass a post-intervention strategy designed to tackle long-term economic and political problems. Outside powers that are considering intervention should realize that interventions entail more than the imposition of economic sanctions or the activation of the military. They should be prepared to make long-term—even open-ended—commitments.

More generally, the development of economic sanctions and military strategies should not be seen as separate undertakings. Economic sanctions strategies should include determinations about when to threaten and escalate the use of military force. The imposition of economic sanctions and the use of military force should therefore be seen as two points on a coercive continuum and two complementary policy options.

In sum, the effective use of economic sanctions and military force depends on:

1. Having a clear purpose;
2. Correctly assessing the target;
3. Leadership;
4. Coalition support;
5. Providing sufficient resources to ensure effective implementation and execution;
6. Having an appropriate strategy, including an exit and post-intervention strategy.

This may seem to be mere commonsense, but the fact of the matter is that many post–Cold War interventions have failed to meet these conditions. They consequently failed to have the desired effects.

The role of the United Nations

The United Nations has an important role to play both in legitimizing and in helping to monitor and implement coercive actions. As far as economic sanctions are concerned, the United Nations Secretariat should advocate a more integrated use of the UN sanctions committees. These committees, set up to examine and promulgate guidelines to facilitate implementation of sanctions regimes, should be given greater authority to interpret sanctions provisions. At present, because sanctions resolutions do not expressly foresee interpretative functions for sanctions committees, individual states are free to reject the guidance and advice given by the committees. Giving the UN sanctions committees interpretative authority over all UN members would increase uniformity and implementation—and hence the effectiveness of these regimes. Establishing only one sanctions committee would go a long way toward achieving this.

Similarly, the economic sanctions monitoring capacity of the United Nations needs to be strengthened. The experience of the European Union in the monitoring and enforcement of sanctions on the former Yugoslavia is very useful in this regard. It showed that, with relatively limited means, one could monitor trade and traffic.

What goes for economic sanctions regimes also goes for military interventions. The United Nations badly needs to update its monitoring and supervisory mechanisms. This becomes all the more important when most of the coercive interventions take place outside the purview of the United Nations. Regular reporting mechanisms need to be established. One could also envisage the establishment of a Security Council supervisory committee for military operations. Such a committee, like the sanctions committees, should be a subsidiary organ of the Council and have the same membership as the Council. This would be preferable to revitalizing and using the Military Staff Committee. Indeed, the Military Staff Committee, because of its limited membership—the chiefs of staff of the Permanent Members of the Security Council—is not appealing to most UN Member States. In as much as possible, the deliberations of this committee should be open to other UN member-states. Non-governmental organizations should be given rights of petition, and the proceedings of this Committee should be made public. Transparency in this domain is essential.

The United Nations can also be instrumental in forging a consensus on the conditions and criteria for humanitarian interventions. The United Nations Secretariat should initiate a wide variety of studies and involve experts and research institutes from around the world.[59] Following its experience during the Cold War in the arms control field, the United Nations may wish to set up different independent groups of non-governmental experts to study the matter of humanitarian intervention and the use of coercive instruments in all its aspects. For example, one group could conduct a systematic study of past state practice and legal arguments and try to identify criteria for humanitarian intervention. The International Legal Commission could also be invited to express its opinion on this issue.[60] Another could tackle the political issues related to intervention by outside powers, including the impact of domestic politics. A third group could look at the operational and military aspects. A fourth group could look at the specific problems of the implementation of peace agreements and how to deal with antagonists like Foday Sankoh. Following these inventory exercises, governmental expert groups could be established. Given the nature of the problem, it will be important to depoliticize the meetings of both the non-governmental and governmental expert groups as much as possible. Only when some intellectual clarity has been reached can one envisage the establishment of governmental groups of experts.

The primary responsibility of the UN Security Council in these matters notwithstanding, the UN Security Council and the UN General Assembly could jointly decide to finance and set up such groups. Ultimately, the results of these studies could be discussed in both the Council and the

Assembly and possibly give rise to a joint declaration or resolution. An amendment of the Charter might follow. This, of course, will only happen—if at all—very far down the road.[61]

Finally, the United Nations should be given a key role in organizing and coordinating the long-term commitments that are needed to eradicate the underlying sources of communal conflict. As noted above, regional organizations should be intimately involved in this process, but the process should ultimately be supervised by the United Nations. This will keep regional politics from taking over.

The United Nations experiences in Kosovo, East Timor, Sierra Leone, and the Democratic Republic of Congo will have long-lasting effects on the organization. While success or failure will depend on the material and political support of states, the UN Secretariat also has an enormous responsibility. It should not squander the meagre resources it has been given.

Unfortunately, the May 2000 crisis in Sierra Leone indicated that the lessons learned in the 1990s—in particular, "thou shalt not send lightly-armed peace-keepers into a violent or potentially violent situation"—were not acted upon. After the Somalia, Rwanda, and Bosnia debacles of the early 1990s, few UN missions were launched; few states had the stomach to deploy the robust type of forces needed. That said, in the wake of the 1999 US–NATO intervention in Kosovo, the UN Security Council established three major missions—in East Timor, in Sierra Leone, and in the Democratic Republic of Congo. All were equipped with a Chapter VII (enforcement) mandate. Unfortunately, resources to carry out such a mandate lagged behind. This mismatch of mandate and resources was reminiscent of the agonizing UN missions of the early 1990s.

The UN Secretary-General should protect the organization from such irresponsible behaviour of states by clearly outlining the options and their respective strengths and limitations.[62] In some cases, he should refuse a mission and make his case publicly. He should be relentless in going public with such information. He should also make information publicly available that is damaging to the Secretariat and shows its failures. The publication of the reports on the fall of Srebrenica and on UN action in Rwanda during the 1994 genocide are, in this respect, encouraging.[63] We await the report on the mission in Sierra Leone and subsequent action.

Notes

1. It may also involve criminal prosecution. This aspect of intervention, although important, will not be covered in this chapter. In the case of the former Yugoslavia and Rwanda, the UN Security Council established International Criminal Tribunals charged

with bringing those responsible for war crimes and other gross violations of human rights to justice.
2. Since 1990, wars have claimed more than 5 million lives. See UN Secretary-General's Commencement Address at Paul Nitze School of Advanced International Studies, Johns Hopkins University, United Nations Press Release, SG/SM/7421 of 25 May 2000.
3. Sanctions to quell internal conflict were imposed on the republics of the former Yugoslavia, the Federal Republic of Yugoslavia, the Bosnian Serbs, Somalia, Haiti, Liberia, Unita (Angola), Rwanda, and Sierra Leone. In the case of Iraq, sanctions were imposed to force Iraq to end its occupation of Kuwait and subsequently to ensure Iraqi compliance with UNSC Res. 687 (1991) of 3 April 1991. In the case of Eritrea and Ethiopia, an arms embargo was imposed to end war between these two countries. In the case of Afghanistan, Libya, and Sudan, sanctions were imposed to force those countries to extradite individuals suspected of terrorist attacks.
4. Military force was authorized in Bosnia, Somalia, Rwanda, Haiti, Zaire, Albania, Kosovo, East Timor, Sierra Leone, and the Democratic Republic of Congo. Troops engaged in all these operations received Chapter VII—enforcement—mandates, and were authorized to use force for purposes other than self-defence. Not all of them did. Military force was also authorized in the case of Iraq. Yet this was a more classical inter-state conflict. The UN Security Council did not authorize the initial military intervention in Kosovo in March 1999, but subsequently authorized an international presence with an enforcement mandate. See UNSC Res. 1244 (1999) of 10 June 1999.
5. For a review of UN economic sanctions regimes see, for example, David Cortright and George Lopez, *The Sanctions Decade: Assessing UN Strategies in the 1990s* (Boulder and London: Lynne Rienner, 2000); and Chantal de Jonge Oudraat, "Making economic sanctions work," in Chester Crocker, Fen Hampson, and Pamela Aall (eds.), *Managing Global Chaos*, 2nd ed. (Washington, DC: United States Institute of Peace Press, 2000). For a review of coercive military operations see, for example, Donald C. F. Daniel and Bradd C. Hayes with Chantal de Jonge Oudraat, *Coercive Inducement and the Containment of International Crises* (Washington, DC: United States Institute of Peace Press, 1999); Chantal de Jonge Oudraat, "L'ONU, les conflits internes et le recours à la force armée," *Annuaire Français de Relations Internationales 2000*, 1 (Brussels: Buylant, 2000); 817–30; and Peter Viggo Jakobsen, *Western Use of Coercive Diplomacy After the Cold War: A Challenge for Theory and Practice* (New York: St Martin's Press, 1998).
6. Realist and neo-realist theory has shown that international cooperation becomes very difficult when actors believe that such cooperation might result in relative gains that can be exploited to the advantage of one and the disadvantage of others. See, for example, John Mearsheimer, "The false promise of international institutions," *International Security* 19/3, (1994/5): 5–49.
7. See also Chapter 3, above.
8. In October 1998, the North Atlantic Council had authorized the Supreme Allied Commander in Europe (SACEUR) to launch air strikes if Milosevic did not comply with UNSC Res. 1199 (1998) of 23 September 1998. NATO's activation order was suspended, but not annulled, after Richard Holbrooke reached an agreement with Milosevic in October 1998.
9. In the 1999 UN General Assembly debate, some states emphasized the need for a set of generally accepted rules and guidelines that would regulate humanitarian interventions. That said, they were clearly in the minority, and they were not very specific. See, for example, the statements of New Zealand, Lithuania, Sweden, Spain, Brazil, Argentina, Egypt, and the Republic of Korea.
10. See "Secretary-General presents his Annual Report to General Assembly," United Na-

tions Press Releases, SG/SM/7136 and GA/9596, 20 September 1999. In March 2000, Kofi Annan also launched a major study on peace operations.
11. See Charter of the United Nations, Articles 39, 42, and 2 (7). Under Articles 24 and 25, states promise to accept and carry out decisions made by the Council.
12. See also, in this regard, the 1991 Annual Report of the UN Secretary-General, Javier Pérez de Cuéllar, A/46/1, September 1991.
13. In 1950, the UN General Assembly had given itself the right to vote on the use of force to restore or maintain international peace and security in case the Council was logjammed. The "Uniting for Peace" Resolution was adopted by the UN General Assembly in November 1950 during the Korea crisis. See UNGA Res. 377, 3 November 1950. The Assembly has invoked the resolution several times, but never to recommend the use of force. Moreover, legal experts disagree over the question of whether the UN General Assembly is, indeed, entitled to intervene in cases where the Council is divided. The International Court of Justice, in its Advisory Opinion of 20 July 1962 on *Certain Expenses of the United Nations*, ruled that *only* the Council could order enforcement actions and authorize the use of force. For details on the legal debate, see René Degni-Segui, "Fonctions et pouvoirs: Article 24," in Jean-Pierre Cot and Alain Pellet (eds.), *La Charte des Nations Unies*, 2nd ed. (Paris: Economica, 1991): 451–8; Anthony Clark Arend and Robert J. Beck, *International Law and the Use of Force* (London and New York: Routledge, 1993): 59–60, 66–7; and John F. Murphy, "Force and Arms," in Christopher C. Joyner (ed.), *The United Nations and International Law* (New York: Cambridge University Press and American Society of International Law, 1997): 108–9.
14. The cases foreseen in Article 53 (1) and Article 107 that permit action against World War II enemy states have become obsolete.
15. See Anthony Clark Arend and Robert J. Beck, *International Law and the Use of Force* (see note 13, above). Arend and Beck argue that (p. 111) ". . . there exists a substantial gap between, on the one hand, the 'restrictionist' views of most states and legal scholars, and, on the other, the consistent practice of those states whose interests (have been) specially affected." Such a significant discrepancy would seem to call into question the existence of any authoritative and controlling rule prohibiting state intervention to protect nationals." See also Natalino Ronzitti, *Rescuing Nationals Abroad Through Military Coercion and Intervention on Grounds of Humanity* (Dordrecht: Martinus Nijhoff, 1985). Ronzitti argues (p. 76) "that a process is under way that might entail the creation of a new rule of customary international law permitting intervention for protecting nationals abroad."
16. See UNGA Res. 2625, 24 October 1970.
17. See Rein Mullerson, "Self defense in the contemporary world," in Lori Fisler Damrosch and David J. Scheffer (eds.), *Law and Force in the New International Order* (Boulder: Westview Press, 1991): 16. Mullerson asserts that the Court unambiguously condemned these doctrines as contrary to international law and cites the following passage: "The Court cannot contemplate the creation of a new rule opening up a right of intervention by one state against another on the ground that the latter has opted for some particular ideology or political system."
18. See, for example, UNSC Res. 1269 (1999) of 19 October 1999. That said, efforts to combat terrorism are seen, first and foremost, as national efforts; states are encouraged to prevent and suppress such activities in their own territories, not uninvited in the territories of other states.
19. See UNSC Res. 748 (1992) of 31 March 1992. Sanctions were imposed under Chapter VII of the UN Charter. They were lifted on 5 April 1999.
20. Sanctions were imposed on Sudan because of Sudan's refusal to extradite three individuals accused of the assassination attempt on the Egyptian President Hosni Mubarak.

INTERVENTION: TRENDS AND CHALLENGES 71

See UNSC Res. 1054 (1996) of 26 April 1996. Sanctions went into effect on 10 May 1996. They consisted of restrictions on the travel of Sudanese diplomatic personnel. Sanctions on the Taliban were imposed because of the Taliban's refusal to hand over Osama Bin Laden and his associates for trial. See UNSC Res. 1267 (1999) of 15 October 1999 for the sanctions on the Taliban (Afghanistan). Sanctions went into effect on 15 November 1999, and consisted of a freeze on financial assets and a boycott of Taliban-owned aircraft.

21. In 1999, seven countries believed to be supporting international terrorism—Cuba, Iran, Iraq, Libya, North Korea, Sudan, and Syria—were subjected to unilateral US sanctions, as were 202 terrorist organizations and 59 individuals. See Office of Foreign Assets Control, US Department of the Treasury, "Terrorism: A Summary of Terrorism Sanctions Regulations, Terrorism List of Government Sanctions Regulations, and Foreign Terrorist Organizations Sanctions Regulations," 25 June 1999. See website: <www.treas.gov/ofac>.

22. The unilateral adoption of economic sanctions for coercive purposes has been condemned in many UN General Assembly resolutions. See, for example, UNGA Res. 2131, 21 December 1965. Yet, unlike the use of force, the Charter does not contain a specific prohibition on the coercive use of economic sanctions, nor does it prohibit states from imposing sanctions unilaterally if they so wish. Moreover, it may be recalled that in the Nicaragua case, the International Court of Justice condemned the US for its military support to the Contras, but it did not condemn the US for imposing an economic embargo on Nicaragua. In sum, there is no legal impediment to the unilateral imposition of sanctions, unlike the use of force.

23. Deterrence can be defined as action that prevents an adversary from doing something that one does not want it to do, and that it might otherwise be tempted to do. Compellence can be defined as action that stops an adversary from doing something that it has already undertaken, or forces to do something that it has not yet undertaken. On the difference between deterrence and compellence, see Thomas C. Schelling, *Arms and Influence* (New Haven: Yale University Press, 1966): 69–91; and Robert J. Art, "To what ends military power?" *International Security* 4/4, (1980): 6–7.

24. Many NATO states had serious misgivings about the legal grounds of NATO's intervention. See Catherine Guicherd, "International law and the war in Kosovo," *Survival* 41/2, (1999): 19–34.

25. Some analysts advocate a new interpretation of Article 2 (4) of the Charter, which prohibits "the threat, or use of force against the territorial integrity or political independence of any state, or in any other manner inconsistent with the purposes of the United Nations." They argue that humanitarian assistance and intervention is not directed against the territorial integrity or political independence of the state. This argument does not seem to be supported by practice. Indeed, humanitarian intervention often entails a profound overhaul of state structures and practices.

26. The relevant Articles in Chapter VIII of the UN Charter are Article 52 and 53. Article 52 (1) reads: "Nothing in the present Charter precludes the existence of regional arrangements or agencies for dealing with such matters relating to the maintenance of international peace and security as are appropriate for regional action, provided that such arrangements or agencies and their activities are consistent with the purposes and principles of the United Nations." Article 53 (1) reads: "The Security Council shall, where appropriate, utilize such regional arrangements or agencies for enforcement action under its authority. But no enforcement action shall be taken under regional arrangements or by regional agencies without the authorization of the Security Council . . ."

27. See Winrich Kühne, *Humanitäre NATO-Einsätze Ohne Mandat?: Ein Diskussions-*

beitrag zur Fortentwicklung der UNO-Charta (Ebenhausen: Stiftung Wissenschaft und Politik, AP3096, 1999).

28. See Michael E. Brown, "The causes and regional dimensions of internal conflict," in Michael E. Brown (ed.), *The International Dimensions of Internal Conflict* (Cambridge: MIT Press, 1996): 590–9.
29. The United States and the United Kingdom defended such a right during the Kosovo crisis. In general, though, the US and European governments made weak legal cases when defending a right to unilateral humanitarian intervention. On the different positions of the NATO members see, for example, Serge Sur, "Les aspects juridiques de l'intervention des pays membres de l'OTAN au Kosovo," *Revue de Defense Nationale* (December 1999): 44–62; Adam Roberts, "NATO's 'humanitarian war' over Kosovo," *Survival* 41/3 (1999): 102–123; and Catherine Guicherd, "International law and the war in Kosovo," *Survival* 41/2 (Summer 1999): 19–34.
30. See, for example, Michael L. Burton, "Legalizing the sublegal: A proposal for codifying a doctrine of unilateral humanitarian intervention," *Georgetown Law Journal* 85 (1996): 417–568; David J. Scheffer, "Toward a modern doctrine of humanitarian intervention," *University of Toledo Law Review* 23 (1992): 252–93; Theodor Meron and Allan Rosas, "A declaration of minimum humanitarian standards," *American Journal of International Law* 85 (1991): 375–81. See also David J. Scheffer, "Challenges confronting collective security: Humanitarian intervention," in David J. Scheffer, Richard N. Gardner, and Gerald B. Helman, *Post-Gulf War Challenges to the UN Collective Security System: Three Views on the Issue of Humanitarian Intervention.* (Washington, DC: United States Institute of Peace Press, 1992), 11–13; John Norton Moore, "The control of foreign intervention in internal conflict," *Virginia Journal of International Law* 9 (1969): 264; and Richard B. Lillich, "Forcible self-help by states to protect human rights," *Iowa Law Review* 53 (1967): 347–51.
31. See Dan Smith, "Interventionist dilemmas and justice," in Anthony McDermott (ed.), *Humanitarian Force*, PRIO Report No. 4, published jointly with the Norwegian Institute for International Affairs (Oslo: PRIO, 1997).
32. Article 3, which is common to all Geneva Conventions, reads as follows:

In the case of armed conflict not of an international character occurring in the territory of one of the High Contracting Parties, each Party to the conflict shall be bound to apply, as a minimum, the following provisions:

(1) Persons taking no active part in the hostilities, including members of armed forces who have laid down their arms and those placed 'hors de combat' by sickness, wounds, detention, or any other cause, shall in all circumstances be treated humanly, without any adverse distinction founded on race, colour, religion, or faith, sex, birth or wealth, or any other similar criteria.

To this end, the following acts are and shall remain prohibited at any time and in any place whatsoever with respect to the above-mentioned persons:

(a) violence to life and person, in particular murder of all kinds, mutilation, cruel treatment and torture; (b) taking of hostages; (c) outrages upon personal dignity, in particular humiliating and degrading treatment; (d) the passing of sentences and the carrying out of executions without previous judgment pronounced by a regularly constituted court, affording all the judicial guarantees which are recognized as indispensable by civilized peoples.

(2) The wounded and sick shall be collected and cared for. An impartial humanitarian body, such as the International Committee of the Red Cross, may offer its services to the Parties to the conflict.

The Parties to the conflict should further endeavour to bring into force, by means of special agreements, all or part of the other provisions of the present Convention.

The application of the preceding provisions shall not affect the legal status of the Parties to the conflict.

The International Criminal Tribunal for the former Yugoslavia was authorized to adjudicate: (1) grave breaches of the 1949 Geneva Conventions, such as willfully killing or causing great injury to wounded soldiers, prisoners of war, or civilians; torture; unlawful deportation; or taking civilians hostage; (2) violations of the laws or customs of war, such as wanton destruction of cities or villages; attacks on undefended civilian populations; and destruction of institutions dedicated to religion, charity, or education; (3) genocide, defined as crimes committed with the intent of destroying in whole or in part a national, ethnic, racial, or religious group; (4) crimes against humanity, defined as inhumane acts such as murder, torture, or rape, committed as part of a widespread or systematic attack against any civilian population on national, political, ethnic, racial, or religious grounds. The Rwandan tribunal was authorized to adjudicate serious violations of humanitarian law in the latter two of these areas as well as violations of Article 3 of the Geneva Conventions. For the statutes of the tribunals see UNSC Res. 827 (1993) of 25 May 1993 and UNSC Res. 955 (1994) of 8 November 1994. The jurisdiction of the (permanent) International Criminal Court is "limited to the most serious crimes of concern to the international community as a whole." The Court has jurisdiction with respect to the following crimes: crime of genocide, crimes against humanity, war crimes, and the crime of aggression.

33. Several NGOs have argued that certain aspects of NATO's bombing campaign were in violation of humanitarian law, in particular the choice of certain targets and the use of cluster bombs. See, for example, the US Human Rights Watch materials on <www.hrw.org/hrw/campaigns/kosovo98>.
34. See Serge Sur, "Les aspects juridiques de l'intervention des pays membres de l'OTAN au Kosovo," *Revue de Defense Nationale* (see note 29, above); Sur considers an intervention by a group of states more desirable than intervention by a single state. Indeed, in the former case it is easier to defend against accusations that the intervention takes place out of self-interest and is mainly self-serving. Yet, this does not seem to be a condition that would make intervention more lawful.
35. Couching this issue in terms of a weakening of state sovereignty is unhelpful and beside the point. Sovereignty has never been an absolute concept. Moreover, military intervention is increasingly used in situations where state institutions have collapsed, and is most often aimed at non-state actors: international terrorists, small military groups, crime syndicates, or individuals advocating genocide. If the sovereignty and independence of states is at risk at the dawn of the twenty-first century, it is because of globalization—economic interdependence and the information technology revolution—not military intervention by outside powers.
36. See Charter of the United Nations, Articles 43, 46, and 47.
37. On a UN Force see, for example, Brian Urquhart, "For a UN volunteer military force," *New York Review of Books* XL/11 (June 1993): 3–4. On peace enforcement units, see the proposal by Boutros Boutros-Ghali in *An Agenda for Peace: Preventive Diplomacy, Peacemaking and Peacekeeping* (New York: United Nations, 1992), para 44.
38. See *The United Nations and Rwanda, 1993–1996*, Blue Book Series, vol. X, (New York: United Nations, 1996).
39. See the Annual Progress Report of the Secretary-General on Standby Arrangements for Peacekeeping, and <www.un.org/Depts/dpko>.

40. On 22 October 1999, the UN Security Council authorized the establishment of a mission in Sierra Leone (UNAMSIL) of up to 6,000 military personnel. See UNSC Res. 1270 (1999) of 22 October 1999. Troop strength was increased in February and May 2000 to 11,100 and 13,000 soldiers respectively. See UNSC Res. 1289 (2000) of 7 February 2000 and UNSC Res. 1299 (2000) of 19 May 2000. A UN Mission in the Republic of Congo following the Lusaka cease-fire of 10 July 1999 would require many thousands of troops. Although the cease-fire agreement provides for the deployment of UN soldiers, thus far the United Nations has only established an observer mission comprising 90 military observers. An advance group entered the country in November 1999. In February 2000, the United Nations Organization Mission in the Democratic Republic of Congo (MONUC) was authorized to deploy up to 5,537 military personnel. See UNSC Res. 1291 (2000) of 24 February 2000.
41. See Brian Urquhart, "Will the world learn from the debacle in East Timor," *The Boston Globe*, 17 September 1999.
42. Even for a limited operation such as Operation Turquoise in Rwanda, France had to hire heavy-lift air transport planes (Antonov An-124s) from Russia.
43. See, for example, Richard Haass, *Intervention: The Use of American Force in The Post–Cold War World* (Washington, DC: Brookings Press, 1999); Richard Haass, *The Reluctant Sheriff: The United States After the Cold War* (Washington, DC: Brookings Press, 1997); Willam J. Durch (ed.), *UN Peacekeeping* (see note 5, above); and Stanley Sloan, *The United States and the Use of Force in the Post-Cold War World: Toward Self-Deterrence?* Report prepared for the Committee on Foreign Affairs, US House of Representatives, August 1994, 103rd Congress, 2nd Session (Washington, DC: GPO, 1994).
44. See Chantal de Jonge Oudraat, "Bosnia," in Donald C. F. Daniel et al., *Coercive Inducement* (see note 5, above): 41–78.
45. The US proposed to take the lead in Somalia on 25 November 1992. An US-led military operation (UNITAF) was authorized by the UN Security Council on 3 December 1992. One week later, UNITAF troops landed in Somalia. On 4 May 1993, the United States handed over command of the operation in Somalia to the United Nations (UNOSOM II). On 13 October 1993, the United States announced that it would withdraw all of its troops from Somalia by the end of March 1994. This doomed the international intervention in Somalia to failure. The last US troops left Somalia in March 1994. They would return briefly one year later, in March 1995, to extract the remaining UN troops from Somalia. Violent conflict in Somalia has persisted. See Donald C. F. Daniel and Bradd C. Hayes, "Somalia," in Donald C. F. Daniel et al., *Coercive Inducement* (see note 5, above): 79–112.
46. See Chantal de Jonge Oudraat, "Haiti," in Donald C. F. Daniel et al., *Coercive Inducement* (see note 5, above): 41–78.
47. See Ivo Daalder and Michael O'Hanlon, *Winning Ugly: NATO's War to Save Kosovo*, (Washington, DC: Brookings Press, 2000).
48. It must also be noted that Nigeria and ECOMOG, contrary to the United States and NATO, intervened upon requests of the sitting, albeit besieged, central governments.
49. This was one of the lessons that the US military had learned during Vietnam. For details, see, for example, Richard N. Haass, *Intervention: The Use of American Military Force in the Post Cold War World* (Washington, DC: Carnegie Endowment for International Peace, 1994); and US Department of the Army, *Peace Operations* (Washington, DC: GPO, Field Manual 100-23, 30 December 1994).
50. The polls were carried out in 1995 by the Program on International Policy Attitudes at the University of Maryland. See Randolph Ryan, "Is the US public bolder than its leaders? Studies suggest Americans might back forceful action to stop ethnic cleansing," *The Boston Globe*, 23 July 1995. See also Sloan, *The United States and the Use of Force*

INTERVENTION: TRENDS AND CHALLENGES   75

in the Post–Cold War World: Toward Self-Deterrence? (See note 43, above). The studies and surveys by the Triangle Institute for Security Studies were carried out in 1999. See Peter D. Feaver and Richard H. Kohn, "Project on the Gap Between the Military and Civil Society: Digest of Findings and Studies, Paper presented at the Conference on the Military and Civilian Society, Cantigny Conference Center, 28–29 October 1999. cm website: <(www.poli.duke.edu/civmil)>. See also Peter D. Feaver and Christopher Gelpi, "How many deaths are acceptable?" (see note 50, above).

51. The poll showed some remarkable discrepancies between the military elite, the civilian elite, and the mass public. Faced with the same question on the Congo, the military elite gave 284 and the civilian elite 484 as the number of acceptable deaths. For Iraq, the figures were: military elite, 6,016; civilian elite, 19,045. Finally, respondents were asked how many American deaths would be acceptable to defend Taiwan against invasion by China. The military elite responded 17,425; the civilian elite, 17,554; and the mass public, 20,172. See Peter D. Feaver and Christopher Gelpi, "How Many Deaths Are Acceptable? (see note 50, above).

52. See, for example, Frederick Forsyth, "Send in the mercenaries," *Wall Street Journal*, 15 May 2000; Jonah Schulhofer-Wohl, "Should we privatize the peacekeeping?" *Washington Post*, 12 May 2000; and William Shawcross, "Send in the mercenaries if our troops won't fight," *Guardian*, 10 May 2000.

53. For details, see David Shearer, *Private Armies and Military Intervention*, Adelphi Paper 316 (London: International Institute for Strategic Studies, 1998); David Shearer, "Outsourcing war," *Foreign Policy* (Fall 1998): 68–81; Deborah Avant, "The market for force: Exploring the privatization of military services," a Paper for the CFR Study Group on the Arms Trade and the Transnationalization of the Defense Industry: Economic versus Security Drivers, 1999; and Abdel-Fatau Musah and J. Kayode Fayemi, *Mercenaries: An African Security Dilemma* (London: Pluto Press, 2000). It may be noted that EO was outlawed in South Africa in 1998.

54. However, after having spent 21 months in the country and enabled the sitting government to get the better of the Revolutionary United Front (RUF), EO's contract was terminated. This, of course, was one of the conditions of the RUF, who also refused the deployment of UN peace-keepers. The ensuing military vacuum led to continued fighting. In May 1997 a military coup took place, derailing all previous peace efforts. See David Shearer, *Private Armies and Military Intervention* (see note 53, above).

55. See, for example, James Rupert, "Diamond hunters fuel Africa's brutal wars: in Sierra Leone, mining firms trade weapons and money for access to gems," *Washington Post*, 16 October 1999. Others have estimated that Sierra Leone loses US $200–300 million annually to illegal diamond trafficking. Most of this illegal trade passes through Liberia which since the mid-1990s has exported 31 million carats—more than 200 year's worth of Liberia's national capacity. See Douglas Farah, "Diamonds are a rebel's best friend: Mining of gems helps Sierra Leone militia stall peace process," *The Washington Post*, 17 April 2000; and Blaine Harden, "Africa's gems: Warfare's best friend," *The New York Times*, 6 April 2000.

56. It should be noted that international criminal prosecution is a third instrument available to states. However, this instrument is not covered in this chapter.

57. For a more detailed development of these conditions see Chantal de Jonge Oudraat, "L'ONU, les conflits internes et le recours à la force armée" (see note 5, above): and Chantal de Jonge Oudraat, "Making economic sanctions work," in Chester A. Crocker, Fen Osler Hampson, and Pamela Aall (eds.), *Managing Global Chaos*, 2nd ed. (Washington, DC: United States Institute of Peace Press, 2001).

58. This is in contrast with what happened in the nineteenth and twentieth centuries. It also underscores the idea that the debate over intervention is perhaps not a debate over the

decline of the sovereignty of the state, but rather a debate over how the state is reasserting its sovereignty.
59. The launch in March 2000 of a major study on peace missions by the UN Secretary-General is in this regard encouraging, but this effort should be multiplied.
60. See, for example, the proposal by Michael L. Burton, "Legalizing the sublegal: A proposal for codifying a doctrine of unilateral intervention," *Georgetown Law Journal* 85 (1996): 417–568.
61. It would entail progress on the question of membership of the Council as well as moves on the veto, both of which are unlikely in the near future.
62. This was a procedure first introduced by UN Secretary-General Boutros Boutros-Ghali. Unfortunately Kofi Annan has abandoned this practice.
63. See Report of the UN Secretary-General, *The Fall of Srebrenica*, A/54/549, 15 November 1999; and Report of the Independent Inquiry into the Actions of the UN During the 1994 Genocide in Rwanda, 15 December 1999. Both reports are available at <www.un.org>.

5
Trends in military expenditure and arms transfers

Elisabeth Sköns

The end of the Cold War brought about a reduction in military expenditure and international arms transfers, both in terms of world totals and in most regions and countries. Both the level of military expenditure and the level of international arms transfers reached a peak in 1987, then stayed roughly constant for two years and began a rapid decline after 1989, the year of the fall of the Berlin wall. Towards the end of the decade the reductions have ceased. Since the mid-1990s, both military expenditure and the level of global transfers of major conventional weapons have stagnated; the volume of arms transfers has even increased slightly. The total reduction in world military expenditure during the period 1987–1998 was one-third in real terms,[1] while the reduction in the volume of international transfers of major conventional weapons was around 40 per cent.[2]

In spite of these reductions, the amount of economic resources used for military activities is still significant both in a global perspective and in individual regions and countries. The estimate for total world military expenditure in 1998 was US $745 billion. This estimate is based on official public expenditure data. In addition, there are the costs of actually fighting wars, which are not always included in official figures. Adding the cost of the consequences of war, including both the short-term costs of refugees and lost production, and the long-term costs of economic reconstruction, military activities represent a significant consumption of global resources—economic, manpower, and technological—in a world of scarce resources, poverty, and hunger.[3]

World military expenditure in 1998 represented an average of US $125 per capita. By comparison, at least half a dozen countries in Africa had an average GNP per capita of less than US $250 in the same year.[4] A comparison with public expenditure on education and health shows that, while military expenditure in 1996 corresponded to 2.4 percent of world aggregate GNP, the comparable shares of education and health were 4.8 and 5.5 percent respectively.[5] If action were taken to redirect some of the resources currently devoted to military purposes to instead meet the needs of the disadvantaged, this would go a long way to alleviating the most serious suffering. But is this possible?

At the same time there are also significant security needs that remain unsatisfied. While there has been a reduction in external armed conflict—conflict between countries—internal security needs are great and possibly increasing. During the 1990s alone more than 4 million people lost their lives in violent conflicts, most of whom were civilians—nine out of ten casualties in civil wars are non-combatants—and by 1997 about 35 million people were displaced either as refugees or within national borders.[6] The question that arises is whether military expenditure is the best or most appropriate way of providing security for states and people.

There are no easy answers to these questions. A chapter on trends in military expenditure and arms transfers cannot address all these issues, which relate to a large proportion of global, international, and national security problems; neither can it ignore them.

Military expenditure is primarily an economic indicator, since it is a measure of economic input. Thus, the decline in world military expenditure shows that there has been a reduction in the aggregate amount of world economic resources devoted to military purposes during the post–Cold War period. It also shows that there has been a decline in military activity, although there is no clear relationship between the input of economic resources into the military sector and the output in terms of military activity or military strength. The link between military expenditure and security is naturally even weaker, since levels of security depend on a range of factors other than military expenditure or even military strength.

International arms transfers represent the flow of weapons between countries. Only transfers of major conventional weapons are discussed in this chapter. There exists no data on international transfers of small arms and light weapons. Most countries lack a domestic capability to produce weapons. For these countries, arms trade data show also their total arms procurement.

Probably the most significant developments in the military sector during the post–Cold War period are the changes in the arms industry. Reductions in military expenditure have resulted in a sharp drop in the demand for military equipment—that is, for the goods and services produced by the arms industry. In combination with the increasing costs for advanced weapon systems, the changing relationship between military and civil technology, and the process of globalization, this has had a profound impact on the arms industry. During the 1990s, the changes in the arms industry in most major centres of arms production include, in addition to sharp production cuts, an increased degree of privatization, concentration, internationalization, commercialization, and competition. There has been increased pressure from the industry to export and increased demand on governments in arms-producing countries to assist the industry in its export efforts. These changes are likely to have a significant impact on arms production, arms procurement, and arms exports.

The trends in military expenditure and arms transfers are described below in section 1. Some insights into the complexity of factors determining military expenditure and arms transfers are given in section 2. The impact of globalization is addressed separately in section 3.

Economic considerations are often perceived as an impediment to reductions in military expenditure. Arms exports are to some extent a function of excess supply, which in the post–Cold War period has been the result of over-capacities in arms production. In the process of reducing this over-capacity, economic considerations have been even more important. Section 4 is therefore devoted to the economics of reductions in military expenditure, arms production, and arms transfers. Finally, section 5 briefly outlines the key challenges for the first years of the new millennium.

1 Trends in military expenditure and arms transfers

Trends in military expenditures

The trends in world military expenditure since the end of World War II can be divided into two periods: first, a period of rapid increase from the end of the war until the peak years of 1987–89; and second, a period characterized by an overall downward trend in expenditure since 1989. The first of these periods roughly coincides with the era of the Cold War, which is generally perceived as beginning in 1947 soon after the end of World War II, and ending with the fall of the Berlin wall in 1989, which marked the beginning of the post–Cold War period.

During the Cold War period (1947–89), which was characterized by rivalry between the two superpowers, the United States and the Soviet Union, world military expenditure was growing rapidly and reached an unprecedentedly high level. More economic resources were used for military purposes after World War II than ever before. During the 1980s the level of world military expenditure was more than ten times higher than in the period 1925–38. This was due primarily to the trends in military expenditure of the two superpowers and to some extent of their allies. By the end of the Cold War period, the United States and Russia accounted for 36 and 23 percent respectively of total world military expenditure.

While expenditure was increasing consistently throughout the Cold War period, the rise was not uniform over time. During periods of large-scale wars, there were steep increases in military expenditure. These were followed by periods of decline and leveling-off, but without a return to pre-war levels. This pattern is clearly seen (table 5.1) in the period of the Korean War (1950–53) and the period of US participation in the Vietnam War (1961–73). During the US presidency of Ronald Reagan (1981–89), the rate of increase was similar to that during those two wars, although the United States was not involved in any major armed conflict. Throughout the 1970s and early 1980s, world military expenditure continued to increase, until it culminated in 1987 at slightly over US $1 trillion and remained roughly constant until 1989, whereafter the post–Cold War decline began.

During the post–Cold War period (1989–98), world military spending dropped by more than one-third in real terms (table 5.2). This decade can be seen as a period of disarmament, marked by downsizing and restructuring of many armed forces in combination with cuts in arms procurement expenditure and also, therefore, in arms exports and arms production. Since 1995, world military expenditure has been fluctuating around a roughly constant level, and towards the end of the decade there were several indications of a renewed period of growth in the early years of the new millennium.

While the overall reduction in world military expenditure since the end of the Cold War has been one-third, there has been wide variation among regions (table 5.3). The deepest cuts have been in Russia and other Central and East European countries as a result of the disintegration of the Soviet Union and the dissolution of the Warsaw Pact. By 1998, Russian military expenditure had declined to less than 5 percent of that of the Soviet Union in 1989. With the other former Soviet republics included in the comparison, their combined military expenditures in 1998 were only 6 percent of Soviet military expenditure in 1989.

Other regions in which substantial reductions in military expenditures have occurred are the African and American continents (cuts of 25 and 30

Table 5.1 World military expenditure, 1949–85

Year	US$ bn[1]
1949	140
1950	150
1951	220
1952	282
1953	290
1954	261
1955	260
1956	260
1957	265
1958	261
1959	271
1960	267
1961	269
1962	324
1963	338
1964	334
1965	336
1966	367
1967	405
1968	430
1969	438
1970	430
1971	429
1972	433
1973	486
1974	501
1975	516
1976	523
1977	532
1978	547
1979	562
1980	567
1981	580
1982	615
1983	632
1984	643
1985	663

Source: SIPRI data as in M. Thee (ed.), "Arms and disarmament SIPRI Findings; 20 years of studies by the Stockholm International Peace Research Institute," Bulletin of Peace Proposals 17/3–4 (1986): 229.

[1] Figures are in US $ billion, at constant (1980) prices and exchange rates.

Table 5.2   World military expenditure, 1989–98

Year	US$ bn[1]
1989	1050
1990	1004
1991	
1992	817
1993	785
1994	762
1995	723
1996	709
1997	721
1998	696

Source: *SIPRI Yearbook 1999: Armaments, Disarmament and International Security* (Oxford: Oxford University Press, 1999), table 7.1.

percent respectively). In Western Europe the reduction during the same period was only 14 percent. The only regions in which expenditures continued to rise during the post–Cold War period were Asia (an increase of 27 percent) and the Middle East (an increase of 17 percent). In the Middle East, where military expenditure fluctuated widely during the 1990s, a huge amount of economic resources were still devoted to military activities by the late 1990s.

Trends in arms transfers

The volume of international arms transfers is primarily a measure of military technology transfer between countries, as embodied in weapons. For countries without a domestic defence industrial base—that is, most countries in the world—it is also a measure of their total arms purchases, while for arms-producing countries, arms import data reflect only part of their arms procurement. Global trends in international arms transfers are difficult to measure. Only a handful of countries provide statistics on their arms exports and imports and very few provide sufficient information to enable comprehensive statistics on their overall arms transfers expressed in monetary terms. Therefore, available data on international arms transfers consist of estimates based on the number of weapons transferred between countries, regardless of how these are financed; whether they are paid in cash, purchased on credit terms, or given away as grant aid. The

Table 5.3 Regional military expenditure estimates, 1989–98

US $ bn[1]

Region	1989	1990	1991	1992	1993	1994	1995	1996	1997	1998	% change 1989–98
Africa											
North	12	11	10	10	10	10	9	9	9	[9]	–25
Sub-Saharan	3	2	3	3	3	3	3	3	3	4	+29
Americas	9	9	8	7	7	6	6	6	6	[6]	–40
North	406	385	338	358	342	325	310	293	295	283	–30
Central	385	369	325	342	325	307	289	273	271	260	–32
South	0.8	0.8	0.6	0.6	0.5	0.5	0.5	0.5	0.4	. .	–50[2]
Asia	20	16	13	15	17	17	21	19	24	. .	+18[2]
Central	104	106	109	115	117	117	121	126	130	131	+27
East	. .	. .	. .	[1]	[1]	[1]	[1]	[1]	[1]	[1]	[+9]
South	92	95	98	103	103	104	107	112	115	116	+25
Oceania	11	11	11	11	12	12	13	13	14	14	+27
Middle East	8	9	10	9	9	9	9	9	9	9	+6
Europe	37	[46]	[64]	[45]	42	41	39	39	44	43	+17
Central/East	483	447	. .	280	265	259	235	234	234	[220]	–55
CIS	[250]	[213]	. .	[59]	[52]	[51]	[36]	[34]	[35]	[21]	[–92]
West	0	0	. .	[50]	[44]	[43]	[28]	[26]	[28]	[14]	[–76][3]
World	232	234	231	221	213	208	199	201	199	199	–14
Change (%)	1 050	1 004	. .	817	785	762	723	709	721	[696]	–34
	–1.8	–4.3	. .	. .	–3.9	–2.9	–5.1	–1.9	1.7	–3.5	–4.5

Source: *SIPRI Yearbook 1999: Armaments, Disarmament and International Security*, (Oxford: Oxford University Press, 1999), table 7.1.
[1] Figures are in US $billion at constant 1995 prices and exchange rates. Figures in [ ] are SIPRI estimates. Figures do not always add up to totals because of the conventions of rounding.
[2] Change over the period 1989–97.
[3] Change over the period 1992–98.

available data also limited to the amount of deliveries which can be identified. Thus, SIPRI data on arms transfers are limited to the information that is available in open sources. For this reason, they are also limited to include only the transfer of defined categories of major conventional weapons, each of which is assigned a value according to its estimated military-technological sophistication. Thus, the SIPRI statistics reflect the trend as provided in open sources on the international transfer of major conventional weapon systems. They do not reflect the actual import cost to the recipient country or the export revenues of the supplier country, but rather the amount of military technology transferred. The only other comprehensive arms trade statistics, those of the United States Arms Control and Disarmament Agency (ACDA) and Congressional Research Service (CRS), are based on similar methods, except they are not based on open sources but on statistics from the US intelligence services. They also have a broader coverage in that they include almost all types of military goods and services.

The longest available time series of world-wide arms transfer statistics are those of ACDA, which begin in the year 1965. They show a slow and steady growth from 1965 up to 1974. In 1975 worldwide deliveries suddenly surged, and had tripled by 1980 in real terms, to culminate in the late 1980s.[7]

SIPRI data on the deliveries of major weapon systems are available from the year 1950, but only for transfers to developing countries. These data show the same general trend: a slow increase up to 1973, after which there was a rapid increase during the 1970s and consistently high levels during most of the 1980s, coming to a peak in 1987. For more recent years, SIPRI data cover transfers to both developing and industrial countries. According to these data, two distinct phases can be identified in the global arms trade during the post–Cold War period: a transitional period of steep decline between 1989 and 1994 (a 40 per cent reduction), and a fairly stable level during the period 1994–98 at this lower level (table 5.4).[8]

Developing and industrial countries have shown different trends in arms imports. In the developing countries the volume of imports of major weapons fell by 45 percent between 1989 and 1992. Yet during the period 1992–97 there was a significant increase, a doubling in real terms, followed by another sharp drop (30 percent) in 1998. Arms imports by the industrial countries declined more or less continuously until 1996. Thereafter they have started to rise again slightly.

It can be clearly seen that throughout the post–Cold War period, the industrial countries as a group have cut their imports of major weapons more than the developing countries (by one-half and one-quarter respectively). This has resulted in a change in their import shares. While at the

Table 5.4 Volume of imports of major conventional weapons, 1988–98

Region	US $ bn[1]										% change
	1989	1990	1991	1992	1993	1994	1995	1996	1997	1998	1989–98
World	33.5	28.7	25.5	22.5	23.8	20.1	20.9	22.0	27.4	21.9	–35
Industrialized countries	14.5	11.2	10.7	11.7	10.7	8.1	6.4	6.0	7.3	7.8	–46
Central/East Europe	5.4	3.7	0.9	0.5	1.5	0.5	0.8	0.7	0.4	0.1	–98
Other industrialized	9.1	7.5	9.8	11.2	9.2	7.6	5.6	5.3	6.9	7.7	–15
Western Europe	6.1	5.2	6.6	8.2	6.2	5.5	3.9	3.9	5.1	6.0	. .
North America	0.5	0.5	1.4	1.1	1.1	1.2	0.7	0.7	1.0	0.6	. .
Developing countries	19.0	17.5	14.8	10.8	13.1	12.0	14.5	16.0	20.1	14.2	–25
LLDCs	3.0	2.7	1.7	0.1	0.4	0.1	0.5	0.2	0.2	. .	. .

Source: Based on *SIPRI Yearbook 1998: Armaments, Disarmament and International Security*, (Oxford: Oxford University Press, 1998), table 8A.1, p. 318; and *SIPRI Yearbook 1999: Armaments, Disarmament and International Security*, (Oxford: Oxford University Press, 1999), table 11A.1.

Note: The SIPRI data on arms transfers refer to actual deliveries of major conventional weapons. The trend-indicator values, developed and used by SIPRI, are not an indicator of the actual financial value of the deliveries, but only an indicator of the volume of international arms transfers. Thus, they are not comparable to economic statistics, such as GDP/GNP figures or export/import figures.

[1] Figures are SIPRI trend-indicator values expressed in US $billion at constant (1990) prices.

beginning of the period the combined arms imports of industrial countries averaged around 40 percent of the world total, this share had decreased to 30–35 percent by the end of the period.

A look at disaggregated data for industrial countries shows that the declining trend is once more almost entirely the result of the reduction in arms imports by Russia, the other former Soviet republics, and its former allies, while the combined arms imports of North America and Western Europe declined by only 1 percent between 1989 and 1998.

The supply of major conventional weapons has always been concentrated to a very small number of supplier countries, while the pattern of recipient countries is somewhat less concentrated. During the period 1994–98, the United States accounted for 48 percent of total world deliveries of major conventional weapon systems, and the five leading supplier countries (including the United States) for 83 percent of the total (table 5.5).

On the recipient side, the country which received most major weapon systems during the period, Taiwan, accounted for 12 percent of the total, while the five leading recipient countries accounted for 36 percent of the total and the 10 leading recipients for slightly more than half (54 percent) of world total arms transfers.

Table 5.5 Leading suppliers of major conventional weapons 1994–98

	1994	1995	1996	1997	1998	1994–98	1994–98 (%)
USA	9.8	9.6	9.7	12.4	12.3	53.9	48.0
Russia	1.2	3.3	3.6	3.0	1.3	12.3	11.0
France	0.8	0.8	1.9	3.3	3.8	10.6	9.4
UK	1.5	1.7	1.8	3.2	0.7	8.9	7.9
Germany	2.6	1.4	1.4	0.7	1.1	7.2	6.4
Total 5	15.9	16.8	18.4	22.6	19.2	92.9	82.7
World total	20.1	20.9	22.0	27.4	21.9	112.3	100.0

Source: *SIPRI Yearbook 1999: Armaments, Disarmament and International Security* (Oxford: Oxford University Press, 1999), table 11.1.

Note: The SIPRI data on arms transfers refer to actual deliveries of major conventional weapons. The trend-indicator values, developed and used by SIPRI, are not an indicator of the actual financial value of the deliveries, but only an indicator of the volume of international arms transfers. Thus, they are not comparable to economic statistics, such as GDP/GNP figures or export/import figures.

[1] Figures are SIPRI trend-indicator values expressed in US $billion at constant (1990) prices.

Table 5.6 Military expenditures as a percentage of GDP, selected countries, 1990–98

Country[1]	Income group[2]	1990	1991	1992	1993	1994	1995	1996	1997	1998
Africa										
Eritrea	low	..	..	..	21.4	13.0	19.9	22.8	13.5	..
Morocco	middle	4.1	4.1	4.3	4.4	4.9	4.7	3.9	..	..
Mozambique	low	10.1	8.7	8.3	7.6	8.8	3.9	3.6	3.7	(4.2)
Rwanda	low	3.7	5.5	4.4	4.5	3.5	4.2	5.3	4.1	4.3
Asia and Oceania										
Brunei	high	..	[6.7]	[6.5]	[6.0]	[6.3]	[5.7]	6.2	6.9	7.6
Cambodia	low	..	..	..	[3.0]	[4.9]	4.2	3.6	3.3	2.7
Pakistan	low	5.7	5.8	6.1	5.7	5.2	5.2	5.1	4.6	4.2
Singapore	high	4.8	4.6	4.8	4.3	4.0	4.4	4.5	4.6	[5.1]
Sri Lanka	low	2.1	2.8	3.0	3.1	3.4	5.3	5.0	4.2	4.2
Taiwan	upper-middle	4.9	4.7	4.5	4.3	4.0	3.8	3.7	3.5	3.5
Turkmenistan	middle	..	..	..	..	1.1	1.4	2.1	4.2	3.6
Europe										
Armenia	low	..	..	..	2.1	..	4.1	3.3	3.8	3.6
Croatia	upper-middle	..	..	7.3	8.2	8.4	9.8	7.5	6.2	6.2
Greece	upper-middle	4.7	4.3	4.5	4.4	4.4	4.4	4.5	4.6	4.8
Russia	middle	[12.3]	..	[5.5]	[5.3]	[5.9]	[4.1]	[3.8]	[4.2]	[3.2]
Yugoslavia (Federal Rep.)	middle	..	..	..	..	5.8	4.2	(6.0)	(7.2)	(5.4)

continues

Table 5.6 continued

Country[1]	Income group[2]	1990	1991	1992	1993	1994	1995	1996	1997	1998
Middle East										
Bahrain	upper-middle	5.1	5.3	5.3	5.0	4.8	5.0	5.0	4.8	5.0
Israel	high	12.3	11.0	10.5	9.4	8.8	8.5	8.7	8.6	8.7
Jordan	middle	9.6	9.5	7.7	7.8	8.2	8.5	9.1	9.3	9.6
Kuwait	high	48.5	116.1	30.8	12.0	13.1	13.9	10.6	8.1	[9.3]
Lebanon	middle	5.0	3.4	5.2	4.0	4.6	4.4	3.7	3.0	[3.2]
Oman	upper-middle	18.3	14.7	16.2	15.4	15.7	14.7	13.0	11.2	(11.6)
S. Arabia	upper-middle	[12.8]	[22.6]	11.7	13.9	11.9	10.3	9.5	12.4	[12.8]
Syria	middle	6.9	10.4	9.0	7.2	7.4	7.1	6.0	5.9	[6.3]
Turkey	middle	3.5	3.7	3.7	3.8	4.1	3.9	4.1	4.1	4.4
UAE	high	4.7	4.7	4.5	4.5	4.3	4.1	[3.7]	3.4	3.3
Yemen	low	8.4	9.1	9.2	9.0	11.3	8.0	6.9	7.4	6.5

Source: *SIPRI Yearbook 2000: Armaments, Disarmament and International Security* (Oxford: Oxford University Press, 2000), table 5.4.
[1] Countries for this table have been selected on the criterion that the share of their military expenditure was higher than 4.0 percent in any of the years 1995–98.
[2] Based on GNP per capita 1995.

Future trends in military expenditure and arms transfers

Towards the end of the millennium, the decline in world military expenditure had slowed down and there were indications that the trend would be reversed in the early 2000s. Expenditures on arms procurement in the European NATO countries has increased by 14 percent since 1995.[9] Defence plans in some of the major spender countries also point towards future increases. The United States, which accounted for more than one-third of world military expenditure in 1998, presented a defence budget for fiscal year 2000/2001 which represented a 1 percent increase in real terms, while procurement expenditure is planned to increase by 19 percent over the five-year period 2000–2005. In 1999, Russia appeared both politically and economically prepared to halt the rapid fall in its military expenditure and announced a planned 50 percent increase in arms procurement. In Europe, new requirements are arising out of new doctrines of military intervention in areas of conflict which are likely to lead to increased military budgets. In Asia the simmering conflict between China and Taiwan has already resulted in increased military budgets and the 1997 Asian financial crisis has not had a strong impact on military expenditure in these countries. In Africa, where military expenditure has been in long-term decline, the bottom was reached in 1995, after which there has been a gradual increase—probably more than SIPRI data show, because of the hidden cost of armed conflicts in the region. Overall, therefore, unless current plans are changed, it can be expected that the first years of the new millennium will become a period of increasing military expenditure.

As regards future trends in arms transfers, most observers agree that, although the early post–Cold War decline in the volume of international arms transfers has been halted, there will not be a return to the previous Cold War levels of arms transfers within the near- or medium-term future. In the three major arms-importing regions—Asia, Europe, and the Middle East—there are no indications of a significant future growth in their arms imports.

The financial crisis in Asia, which started in August 1997, has resulted in the cancellation of orders and arms import programmes in the affected countries. While some of these economies are now recovering and are likely to revive some of their cancelled programmes, this will not suffice for a return to previous levels.

In Europe, the Central and East European countries have expressed significant requirements for new arms imports, but they lack the financial means to implement them. In the West European countries, the change from territorial defence forces to forces for military action in conflicts abroad is likely to lead to demands for new equipment for peace-keeping forces. However, this emerging demand will be met both by domestic production and imports, and while the degree of imports is difficult to assess it is not a matter of the huge quantities of Cold War imports of large and sophisticated weapon platforms.

While the demand for weapons in the Middle East continues to be significant, there is a general consensus that Middle East arms purchases are not likely to return to previous levels. This is due to domestic pressure to spend more of the oil revenue on social programs to accommodate growing populations, the turbulence in oil markets which has led to new caution in making major economic commitments for the future, and problems of absorbing weapons already received.

2 Determinants of military expenditure and arms transfers

Determinants of military expenditure

The determinants of military expenditure include both the driving forces for increasing military expenditure and the various forms of constraints which set limits on these forces. Actual military expenditure trends can be seen as a synthesis of these two types of determinant: the driving forces, seeking to maximize military expenditure, and the constraints on those forces.[10] The main conventional rationale for military expenditure is related to international security; to protect state and people against external armed aggression. However, with the end of the Cold War, this factor is diminishing in importance. The prevalence of international armed conflict has decreased dramatically. Today, most major armed conflicts are generally internal.[11] At the global level, there is little similarity between the patterns in global military expenditure and in armed conflict; military expenditure is concentrated in the industrial world (see table 5.3), but the majority of armed conflicts are located in the developing world. However, this is not always true at the regional and national level. In a study of 40 African countries covering the period 1960–91, a positive correlation was found between wars and military expenditure in 71 percent of those countries.[12] Also, if the level of military expenditure is compared with national output, it is clear that most of the countries with the highest ratio of military expenditure to national output (GDP) are countries involved in major armed conflicts (table 5.6).

While security-related factors and the prevalence of armed conflict are some of the driving forces of military expenditure, these forces also include non-security-related factors. Political and economic factors, often purely domestic in character, also act as driving forces. Nation-building and the positioning of states in the international power structure are to some extent based on the build-up of a strong defence establishment. Military forces are not used exclusively for territorial defence but also for repression of a country's own population, to secure the power of regimes without a democratic power basis. Driving forces of an economic nature are best exemplified by those of the military industrial complex; that is, the interplay of interests of the arms industry, government, and the military establishment, which manifests itself in, for example, the lobbying of arms-producing companies, inter-service rivalry, and the efforts of politicians to supply military contracts to their local home electoral constituencies.[13] During the Cold War, the main driving force for high and rising military expenditure was the competition for strategic military superiority between the United States and the Soviet Union, reinforced by exaggerated threat perceptions on both sides (political) and the pull from the military industrial complex in both countries (economic and political).

The constraints on high military expenditure are mostly economic in nature but, at least in democratic countries, there are also political constraints, in terms of competing demands on public resource allocation by the electorate. Economic constraints have been one of the most important factors behind the sharp reduction in Russian military expenditure. The disintegration of the Soviet Union in 1991 and the subsequent transition of the economic, political, and military system of its successor state, the Russian Federation, led to a dramatic reduction in Russian military expenditure. The largest cut in Russian military expenditure actually occurred in 1992, under pressure from the liberal economic reforms of Finance Minister Gaydar. Later into the decade, difficulties implementing adopted defence budgets into actual expenditures have continued to undermine Russian military expenditure plans. In Africa too, the long-term decline in military expenditure was the result more of scarce economic resources than of the absence of wars and internal conflicts, of which there were plenty on the continent, particularly in the Horn of Africa and in Southern Africa. Also in Europe, although to a lesser extent, the cuts in military spending have been reinforced by their coinciding with periods of restrictive overall budgetary policies.

In Asia and the Middle East, on the other hand, many countries have experienced few economic constraints, at least until recently. Thus, it has been possible to raise military expenditure significantly due to high economic growth rates in Asia, high oil revenues in some of the Arab Middle East states, and large amounts of US military and economic aid to Israel.

Determinants of arms transfers

International arms transfers are determined by three broad categories of factors: politico-military, technological, and economic. These factors all operate at the international, regional, and national levels in the major supplier and recipient countries that dominate the arms trade.[14] The arms transfer and production system can be perceived of as located at the intersection of three important sets of forces for change in international relations that are seldom considered together: the pursuit of wealth, power, and victory in war.[15] First, the production of and trade in weapons are to some degree subject to the same economic pressures as are non-military goods; second, attempts by states to change their position in the arms transfer and production system reflect shifts in the international power hierarchy; and third, war often provides a dramatic catalyst to military innovation and production.

The system itself is based on a three-tier structure of arms-producing countries. The first tier, during the Cold War, consisted of the United States and the Soviet Union. Their near-monopoly on modern military technology granted them a capability to use arms transfers as effective tools of foreign policy. The second tier consisted of 10–15 other industrial countries with less, but still significant, capabilities in arms production and innovation. Their motivation for participating in the arms transfer system is different from that of first-tier suppliers: low levels of domestic procurement and relatively small research and development establishments force a greater reliance on arms exports.

Throughout the 1970s and 1980s sophisticated weapons were further diffused throughout the system to what became the third tier: several states in the developing world (Brazil, China, Egypt, India, Israel, and others) which sought to acquire not only the weapons but also the means of reproducing them, in order to establish a strong regional political or military presence. However, the advance of third-tier producers was hindered by their weak economic, industrial, and technological infrastructures. These states, therefore, relentlessly pursued arms exports in order to maintain their fragile defence industrial bases, although with limited success.

During the post–Cold War period the system of world arms production and trade has maintained the three-tier structure, while the positions of the participating states have changed fundamentally. During the mid-1980s, the two superpowers each accounted for roughly one-third of global arms production, 13 second-tier industrial countries accounted for another 25 percent of the world total, while 15 third-tier states in the developing world accounted for the remaining 10 percent.[16] By the mid-1990s there was still a strong concentration of world arms production. The 10 largest arms-producing countries accounted for close to 90 percent of world arms production. The main change is that the first tier has been reduced to one country, the United States, which alone accounted for almost 50 percent, while Russia, which took over most of the arms

Table 5.7 Largest arms-producing countries, 1996
Figures are in US $billion, current prices. Figures in italics are percentages

	Arms production estimates based on			
Country	Procurement data[1]	Company data[2]	Arms prod. as %age of world total	Arms exports[c] as share of production
USA	95	. .	*46–49*	Medium
UK	20	. .	*10*	Very high
France	20.5	19	*9–10*	High
Japan	9	. .	*4–5*	Low
Germany	. .	8	*4*	Medium
Russia	7–9	. .	*3–4*	Very high
Italy	3.5	4	*2*	Medium
Canada	. .	3.8	*2*	High
South Korea	. .	3.7	*2*	Low
Israel	. .	3.5	*2*	Very high
Total of top 10	170–180	170–180	*80–90*	
Total world	195–205	195–205	*100*	

Source: *SIPRI Yearbook 1999: Armaments, Disarmament and International Security*, (Oxford: Oxford University Press, 1999), table 10.7.

[1] Data are for government expenditures on arms procurement and military research and development plus arms exports minus arms imports.

[2] Data are for the sum of arms sales in the national arms industry as provided by national government organizations or defence industry associations. In a few cases data are SIPRI estimates for aggregate arms sales by companies within the country.

[3] Data on arms exports are from reports by governments and defence industry associations. Export share categories: low, 0–9%; medium, 10–19%; high, 20–39%; very high, ≥ 40%.

production of the Soviet Union, ranked fifth in size and accounted for only 3–4 percent of global arms production.[17] During the years since 1996, the concentration in global arms production has, if anything, become even greater.

The post–Cold War period has also seen another significant change in the international arms transfers and production system: towards a diminishing role for political factors and a growing role for economic factors. This is primarily the result of the end of superpower rivalry and its replacement by a unipolar system in which foreign policy incentives have less relevance, and the decline in domestic armaments markets in almost all arms-producing countries, including the only remaining superpower, the United States. These two factors have contributed to an increased pressure for exports and intensified competition among weapon suppliers to win the few large contracts on the now smaller world arms market. Companies are lobbying for financial and other support from their home governments, for the promotion and marketing of their weapon systems, for example. Governments are becoming increasingly involved in the negotiation of large arms deals and of the various types of offset offers which constitute a normal part of any large arms deal today. Such offset agreements are normally worth as much as the arms deal itself, often reaching more than 150 percent of the original deal. Thus, while offsets are regarded as an unfair trading practice in most sectors of the civil foreign trade, in the international arms trade they constitute the norm.

Another indication of the strong export pressure in the current arms trade is the fact that governments also provide financial support for arms exports, in the form of export credit guarantees, but also in more direct forms. A recent study of US government funding of foreign arms purchases from US corporations showed that more than half of US weapon sales are now financed by taxpayers instead of foreign arms purchasers. These subsidies included loans, grants, and government promotion activities for US arms exports.[18] Similar tendencies have been identified in other major arms supplier countries.[19]

3 The impact of globalization on military expenditure and arms transfers

Although the term "globalization" did not appear until recently, the notion of globalization has existed for a long time.[20] The concept is being used for a wide variety of phenomena and trends, and the descriptions of current trends in globalization and the conclusions regarding its impact differ accordingly. There exists not one discourse of globalization but several. In a recent survey of the debate and literature on this matter, five major discourses on globalization are identified, basically falling into the areas of economics, sociology, political science, culture, and ecology.[21] All these aspects of globalization, together with the globalization of technology, have an impact on the trends and patterns in military expenditure and arms transfers, directly or indirectly, by their impact on the causes of military expenditure; arms production and arms transfers.

These factors have affected military expenditure and arms transfers in several ways, perhaps primarily through their effect on the arms industry. While the military sector has been the sector most resistant to privatization, commercialization, and reduced political control, all these trends are currently affecting the production, procurement, and international transfer of arms. The arms industry is increasingly being privatized and commercialized. The European arms industry is going through a process of internationalization, until now relatively limited and primarily through cross-border joint ventures, but also more recently (during 1999) through cross-border mergers of arms producing companies. European companies are also acquiring arms-producing companies in other continents; recent examples include Australia, South Africa, and South Korea, while trans-Atlantic military–industrial links are still rare in spite of the lively debate on both sides of the Atlantic about their potential.

The increasing privatization, commercialization, competition, and internationalization of arms production has led to an increased pressure from the arms industry to export their excess supply of weapons, and thus to increased commercialization of the arms trade, in which marketing and generous sales terms play an increasing role. At the same time, increased internationalization means reduced possibilities for national governments to implement national arms export regulations, since companies can choose to export their products from a business unit in another country with more liberal export regulations. For this reason, national export laws are becoming increasingly irrelevant. This points to the need for common or international export rules.

However, globalization may also render international control more difficult. The globalization of technology in general, and in the context of a gradual closing of the gap between military and civil technology, will make it increasingly difficult to control the international transfer of militarily relevant technologies in the future. The challenge is to achieve international limitations in the transfer of military technology without resorting to controls which will inhibit international transfers of all types of advanced technology; that is, civil technologies which would benefit economic growth in the recipient countries.

A relatively new development is the impact of globalization on armed conflicts and the financing of those conflicts. The fragmentation and decentralization of the state have produced a new type of war, and with it the increased financing of wars outside traditional government defence budgets. As described by Mary Kaldor,[22] these new wars take place in the context of extreme globalization, under which territorially-based production has more or less collapsed and production continues only of a few valuable commodities (diamonds, emeralds, drugs), which provide a source of income for whoever can provide "protection." These wars are fought by various types of fighting units, public and private, state and non-state, including regular armed forces or remnants thereof, paramilitary groups, self-defence units, foreign mercenaries, and regular foreign troops, usually under international auspices. Under these conditions, governments, like privatized military groups, need alternative sources of funding for their military activities, many of which involve criminal activities. These fall into the following categories: (1) "Asset transfer," i.e., the redistribution of existing assets to benefit the fighting units (including looting, robbery, hostage-taking, and deriving profits from control over market prices); (2) "war taxes" or "protection" money from the production of primary commodities and various forms of illegal trading; (3) external assistance, in particular for imports, such as remittances from abroad to individual families, direct assistance from the Diaspora living abroad, and assistance from foreign governments; and (4) humanitarian assistance diverted by governments and warring factions for their own use. For countries involved in such new wars, data on government military expenditure are irrelevant for measuring military expenditure. What is more important is that the set of social relationships formed by these systems for financing wars constitutes strongly resisting factors for the ending of war.

Privatization of security is also an increasing trend in countries which are not involved in regular armed conflict but where there is a demand for more security services than the government can offer. There is an emerging group of private security companies whose main task is the provision of security in many developing countries, especially in Africa.[23] The demand for private security services has emerged from a combination of factors, including from Western governments seeking to reduce defence budgets, African governments in search of security, international mining corporations, and rebel movements. They provide a variety of services, ranging from guarding installations, protecting convoys, and supporting humanitarian assistance operations, to performing reconnaissance and intelligence services, providing logistical and transport support, military training, strategic planning, and engaging in combat. These companies have developed to fill the need for security in the current context of conflict in Africa, operating in weak states with limited government legitimacy and with limited economic resources, and in which the international community is increasingly reluctant to intervene.

4 Economic aspects of military expenditure and arms transfers

The experiences in many countries that have cut their armed forces, arms production, and military expenditures are that these cuts have had adverse economic effects in terms of economic decline, especially on a local and regional level, and in terms of unemployment. Such negative economic consequences constitute obstacles to reductions in military expenditure even if there is scope for cuts from a security perspective.

The question under consideration is whether cuts in military expenditure lead to the release of economic resources for other competing demands. Is there a so-called "peace dividend"? This question can be perceived in two parts, the more long-term and the short-term. First, are there economic gains in the long-term from reductions in military expenditure? This issue can be analysed by looking at the economic impact of current military expenditure. If the overall impact is negative, there should be something to gain by reducing military expenditure. Second, what are the nature and costs of the adjustment process involved in transferring economic resources from military use to non-military use?

From a purely theoretical perspective, there is no consensus on the economic effects of military spending: the two main existing schools (neo-classical and Keynesian) provide different answers.[24] Applied empirical studies show that, in advanced economies, military expenditure has a negative effect on economic growth through its effect on investment.[25] Empirical studies for developing countries suggest that there is no evidence of a positive effect of military expenditure on economic growth and that a negative impact is likely.[26] In general, these conclusions refer to a *ceteris paribus* comparison, when nothing else is changed. They do not assume a policy of conversion to redirect the saved money from reduced military expenditure into alternative uses, such as non-military government expenditure or investment.

Since military expenditure has no positive effect on the economy, it follows that there should be no negative impact on the economy of cuts in military expenditure in the long-term; that is, after the completion of such cuts. In this sense there is a peace dividend (an economic gain) to be had from cuts in military expenditure. This has also been demonstrated in a series of case studies using input–output simulations of military expenditure reductions.[27] However, this does not mean that reductions in military expenditure are without negative economic consequences. During the period of adjustment to a situation of a lower level of military spending, a multitude of adverse economic consequences are likely to be confronted on the macroeconomic, regional, and local levels, on the company level, and on the labour market. Such short-term economic adjustment problems have led many analysts to conclude that there is no peace dividend to be achieved from reduced military expenditure, but the proper conclusion to draw is that such reductions have not been associated with the proper policy, a policy directed at facilitating the conversion of military resources to civil purposes; that is, an active conversion policy.

Conversion policies can address anything from the demobilization of soldiers, base closures, and the diversification of arms-producing companies to the transfer of military technology to civilian purposes. Such activities, which are annually documented by the Bonn International Centre for Conversion (BICC) had given extensive results by the late 1990s. In its most recent survey of disarmament and conversion, the achievements through 1998 were summarized as follows:

while a reversal of the disarmament and conversion process in some countries or regions cannot be excluded, it must be emphasized that behind the noisy headlines of the many conflicts, there exists a string of positive, often silent achievements. Clearly, in total the 1990s balance sheet of disarmament and conversion is positive. Global disarmament continued even in 1997 and 1998, although at a slower pace, and so did conversion. Despite the difficulties of implementing disarmament, numerous practical conversion projects are underway or have already been completed.[28]

While efforts at the micro level to convert military bases, retrain former soldiers, and diversify arms-producing companies are important contributions to the adjustment involved in reallocating military expenditure to sustainable non-military use, these efforts alone are not sufficient. This can be clearly seen in the Russian experience, where the ambitious conversion plans of the early 1990s faltered primarily because of the lack of two basic elements: investment capital and a functioning market for civil goods and for labour. Diversification of production requires a significant amount of investment, both for the conversion of production facilities and labour through reconstruction and retraining, which seldom occurs, and even more so for the expansion of civil production by new investment and new recruitment, which is the more feasible strategy. Therefore, the adjustment from military to civil use of economic resources, in addition to practical conversion measures, "requires a more general policy which sees conversion as an integral part of a policy of industrial restructuring and regeneration."[29] Conversion must be seen as an investment process.

This conclusion applies in particular to the arms-producing industrial countries. However, it is also of relevance to developing countries, although in a somewhat modified form, since most have no arms production and since the large part of their military expenditure is spent on military personnel. Demobilization can also have severe social costs. Therefore, abrupt declines in military expenditure, when combined with conditions of economic decline stemming from low prices of exports, reduced foreign assistance and poor macroeconomic policies, would lead to high costs, a long transition period, low benefits, and thus a low (or even negative) return from disarmament. This may prove to be the case in several such countries today, unless countered by international technical and financial assistance and informed national macroeconomic, trade, and defence economic policies. In developing countries, though, the prospects of achieving a peace dividend might be improved because they probably have smaller stocks of military capital and relatively greater flows of resources into and out of the military sector.[30]

Few studies have been made on the actual reallocation of public expenditure from military to civilian purposes. However, a recent survey by the International Monetary Fund (IMF) showed that reductions in military spending in some countries have been accompanied by increased public expenditure on health and education. In 61 countries for which health and education data were available for the period 1993–97, the share of these expenditures increased during the period, both as a share of GDP and of total government expenditure, while the shares of military expenditure declined.[31] The tabular data provided indicate that the increased shares of health and education were the result of the fact that expenditure on health and education did not decline as much as military expenditures.

5 Key challenges

Our current world is one in which military activities annually absorb an amount of economic resources corresponding to the annual income of half of the world's population, while at the same time there is an enormous need for these resources to address poverty, hunger, and preventable diseases. Furthermore, in spite of the amount of resources spent ultimately for security purposes, the actual security of states and human beings in many regions is extremely low. The overall challenge lies in how to reduce military expenditure and international arms transfers and channel the released resources into economically and socially more beneficial uses, while at the same time not reducing, but rather enhancing, the security of the world population. As insurmountable as this challenge appears, it must be addressed.

Any policy aimed at the reduction of military expenditure and international arms transfers, whether on a worldwide, regional, or local scale, would clearly have to address a whole range of factors that contribute to current levels of military expenditure and arms transfers. This range would comprise at least six different factors: (1) the root causes of the need for military forces; (2) a set of security-related factors behind military expenditures; (3) the organization of the military sector itself; (4) vested economic and political interests in sustaining military expenditure; (5) arms control and disarmament agreements and activities; and (6) the planned transfer of released resources to productive or social use. A condition for being able to address most of these challenges is an open and democratic political decision-making process for issues related to them. Therefore, the challenge of increased transparency in the military sector must be discussed in some detail.

The basic challenge is how to address the root causes of military forces and conflict. A second challenge is how, given the need for military forces, to develop policies and measures which improve security regimes and security in all its aspects: international, regional, national, and human; and, in particular, how to develop new non-military policies and measures of providing security. These are factors traditionally belonging to the domains of national and international security, but also, increasingly, to other domains, with the current transformation of the security concept to a broader scope, including not only military security of the state but also economic, social, and environmental security for both states and people. In particular there is a need to develop non-military methods of peace enforcement and to avoid the use of military means to prevent the outbreak of armed conflict or stop its continuation. The new phenomenon of using private security groups or forces for the provision of military security, particularly in Africa, deserves special attention. These security groups are primarily private companies, providing security services to foreigners for profit. The main task of these companies is to fill the void created by inefficient armed forces. Many of them have been involved in one way or another in Africa's many conflicts, supporting either the government or the rebels. However, since they are profit-orientated, there are doubts about their sincerity in bringing about an enduring peace where they operate. How to regulate their activities is a source of concern for the international community.

A third challenge is to ensure that there is a proper match between existing security requirements and the size of the military establishment, and to reduce waste and inefficiencies, which are common in the military sector and often made possible by the fact that military establishments are shrouded in secrecy and often politically and economically protected.[32]

A fourth challenge is how to remove obstacles to reductions in military expenditure, which stem from domestic, personal, economic, and political, rather than international security-related, factors. These refer to the vested interests not only of the military establishment itself, but also of the ruling regimes in many countries, of the companies and countries involved in the production and sales of military goods and services, and of the politicians with electorate constituencies in regions depending on military contracts. Vested interests in war are an increasing challenge, primarily for the prospects of conflict resolution and successful peace settlements. Both these challenges can be met only by studying the causes and mechanisms of vested interests and devising measures addressed at these causes, not their effects.

The fifth challenge is to cement any progress reached in international agreements on arms control and disarmament, primarily because this creates some resistance against any reversal of progress. In particular, there is a need to develop new forms of arms control measures that are relevant in the post–Cold War environment. While the traditional arms control that developed during the Cold War was designed to manage arms competition among antagonistic states, what is needed today are arms control measures which can be applied in the context of internal armed conflict fought by sub-state or non-state actors, in particular to maintain peace and resolve conflict in countries where civil wars have been settled by peace agreements. Although much remains to be done in this area, some experience has been gained and analysed. A study by the Lessons Learned Unit of the UN Department of Peacekeeping Operations on disarmament, demobilization, and reintegration[33] has developed a number of recommendations which also include the need to address the new channels available for financing war, and the conversion of military forces through their reintegration and rehabilitation. These are measures which require significant assistance from the international community, both in terms of sanctions and financial assistance. Another summary has identified several categories of arms control mechanisms that are particularly well suited to post-conflict environments: disengagement, demilitarization, disarmament, and confidence-building measures.[34]

Finally, a sixth challenge related to the above is to find policies to redirect economic resources that have been released from cuts in military expenditure into uses which are beneficial to economic and social development in the long run. The transfer of resources from military to non-military uses requires a conversion policy for its implementation. It also requires financial capital for investment in alternative economic activities. Many countries in the developing world would require development aid to assist in the conversion process.

There are no easy solutions to this broad range of challenges, and the identification of such solutions is beyond the scope of this chapter. However, an important condition for the resolution of these problems is increased transparency in the military sector, in order to promote democratic and participatory decision-making in setting the priorities of military and non-military expenditure in the allocation of central government expenditure. In addition, increased information and knowledge about the characteristics and functions of the military sector, and about the relationship between military expenditure, conflicts, and economic development, are essential for any future change, whether in the short or medium term. Thirdly, the nature of these challenges, and the state of the economies in the most seriously affected countries, is such that any progress in addressing them requires the involvement of the international community. Such involvement includes many different types of activities. The most difficult to achieve is probably the commitment of economic resources for the various ends outlined above. Perhaps the most immediate task is to make a convincing argument for such financial commitments; one of the main arguments here is that the long-run cost of not addressing these challenges is likely to exceed by far the short-run costs of addressing them today.

Another overall challenge is to reconsider the relationship between security and economic development. These two issue areas have been, and are still to a great extent, treated as entirely separate fields; they are dealt with by different organizations, both nationally and internationally and also within the UN system, and by different types of policies and measures. In practice, however, they are increasingly intertwined. Military expenditure constitutes a significant economic burden in many developing countries, which inhibits economic and social development. Lack of security inhibits economic activities and armed conflict exerts a disastrous negative impact on economic development. The conflict prevention perspective is now being integrated into national development policy and cooperation in many countries. The World Bank has created a post-conflict unit to facilitate assistance in reconstruction activities after the cessation of hostilities. Security can no longer be understood mainly as military security. An expanded security policy should also integrate development policy in terms of a global security policy which covers economic, social, ecological, and political relationships in other regions of the world. It is possible that the United Nations could have a role to play in promoting the necessary fundamental change in security policy that is already emerging.

The need for increased transparency in military matters

Openness and democratic participation in the formation of defence and security policies, in arms procurement decision-making and in budgeting processes, constitutes a central challenge. Transparency in defence budgeting and the activities financed by defence budgets is important for two major reasons: (1) for establishing national priorities between military and non-military sectors in the allocation of public expenditures; and (2) for building confidence and security between neighbour states. Domestic transparency in military matters facilitates the identification of excessive military spending and can in itself lead to reductions in military expenditure in cases where factors other than those related to security determine the amounts of money allocated to defence.

This facilitates the identification of excessive military expenditure and the establishing of priorities in the allocation of public resources among military and non-military purposes that are in line with the interests of the population. In many countries there is very little information available about the military sector, not only for the taxpayer and the electorate, but also for the members of parliament responsible for approving government proposals on military matters.

Information exchanges with neighbour states can also lead to reduced levels of military expenditure by reducing threat perceptions and preparing the ground for arms control and disarmament agreements.

While increased transparency on the national and subregional level is most important, international initiatives may reinforce demands for national transparency and also contribute to the provision of data. Here, the international community and the United Nations have a role to play in promoting the concept of transparency and setting standards. Existing initiatives include those of the United Nations for reporting military expenditure and international arms transfers. While the response rate to the latter is relatively high, the reporting of military expenditure has a much lower turn-out, and this measure is therefore currently under review by member governments.

The UN reporting instrument on military expenditure

The UN call to its Member States to annually report the size and structure of their military expenditure[35]—which was originally established as a first step towards a reduction of military budgets—is currently a rather lame measure. The response rate is low, averaging around 30 countries out of a total of 187 UN Member States, and these are to a great extent those which are already most transparent in military matters. Some improvement is required and the reporting instrument is therefore currently under review.[36] The most important changes required are the taking of a more active approach by the UN Secretariat to encourage Member States to report and the creation of some political momentum behind the initiative.

Today, the UN Secretariat is not authorized to do much more than passively receive and file the reports. The much greater response rate by other organizations, including SIPRI, shows that a more active approach could give better results. However, for broad participation in the UN reporting system, this would not suffice. Incentives to report require a political context.

Information exchanges on a regional basis for confidence-building, modelled after the Organization for Security and Cooperation in Europe (OSCE) system, could provide one such context. Broader proposals to reduce military expenditure by specific percentages (as was the original intention with the UN system), still kept alive in the academic community, may be too crude and general to be feasible. However, it might be possible to develop similar proposals on a regional basis, including measures tailored to the security environment of a particular region. Another useful initiative would be to set up "transparency institutes" with the task of compiling and providing information on military matters, and providing support to parliamentarians and civil society for an informed debate on budget priorities, arms procurement, arms imports, economic impacts, and so on. Today, the most basic information for an open debate on these issues is lacking in many countries.

The UN Register on Conventional Arms

The response rate to the UN Register on Conventional Arms (initiated in 1991)[37] is higher; 97 Member States reported in 1998. The report for 1999, which was released in August 1999, included responses from 64 countries with some additional replies expected later.[38] Much remains to be improved, however. Transparency in the international arms trade is still very limited. The UN Register provides little detail on the items reported. Small arms and weapons of mass destruction are not included at all, and neither are technology transfers for the manufacture of weapons. Reporting on procurement from national production and on military holdings, which has been included in the reports to the UN Register since 1998, is still unsatisfactory. The group of government experts charged with the task of reviewing the Register will convene again in 2000, and it is hoped that the gradual improvement of the register will continue.

Transparency in arms production

The area in which there is the least transparency is arms production; this is due, basically, to commercial considerations. Arms-producing companies release little information on their arms sales and governments are reluctant or unable to put pressure on them. With the internationalization of arms production, this becomes even more difficult on the national level. Still, arms-producing companies are powerful actors and will probably have significantly increased leverage in the evolving international system for arms production and exports. With arms sales ranging up to US $15–20 billion per year, and with an increasingly oligopolistic industrial structure, the power balance between state and industry is shifting in favour of the latter. There is a need, therefore, for policy proposals to introduce some transparency in the activities of the arms industry, with a long-term view towards some type of regulatory measure of their activities, preferably on an international basis.

Notes

1. E. Sköns et al., "Military expenditure," *SIPRI Yearbook 1999: Armaments, Disarmament and International Security* (New York: Oxford University Press, 1999): 269–70.
2. B. Hagelin, P. D. Wezeman, and S. T. Wezeman, "The volume of transfers of major conventional weapons," *SIPRI Yearbook 1999: Armaments, Disarmament and International Security* (Oxford: Oxford University Press, 1999): figure 11.1, p. 422.
3. According to one calculation, world military expenditure corresponded to the combined annual income in the poorest countries representing 49 percent of the world population in 1992. United Nations Development Programme (UNDP), *Human Development Report 1994* (New York: Oxford University Press, 1994): 48.
4. World Bank, *Entering the 21st Century: World Development Report 1999/2000* (New York: Oxford University Press, 2000): 230–31.
5. UNDP, *Human Development Report 1999* (New York: Oxford University Press, 1999): appendix table 13, p. 191.
6. N. A. L. Mohammed, "Civil Wars and Military Expenditures: A Note," Paper prepared for the conference on "Civil Conflicts, Crime and Violence," by the World Bank's Development Economic Research group (DECRG), Washington, DC, 22–23 February 1999, p. 5. Available also on website: <http://www.worldbank.org/research/conflict/papers.htm>.
7. US Congressional Budget Office, *Limiting Conventional Arms Exports to the Middle East* (Washington, DC: Congress of the United States, Congressional Budget Office, 1992): 6, figure 2.
8. B. Hagelin, P. D. Wezeman, and S. T. Wezeman, "The volume of transfers of major conventional weapons," *SIPRI Yearbook 1999: Armaments, Disarmament and International Security* (Oxford: Oxford University Press, 1999): 422–23 and appendix 11A.
9. NATO, "Financial and Economic Data Relating to NATO Defence," Press release M-DPC-2 (1999)152, of 2 December 1999, on website <http://www.nato.int/docu/pr/1999/p99-152e.htm>, version current on 2 December 1999.
10. R. Smith, "The demand for military expenditure," in K. Hartley and T. Sandler (eds.), *Handbook of Defense Economics*, Vol. 1 (Amsterdam: Elsevier, 1995): chapter 4.
11. M. Sollenberg, P. Wallensteen, and J. Andrés, "Major armed conflicts," SIPRI Yearbook 1999 (see note 8, above), chapter 1.
12. NAD. Mohammed, "What determines military allocations in Africa: Theoretical and empirical investigation," *Defence and Peace Economics* 7/3 (1996): 203–31.
13. G. Chapman and J. Yudken (1992), Briefing Book on the Military-Industrial Complex, Council for a Liveable Education Fund, Dec. 1992; and J. P. Dunne, "The defense industrial base," in K. Hartley and Sandler (eds.), *Handbook of Defense Economics* (see note 10, above): chapter 14.
14. For theories on the determinants of arms transfers, see K. Krause, *Arms and the State: Patterns of Military Production and Trade* (Cambridge: Cambridge University Press, 1992); and S. G. Neuman and R. E. Harkavy, *Arms Transfers in the Modern World* (New York: Praeger, 1979).
15. Krause, *Arms and the State* (see note 14, above): 2 and 97–98.
16. Krause, *Arms and the State* (see note 14, above): 93, table 10.
17. E. Sköns and R. Weidacher, "Arms production," *SIPRI Yearbook 1999* (see note 8, above), table 10.7, p. 408.
18. W. D. Hartung, "Corporate welfare for weapons makers: the hidden costs of spending on defense and foreign aid," *Policy Analysis*, (Washington, DC: Cato Institute, 1999): 350.
19. US General Accounting Office, *Military Exports—A Comparison of Government Sup-*

port in the United States and Three Major Competitors, Report to Congressional Committees, GAO/NSIAD-95-96, (Washington, DC: US General Accounting Office, 1995).
20. E. Rothschild, "Globalization and the return to history," *Foreign Policy* (Summer 1999): 106–116.
21. G. Therborn, "Challenges and issues of globalizations," Paper presented to the Conference on Globalizations, Swedish Council for Planning and Coordination of Research (FRN), Stockholm, 22–24 October 1998. (Papers to be published in a special issue of the journal, *International Sociology*).
22. M. Kaldor, *New & Old Wars: Organized Violence in a Global Era* (Cambridge: Polity Press, 1999).
23. Abdel-Fatau Musah and J. Kayode Fayemi, (eds), *Mercenaries: An African Security Dilemma* (London: Pluto Press, 2000); J. Cilliers and P. Mason (eds.), *Peace, Profit or Plunder? The Privatisation of Security in War-Torn African Societies* (Pretoria: Institute of Security Studies, 1999); Consultation on The *Privatization of Security in Africa*, Summary report, Overseas Development Council, Washington, DC, 12 March 1999.
24. P. J. Dunne, "The economics of war and peace: Opportunities in the post–Cold War world," inaugural lecture at Middlesex University Business School, Hendon, London, 6 February 1997.
25. R. Smith, "Military expenditure and investment in OECD countries, 1954–73," *Journal of Comparative Economics* 4/1, (1980): 19–32.
26. J. P. Dunne, "Economic effects of military expenditure in developing countries: A survey," in N. P. Gleditsch et al. (eds.), *The Peace Dividend* (Amsterdam: Elsevier, 1996), chapter 23.
27. N. P. Gleditsch et al. (eds.), *The Peace Dividend* (see note 26, above).
28. Bonn International Conversion Centre (BICC), *Conversion Survey 1999: Global Disarmament, Demilitarization and Demobilization* (Baden-Baden: Nomos Verlagsgesellschaft, 1999): 13–18.
29. Dunne (1997) (see note 24, above).
30. UNIDIR, *Economic Aspects of Disarmament: Disarmament as an Investment Process*, (New York: United Nations, 1993): 71–72.
31. "Military spending continues to stabilize; some countries increase social spending," IMF Survey, 7 June 1999: 186–88.
32. This challenge is illustrated in several case studies in R. P. Singh, (ed.), *Arms Procurement Decision-Making*, vol. I (Solna (Sweden): SIPRI, and New York: OUP, 1998).
33. L. T. Kapungu, Lessons Learned Unit, Department of Peacekeeping Operations (UN), "Arms control and peace settlements and the challenges of substate activities," Paper prepared for the 1999 Nobel Symposium, A Future Arms Control Agenda, Stockholm, 30 September–October 1999.
34. N. Ball, Overseas Development Council (Washington, DC), "Arms control as a conflict-management tool," Paper prepared for the 1999 Nobel Symposium, A Future Arms Control Agenda, Stockholm, 30 September–2 October 1999.
35. Report of the Secretary-General, Objective Information on Military Matters, Including Transparency of Military Expenditures, United Nations General Assembly, UN Doc. A/54/298, 22 September 1999 (URL: <http://www.un.org/Depts/dda/CAB/rep542981.pdf).>
36. See for example, Draft Resolution of the First Committee, Objective Information on Military Matters, Including Transparency of Military Expenditures, UN Doc. A/C.1/54/L.27, 22 October 1999. See website: <URL: http://www.un.org/Depts/dda/CAB/res54l27e.pdf>.
37. Report of the Secretary-General, General and Complete Disarmament: Transparency in Armaments, Report on the Register of Conventional Arms, UN Doc. A/47/342, 14 August 1992.

38. Report of the Secretary-General, The United Nations Register of Conventional Arms, United Nations General Assembly, UN Doc. A/54/226, 13 August 1999. See website: <http://www.un.org/Depts/dda/CAB/rep542261.pdf>.

6

"Alliances" and regional security developments: The role of regional arrangements in the United Nations' promotion of peace and stability

Brian Job

Recognizing that almost all states conduct significant components of their economic, political, and security affairs within their regional geographic contexts, the UN Charter holds that regional agencies or "regional arrangements" would and should play a major role in sustaining international peace and stability since the Second World War. Thus, in Chapters VI (Article 33 (1)) and VIII, Member States were advised, as a first resort, to attempt to settle disputes through regional agencies or arrangements before approaching the Security Council. In turn, regional agencies or arrangements were to keep the Security Council fully informed of their activities, or planned activities, and were called upon not to undertake enforcement actions without the authorization of the Security Council, (Chapter VIII, Article 53 (1)).

However, while the post–1945 period did see the establishment of a wide variety of regional organizations, these did not by and large operate in parallel with the United Nations as the drafters of the Charter had intended. Instead, international relations came to be rigidly defined by a small number of regional arrangements, namely the set of collective defence arrangements (alliances) that underpinned the Cold War. Their ideological differences and associated defence and security policies significantly inhibited the ability of the United Nations to fulfill its potential mandate, as defined by the Charter, on a number of issues. UN peacekeeping efforts, for instance, succeeded, but could only be applied to those conflicts in which the contending superpowers either had no interests or perceived overriding mutual interests in forestalling the spread or escalation of regional wars.

The end of the Cold War, the unravelling of the Soviet Union, and the general movement towards a global, free-market economy had a dramatic impact on both the United Nations and regional security arrangements. First, for the latter, much if not all of their rationale simply disappeared, either resulting in their complete collapse (as with the Warsaw Pact), or necessitating a process of redefinition in the emerging new world order (as with NATO). Second, the removal of the Cold War "overlay" on regional affairs—the lifting of the template of superpower ideology, intervention, and clientelism—transformed the dimensions of conflict within the system. On the one hand, internationalized civil wars such as those in Angola and Afghanistan lost their momentum with the withdrawal of superpower involvement. Inter-state tensions and overt conflicts dropped significantly. But, on the other hand, intra-state conflict increased dramatically, marked by internecine communal struggle and shocking levels of destruction and lethality, particularly targeting civilian populations. For the United Nations, the result was a renaissance of sorts in the early 1990s. With the Security Council unlocked, an activist Secretary-General in office, and a sense of relative equanimity among the major powers, the United Nations was called upon by its members to assume a dramatically expanded role in international peace-related activities. It did so not only by launching a barrage of new peace-keeping missions but also by authorizing and helping to organize coalitions of Member States to utilize force to implement its resolutions. Accordingly, a major war was undertaken in 1990–91 against Iraq because of its aggression against Kuwait; and, by July 1993, over 78,000 UN peace-keepers were deployed around the world.

Paradoxically, however, the end of the decade finds the United Nations in crisis rather than triumph. Its peace-keeping momentum has been reversed. By mid-1999, only 12,000 personnel served in UN missions. Gaining approval for new missions with relevant mandates and adequate deployments is now extraordinarily difficult, and usually unsuccessful as far as mandates and deployments are concerned. Fiscal exigencies have grown so severe that calculations of cost forestall the creation of missions or drastically limit their dimensions and their timetables. Member States have been burned by the experience of their forces in UN missions in the complex crisis situations of Bosnia, Somalia, and Rwanda. Governments in key states, focused on the downside risks of engagement in countries in which they have no direct interests, refuse to summon up the necessary political will to mobilize and support UN action. The United Nations finds itself bogged down with missions such as Cyprus, Lebanon, and Iraq (although not with UN troops in the latter case) on the one hand, while unable to take on fully the demands of major systemic humanitarian and security crises, such as those in contemporary sub-Saharan Africa.

In this context (admittedly one that has been painted rather darkly), it is especially appropriate to re-examine the role of regional arrangements in advancing peace and stability, in terms of their transformation in the post–Cold War security context and in terms of their capacity to interrelate effectively with the United Nations, as envisaged under Chapter VIII. As the Secretary-General has stated, while the UN Security Council must retain primary responsibility for peace maintenance and activities, regional action as a matter of decentralization, delegation, and cooperation with the United Nations' efforts could not only lighten the burden of the Council but also contribute to a deeper sense of participation, consensus, and democratization in international affairs.[1]

This chapter undertakes this consideration in the following manner. First, it surveys the nature of multilateral regional arrangements, reviewing the rationale for the different forms and functions of arrangements that states undertake and then looking at the shifts in the patterns of regional security arrangements and activities in the post–Cold War decade.

The second section of the chapter looks at where and how regional security mechanisms have been effective in advancing regional peace, stability, and conflict management. Particular attention is paid to recent experience in two regions, Europe and the Asia–Pacific region. In both instances, prevention through confidence-building, good offices, monitoring, inclusive dialogue, and consultation appears to be the key. "Nesting" of institutions with overlapping memberships is a particularly desirable feature as well, as demonstrated in the European context. It appears, however, that if and when serious inter-state or intra-state conflict does break out, regional arrangements are unlikely to be able to cope by themselves, necessitating recourse to the global level, i.e., UN conflict management. The successful articulation of the regional and global dynamics involved thus hinges on two factors: first, the effectiveness of regional mechanisms in preventing conflict from breaking out in the first place, and second, the extent to which the United Nations has anticipated the need for its engagement and is capable of mobilizing an adequate response on both political and logistical fronts.

Finally, a third and more basic set of issues needs to be raised. These concern the extent to which conflict of the type that is likely to predominate into the coming decades, namely intra-state, communal warfare in weak, failing, or predatory state environments, can be managed by arrangements (both regional and global) that are basically designed to preserve and protect the prerogatives of states. Already we see increasing tensions arising over issues that derive from this fundamental dilemma. The recent Kosovo crisis, for instance, pitted those who argued for humanitarian intervention by a regional actor (NATO) acting without the authorization of the Security Council against those who argued for principles of sovereignty and non-interference, and for their right to exercise their vote or veto for these principles within the United Nations. Phrased another way, are our existing regional and global security arrangements, however well they might function, essentially unable to protect and advance human security adequately in the twenty-first century? To what extent must we seriously consider developing new institutional forms for security and peace management, forms that provide for inclusion of non-state actors such as NGOs and directly facilitate alternate strategies of preventive diplomacy and peace building?

Multilateral regional arrangements

Forms of multilateral security management

The form and function of the security arrangements that states undertake reflect their understanding of their individual security situations and the extent to which these are shared or threatened by other actors. Both "objective" and subjective factors are involved; perceived threats are "real" in that they determine state behaviour. Within a given regional or global distribution of power, a variety of security arrangements is possible, depending upon the security perceptions and resulting policies of key state actors.

In principle, one can envisage a spectrum of security conditions ranging from a state of anarchy at one extreme—a Hobbesian state of nature pitting all against all—to a state of cooperation and mutual understanding at the other. In practice, one finds that security arrangements cluster in three categories between these extremes, each category reflecting a different form of mutually perceived security dilemma and accordingly resulting in different forms of security practices and institutional arrangements. Table 6.1 provides a brief overview.

Collective defence

The traditional remedy to the classic security dilemma has been the formation of alliances. In order to advance their interests, states undertake commitments to come to the defence of one another, should one be threatened or attacked by a defined perceived adversary. Alliance arrangements, both formal and informal, are by definition exclusionary, their membership is purposely limited to those states who share perceived opponents and are willing to undertake similar mutual obligations. Military prepara-

Table 6.1 Forms of multilateral security management

	Perceived security situation	Organizational arrangement	Examples
Collective defence	Perceived, identified threat from one or more states outside the group, alleviation of threats/conflict through military preparation and deterrence	**Alliance**[1]—formal association of states for the use of force, in specified circumstances, against states outside their membership—exclusive orientation **Alignment**—informal arrangement among states of perceived similar security interests, some of which may be linked through alliance arrangements	NATO, Warsaw Pact, ANZUS[2]
Collective security	Perceived potential threat, but from no immediately identifiable state, alleviation of threats/conflict through threat of joint, overwhelming military response	**Collective security institution**—association of states, committed to collective response to thwart aggression against any member—inclusive orientation **Concert**—association of major powers for management of security affairs according to their common interests—exclusive orientation	League of Nations Concert of Europe Note: UN as a combined concert/collective security institution
	Perceived advantage in mutual cooperation on security related matters, no immediately perceived/acknowledged threat, alleviation of threat through cooperation	**Strategic partnership**[3]—agreement, usually bilateral, of states to consult, cooperate on matters of perceived common security interests—exclusive orientation	Russian–Chinese "strategic partnership"

Cooperative security	Perceived sense of common interests in mutual security, alleviation of threats/conflicts through preventive measures, confidence building, etc.	**Security dialogue organizations**—organizations of states to facilitate communication, confidence building, mutual trust among members—inclusive orientation	
		"Track 1"—arrangements engaging official representatives of governments, i.e., official, diplomatic arrangements	OSCE, ARF
		"Track 2"—arrangements engaging experts, academics, "officials acting in their private capacities" from member states, i.e., unofficial arrangements	CSCAP[4]
		Security community—organization of states who perceive no future threat from each other, i.e., see no viability in the use of force to settle differences—exclusive orientation	
		Pluralistic security community—group of states acting on the basis of shared norms, consultation/consensus to achieve common positions	ASEAN[5]
		Integrated security community—association of states in which identities and policy-making are unified through formal institutional arrangements and actions	European Community[5]

---

[1] This definition of alliance follows Glenn Snyder, in his *Alliance Politics*. (Ithaca: Cornell University Press, 1997): chapter 1.
[2] Bilateral alliance examples would include the US–Japan alliance (involving a formal, but non-symmetrical, set of commitments. There is a large number of other forms of bilateral defence agreements, for example those involving Canada and the US, the US and Israel, etc.
[3] China uses the term "strategic partnership" to describe its recently formed bilateral arrangements, maintaining that such arrangements are distinctive from alliances in that they are not oriented against any outside party.
[4] Council for Security Cooperation in the Asia Pacific.
[5] There is debate among scholars as to whether or not ASEAN and the European Community fully qualify for these designations, but certainly each displays significant characteristics of these two forms of security community.

tion for collective defence, and maintenance of deterrence postures, therefore, are the key avenues for alleviating threats and conflict. In these circumstances, as typified during the Cold War, peace between the central opponents may be sustained, but with concomitant increases in tension, arms races, strained communication, and brinksmanship diplomacy.

Collective security

A collective security arrangement entails an "all-for-one" commitment by members to respond collectively and automatically to assist a threatened or attacked member. The states in the group perceive the possibility of threat, but not from an immediately identifiable source (otherwise they presumably would constitute a collective defence arrangement). They seek, therefore, a wide, inclusive membership, seeking to forestall conflict by engagement and consultation (community-building), and by creating the prospect of an overwhelming response to aggression should it occur. The historical experience of attempts at global or broad regional collective security arrangements has not been particularly satisfactory, in large part because of the failure of members to summon sufficient political will to confront, early on, the behaviour of a violator.

A concert, on the other hand, is an exclusive arrangement; in essence, a "committee of great powers" based upon their perceived mutual interests in sustaining the status quo and channelling their competition to the periphery of the (regional) system. In this limited context, it functions as a collective security mechanism among the great powers. Analysts and practitioners, however, have come to link the notions of concert and collective security in another fashion, namely in arguing that a broadly-based, inclusive collective security arrangement requires embedded within it an exclusive concert of powers if it is to function effectively. This was, of course, the central logic of the drafters of the UN Charter.

Cooperative security

Cooperative security is premised on a radically different appreciation of the security dilemma. Security is conceived as being a mutually determined phenomenon, in which no single actor can achieve security through unilateral means. In order to enhance security, therefore, communication, transparency, and dialogue need to be fostered. Advancement of cooperative security necessitates the inclusion of non-likeminded actors to promote reassurance, confidence-building, and mutual trust. Thus, to the best extent possible, potential adversaries are to be engaged rather than excluded.

In order for a cooperative security arrangement to germinate there must be (a) a common appreciation of the notion of mutual security, (b) acceptance of certain shared norms about the value and process of dialogue, and (c) the absence of ideological schisms or perceived danger of imminent threat or aggression. In practical terms, cooperative security arrangements are dialogue mechanisms, oriented to inclusion, consultation, and confidence-building. Their emphasis is as much on process as on specific results; they are engineered for mediation rather than arbitration and do not organize for peace-keeping or peace enforcement *vis-à-vis* each other. The term "dialogue organization" aptly describes a cooperative security arrangement, which can be either established to function at official levels involving only state representatives—that is, on a "Track 1" basis—or to function at unofficial levels involving civilians (usually academics, security experts, and officials attending "in their private capacities")—a "Track 2" basis. The pace of security dialogue organizations is often very slow and incremental, a characteristic that has led to their being labelled "talk shops" by realist sceptics.

If the norms of cooperative security are accepted by an interacting group of states, to the point where they no longer regard force as a viable instrument of interaction among each other, and additionally do not perceive the need to defend against each other, they are said to constitute a *security community*—a so-called *pluralistic security community* if they engage in tightly-knit interactions that lead to common policy stances, an *integrated security community* should they create institutional mechanisms that formulate policies on behalf of the membership.

Note that a pluralistic security community can be fostered within an alliance, i.e., among its members themselves, through the promotion of common values, rationalization of policies beyond narrowly defined matters of military cooperation (e.g., technological development and industrial policy), establishment of permanent institutional infrastructures, and so on.

Regional security arrangements in the post–Cold War era

The Cold War was sustained by the confrontation of regional collective defence arrangements, most notably of course NATO and the Warsaw Pact, but also the various bilateral alliances (such as the United States' alliances with its Asian partners and the Soviet Union's "friendship agreements" with client states) and informal defence arrangements (for example, the many regime support agreements involving the superpowers and client regimes in Asia, Africa, and the Americas). Other regional arrangements were formed, many on a regional basis, among newly independent states seeking to reinforce their nation-building agendas and to advance, to the extent possible, a non-aligned presence within the international system. However, these organizations, such as the OAU, the OAS (of longer standing), and the Association of South-East Asian Nations (ASEAN) were not equipped or able to undertake regional conflict management actions during the Cold War years. Ignored or overruled by the superpowers, preoccupied with internal affairs, and lacking collective agreement on norms of regional conduct, they were relegated to the sidelines.

By and large, the cooperative relationship between regional arrangements and the United Nations envisaged in the Charter was moribund during the Cold War. The striking exception to this statement (both concerning itself and its interaction with the United Nations, the European Community, and other regional organizations) was the Conference on (now Organization for) Security and Cooperation in Europe (CSCE). Established in the mid-1970s, the CSCE, functioning as a security dialogue organization to promote implementation of the Helsinki Accords, became arguably the single most important bridging mechanism in overcoming the divisions of Europe.

The end of the Cold War was a remarkable turning point in the international relations of regions and the role of regional security arrangements. In retrospect, one can point to five key developments.

First, the prominent regional security institutions of the Cold War, i.e., the collective defence arrangements, having lost their rationale, faced either dissolution (as happened to the Warsaw Pact) or the prospect of "reinventing" themselves in the context of the post–Cold War period. Thus, NATO struggled to redefine its Strategic Concept, undertook to engage all members of the former Soviet Union in security dialogue (in the Partnership for Peace), enlarged its regional footprint by admitting new members, and, acting both unilaterally (as in Kosovo) and through the United Nations, deployed its substantial military capabilities in peace enforcement operations. Within the Asia–Pacific region, the most prominent formal security relationship of the Cold War, the US–Japan defence agreement, has been recast to emphasize its role as a foundation of regional security (although China, among others, regards the US–Japan relationship as less benign).

A minor but interesting counterpoint to this redefinition of alliances by the United States and its Euro–Atlantic and Asian partners has been the tack taken by China, which has formulated a series of bilateral arrangements with other states that it calls "strategic partnerships." These involve cooperation on security matters, including regularized consultation, sales of arms, and technology transfer. Chinese analysts and officials maintain that these are not alliances, in that they are not targeted against any country. But neither do they reflect collective security or cooperative security principles.

Second, the ending of ideological confrontation and the abandonment of state-controlled economies gave impetus to movements of democratization and opening of political systems and to adoption of free-market principles around the globe. Regional institutions have become the primary promulgators of these new norms in the post–Cold War order. Thus, the OAS, for instance, has revitalized itself around the priorities of democratization and human rights. In Europe, the efforts of the OSCE are enjoined by the Council of Europe, the West European Union, and the European Union—all with agendas to advance the establishment of open markets, open societies, and human rights. In the Asia–Pacific region, the APEC forum and parallel Track 2 organizations, such as PBEC, riding the wave of economic growth in the region throughout the 1980s and into the 1990s, championed the cause of free trade within Asia and across the Pacific.

Third, the states of Africa, finding themselves largely abandoned and ignored in the post–Cold War order, have struggled to reinvigorate and create viable regional institutions. In the immediate aftermath of the withdrawal of major power intervention in key conflicts in the Horn of Africa and in Angola, there were hopeful signs of achievement of peaceful settlements. These proved to be short-lived, as these areas, along with much of sub-Saharan Africa, became caught up in the turmoil of communal conflict, economic decline, and natural disasters, in weak, failed, and predatory state environments. In an attempt to redress and reverse these trends, African states have looked to the Organization of African Unity to assume broader and more proactive roles in preventive diplomacy, conflict resolution, and peace-keeping. Whether or not affected states will be willing to cooperate with OAU missions, provide the necessary financial and human resources, countenance interventionary actions in Member States, and cooperate more effectively with UN efforts at peace-keeping and peace-building remains to be seen. Also of note is an interesting feature of developments in Africa: the undertaking by what are nominally "economic organizations," such as ECOWAS, the Intergovernmental Authority on Development (IGAD), and the Southern African Development Community (SADC), of peace-keeping and peace-making missions.

Fourth, the ending of the Cold War was brought about through a coinciding of structural and ideational shifts, the latter essentially being the replacement of traditional, polarized security views by the principles of cooperative security. Security dialogue mechanisms, such as the CSCE, were key instruments in effecting this transformation in Europe. Accordingly, their role within the European context has been cemented in within the region's security architecture. Institutions such as the Council of Europe, European Union, and Western European Union have moved to assume more proactive roles in promoting democratization, civilian–military relations, monitoring and negotiating on human rights matters, and confidence-building in zones of tension.

The trend of more proactive security dialogue organizations, however, was by no means limited to the European context; indeed, it is perhaps the single most notable development in regional arrangements across all regions. In the Asia–Pacific region, for instance, the existing ASEAN assumed regional leadership in establishing the bases for a regional multilateral security framework. Over the course of the 1990s, it expanded its own agenda of activities, enlarged its membership to encompass all of Southeast Asia and engineered the establishment of regional Track 1 and Track 2 security dialogue organizations; the ASEAN Regional Forum and the Council for Security Cooperation in the Asia–Pacific region respectively. Regional and subregional dialogue activities outside the ASEAN rubric multiplied rapidly throughout the region as well, sponsored by individual states including Canada, Australia, Japan, the United States, and South Korea; these include universities and think tanks, foundations, and NGOs.

Maintaining peace and security in the post–Cold War decade

Before proceeding, we should recall several distinctive features of the record of conflicts over the last decade. Overt inter-state conflict, while never more frequent than intra-state conflict during the post–Second World War era, has essentially been reduced to one or two outbreaks per year—these are generally in traditional regional crisis points such as South Asia. The most prevalent form of conflict, in terms of numbers of wars and lethality, is now that which occurs within states. Since 1989 the number of "major" ongoing conflicts has declined, particularly since 1993; although 1998 showed a slight increase to a total of 27 in 26 locations. This latest increase is due to the shift from Asia to Africa as the most troubled region in the world; of the 13 conflicts registering over 1,000 deaths in 1998, nine were within African states.[2]

This record is relevant to the assessment of peace-keeping, peace enforcement, and post-conflict peace-building efforts; that is, activities that were implemented after conflict broke out. Additionally, it provides information concerning the record of attempts, if any, at preventive diplomacy in these instances. What it does not shed light upon are all those activities undertaken in cases where conflict has been averted, the "dogs that have not barked" cases. Surprisingly, there appears to be no single repository of this information, i.e. a consolidated record of peace-related activities by regional organizations.

Table 6.2, assembled largely from a 1999 UN report, provides a cursory overview, organized by region and organization. While it must be

Table 6.2 Regional, subregional, and interregional organizations: Peace-keeping and peace-related activities

Organization	Region	Type of organization[1]	Co-op. with UN[2]	Peace/security-related activities[4]	Selected examples
Americas					
Organization of American States (OAS)	Americas	Security organization[2]—alliance	Yes	Preventive diplomacy, peace-making, peace-building, human rights monitoring	Numerous electoral assistance missions, human rights monitoring, mine-clearing assistance
Caribbean Community	Americas	Security organization[2]	Yes	[preventive-diplomacy, peace-making, peace-building][5]	
Rio Group	Americas	Dialogue organization			
Africa					
Organization of African Unity (OAU)	Africa	Security organization[2]	Yes	Preventive diplomacy, peace making, peace-keeping, [humanitarian assistance]	Numerous diplomatic initiatives for political settlements, military observer groups, observer missions
Central African Customs and Economic Union (CACEU)	Africa	Economic organization	Yes	[peace building]	
Economic Community of West African States (ECOWAS)	Africa	Economic organization[2]	Yes	peace making, peace-keeping	Deployment of peacekeeping forces (ECOMOG), diplomatic assistance to peace agreements

continues

Table 6.2 continued

Organization	Region	Type of organization[1]	Co-op. with UN[2]	Peace/security-related activities[4]	Selected examples
Africa *continued*					
Intergovernmental Authority on Development (IGAD)	Africa	Economic organization	Yes	peace support	Diplomatic initiatives for peaceful settlement in Sudan and Somalia
Southern African Development Community (SADC)	Africa	Economic organization	Yes	peace making, peace-keeping	Diplomatic initiatives for peaceful settlement in the Congo
Asia/Pacific					
Indian Ocean Council (IOC)	South Asia	Dialogue organization			
Association of South-east Asian States	Southeast Asia	Dialogue organization[2]	Yes	Preventive diplomacy, confidence building	Diplomatic initiatives for peaceful settlement in Cambodia
ASEAN Regional Forum	Asia Pacific	Dialogue organization[2]		Confidence building	
Australia–New Zealand–United States Security Treaty (ANZUS)	Australasia	Security Organization–Alliance			

120 BRIAN JOB

"ALLIANCES" AND REGIONAL SECURITY DEVELOPMENTS   121

Europe

Organization for Security and Cooperation in Europe (OSCE)	Europe	Security organization—cooperative security	Yes	Preventive diplomacy, peace-making, humanitarian assistance, human rights monitoring, election supervision, [peace-keeping]	Peacemaking missions, observer missions, electoral supervision, implementation of Dayton Agreement, monitoring of local police, cooperation with the EU on sanctions, cooperation with the UN on political settlements
European Union (EU)	Europe (+)	Economic organization[2]	Yes	Preventive diplomacy, post-conflict development assistance, conflict prevention	Observer missions, peace-making co-sponsored with UN, sanctions assistance, humanitarian assistance
Western European Union (WEU)	Europe (+)	Security organization[2]	Yes	Peacekeeping, conflict prevention, post-conflict development assistance, [human rights]	Mine-clearing operations, embargo enforcement, monitoring and enforcement of sanctions
Council of Europe (COE)	Europe	Dialogue organization		Human rights	Human rights monitors, Commission and Court of Human Rights
Euro-Atlantic Partnership Council (EAPC)	Europe	Dialogue organization			
Partnership for Peace (PFP)	Europe	Dialogue organization			
Commonwealth of Independent States (CIS)	Europe	x[6]	Yes	Peace-making, peace-keeping, peace accords	Peace-keeping force deployments

continues

Table 6.2 continued

Organization	Region	Type of organization[1]	Co-op. with UN[2]	Peace/security-related activities[4]	Selected examples
Europe *continued*					
Black Sea Economic Cooperation (BSEC)	Europe	Economic organization	Yes	[Peace-building]	
Middle East					
Gulf Cooperation Council (GCC)	Middle East	Dialogue organization			
Transregional					
North Atlantic Treaty Organization (NATO)	Europe (+)– Atlantic	Security Organization[2]– Alliance	Yes	Peace-keeping, peace support	Monitoring and enforcement of embargoes, enforcement of no-fly zones, air protection, implementation of Dayton Accord, peace-making mission
Asian-African Legal Consultative Committee (AALCC)	Asia, Africa, Middle East	Dialogue organization ?	Yes	[Preventive diplomacy, peace-making, peace-building]	Promotion of safety zones for refugees
Commonwealth Secretariat	Africa, Asia, Pacific, Caribbean, UK, Canada	Dialogue organization[2]	Yes	Preventive diplomacy, peace-making, peace-building	Observer mission (South Africa), diplomatic missions

| League of Arab States (LAS) | Africa, Middle East | Dialogue organization | | Yes | Preventive diplomacy, peace-making, [peace-keeping, peace-building] | Diplomatic initiatives for peaceful settlement |
| Organization of the Islamic Conference (OIC) | Africa, Asia, Europe, Middle East | Dialogue organization | | Yes | Preventive diplomacy, peace-making, [peace-building, peace-keeping] | Diplomatic initiatives for peaceful settlement |

Primary source: *Cooperation Between the United Nations and Regional Organizations/Arrangements in a Peacekeeping Environment: Suggested Principles and Mechanisms*, March 1999 <http://www.un.org/Depts/dpko/lessons/regcoop.htm>

Supplementary sources: Carnegie Commission on Preventing Deadly Conflict, *Preventing Deadly Conflict*, Final Report, Appendix 2. *CIA Factbook*, 1999.

Peck, Connie, *Sustainable Peace: The Role of the UN and Regional Organizations in Preventing Conflicts*, Carnegie Commission on Preventing Deadly Conflict (Lanham: Rowman and Littlefield, 1998).

Notes:

[1] This designation follows the categories utilized in the Final Report of the Carnegie Commission on Preventing Deadly Conflict, Appendix 2, "Regional Arrangements".

[2] Indicates a regional organization included in the Carnegie Commission's Report, Appendix 2. Designations of the remaining organizations were determined by the author.

[3] A "yes" indicates that the regional organization is one of the 16 organizations, as of March 1999, which "are cooperating or have shown interest in cooperating with the UN in peacekeeping and other peace-related activities." Taken from *Cooperation Between the United Nations and Regional Organizations/Arrangements in a Peacekeeping Environment: Suggested Principles and Mechanisms*, March 1999. Source: <http://www.un.org/Depts/dpko/lessons/regcoop.htm>

[4] Square brackets [] indicate potential activities, per designation from UN Report cited in above note.

[5] One no longer finds reference to the Rio Treaty as a viable regional security arrangement in the Americas.

[6] x indicates uncertainty over the appropriate characterization of a particular organization.

viewed as a sample, rather than a comprehensive treatment of regional security organization activities (and does not include bilateral arrangements such as the US–Japan defence agreement), several features appear to merit notice. First, the surprising range and variety of organizations and the broad repertoire of peace-related activities that they initiate. Second, the preponderance of regional institutions operating within the European context. Third, and less surprising, is the dearth of regional institutionalization in the Middle East, although several trans-regional organizations include these areas within their mandate. Fourth, there are no regional or subregional "security organizations" within the Asia–Pacific region. Indeed, the end of the Cold War found this region without any equivalent to the OAU, the OAS, or OSCE, i.e., any region-wide institutional building blocks for promoting multilateral security regionalism.

Peace-related activities at the regional level

A review of recent academic literature, official and unofficial reports, and UN and other international organization documents suggests that there are four important dimensions to achieving effective prevention, management, and resolution of conflict on a regional basis. These are:

- an emphasis upon preventive diplomacy,
- inclusive engagement,
- "nesting" of institutions, and
- matching resources to mandates.

It is a truism to state that preventing conflicts from breaking out is the most effective strategy of peace-keeping. Yet, one is struck by the generally low levels of support and resource allocation for preventive diplomacy across all regions. While this is less true of Europe (and perhaps also of the Americas), and the situation appears to be improving, albeit slowly, in Africa, surprisingly little progress appears to be being made in this direction in Asia. In part, this may be a result of a general aversion to formal institutionalism shared by Asian states. Secretariats, for instance, either do not exist at all, or they are staffed at the bare minimum levels necessary to circulate information and schedule meetings. Certainly, this has been true of ASEAN, and even more so for the ASEAN Regional Forum (ARF). Neither of these groups has the capacity to engage in monitoring and early warning; neither has been given general mandates by their respective memberships to their Chairs or Secretariats to engage in proactive diplomatic initiatives to decrease tensions and to facilitate dispute resolution. Norms of non-intervention remain so strong that virtually any form of preventive diplomacy is seen as being intrusive and a threat to principles of state sovereignty.

The development of regional peace and stability can only proceed on the basis of inclusion and engagement. This, of course, was the primary lesson of the process of ending the Cold War. Adversaries have to be engaged; a process has to be set in motion leading towards mutual understanding of each side's perspective. To a substantial extent, all regions in the post–Cold War period have moved towards inclusive regional arrangements. Certainly Europe has, and the Americas have too, with the exception of the US–Cuba standoff. The Middle East remains a fractured and exclusionary context; its peaceful settlement processes will continue to founder until all accept the legitimacy of each other's existence and join in security dialogue. In Asia, inclusion of the non-likeminded has been a recent and difficult process. ASEAN has sought successfully to incorporate all the states of Southeast Asia within its membership and is experiencing substantial (hopefully short-term) growing pains as a result. In Northeast Asia, inclusion and engagement has been most difficult; on a grand scale regarding China, and in more immediate and critical ways concerning North Korea. While the latter, for instance, is a participant in regional, Track 2 dialogues sponsored by the Council for Security Cooperation in the Asia–Pacific (CSCAP) region, it is not a member of the ARF. It refuses to join any Track 1 subregional institution for Northeast Asia. Resolution of the impasse on the Korean Peninsula can be facilitated through multilateral, regional arrangements, but its solution will remain dependent upon the North and the South taking decisive steps that neither, especially the Democratic People's Republic of Korea (DPRK), appears prepared to do in the near future.

Preventive diplomacy is most effectively practiced in Europe. The successful mediation efforts led by the OSCE in diffusing the minority issues in the Baltic states are a prime example. Three features of the European context stand out in comparison with other regions. Regional organizations have long been established in Europe; the OSCE, for example, has a 25-year track record. The political security culture of Europe supports the building and growth of formal institutions at the regional level, allowing them to accumulate experienced staff and to operate (in relative terms) with adequate resources. In the aftermath of the Cold War, a network of overlapping institutions has developed which can call upon and count upon each other to take up different aspects of the peace maintenance challenge in any given conflict situation. The individual state, especially one in the "at risk" peripheries of Europe, finds itself "nested" within an institutional context by virtue of its membership in, or existence within, the area of responsibility of at least several different regional institutions.

Table 6.3 Budget estimates of organizations and their peace-related programmes, 1997

Organization	US$ m
ASEAN	5.0
OAS	91.2
OAU (but unpaid)	30.0
COE	161.0
OSCE	49.4

Matching resources to mandates is a perennial and pervasive problem of international governance at all levels. Certainly, this is a systemic and general condition of virtually all collective security and cooperative security orientated arrangements in today's world. (Collective defence arrangements, on the other hand, appear to exist much more comfortably in this regard—the sustaining of a perceived threat being the key to sustaining resources.) In some regions, however, the situation is much less satisfactory than others. Connie Peck, in her recent book, presents the following data that drive this point home.[3] The comparison is stark. One European organization has more resources at its disposal than those of the combined OAS and OAU *and* those of the Asia–Pacific region (since one can assume that the total of the ARF budget and regional Track 2 institutional budgets will be even smaller than those of ASEAN). While Member States in these other regions can and do bear costs of seconding bureaucrats, supporting missions, etc. for their respective regional institutions, the indisputable conclusion is that regional security arrangements are woefully under-funded. The relative success of European institutions is thereby demonstrated from yet another perspective.

Regional arrangements and the United Nations

As stated at the beginning of this chapter, while the Charter provides for regional security arrangements, the authority and ultimate responsibility for peace-keeping and peace-related activities remains with the United Nations.

The experience of the last decade clearly supports arguments for the engagement of regional security mechanisms, preferably as a matter of first resort, in attempting to prevent and manage conflict. Regional institutions presumably have the advantages of familiarity and proximity. They are likely to have direct interests in seeing tensions reduced and conflicts ended, given the likelihood of the spillover effects of economic uncertainty, voluntary and involuntary flows of refugees, cross-border incursions, and so on. They are sensitive to the nuances of regional and local political and security cultures; they have first-hand knowledge of the issues involved. They are likely to be more functionally capable in terms of language and logistical matters. They have an incentive to stay the course and see post-conflict peace-building efforts satisfactorily concluded, because they will reap the benefits of a stable environment and suffer the consequences of further regional instability.

But there are disadvantages and drawbacks to intraregional efforts at conflict management. Regional institutions may well be dominated by the interests of one or more regional powers. Member States, directly or indirectly, may be party to the disputes in question, thus compromising their willingness to become engaged and/or their impartiality once engaged. Member States may find that engagement in the conflict situation of one of their neighbours could bring with it the risk of domestic destabilization. Regional institutions themselves, as discussed above, lack adequate resources to plan and support major peace-keeping missions. (NATO would be the singular exception.)

The track record of regional security institutions in dealing with regional conflict looks decidedly mixed (although, again, this is an issue that does not appear to have been systematically scrutinized by scholars or policy-makers). Their efforts are almost certainly better focused on activities orientated towards conflict prevention, including all forms of preventive diplomacy—diplomatic initiatives, providing good offices, monitoring and observation, fact finding, and so on. Such activities are less expensive, less logistically complicated and very dependent upon the ability to understand local issues and to gain trust from all sides. Once serious conflict breaks out, the potential for successful action by regional security arrangements is small. Even in Europe, once war broke out in the former Yugoslavia European institutions were stymied, either unable or unwilling to respond with sufficient political and military clout.

The United Nations, on the other hand, holds the mandate for action in such circumstances, has an extended history and experience in peace-keeping, and has substantial institutional capabilities to deal with the spectrum of problems involved in responding to a complex humanitarian or conflict crisis. As a global institution, it can call upon members from outside a region in order to assemble forces that are as neutral as possible. Through the Security Council, the entire UN membership can be called upon to act in dealing with the participants in a particular conflict. These are all positive and important factors, ones that have contributed to the United Nations' record of mounting a total of 49 peace-keeping missions.

However, the United Nations is also in crisis. It lacks the infrastructure and financial resources to adequately meet its peace-keeping responsibilities. Mired in debts arising from unpaid dues and assessments, it essentially has to pick and choose its missions and determine their strength and longevity on the basis of cost criteria. In moments calling for action, it finds itself paralyzed either because of a general lack of political will to mobilize on behalf of a country or countries that hold little intrinsic geopolitical relevance to the powerful members of the United Nations, or because these same members perceive that other interests are at stake and refuse to authorize the United Nations to act. One sees little at this moment to suggest that the momentum of UN peace-keeping is going to reverse its downward course. The number of missions undertaken has declined from the highs of early to mid-1990s; the number of troops deployed under UN Blue Helmets is shrinking. Furthermore, recent reports critical of UN conduct or failure to act in past missions have created a pall over the prospect of future UN actions in unfriendly developing-country environments.

Indeed, the United Nations finds itself dependent on the support of a small number of nations, but also on the force capabilities of the United States and its NATO allies. It is inconceivable, at present, that the United Nations could mount a major peace enforcement mission without the assistance, if not the direct involvement, of the United States. On the other hand, as the Kosovo crisis of 1999 demonstrated, there is yet an additional vulnerability for the United Nations; namely, that it will not be able to sustain its authority over peace enforcement behaviour by regional institutions, should they choose, as the United States did, to act on their own. While this precedent has been loudly decried by other major powers, it would be overly optimistic to assume that, should an appropriate cause arise, they too would not undertake unsanctioned action to resolve a regional humanitarian crisis in their own interests.

What is to be done? The larger remedies are obvious and have been amply rehearsed in the media, aimed at the appropriate attentive publics. On the basis of the issues explored in this chapter, specifically the role of regional security arrangements and their articulation with the United Nations, several avenues should be pursued.

First, the greatest marginal pay-off of investment of resources in peace-related activities would appear to be the enhancement of preventive diplomacy capacities, particularly those of regional security institutions.

Second, more attention should be paid to the articulation of regional and UN mechanisms. There is undoubtedly duplication of efforts in certain areas and mutual neglect in others.

Third, more attention should be paid to facilitating the articulation of regional Track 1 and Track 2 security programs *and* to the inclusion of non-state actors (i.e., representatives of civil society) and NGOs.

Fourth, once a conflict goes beyond its "tipping point" and explodes into deadly violence, the United Nations remains the best last resort. Its peace-keeping capabilities, despite their flaws, bring to bear the best combination of political legitimacy and functional expertise.

Human security in a system of states: A fundamental challenge

The chapter closes with some brief thoughts on a challenge for the United Nations of the new millennium. To many observers, there is a fundamental distinction emerging between the nature of the problem to be addressed, namely deadly conflict, and the institutional forms that are available and responsible for action. This can be succinctly expressed in the question: is the system of states capable of providing for and protecting human security?

The preponderance of conflict and human destruction we see today, and are likely to see well into coming decades, is characterized by three features: (a) it is intra-state and transnational, occurring within the boundaries of states but with no respect for them. It is affected by and affects forces that communicate and transmit influence beyond the control of states; (b) it is exacerbated, rather than controlled or alleviated, by the states in which it occurs. That is, the forces of the state are unable or unwilling to restore order and provide for the security of its citizens. In popular terminology, the problem is of weak states, collapsed states or predatory states; (c) its effects upon society are far-reaching, to the point that the minimal conditions of civilian life are no longer attainable, the social fabric of societies is destroyed, and the environment is despoiled. The label "complex humanitarian emergencies" is now used to refer to such conflicts. Their resolution and redress involves the mobilization of vast amounts of human and fiscal resources, over a period of decades.

In its present incarnation, the contemporary state-centric order, including its regional and international institutions, appears increasingly ill-suited for remedying the human security dilemma presented by contemporary conflict. The UN system, at its core, remains devoted to the preservation of the prerogatives of its Member States. Similar institutional logic and behaviours prevail at the regional institutional level. States, concerned with protecting their sovereignty, continue to opt for non-interference rather than action on the part of civilian populations. While there have been movements away from this Westphalian notion of sovereignty throughout the last decade, the emerging alternative strategies and thought processes do not necessarily appear particularly palatable nor more likely to advance the condition of human security. Thus, in the recent Kosovo conflict, one sees the arguments of humanitarian intervention triumph over the calls for respect of state sovereignty and non-intervention. The result, however, is the employment of a conflict strategy that has even greater destructive consequences for relevant civilian populations (thus, human security is further degraded) in order to avoid putting at risk the citizens of those states who prosecute the conflict.

The answer to this challenge must lie in altering the representative character of global and regional security institutions. States almost certainly can no longer be regarded as the sole responsible actors. However, difficult and awkward elements of civil society will have to be incorporated directly into the security architectures of the future. This is the security dilemma of the twenty-first century and the new millennium.

Notes

1. As quoted in "Cooperation Between the United Nations and Regional Organizations/ Arrangements in a Peacekeeping Environment: Suggested Principles and Mechanisms," March 1999, p. 4/18, <http://www.un.org/Depts/dpko/lessons/regcoop.htm>
2. These data are taken from Peter Wallensteen and M. Sollenberg, "After the Cold War: Emerging patterns of armed conflict, 1989–1994," *Journal of Peace Research* 32/3, (1995): 345–60; and *SIPRI Yearbook 1999* (Oxford: Oxford University Press, (1999): Chapter 1.
3. Connie Peck, *Sustainable Peace: The Role of the UN and Regional Organizations in Preventing Conflicts*, Carnegie Commission on Preventing Deadly Conflict, (Lanham: Rowman and Littlefield, 1998): 221.

7
Weapons of mass destruction

Trevor Findlay

As the twenty-first century dawns, weapons of mass destruction (WMD) continue to be one of the scourges of humankind. Nuclear weapons, the most feared and destructive, remain ensconced in the strategic calculations of greater and lesser powers, and in the armouries of at least eight of them. Only two years before the end of the last millennium, two new declared nuclear weapon possessor states suddenly appeared. Although deliberate nuclear war seems a remote possibility, with the exception perhaps of India and Pakistan, accidental nuclear war remains frighteningly possible. With even deep cuts stalemated, the promise of nuclear abolition, so tantalizingly raised by Ronald Reagan and Mikhail Gorbachev in the mid-1980s again seems a distant prospect. Even the anti-ballistic-missile debate has re-emerged to complicate nuclear arms control. The danger of "nuclear leakage" from Russia remains high. While chemical and biological weapons have been subjected to impressive constraints under international law, the threat of their acquisition and use will remain as long as the bans are not universal and transparency is incomplete. Less tractable than control over weapons of mass destruction themselves has been control over their means of delivery, with ever more states acquiring, in particular, ballistic missile capabilities.

This chapter seeks first to assess the short- and medium-term outlook in the twenty-first century for weapons of mass destruction. Second, it examines the contradictory effects of globalization. Finally, it attempts to identify the major challenges ahead and the actors and measures that hold the most promise of tackling them.

Outlook for the beginning of the new millennium

Judging the proliferation outlook at any point in time is a task riven with pitfalls. The passing of the second Christian millennium is no exception. Since weapons of mass destruction programmes are by their very nature secretive, assessing the truth is inherently difficult. The subject is plagued by speculation, rumour, exaggeration, and worst-case scenarios, often based on little evidence. Intelligence and defence communities are prone, for self-serving reasons, to exaggerate the threat and underestimate the normative, political, legal, economic, and practical barriers against rampant proliferation of weapons of mass destruction. The peace movement often falls victim to the same temptation, hoping that through exaggeration will come redemption. The media remains to a large extent interested in sensationalism and scaremongering to increase its market share. Pundits and commentators recycle such reports, which even insinuate themselves into official and academic analyses.

With these caveats in mind, and viewed globally across the three types of weapons of mass destruction (nuclear, chemical, and biological), the current situation has some encouraging, albeit much overlooked, characteristics—despite recent setbacks. First, the vast majority of states are now committed not to acquire any weapons of mass destruction by virtue of their membership in the Nuclear Non-Proliferation Treaty, the Comprehensive Nuclear Test Ban Treaty, the Chemical Weapons Convention, and the Biological Weapons Convention. For the vast majority of these states, compliance will be axiomatic. In any event, compliance by all state parties is, or will shortly be, subject to verification by four increasingly sophisticated multilateral verification systems.[1] Hence, taking into account the current and potential likely possessors, the problem lies in a tiny minority of states, and even these are not involved in all types of WMD.

Second, since the end of the Second World War, the use of WMD has been (admittedly through a combination of good luck and good management) almost non-existent, with only chemical weapons making a brief confirmed appearance. Third, WMD are a problem now effectively confined to the northern hemisphere. While the southern hemisphere would certainly be affected by a nuclear exchange or large-scale biological warfare, and individual countries could be specifically targeted by WMD, the fact remains that Africa, Southeast Asia, Oceania, and Latin America are essentially free from nuclear, chemical, and biological weapons.

Beyond these global trends, however, the situation is decidedly mixed, with each type of weapon of mass destruction in a different situation in different regions. The greatest threat of new acquisition and use of WMD comes from the Eurasian landmass, particularly the Middle East, South Asia, and East Asia.

Nuclear weapons

Predictions that by the end of the century there would be twenty or more nuclear weapon states have proved false, largely because of the successful pursuit of nuclear non-proliferation and arms control strategies. There is no reason to suppose that this will change adversely in the twenty-first century. The NPT, the five existing nuclear-weapon-free zones (Antarctica, Africa, Latin America, Southeast Asia, and the South Pacific) and soon a sixth in Central Asia, and a web of nuclear safeguards overseen by the International Atomic Energy Agency (IAEA), ensure that the vast majority of states will never seek to acquire nuclear weapons and their compliance will be verified. Two recent aspirants to the nuclear club, Iraq and North Korea, have been at least temporarily thwarted, while four states—Belarus, Kazakhstan, South Africa, and Ukraine—have voluntarily surrendered their nuclear weapons. The accession of Brazil to the NPT in 1999 brings the last country with a significant indigenous, but unrealized, nuclear potential into the treaty. The only significant holdouts from the NPT are Israel, India, and Pakistan. Also a cause for optimism is the new IAEA Strengthened Safeguards System which, in greatly increasing the scope of traditional safeguards and giving the agency an enhanced ability to uncover non-declared nuclear activities, will help detect and deter future attempts at non-compliance with the NPT like the Iraq and North Korean cases.

There have been no atmospheric nuclear tests for twenty years. The CTBT, the jewel in the crown of nuclear arms control in the 1990s, has codified the almost universal norm against nuclear testing in any environment. It has acquired a large number of signatures and been ratified by France and the United Kingdom. All the other recognized nuclear weapon states (NWS) have at least signed it, committing them not to frustrate the purposes of the treaty by conducting nuclear tests unless they specifically renounce it. In addition, they have all imposed unilateral testing moratoria on themselves. Since the NWS presumably resigned themselves to forgoing the testing option before signing (and began to prepare alternatives), it is unlikely they will ever resume testing, even if the treaty does not enter into force soon. Despite India and Pakistan's spasm of nuclear testing in May 1998, they too have declared moratoria. The twentieth century may indeed have seen both the beginning and the end of nuclear testing.

The number of nuclear weapons in existence is now the lowest since the 1970s, as is the total megatonnage. Both the United States and Russia continue to dismantle nuclear weapons under their 1994 START I agreement to a level of 1,600 deployed delivery vehicles with 6,000 accountable warheads by December 2001.[2] In addition, an entire class of nuclear weapons has been banned by the 1987 Intermediate-range Nuclear Forces (INF) Agreement. Compliance has been good and the verification system has worked well for both agreements. Meanwhile, US short-range and tactical nuclear weapons have been withdrawn in large numbers from deployment abroad.

On the other hand, the Russian and US nuclear arsenals remain obscenely large; there is no momentum to dramatically reduce them further, much less evidence of a willingness to achieve eventual nuclear disarmament. Although they have been de-targeted, ballistic-missile-delivered nuclear forces remain on hair-trigger alert, an inexplicable hangover from the Cold War. Preliminary talks have begun on START III, which presidents Boris Yeltsin and Bill Clinton agreed to in Helsinki in 1997 and which should reduce US and Russian arsenals to 2,000–2,500 strategic nuclear warheads each, but actual negotiations, at US insistence, are linked to ratification of START II. START II, which envisages cuts in deployed strategic nuclear weapons to 3,500 each side by 2003, was for a long time only ratified by the United States, while ratification by Russia was held up in the Duma until mid-April 2000. Linkage politics had clearly been at work here too, with Russian politicians holding ratification hostage to NATO expansion and then the NATO bombing of Kosovo, but more enduringly to US attempts to rewrite the Anti-Ballistic-Missile (ABM) Treaty to accommodate limited missile defences. Even if START II were implemented tomorrow, the number of extant nuclear weapons would be surprisingly large; the combined US/Russian total, including tactical, short-range, and cruise missile warheads, spares, stockpiles, and reserves, would be 10,000–11,000 weapons.[3]

American attempts to find a technological solution to proliferation problems, by deploying a pared-down version of the discredited Strategic Defense Initiative (SDI) to counter future (not yet actual) long-range delivery capabilities by "rogue states," are alarming not just Russia, but also China and US allies in NATO. Both Russia and China have indicated that they will respond with new weapons systems of their own. Most worryingly, US plans threaten to destroy the Cold War consensus that the ABM Treaty's ban on anti-ballistic-missile systems was a key concomitant of efforts to achieve a balanced, steady reduction in strategic nuclear arsenals. START III is thus stultified.

Threats to rearm notwithstanding, Russia's economic meltdown since the collapse of the Soviet Union has put its nuclear capability into steep and probably irreversible decline. Igor Khripunov claims that continued economic turmoil and slow recovery could reduce Russia's strategic nuclear arsenal to 300–350 warheads early in the new century.[4] Yet, perversely, the accompanying decline in Russian conventional military capabilities has produced pressures to increase reliance on nuclear weapons, including tactical weapons. Russian nuclear doctrine has been amended to accommodate first use, and there are periodic calls for development of new nuclear capabilities, including the arming of the new Topol-M ballistic missile with multiple warheads ("mirving"), rather than the single warhead that would be compliant with START II and beyond.

Of the other NWS, China continues to modernize its nuclear arsenal slowly, notwithstanding allegations in the May 1999 Cox Report that espionage would enable it to rapidly match certain US capabilities. The size of China's arsenal, although secret, probably remains small, at about 400 warheads (strategic and tactical).[5] Britain and France have meanwhile been quietly reducing both their weapon holdings and the variety of their delivery systems. Britain now relies entirely on a small submarine-based nuclear deterrent, with fewer than 200 warheads, while France has abolished the land-based leg of its triad and is likely to have around 400 weapons by 2005.[6] Both the French and British arsenals are the smallest they have been for decades, but their reductions have now stopped to preserve what these countries perceive to be a minimum deterrent. France is modernizing its force.

India and Pakistan are of much greater concern than the older nuclear weapon states, since they are engaged in perpetual low-level armed conflict involving bitter territorial disputes. Although they have been known to be nuclear-capable for decades, their sudden spasm of tit-for-tat nuclear testing in May 1998 was a bitter blow to non-proliferation and arms control efforts. With sustained efforts by both countries to acquire ballistic missile delivery systems, the publication of India's draft nuclear doctrine calling for a sophisticated nuclear triad, and the Pakistani military's October 1999 coup, the situation is extremely worrying. Meanwhile, the one extant undeclared nuclear weapon state, Israel, maintains both a sophisticated nuclear arsenal of an estimated 100–175 weapons and an implausible pledge that it will not be the first to "introduce" nuclear weapons into the Middle East.[7]

The situation with regard to the other states with known nuclear ambitions, Iraq and North Korea, is less dramatic, but worryingly uncertain. Iraq was subjected to an unprecedentedly intrusive multilateral verification regime which, despite Iraqi obfuscation and chicanery, managed to obtain a detailed picture of the country's attempts to acquire all three types of weapons of mass destruction, and to demolish substantial elements of such capabilities and their accompanying infrastructure, including long-range ballistic missile delivery systems. Unfortunately, the UN Special Commission (UNSCOM) was expelled in December 1998 and Iraq has since remained uninspected.[8] Iraq has, to date, rejected cooperation with UNSCOM's successor, the UN Monitoring, Verification, and Inspections Commission (UNMOVIC). However, sanctions remain in place and Iraq's import activity is being monitored.

North Korea is another *sui generis* case. Its suspected violation of the NPT and threatened withdrawal from the Treaty was met with a 1994 agreed-upon framework brokered by the United States which offered the country a proliferation-resistant nuclear power capacity in return for a verified freeze of its existing nuclear activities. The deal has remained unconsummated in key respects. While North Korea has repeatedly tested the limits of the agreement and refused comprehensive access to its nuclear facilities and materials by the IAEA, it has not completely reneged on its commitments and offers periodic gestures, such as permitting the United States to inspect a suspected underground nuclear site in May 1999.

All of these proliferation challenges will remain with us into the new millennium. On the other hand, given the tightening web of agreements, enhanced verification and monitoring, and the transparency that comes with globalization, new proliferators who attempt to build a nuclear arsenal from scratch are much less likely to appear without significant advance warning. More likely is the sudden acquisition by a would-be proliferator of a nuclear weapon or nuclear materials from an outside source.

In this context, apart from the India–Pakistan nuclear standoff, the most dangerous proliferation scenario at the outset of this new millennium is the crumbling nuclear infrastructure of the former Soviet Union. While command and control and physical safeguards on strategic nuclear weapons are regarded as generally satisfactory, the situation with regard to non-strategic nuclear weapons, nuclear components, and fissionable materials is of major concern. Poor physical security, lax controls, non-existent accounting for nuclear materials, and the collapse of funding for the Soviet "nuclear cities," nuclear laboratories, and their staff, have rendered "nuclear leakage" from Russia a greater threat than its possible use, either accidental or deliberate, of nuclear weapons. While there have been no confirmed cases of leakage of weapons-grade nuclear materials from Russia, the danger persists. The United States in particular has responded with several imaginative cooperative programmes, including the so-called Trilateral Initiative with the IAEA. Yet the rest of the world, including Europe, which should have so much to fear from the situation, has done little.

Multilaterally, progress towards nuclear disarmament appears to be logjammed. While non-entry-into-force of the CTBT is unlikely to result in resumed nuclear testing, it does preclude full implementation of its verification system. In addition, a major undertaking by the NWS to the non-NWS will remain unfulfilled. This greatly compounds the suspicion of the non-NWS that the nuclear powers have no intention of achieving complete nuclear disarmament, as they are committed to do by the NPT—a commitment reinforced by the July 1996 Advisory Opinion of the International Court of Justice. Many fear that one of the grand bargains encapsulated in the NPT—the disavowal of nuclear ambitions by the vast majority of "have–nots" in return for eventual nuclear disarmament by the "haves"—will break down. For their part, the non-NWS have been unacceptably lax in fulfilling their legal obligations to conclude full-scope safeguard agreements with the IAEA and to sign and ratify additional protocols to strengthen such safeguards.

The poisonous atmosphere between the two groups has frustrated the multilateral disarmament process in the Conference on Disarmament (CD), which is rapidly losing credibility. The negotiation of an almost universally supported Fissile Material (Cut-Off) Treaty (FMT) has been inexplicably blocked by the demand of some members for the commencement, at the very least, of discussions on nuclear disarmament. Even the ABM issue has soured the atmosphere, with China demanding that the outer space issue be given attention before it will agree to FMT negotiations. The NPT Review Conference in April/May 2000 will be a bitter affair, although no state party is likely to be willing to push the Treaty to the brink, since its benefits continue to vastly outweigh its perceived shortcomings.

Although difficult to quantify, the voices in favour of nuclear disarmament apparently continue to gather strength. Officially sponsored reports like the Canberra Commission and the Tokyo Forum, the initiatives of the seven-nation New Agenda Coalition (Brazil, Egypt, Ireland, Mexico, New Zealand, South Africa, and Sweden), and non-governmental activities such as the Middle Powers Initiative and Agenda 2000, are keeping the public aware of the nuclear issue and maintaining pressure on governments. Even a draft nuclear weapons convention has been prepared to demonstrate the feasibility, at least on paper, of a ban on nuclear weapons.[9] It has been tabled by Malaysia in the UN General Assembly. Perhaps as important, a steady stream of retired political leaders, government ministers, military officers, and others who once held high office in the NWS are adding their voices to the calls for nuclear disarmament.

Nonetheless, public opinion remains largely apathetic. There also remain significant pockets of opposition to nuclear disarmament or even nuclear arms control in political parties, defence departments, nuclear weapon laboratories, and research organizations in the NWS and elsewhere. Despite periodic rhetorical flourishes, none of the NWS has evinced a commitment to total nuclear disarmament or even to declaring that the only purpose of nuclear weapons is to deter their use by others, as called for by the Canberra Commission. While so-called negative security assurances by the declared NWS have been given the legitimacy of a 1985 Security Council resolution, even these have been undermined, at least in the case of the United States, by a willingness to consider use of nuclear weapons against non-NWS which use chemical or biological weapons. The CD has abandoned hope of ever negotiating a treaty on the subject.

Overall, US "counter-proliferation" policy contains the worrying implication that the United States is willing to forgo multilateral approaches in favour of unilateral approaches, as demonstrated by its bombing of a factory in Sudan in 1998 which was allegedly connected with chemical weapons production and/or storage. As long as the NWS refuse to pursue more seriously their obligations under the NPT, their efforts to counter proliferation by other means will be viewed as hypocritical.

Chemical weapons

The situation with chemical weapons is fundamentally different from that of nuclear weapons to the extent that there exists an almost universal norm against their acquisition and use, a strong multilateral disarmament regime binding states to a total ban, and a verification regime to ensure that such commitments are complied with. The Chemical Weapons Convention currently has 121 parties and 48 signatories (the major gap is in the Middle East, where several Arab countries have declined to become parties on the grounds that Israel retains nuclear weapons). The Organization for the Prohibition of Chemical Weapons (OPCW) is firmly established in the Hague and is carrying out its verification activities professionally and effectively. The greatest problem encountered to date is the inability of Russia to meet its obligations to rid itself of chemical weapons stocks by the due date. However this is a resource problem rather than one of political will. Certain steps by the United States to unilaterally modify its legal obligations under the convention are also of concern. To date, however, there has been no known deliberate substantive violation of the CWC and its implementation has immeasurably increased knowledge and awareness of both former and potential chemical weapons capabilities. The task in the coming decades will be to ensure that those states suspected of having chemical weapons capabilities or intentions are brought into the regime. A useful incentive will be the restrictions on trade in certain chemicals with non-CWC parties which were imposed from the end of 1999.

Biological weapons

The case of biological weapons is also heartening to the extent that there is an international norm and a multilateral treaty, dating to 1972, which is now being provided with a long-overdue verification system. An ad hoc group of parties is currently negotiating a protocol to the Biological Weapons Convention and narrowing differences on a complex text.[10] The need for a verification system has been demonstrated not only by the case of Iraq, but also that of the former Soviet Union. It has recently been confirmed that the Soviet Union maintained a biological weapons capability after it became a party to the BWC. Rapid developments in the biological sciences, including genetic engineering and the spread of biotechnology to increasing numbers of countries since the treaty was negotiated, make the establishment of a verification system imperative. Unfortunately, pressures from the lucrative biotechnology industry and national security sensitivities may combine to produce a less authoritative verification regime than that of the CWC. In any event, a new multilateral verification agency, an Organization for the Prohibition of Biological Weapons (OPBW), is likely to be established, albeit one that is smaller and less systematically intrusive than the OPCW. Nonetheless, it is encouraging that the negotiations have come so far and that the endgame appears in sight. One of the tasks in the coming decade will be to achieve universality of membership of the BWC and to ensure as many parties as possible sign and ratify the new Protocol.

Delivery systems

Since it is pointless having weapons of mass destruction unless they can be delivered effectively (or at least convincingly to those one is attempting to deter), the proliferation of means of delivery cannot be left out of any assessment of the proliferation situation. Here, the outlook is even murkier than it is in the case of the weapons themselves. Many delivery systems, from artillery shells to aircraft, are dual-use, capable of delivering conventional weapons as well as WMD. Apart from the START and INF treaties' limits on ballistic missiles, the main constraints on delivery systems are ad hoc groupings of states which seek to impose export controls on systems, components, and technology.

The most notable is the Missile Technology Control Regime (MTCR), which has expanded both in membership and in the scope of its controls since the end of the Cold War. Major developing countries, however, see it as a cartel intent on denying them state-of-the-art technology. Unilateral export controls by the United States, in league with other technologically advanced countries, strengthen this impression, as do export control regimes in relation to WMD and conventional weapon capabilities, notably the Nuclear Suppliers Group, the Zangger Committee, the Wassenaar Arrangement, and the Australia Group.[11] While these regimes have done a reasonable job of controlling technology transfers to "pariah states" and slowing the transfer of goods and technology needed to produce weapons of mass destruction, countries such as India, Pakistan, Syria, North Korea, Iran, and Iraq continue to have ambitions for acquiring long-range missile delivery systems. They are unlikely ever to forgo these ambitions as long as the NWS reserve the right to retain these capabilities themselves. Some of these states and others, including China, which remain outside the control regimes, also appear content to assist proliferation by others, regardless of the regional or global consequences.

The effects of globalization

As in many other areas, the effects of globalization on the proliferation and control of weapons of mass destruction have been and will continue to be simultaneously beneficial and harmful. In making it harder to control knowledge, technology, and expertise, globalization makes it harder to control the spread of weapons of mass destruction. Information on how to construct a nuclear weapon, combine the chemical precursors necessary to make chemical weapons, or obtain the growth cultures necessary for rapid production of biological weapons may be posted on and downloaded from the internet in an instant. Modern telecommunications permit similarly rapid person-to-person exchanges of information. The globalization of markets and finance and the ubiquity of modern global travel and trade make it impossible to completely prevent illicit goods and services from being exported, as the trade in drugs and endangered species illustrates. It also means a blurring of the distinction between civilian and military items. Critical technologies, such as advanced machine tools and testing equipment, information technologies, and biotechnology, have WMD or other military applications, but are also essential to the development of a legitimate modern industrial economy. In recognition of this, the United States recently relaxed export controls on supercomputers.[13]

However, globalization is also having benign effects on non-proliferation and arms control efforts. Information technology is permitting a wider dissemination of information more quickly to all parts of the globe, enhancing transparency and empowering those seeking to contain or end the WMD threat. Governments are finding it increasingly difficult to control the flow of information in and out of their territory, providing a boost for democracy, advocacy, and unofficial monitoring. Societal verification, so long regarded as utopian and naive, will be facilitated by such developments.

Globalization is also permitting official global verification networks to be more effective than they could be even a decade ago. The Provisional Technical Secretariat for the CTBT Organization in Vienna, for instance, plans to become the focal point for a global 24-hour network of 321 monitoring stations, linked in real-time via satellite, to detect and identify illicit nuclear tests. Modern communications and off-the-shelf equipment permit monitoring stations to be located in the remotest and harshest environments. The IAEA and OPCW are also globally networked and their operations have been enhanced as a result of the same technological revolution. A global network of commercial satellites can now provide imagery, at low cost, that matches the resolution and quality of that of secret US military satellites. This will prove a boon for official and unofficial monitoring efforts alike. The posting of high-resolution satellite imagery on non-governmental websites, as the Federation of American Scientists has done with photos of North Korea's meagre missile test facilities, is just the beginning of a new era of global transparency.

The creation of global news networks has also resulted in non-proliferation issues becoming better and more rapidly known. The nuclear tests by India and Pakistan were known around the globe almost as soon as they were announced, and reactions were registered immediately in the global media. Such a development permits faster mobilization of efforts designed to counter such developments.

Key challenges and responses

Despite the promise of the end of the Cold War that multilateralism would be the wave of the future, and the promise of globalization that interdependency will advance inexorably, one of the contradictory motifs of our time appears to be a loss of faith in the arms control and disarmament process. There has been a scandalous lack of vision and determination on both sides of the former East–West divide to take advantage of the end of the Cold War. Much strategic thinking appears to neglect the fact that communism is dead and the Soviet empire dismantled. Significant political opposition exists in the polities of both the United States and Russia to arms control and disarmament *per se*; the preferred alternative is seen as strong national defence capabilities, whether conventional or nuclear. Isolationism and unilateralism are constant themes in both US and Russian history, and it is difficult to see how outsiders can influence such phenomena since interference from outside simply confirms the worst fears of those favouring such isolationism. The United Nations is particularly powerless to act in such circumstances.

The United States bears the greatest responsibility for displaying leadership, being the superpower which not only "won" the Cold War but whose governmental system remained intact, whose economy has subsequently boomed, and whose nuclear and conventional forces are overwhelmingly powerful. As the dominant world power the United States is able to be magnanimous, generous, and creative—all in its own self-interest—in pursuit of its avowed aim of abolishing all weapons of mass destruction. Its timidity in pursuing nuclear reductions in the past five years, its mishandling of CTBT ratification, its retrograde policy towards verification of the BWC, and its unilateral reinterpretation of the CWC are all evidence of poor leadership.

The United States in particular holds the key to progress in almost every aspect of the proliferation problem. Most notably, it could unblock the nuclear logjam virtually overnight. In significantly reducing its own reliance on nuclear weapons and moving towards nuclear disarmament, it would encourage Russia to be more at ease with its own enforced nuclear disarmament, incline others to view more favourably the perceived US need for limited missile defences, help kick-start the FMT negotiations, restore the faith of the non-NWS in the NPT, and expose the likes of India in mounting its anti-NPT campaign. In the case of biological weapons, its influence could bring the Protocol negotiations to an early and successful conclusion, while in the chemical weapons area it could bolster faith in the treaty as originally conceived through unilateral action and multilateral persuasion. This is not to absolve other states of responsibility, particularly the other Permanent Members of the Security Council and all other WMD possessors, but to emphasize that with wealth, power, and privilege comes responsibility. Some of the key challenges which require US leadership, along with the participation of other key states, are described below.

Rejuvenating the nuclear arms control process

Bilateral arms control/disarmament appears trapped in a legalistic, treaty-bound paradigm, when less conventional, more creative means would do just as well. The decision of President George Bush in 1991 to withdraw most US tactical nuclear weapons from deployment and reduce the alert status of US nuclear bombers was just as effective an arms control measure as were laboriously negotiated treaties like the Threshold Test Ban Treaty (TTBT) and the Peaceful Nuclear Explosions Treaty (PNET). The United States could simply bypass the current nuclear disarmament deadlock by removing the warheads from, for example, 1,000 nuclear missiles, placing them in "bonded" storage (or strategic escrow) away from their delivery systems, and inviting the Russians to observe the process.[14] The Washington-based Henry L. Stimson Centre has proposed a broader series of parallel, reciprocal, and verifiable steps to "jump-START" the nuclear arms control process and reduce nuclear weapon arsenals to 1,000 each within a decade.[15] Cradle-to-grave transparency on the status of all US and Russian nuclear weapons, agreement with other NWS on a 1,000-weapon ceiling, and enhanced reciprocal verification measures are also proposed. Other unilateral steps, including action by the smaller NWS, are also possible. Confidence-building measures, such as announcing the size of one's nuclear arsenal, could be taken by China as a cost-free enticement to others to do likewise.

Tackling Russian "nuclear leakage"

Despite being one of the major proliferation threats, not nearly enough has been done to contain the prospect of nuclear leakage from Russia. Most states have been content to let the United States bear the major burden of tackling this legacy of the Cold War, despite the fact that many states were allied with one side or other during the Cold War and received benefits (and incurred costs) from having been involved. The fact that the European Union has not been more closely involved is surprising. Since the United States obviously regards its assistance programmes with Russia as an investment in its security, it is hard to see why others, particularly the other NWS, do not think the same way. Even at the cost of US $100,000 per warhead, the total cost for the irreversible dismantlement of 10,000 Russian warheads over five years would only be US $10 billion.[16] The United Nations, with sensitivity, could act as a catalyst in helping obtain further assistance for Russia, as it does in the case of other urgent international crises.

The verification challenge

There is a need for effective and efficient verification regimes to ensure compliance with total bans on weapons of mass destruction. Even strong supporters of global bans will still require the reassurance of universal compliance that verification can provide. Whether and how verification can provide sufficient confidence remains controversial, as the recent ratification debate over the CTBT in the US Senate demonstrated. Valuable lessons for future arms control and disarmament initiatives, including in the nuclear area, have been and will continue to be learned from the experiences of the unparalleled new multilateral disarmament verification organisations. Yet, the vast bulk of research on verification and monitoring currently occurs in the United States. The burden needs to be spread more equally, not only because other states need to be convinced of the verifiability of disarmament agreements, but because multiple efforts are likely to produce innovative verification techniques and technologies. The United Kingdom and medium powers such as Australia, Canada, Finland, and Sweden have all made powerful contributions to verification regimes in the nuclear testing and chemical weapons fields. The United Nations could also play a role by boosting its verification research capabilities.

The compliance lacuna

The international community needs to give much greater attention to the range of responses that are available if non-compliance with disarmament and non-proliferation agreements is detected and proven. The great lacuna in multilateral agreements is the lack of a reference to penalties. All is left vaguely to the will of the Security Council, whose recommendations may or may not be forthcoming. Negotiators should in future consider drafting penalty clauses into treaties which set out in advance the action that will be taken when non-compliance is determined by the relevant treaty authority. The advent of the International Criminal Court should make it easier for individuals who violate international agreements, and government leaders and officials responsible for state violations, to be prosecuted. The passing of domestic legislation to incorporate international law into domestic law should also be explicitly required in future arms control treaties, and each state should establish extraterritorial jurisdiction over nationals engaged in banned activities outside their country of origin.

Reviving the role of the United Nations

The United Nations' need to act, and to be seen to act, impartially and objectively has both comparative advantages and disadvantages in non-proliferation and disarmament matters. Its comparative disadvantage is that it cannot easily lobby individual governments to move in a particular policy direction, nor can it pursue initiatives that are way ahead of the views of the majority or the most influential of its Member States. It has, for instance, no role in pressing legislators to vote for ratification of a particular treaty, or in pressuring a particular state to engage in disarmament negotiations. Unlike in other areas, such as the resolution of armed conflicts among its Member States or tackling humanitarian crises, the United Nations' ability to intervene is severely constrained. Its role in bilateral nuclear arms control is essentially non-existent.

On the other hand, the United Nations can use its impartiality and objectivity to good effect: in acting as an information resource for the global community on proliferation and disarmament problems and solutions; in facilitating creative thinking on non-proliferation and disarmament problems; in assisting in the negotiation of agreements; and in helping to effectively and efficiently implement agreements once they have been negotiated. Yet the United Nations' role in all three areas has been lacklustre due to a lack of resources and creativity. Both of these shortfalls should be addressable.

The UN Secretariat's role has been hampered by limited staff and resources—including, at one stage, the severe downgrading of disarmament as a major focus of the United Nations' work, leading to a loss of collective memory and momentum. Fortunately, the Department of Disarmament Affairs has been restored, but it still lacks the resources and staff to perform the role that it should have as a repository of information and data on proliferation and disarmament issues and as a catalyst for forward thinking. There is no inherent reason why, given the right financial support, the United Nations should not be able to take advantage of the communications revolution, including the fall in information technology costs, to establish something like the Nuclear Proliferation Data Exploitation Centre recently announced by the US government.

Intended to shift the focus of disarmament efforts to the world's regions, the performance of the Regional Disarmament Centres has been mixed at best. Located in remote areas, with little or no staff and resources, they were a brave experiment which has largely played itself out. They should be scrapped in favour of more innovative regional initiatives, utilizing modern information technology to create virtual regional webs rather than static centres.

The UN Institute for Disarmament Research (UNIDIR) has been treated as a pauper, required to beg governments for funding. It is impossible to conduct sustained, long-term, high-quality research under such conditions. It should be given regular UN budgetary support and connected to a proper academic institution, rather than be left adrift in a UN bureaucratic structure. The United Nations University would appear to be an appropriate partner. The UN leadership should be involved in high-level funding approaches to private foundations for support for UNIDIR. UNIDIR should also be given responsibility for the UN Disarmament Fellowship Programme and include training within its mandate, perhaps in cooperation with the United Nations Institute for Training and Research (UNITAR). Lack of capacity in developing country delegations to disarmament discussions can have major repercussions for reaching agreements.

The United Nations also needs to revise its methods of working with non-governmental organizations and other elements of civil society in the disarmament and non-proliferation fields. Often, UN officials treat NGOs with as much disdain and suspicion as some governments do, despite the fact that the United Nations relies on NGOs for support, information, and assistance. The partnership between the United Nations and civil society can be a powerful one when handled properly, as evidenced in UN peace operations.

The UN Disarmament Commission (UNDC) appears by all accounts to be a waste of time and resources. It has produced very little beyond regurgitation of First Committee policy pronouncements and lowest common denominator texts. It has often failed to complete the simplest of assignments due to its consensus rule. It should be abolished and the financial savings diverted to UNIDIR to conduct expert studies.

Constant demands for reform of the Conference on Disarmament have had little effect except to increase its membership, thereby rendering the single multilateral disarmament body even more unworkable. Urgent reforms should include abolishing the bizarre procedure whereby the agenda and establishment of subsidiary bodies and their mandates is reviewed at the beginning of every year. This simply gives an opening for extraneous political issues of the day to be injected by those intent on derailing real progress. A second major reform would be to scrap the consensus rule for both the commencement and conclusion of negotiations. The CTBT was a poor example in this respect: not only did India prevent the CD from referring a treaty to the UN General Assembly which was otherwise unanimously agreed upon, but the Treaty itself contains tortuous entry-into-force provisions which permit its opponents to sabotage it. There would appear to be no reason why the model of the Landmine Convention should not be followed: states interested in concluding a treaty could do so without a small number of states holding them to ransom. It would be up to the negotiating states to decide if they were willing to incur the risk that major states may not wish to sign or ratify their treaty. Those states which do not approve the final draft of a treaty (sometimes even after their concerns have been taken into account) simply do not have to join it. If the CD does not reform itself, it seems inevitable that "coalitions of the willing" will be increasingly tempted to negotiate treaties themselves.

New partnerships

State-centrism still predominates in the non-proliferation and disarmament fields. Although this is understandable, since matters of state security and high politics are involved, this should not mean the exclusion of other players. Most governments remain impervious to the valuable role that civil society, including non-governmental organizations, academics, and informed publics, can play. Non-governmental organizations are still often kept at arms length from official delegations at negotiating meetings, review conferences, and expert colloquia. Only a few countries have followed Canada's lead in regularly including NGO representatives in official delegations. Many developing country delegations appear fearful of NGOs, despite the assistance such groups could render to their under-resourced personnel.

The contrast with the Climate Change Convention community, where NGOs and governments have developed a useful partnership, is stark. The negotiation of the Landmine Convention was a breakthrough in the disarmament field in this regard. A consortium of non-governmental organizations, the International Campaign to Ban Landmines (ICBL), was instrumental in advocating the treaty, helping negotiate it, and subsequently helping monitor its implementation through an NGO consortium called Landmine Monitor. A similar phenomenon has occurred in a related field, namely the successful negotiation of the Statute for the International Criminal Court.

Conclusion

Despite half a century of efforts to rid the world of the three categories of weapons of mass destruction, the setbacks have outweighed the victories. While total numbers and megatonnage of nuclear weapons have waxed and waned, and the number of NWS has reached nowhere near the feared twenty, absurdly large nuclear weapon arsenals, still deployed on hair-trigger alert, could destroy humanity either directly or through nuclear winter (a concept that seems quaintly outmoded but remains nonetheless all too possible). Scandalously, this is at a time when the ideological conflicts which caused such problems for international relations over most of the last century have vanished, and substantive differences between the major world powers are no longer a matter of life and death. Chemical and biological weapons have been more readily kept at bay, but still promise mass destruction unless treaties are implemented, effectively verified, and applied universally.

At the outset of this new millennium, what is required above all is a dramatic new initiative to break the gridlock that has developed between nuclear disarmament, ballistic missile defences, and nuclear non-proliferation. Only the United States, the predominant world power, is in a position to take a unilateral leap or propose a package deal to move the process forward. Other challenges must also be met, including preventing nuclear leakage from Russia and dealing with the few states that flaunt international opinion and non-proliferation norms in one or more of the categories of weapons mass destruction—India, Iraq, Israel, Pakistan, and North Korea. More generally, greater attention must be devoted to verification and compliance to ensure that they do not become barriers to disarmament efforts, but rather provide the necessary confidence for proceeding. Finally, the United Nations must face up honestly to its shortcomings in the non-proliferation and disarmament field, and harness the new creative and community-building possibilities of globalization to advance the cause.

Notes

1. Managed by the International Atomic Energy Agency (IAEA), the Organization for the Prohibition of Chemical Weapons (OPCW), the Comprehensive Nuclear Test Ban Treaty Organization (CTBTO) and, perhaps, an Organization for the Prohibition of Biological Weapons (OPBW).
2. Thomas B. Cochran, Robert S. Norris, and Christopher E. Paine, "Progress in nuclear weapons reductions," in Joseph Rotblat (ed.), *Nuclear Weapons: The Road to Zero* (Boulder: Westview Press, 1999): 158.
3. Cochran et al. (eds.), *Nuclear Weapons* (see note 2, above): 177.
4. Igor Khripunov, "Russia at the crossroads of arms control," *The Monitor: Nonproliferation, Demilitarization, and Arms Control* 5/1–2 (1999). 16.
5. It recently tested a new ICBM, the Dong Feng (DF)-31. See *Arms Control Today*, July/August 1999, p. 27.
6. Cochran et al, (eds.), *Nuclear Weapons* (see note 2, above: 172–3. "Triad" refers to three types of nuclear launch option: from a land base, a submarine base, or the air.
7. David Albright, Frans Berkhout, and William Walker, *Plutonium and Highly Enriched Uranium 1996. World Inventories, Capabilities and Policies* (Oxford: Oxford University Press for SIPRI, 1997): 262. See also Avner Cohen, *Israel and the Bomb* (New York: Columbia University Press, 1998).
8. Except for one routine inspection by the IAEA of Iraq's declared nuclear facilities in January 2000.
9. See Model Nuclear Weapons Convention attached to *Security and Survival: The Case for a Nuclear Weapons Convention*, International Association for Lawyers Against Nuclear Arms (IALANA), International Network of Engineers and Scientists Against Proliferation (INESAP), and International Physicians for the Prevention of Nuclear War (IPPNW), Massachusetts, 1999.
10. For details see Stephen Pullinger, "The Emerging Verification Protocol," Briefing Paper no. 2, Preventing Deliberate Disease series, International Security Information Service (ISIS), London, July 1999.
11. For details see Ian Anthony and Jean Pascal Zanders, "Multilateral weapon and technology export controls," in *SIPRI Yearbook 1999: Armaments, Disarmament and International Security.* (Oxford: Oxford University Press for SIPRI, 1999): 692–700.
12. A plausible definition of globalization is "an increase in the amount and speed of interstate phenomena" (Robert A. Denemark, "World system history: From traditional international politics to the study of global relations," *International Studies Review* 1, special issue, "Prospects for international relations: Conjectures about the next millennium" (1999): 49.

13. *Arms Control Today*, July/August 1999, p. 25.
14. Stansfield Turner, "Clinton can cut nuclear arms without a treaty," *International Herald Tribune*, 2 November 1999, p. 8.
15. *Jump-START: Taking the Initiative to Reduce Post–Cold War Nuclear Dangers*, (Washington DC: Committee on Nuclear Policy, February 1999).
16. Oleg Bukharin and Kenneth Luongo, "US–Russian warhead dismantlement transparency: The status, problems, and proposals," Princeton University Center for Energy and Environmental Studies (PU/CEES) Report no. 314, April 1999, p. 11.

8
"New" and "non-traditional" security challenges

Paul Stares

I believe that the biggest problems to our security in the twenty-first century and to this whole modern form of governance will probably come not from rogue states or people with competing views of the world in governments but from the enemies of the nation-state, from terrorists and drug runners, and organized criminals who, I predict, will increasingly work together and increasingly use the same things that are fueling our prosperity: open borders, the internet, the miniaturization of all sophisticated technology, which will manifest itself in smaller and more dangerous weapons. And we have to find a way to cooperate, to deal with enemies of the nation-states, if we expect progressive governments to succeed.

President Bill Clinton, 21 November 1999

The security of people recognizes that global security extends beyond the protection of borders, ruling elites, and exclusive state interests to include the protection of people. It does not exclude military threats from the security agenda. Instead, it proposes a broader definition of threats in light of pressing post-cold war humanitarian concerns.

Commission on Global Governance, 1995

Since the end of the Cold War, so called "new" and "non-traditional" security challenges have become a source of growing concern around the world. Indeed, many expect that they will become the dominant security challenges of the new millennium. But what are they and how do they differ from "old" and "traditional" security problems? Do they warrant such concern? How should they be addressed—using traditional approaches and instruments or novel ones? And what should be the role of the United Nations in tackling them? Depending on whom one asks, the answers to these questions are likely to vary wildly. In general, however, the spectrum of opinion typically gravitates toward one of two poles that represent competing "security paradigms."

At one end, there are orthodox beliefs about the primary object of security, namely that it is to ensure the survival of the nation state (or ruling regime) from external attack and subjugation or internal subversion and overthrow. In both cases, the threat and use of countervailing force to deter and defend against the enemies of the state are the primary means by which security is sought and maintained. Thus, for adherents of this security paradigm, "new" and "non-traditional" threats can simply mean a different set of enemies or, alternatively, novel means of inflicting harm upon the state.

At the other end of the spectrum, there is a normative reconceptualization of security that puts primary emphasis on protecting the well-being of people and the planet in general, rather than the survival of the state. The range of conceivable security concerns thereby broadens dramatically—some would argue limitlessly—to include a host of economic, social, political, environmental, and epidemiological problems. Whether they emanate from outside or inside the boundaries of the state is immaterial to their consideration as security threats. Likewise, whether they are the product of deliberate or inadvertent acts is irrelevant. The harmful impact on the individual or the surrounding ecosystem is what matters. What makes these problems "new" and "non-traditional" threats, therefore, is not that they are truly novel phenomena or products but rather that they are now treated as security concerns.

One can argue that the two paradigms are not mutually exclusive. Defence of the state as a policy goal can coexist alongside a desire to improve the human condition regardless of geographical location and citizenship. Indeed, some have made such a case in suggesting the complimentarity of "national" and "human" security concerns. Others, however, would doubtless disagree, arguing that the state—its selfish priorities and sovereign encumbrances, to say nothing of the sometimes negligent and repressive treatment of its citizens—can be as much a part of the problem as the solution. Either way, there are overlapping concerns and important linkages between the two paradigms. More importantly, the approaches that are being proposed and practiced to address both "national" and "human" security concerns are quite similar. This could be interpreted as evidence that a "paradigm shift" is under way and already well advanced. However, the considerable resilience of the state along with traditional security practices should caution us that this is not imminent. Rather, it can be attributed to the impact of globalization and the policy logic that it engenders.

The impact of globalization

Globalization—hereafter used to describe the growing interdependence of social, political, and, above all, economic activity as a result of the increasingly unhindered movement of goods, services, information, and ideas around the world—can be seen to be having both positive and negative effects on national and human security agendas.

National security agendas

In a sense, traditional national security concerns have long been "globalized" as a consequence of the Cold War. Through the intercontinental reach of modern weaponry, the extension of alliance relationships, and the use of clients in miscellaneous proxy wars around the world, the US–USSR confrontation progressively evolved into a global contest. Every country on the planet became to a greater or lesser extent embroiled in the Cold War, and all were likely to suffer either directly or indirectly if it turned "hot."

The end of the Cold War—in part the result of the forces of globalization—has clearly brought relief from such fears. This has not been to the extent that one might have expected, however; many thousands of nuclear armed missiles still stand at the ready to be used in a matter of minutes. For some countries, moreover, traditional security concerns remain just as real and may even have grown worse. One can cite in this respect some states in the former Soviet Union, the Middle East, and East Asia. For those countries who have clearly benefited most by the demise of the superpower confrontation—principally in Western Europe and North America—new fears have emerged that can be partly attributed to the effects of globalization.

The first is the threat from so called "rogue states"—essentially countries that are perceived to generally flaunt accepted rules of international behaviour, thereby undermining peace and stability. Though they can be considered to be just a new name for an old problem, rogue states have arguably grown more menacing because of the military capabilities they can potentially acquire in the form of weapons of mass destruction (nuclear, chemical, and biological), along with the associated means to deliver them over long distances. Globalization has exacerbated this concern by lowering the barriers to the worldwide diffusion of the relevant technologies, materials, and expertise for rogue states to develop or purchase such weapons and delivery systems.

Similar fears make up the second new type of security concerns, which stem from the growing empowerment of non-state actors such as separatist movements, religious cults, anti-government extremists, and other groups that use terrorist tactics, as well as organized crime syndicates including, most prominently, drug trafficking "cartels." Though, again, this threat is hardly a product of the post–Cold War era, the capacity of such groups to pursue their goals has increased considerably as a result of globalization. Access to financing and advanced weaponry—including even WMD—has become easier for the same reasons as it has for rogue states, perhaps more so. Their ability to operate globally has likewise grown not only because international travel is easier, and harder to monitor, but also through the increasing use of cooperative arrangements or "strategic alliances" with like-minded groups around the world. Networks based on globally dispersed emigrant communities have also added to the reach of non-state actors.

Besides the physical threat that such groups can pose to people and property, there is also rising concern about their ability to disrupt the vital computer-based information systems that modern societies increasingly depend upon through the use of so called "cyber warfare" tactics. And in cases where these groups are able to draw on profitable illicit business enterprises, the corruption of state officials at every level, including the highest echelons of government, represents an extremely pernicious threat, as numerous cases have demonstrated. Overall, some consider the growing threat posed by transnational terrorism and organized crime to be greater than that represented by rogue state actors.

Human security agendas

For adherents of the human security paradigm, globalization has a paradoxical meaning. On the one hand, it arguably buttresses their case for a reordering of policy priorities. By making the world more integrated and interdependent, globalization has rendered the classic threat of inter-state war less likely if not obsolete. Aggression and territorial aggrandizement are simply becoming too difficult and costly for states to contemplate. The propagation of democratic values and practices around the world— again helped by globalization—and the pacific tendencies this allegedly fosters further reinforces this trend. The rationale for large standing (or rapidly mobilizeable) national armies to defend the boundaries of the state thus diminishes. Certainly, such concerns have receded among the countries of Western Europe and North America to the point of effectively vanishing as serious security imperatives. A similar transformation is expected to eventually take place in the rest of the world, though some regions clearly lag behind others in this trend.

On the other hand, the downside of globalization is that it is engendering a growing sense of exposure or vulnerability to what has previously seemed distant or inconsequential, whether it be far-away conflicts, contagions, crop failures, or currency fluctuations. The effects of such events can now resonate around the world more rapidly and touch the lives of many more people than was previously the case. The magnitude of the underlying forces propelling globalization, moreover, is engendering a growing sense of individual helplessness and resignation.

Of course, not all of the threats to human well-being should be laid at the door of globalization. Very basic factors of a racial, ethnic, biological, geographical, and climatic nature are often the chief culprits. Yet globalization is an important factor in many of the commonly cited items on the human security agenda. These include:

- Racial and ethnic conflict: communal strife can be attributed in part to new ideas and cultural influences that challenge the prevailing sociopolitical order, as well as new economic pressures that may erode the traditional base of employment and wealth and/or create new ones that open up schisms within society. As noted earlier, civil conflicts can also be inflamed and cause greater harm to non-combatants by the ability of warring factions to gain access to modern weaponry.
- Economic insecurity: the progressive lowering of physical, political, and economic barriers to the movement of capital and commerce has increased the exposure of firms and their workforces to foreign competition and the vicissitudes of the global marketplace in general. As the recent Asian financial crisis indicated, the economic fortunes of countries and their citizens can plummet with little or no warning, leaving many unemployed and even destitute. Events at the 1999 WTO summit in Seattle point to the widespread sense of unease and discontent with the effects of economic globalization.
- Environmental degradation: the expansion in global economic activity has accelerated the damage, destruction, and modification of local ecosystems and the planet's climate in general (due most importantly to global warming, ozone depletion, deforestation, and desertification). At the same time, the natural resources of the Earth (fresh water, arable land, fish stocks, and sources of energy) essential for sustaining life and, more generally, for fostering continued economic growth, are also diminishing. Besides the immediate social and economic consequences, environmental degradation may also increase the risk of conflicts over access to scarce resources.

- Epidemiological threats: the dramatic growth in personal travel, whether for business or pleasure, and the expansion of global trade have increased the risk of outbreaks of infectious disease in one part of the world spreading to others. The AIDS pandemic represents the most obvious case, but there are many other examples.

These "new" security concerns are not mutually exclusive; important overlaps and linkages exist. Thus, the most commonly cited "rogue states" are known to be internally repressive of their people. The typical methods employed by the "international community" to contain and punish them—economic sanctions and sometimes military action—also affect the well-being of their citizens, arguably to a greater extent than that felt by members of the ruling regime. Similarly, measures taken to deal with non-state actors can be equally repressive and harmful to the general population. Recent examples include Kosovo, East Timor, and Chechnya, where separatist movements were in each case cited as "national security threats" justifying severe and, to many observers, inhumane countermeasures by the armed forces of Serbia, Indonesia, and Russia, respectively.

Conversely, many of the challenges that make up the human security agenda can have national security implications of the traditional kind. Civil conflict can embroil neighbouring countries in the form of cross-border migration and incursions by the warring parties. This can raise tensions and even lead to conflict at the international level. Again, Kosovo is a recent prime example. Not only did the fear of a widening conflict force NATO to act, but a failure to respond was widely perceived to risk undermining the credibility of the alliance's traditional security commitments. Environmental degradation and resource scarcity may also exacerbate, if not cause, international friction.

Addressing the challenges

Regardless of which security paradigm one favours, the logic of international cooperation and collective action to address the new or non-traditional security issues has become readily apparent for several commonly cited reasons.

First, many of the issues are beyond the capacity of individual states to tackle alone, though, clearly, independent measures can be taken to reduce their vulnerability to certain threats.

Second, the increasing interdependence of security—in which events in one part of the world can undermine the security of people in another—necessitates broad cooperation that spans not just national borders but also regional boundaries.

Third, the empowerment of transnational non-state actors as security threats necessitates international cooperation to deny them access to sanctuaries, weaponry, financing, and other resources.

States, of course, have long sought the cooperation of others to enhance their security—principally through peacetime defence alliances and wartime coalitions. These have typically been directed, however, at specific military threats, and have therefore been limited in geographical scope and duration. New or non-traditional security threats call for broader, deeper, and more durable forms of international cooperation—broader in that they have to be globally inclusive, deeper in that they require states to accept further limits on their sovereignty, and durable in that they have to be sustainable over the long term.

Such cooperation is the functional equivalent of what is often loosely referred to as "global governance"—essentially, norms and rules of behaviour that regulate international society for the common good. Global governance defined this way is already well advanced, even if it is not widely appreciated. It can be seen to have progressed, albeit haltingly, in two phases, with some evidence that we may now be entering a third.

The first phase of global governance effectively started at the end of the nineteenth century with the dramatic expansion of world trade, communications, and travel. States increasingly acknowledged the need to regulate cross-border activities in the interests of public safety, efficiency, and mutual economic benefit. Though they focused predominantly on peacetime interactions, efforts were also made to regulate hostile relations between states by proscribing the use of certain "inhumane" weapons and establishing codes of conduct for the treatment of the wounded and prisoners of war. Though some of these agreements worked better than others, efforts to outlaw aggressive war and establish a collective security system failed entirely.

The second phase began with the establishment of the United Nations and its constituent elements in 1945. This phase is characterized by the extension and intensification of previous efforts not just to regulate international behaviour, but also to control the use made of the global commons (the atmosphere, the oceans, and outer space) and, increasingly, to regulate the domestic conduct of states. As a consequence, an enormous corpus of international regulatory arrangements is now in effect, many of which are designed to address both traditional and non-traditional security concerns.

The most important and well established of the former are enshrined in the Charter of the United Nations, which among other things commits states to respect the territorial integrity and sovereign equality of other states, to not interfere in their internal affairs, and to settle international disputes peacefully. It also provides the legal basis by which states can individually and collectively respond to threats to international peace and security including, if necessary, the use of force. The security of states has also been enhanced by several global arms control and disarmament regimes limiting weapons of mass destruction and other types of weaponry. More recently, global efforts to tackle terrorism and organized crime by limiting the opportunities for money laundering have been implemented.

At the same time, several global regimes have been put in place that directly address the key human security issues outlined above. Among other things, these commit states to respect basic human rights, to protect the environment from pollution and other harmful effects of human development, to reduce human suffering in wartime (including most recently a global ban on the production and use of anti-personnel landmines), to ensure free and fair trade, and to limit the spread of infectious diseases. Given the inherent nature of the international system, however, the effectiveness of these agreements and regimes has ultimately rested on the inclination or capacity of the state parties to comply with them. Some agreements have consequently fared better than others.

However, in what could herald a new phase in the evolution of global governance, states have shown a greater willingness since the end of the Cold War to buttress new or existing international regimes with the threat of sanctions and other punitive measures, including the use of force, to ensure compliance. International organizations established to monitor and manage various cooperative arrangements have, in several cases, been empowered to perform these functions, albeit still with the acquiescence of Member States.

Another feature of this putative new phase in the evolution of global governance has been the greater engagement of non-governmental organizations in both the process of rule-making and implementation. In addressing many of the new and non-traditional security challenges, the role of the non-governmental or private sector has become essential. For example, banks and other financial institutions have come to represent the first line of defence in combating the money laundering activities of organized crime. The assistance of domestic and industrial chemical producers is likewise necessary to restrict the diversion of materials in the manufacture of illicit drugs and chemical weapons. Airlines, shipping agencies, and port authorities can help in deterring and detecting illegal smuggling. Various human rights watchdog groups often provide early warning of communal violence, while humanitarian relief agencies can help reduce the consequences. These are just a few examples.

How these trends develop and what course global governance in general takes in the future will greatly depend on the extent to which sovereign states are prepared to cede to international bodies above them, and non-governmental organizations below them.

The role of the United Nations

The United Nations can play an important role in helping to address many of the new and non-traditional security challenges by contributing what can be described as "the four Ls": leadership, legitimacy, labour, and logistics:

Leadership: when addressing a particular problem, preventive or proactive approaches are generally recognized to be more efficient and less costly than remedial measures. New and non-traditional problems are no different. Mobilizing the necessary political will for collective action, whether it be under the direct auspices of the United Nations or those of so-called "coalitions of the willing," has often proved difficult, however; in some cases it has failed altogether. This problem is even greater when the threat is still distant and open to doubt. To overcome this obstacle, the United Nations can serve not only as the international community's early warning system but also as its primary mobilizing force for action.

Legitimacy: the effectiveness of multilateral initiatives to address specific problems derives largely from the perceived legitimacy of the endeavour. While legitimacy can be built on various factors, the degree of inclusiveness and the moral weight that this can convey is especially important. Given that almost every state is a member of the United Nations, the legitimacy invested in decisions and actions taken by the body is obviously enormous. In particular, for sanctioning enforcement actions that may entail breaching the sovereignty of a state, the ultimate approval of the United Nations is arguably indispensable.

Labour: all cooperative endeavours inevitably entail discussions, sometimes acrimonious, about burden-sharing. Left unresolved, they can prove divisive to the extent of undermining the viability of collective actions. The perennial debates about UN funding bear out the persistence of this problem. The greatest burden that a state will potentially have to bear, however, is that its citizens may lose their lives for the common good. The fear of suffering such losses, especially for causes that may not have a direct bearing on their national interests, often dissuades states from committing personnel. Though the possible loss of life by UN personnel is no less a concern, fewer obstacles stand in the way of their timely use in the service of the international community. At the same time, they are also viewed as more impartial than nationally affiliated personnel, which in certain situations is a distinct advantage.

Logistics: the global reach of UN organizations and networks provides a vital resource for addressing new and non-traditional security problems. As indicated earlier, many are already dedicated to this task.

Like any large organization, the United Nations needs to adapt constantly to new demands placed on it that over time may exceed its original purpose. It is already making a valuable contribution to tackling many of the new or non-traditional security challenges. With the necessary support and commitment of the international community, it can clearly do more.

Governance

9
Recasting global governance
Samuel Makinda

There is no universally accepted definition of "governance," but this term is often used to refer to interpretations of order, stability, and politico-economic management.[1] The Commission on Global Governance has, for instance, defined governance as "the sum of the many ways individuals and institutions, public and private, manage their common affairs." It has posited that governance is "a continuing process through which conflicting and diverse interests may be accommodated and cooperative action may be taken."[2] The World Bank and the International Monetary Fund, on the other hand, use "good governance" to refer to a particular type of political and economic order. For them, "good governance" is associated with the spread of democracy and transparency in governments and free markets. "Good governance" is the opposite of arbitrary and self-seeking rule, corruption, and cronyism, which have been endemic in some developing societies. However, the World Bank and IMF's version of "good governance" has been costly to developing-nation peoples. Although the World Bank and the IMF started to emphasize different priorities following the crises in East Asia in the late 1990s, their "good governance" is still associated with reduction in public expenditures, emphasis on exports, and charges in hospitals and schools.

The concept of global governance, as distinct from "good governance," refers to formal and informal sets of arrangements in global politics.[3] It implies that states alone cannot manage global affairs, and therefore it accords roles to international governmental organizations (IGOs), non-governmental organizations (NGOs), and multinational corporations (MNCs). Global governance refers to transnational networks, institution-building, norm entrepreneurship, regime creation, and the management of global change. It covers many issues, such as women's rights, human rights, development, democratization, the environment, security, and investments. Its recent achievements include the treaty banning landmines, the Kyoto climate convention, the International Criminal Court, the World Trade Organization, and the "new generation" UN peace-keeping operations. In a nutshell, global governance describes regimes or systems of rule, embracing both formal and informal regulatory mechanisms.[4]

Underlying global governance are tolerance and a willingness to manage differences and reconcile self with other, us with them, and inside with outside. This can take place only where there is a common set of values, norms, beliefs, ideas, and institutions. As these values evolve, the nature of global governance has necessarily to change. Indeed, global governance "is a broad, dynamic, complex process . . . that is constantly evolving and responding to changing circumstances."[5] However, it is power that determines whose interests, rules, and standards become "global." Thus, while global governance requires tolerance and accommodation of conflicting interests across national, racial, class, gender, and ethnic boundaries, it is often the preferences of the most powerful actors that are accommodated.

The purpose of this chapter is to demonstrate that global governance can be understood from several perspectives. I will do so by focusing on three themes: state sovereignty, globalization, and Western hegemony. In the next section, I will explain briefly the theoretical approaches that are used in this chapter. I will then describe how the global "interpretive community" has sought to influence perceptions of global governance. This will be followed by an analysis of how sovereignty has evolved. In the final section, I will discuss the impact of globalization. I will conclude that the United Nations can help to shape global governance.

Theoretical context

Explaining and understanding global governance requires interpretation. Interpretation, in turn, takes place within a theoretical framework. As global governance is a multi-faceted process, the study of it requires a theoretical framework that goes beyond a single paradigm. I will, therefore, employ a pluralist approach that is informed by insights gained mainly, but not exclusively, from realist, liberal, and constructivist research programmes.[6] My task is complicated by the fact that there are several variants of realism, liberalism, and constructivism. Moreover, even when taken together, these three paradigms cannot shed light on every facet of global life. I have chosen them because they go a long way toward explaining power, order, norms, and change. As Stephen Walt has argued: "The 'compleat diplomat' of the future should remain cognizant of realism's emphasis on the inescapable role of power, keep liberalism's awareness of domestic forces in mind, and occasionally reflect on constructivism's vision of change."

Realist accounts of global politics tend to emphasize the way in which states use power to maximise their national interests. They posit that the most important international actors are sovereign states, which are rational and operate in an inherently competitive, anarchic, and self-help environment.[8] Realists assume that sovereignty makes states functionally similar.[9] They also emphasize the strategies that states devise in efforts to improve their standing in international economic competition, influence weaker states, or compete for international prestige. Thus, realists focus on military balancing and "positional competition" in economic, technological, and other non-military matters.[10] They acknowledge the existence of globalization, civil society, and transnational forces, but they make no room for them in their analyses. While realism may be helpful in highlighting the role of power and self-interest in global governance, it discounts the function of ideas, culture, institutions, and norms, except as instruments in power politics.

At a glance, liberalism would appear to be the most appropriate approach to use in the study of global governance because, as Michael Doyle has observed, it is identified "with an essential principle, the importance of the freedom of the individual."[11] Liberalism can adequately explain the interactions of states, civil society, MNCs, and IGOs in global governance. The liberal perspective on global politics posits that there "is at the minimum a heterogeneous state of peace and war" which could "become a state of global peace, in which the expectation of war disappears."[12] Liberals believe that IGOs, such as the United Nations, play a vital role in world politics. They acknowledge that "states live under international anarchy," but they argue that "states are inherently respectful of international law" and that they "do not experience a general state of war."[13] Liberals reject the realist claim that states are functionally similar units. Doyle, for example, has argued that states "are inherently different 'units,' differentiated by how they relate to individual human rights."[14] In general, liberals believe that the interests of states extend beyond security and include the protection of human rights.

Constructivism is concerned with the way in which norms, rules, and institutions constitute the identities and interests of states and other international actors. It claims that the structures of human association, including international society, are determined primarily by shared ideas and culture rather than material forces. While realists claim that it is the distribution of capabilities that determines the nature of the international system, constructivists argue that those capabilities have meaning only because of the ideas we attach to them. Constructivists claim that it is the distribution of ideas and culture that determines the shape of the international system.[15] As constructivism focuses on the roles of norms, ideas, and culture in constructing international structures, it would have plenty to say about how global governance is constituted.

As already indicated, global governance is about norms and power. It consists of ideas, culture, and material forces. It also helps generate norms, ideas, and culture. Global governance involves states and non-state actors, and it affects life from the local to the global levels. However, it is the theoretical frameworks utilized to understand it that determine the way norms and power are interpreted. It is for this reason that I have elected to employ a pluralist theoretical approach.

The interpretive community and global governance

Global governance, which is essentially a product of liberal thinking, concerns so-called global values, norms, standards, and rules. The majority of values that are considered global are Western, and so global governance basically facilitates, and reflects, Western hegemony. Western hegemony here refers to the dominance of Western institutions, interests, standards, and NGOs. The "global civil society" is based on Western mores. In global governance, non-Western states and NGOs have had to redefine their interests and identities in relation to Western norms and power. Severe socio-economic problems have delivered developing-nation political leaders and NGOs into the hands of the West, thereby making Western hegemony appear like an "empire by invitation."

The dominance of Western institutions is partly due to the function of an "interpretive community" that constantly explains, promotes, advocates, and justifies global governance. The "interpretive community" has been extremely successful in portraying Western ideas, values, and preferences as global. The term "interpretive community" is used in this chapter to refer to any group of people who are committed to providing justification and legitimating principles for particular institutions, values, or practices. Members of an "interpretive community" may come from different professional backgrounds; they may be scholars, journalists, international civil servants, and NGO workers. They may also be recruited from different countries and might not even be aware that they operate as a part of a global "interpretive community." What they have in common is a conviction that they are interpreting reality, when in fact they may only be expressing aspirations. Sometimes the ideas of an "interpretive community" may influence practice.

In the post–Cold War era, members of a global "interpretive community" have converged on several themes, including a new world order, globalization, and new forms of sovereignty and security. For example, in December 1988, Soviet President Mikhail Gorbachev used the phrase "new world order" in his address to the United Nations to underline the new strategic thinking and the global restructuring he envisaged, but the "world" simply ignored it. However, when US President George Bush used the same phrase two years later, the "world" took notice. In condemning Iraq's invasion of Kuwait in August 1990, Bush talked of a new world order "where the rule of law supplants the rule of the jungle, a world in which nations recognize the shared responsibility for freedom and justice." This liberal aspiration contrasted sharply with the realist logic of power politics, in which war between states is always considered a possibility. It was no more than a wish for a different type of international system in the post–Cold War era, but other world leaders, scholars, and journalists subsequently started talking of a new world order as if it were a reality. Bush's aspiration did not spell an end to power politics; instead it gave impetus to a rethinking of norms in world politics, and this, in turn, energized efforts to portray Western values, standards, and institutions as global norms.

It was in this intellectual climate that the Commission on Global Governance issued a report which defined sovereignty as an institution that is ultimately derived from the people: "It is a power to be exercised by, for, and on behalf of the people of a state." This report implies that sovereignty should be respected only if the people of a state have had an opportunity to exercise their political, economic, and cultural rights. The report also argues that "the principle of sovereignty and the norms that derive from it must be further adapted to recognize changing realities." Furthermore, "global security extends beyond the protection of borders, ruling elites, and exclusive state interests to include the protection of people."[18] The Commission was simply expressing aspirations that may become practice one day.

At about the same time, a former Australian foreign minister, Gareth Evans, argued that the concept of security, "as it appears in the [UN] Charter, is as much about the protection of individuals as it is about the defence of the territorial integrity of states."[19] In April 1991, former UN Secretary-General Javier Pérez de Cuéllar had argued that state sovereignty needed to be reassessed in response to "the shift in public attitudes towards the belief that the defence of the oppressed in the name of morality should prevail over frontiers and legal documents." Similarly, his successor, Boutros Boutros-Ghali, argued that the time of absolute and exclusive sovereignty had passed.[20] The current UN Secretary-General, Kofi Annan, went further in redefining sovereignty, when he told the General Assembly in September 1999 that his interpretation of the UN Charter was that it aims "to protect individual human beings, not to protect those who abuse them." Annan argued, in his speech to the General Assembly in 1999, that sovereignty had been "redefined by the forces of globalization and international cooperation," and that the state was the "servant of its people, and not *vice versa.*"

The conclusions of the Commission on Global Governance and those of UN secretaries-general and other analysts in recent years suggest that the rethinking of norms has given rise to an interpretive community which is ready to argue for changes in the practices of sovereignty. By arguing for liberal interpretations of the UN Charter, they have promoted a particular view of global governance. However, the views of an interpretive community, without changes in the practices of the majority of international actors, cannot constitute a shift in the meaning of sovereignty. According to some analysts, it was not possible in the 1990s to see a clear-cut turn in state practices. As Adam Roberts has observed, while idealists have hoped that "the sovereignty of states would take second place to human rights," humanitarian action in the 1990s "owed much to political considerations that were often tinged with an element of *realpolitik.*"[21]

It is such interpretations that set the stage on which "NGOs and ... IGOs grope, sometimes cooperatively, sometimes competitively, sometimes in parallel, towards a modicum of global governance."[22] What these interpretations do not say is that global governance links together "global civil society," individuals, the state, and market forces. It is also about the generation of, and the response to, "shared" values and institutions, which give rise to processes for identifying issues, forming an agenda, arriving at outcomes, and making arrangements to implement them.[23] However, as the preceding paragraphs show, global governance has definite implications for interpretations of sovereignty.

Sovereignty and global governance

State sovereignty is like a living organism; it casts off its meanings as it evolves in response to the demands of global governance. In simple terms, sovereignty can be described as a principle that legitimizes internal political organization and serves as a mechanism for enhancing international order. It is, therefore, linked to both internal and global governance. As Thomas Biersteker and Cynthia Weber have argued, state sovereignty is "a political entity's externally recognized right to exercise final authority over its affairs."[24] With regard to internal political control, sovereignty revolves around population, territory, and recognized authority. Alan James has added a constitutional dimension to this, claiming that "sovereign states are those territorially-based entities which are independent in terms of their constitutional arrangements."[25]

For the purposes of this chapter, I shall distinguish between three types of sovereignty. The first is external or juridical sovereignty, which is based on the notion that, theoretically, "the state has over it no other authority than that of international law."[26] The second is internal or empirical sovereignty, which is based on the view that states have the right (and capacity) to control the people, resources, and institutions within their territories. The third is individual or popular sovereignty, which is predicated on the claim that all people are entitled to fundamental freedoms and that states exercise control over them only with their consent. Empirical sovereignty and juridical sovereignty accord states rights and responsibilities that other international actors do not have.

The concept of global governance implicitly questions some understandings of sovereignty because it is based on the assumption that states and non-state actors are partners in the management of global affairs. Realists, who claim that states are the most important international actors, would regard global governance as a diminution of sovereignty. The realist view of sovereignty is that theoretically each state is free to pursue its domestic and external affairs without outside interference. Hence Hans Morgenthau's definition of sovereignty as "centralized power that exercised its law-making and law-enforcing authority within a certain territory."[27] On the other hand, liberals, who subscribe to the view that transnational forces play important roles in world politics, regard global governance as a necessary process of addressing anarchy in the absence of central authority. Liberals believe that sovereignty gives states the right to exercise control within their territories, but that this control is to be exercised with some degree of consent and legitimacy from society. For this reason, liberals associate empirical sovereignty with popular sovereignty. Constructivists, who consider sovereignty to be socially constructed, regard global governance as a part of the social construction and reconstruction of international society.

A closer examination of the different perceptions of sovereignty will shed more light. The realist perspective of sovereignty, which is state-centric and absolutist, is often traced back to Jean Bodin in the fifteenth century. Bodin defined sovereignty as "the absolute and perpetual power" of the ruler.[28] Later, Thomas Hobbes elaborated similar views in his *Leviathan*. Both perceptions of sovereignty reflected the overriding concern for order and security in France and England, respectively. As Alexander Murphy has argued, Bodin's main concern was to promote peace.[29] Endorsing Bodin and Hobbes, Hinsley has argued that sovereignty refers to "a final and absolute political authority in the political community."[30] Some writers have continued to view sovereignty from this perspective alone, thereby entrenching the realist viewpoint. However, Hinsley and many others have argued that in practice there have been limitations to the exercise of sovereignty, with Hinsley observing that sovereignty is not a fact but a concept of how political power is exercised. This state-centric perspective is a normative position that originated from absolutist Europe. Indeed, Reus-Smit has argued that the moral purpose of the state in absolutist Europe was to preserve a "divinely ordained" and hierarchical order, and this gave rise to an authoritative norm of procedural justice.[31]

The liberal view of sovereignty may be traced back to John Locke and Thomas Paine. Paine, for example, associated popular sovereignty with international peace. In reference to the American Revolution in 1791, he argued: "Monarchical sovereignty, the enemy of mankind, and the source of misery, is abolished; and sovereignty is restored to its natural and original place, the nation . . . Were this the case throughout Europe, the cause of war would be taken away."[32] Locke's ideas, which defined sovereignty in relation to the consent of individuals and civil society, were also consistent with liberal democracy. In the early twentieth century, liberal scholars, who were opposed to the Austinian juristic theory of the state, defined sovereignty in terms of people's rights. For example, Harold Laski claimed that sovereignty belonged to the people. In recent times, some liberals have argued that transnational forces and NGOs have a legitimate role in world politics, and that sovereignty should not stand in their way. The liberal perspective on sovereignty readily accommodates the norms, power structures, and regulatory mechanisms that underpin global governance.

Constructivists have had a lot to say about sovereignty in the past decade. Indeed, some of the severest critics of our knowledge of sovereignty have been constructivists and critical theorists. Rob Walker, for instance, recognizes sovereignty as "the primary constitutive principle of modern political life," but he argues that its history has not been properly explained and suggests that it is necessary "to be wary of the conventional history of . . . state sovereignty."[33] Constructivists are critical of those who treat sovereignty as an unchanging institution. Reus-Smit, for example, has argued that it is the constitutional structures of society that determine the nature of sovereignty. The norms that underpin global governance are part of these constitutional structures.

The assumptions that underpin sovereignty date back to the Peace of Westphalia, which inaugurated a new "international" legal order for Europe. The Westphalian regime, which brought about a break from the previous religious order, is best remembered for making the territorial state the cornerstone of the modern international system. Since then, the development and reinterpretation of sovereignty have closely mirrored the evolution of the state and the prevailing norms of global governance. However, sovereignty has not always been honoured. In Europe, sovereignty was occasionally subverted with a view to maintaining the balance of power. This is partly why Stephen Krasner has claimed that breaches of the Westphalian model "have been an enduring characteristic of the international environment."[34] Krasner has more recently written of sovereignty as "organized hypocrisy." Others have suggested that sovereignty can be understood only with reference to particular historical periods.

Sovereignty has undergone various transformations in accordance with the prevailing norms of global governance. Whenever serious crises undermine the legitimizing principles of sovereignty, new norms are negotiated, and these norms often reflect the preferences of the hegemonic states. It is the processes of negotiating the rules for sovereignty which Biersteker and Weber had in mind when they argued that sovereignty was socially constructed.[36] They posited that it is "the practices of states and non-state agents [that] produce, reform, and redefine sovereignty and its constitutive elements." In such social interactions, all participants help to shape, and are also shaped by, the structure of the system, in varying degrees. A global structure that is characterized by power politics and secret diplomacy is likely to favour the notion that sovereignty resides with governments. However, a global order which is committed to the promotion of democracy and human rights would favour popular sovereignty. Thus, it is the norms, values, and institutions which underpin global governance that determine the nature of sovereignty.

Westphalian sovereignty was perceived to reside with political leaders and governments. Under this system, the defence of sovereignty provided governments with an excuse to impose dictatorial rule. This autocratic sovereignty was undermined first by the 1776 American revolution, with its emphasis on popular sovereignty, and then by the 1789 French revolution, with its ideas of equality, fraternity, and liberty. After the Napoleonic wars, the Vienna Congress in 1815 was hostile to populist ideas and legitimized neo-Westphalian sovereignty based on monarchical control. This changed after World War I, when the 1919 Versailles Conference legitimized sovereignty based on the nationalist norm. However, this norm did not apply to African and Asian political entities, which had become subject to European colonialism. Thus, in its evolution, sovereignty has oscillated between governmental "proprietorship" and popular "possession."

Sovereignty has closely been identified with territory for more than 350 years, but the inviolability of territorial integrity and the non-intervention norm were given more emphasis at the end of World War II. This extra emphasis privileged the state over its people. The Cold War, which, in Alexander Wendt's words, "was a structure of shared knowledge that governed great power relations," ensured that this state-centric interpretation of sovereignty reigned supreme.[36] During this period, recognition of new states was determined by whether or not they were ready to respect the non-intervention norm and to uphold juridical sovereignty. Popular sovereignty and good governance had no room in this scheme, partly because the two superpowers—the United States and the Soviet Union—could not agree on what form of internal governance was desirable. With the end of the Cold War, Western powers have emphasized normative values and empirical sovereignty, and this has given the impression that sovereignty is increasingly being associated with the democratic norm. However, the emphasis which the Western states and international financial institutions have placed on liberal democracy and popular legitimacy appears to be geared towards consolidating Western hegemony. The processes of globalization have facilitated this.

Globalization and global governance

Global governance and globalization have a chicken–egg relationship. One is said to be a cause, or product, of the other. This chapter will not engage in the argument as to whether globalization precedes global governance or *vice versa*. Neither of them can be traced to a specific date. What is clear is that globalization has become one of the most commonly used terms in international relations, although (or because) its meaning remains imprecise. Jan Aart Scholte has argued that globalization "refers to processes whereby social relations acquire relatively distanceless and borderless qualities."[38] This is a useful starting point, but it does not say much about the globalization processes themselves. As with many social phenomena, the theoretical framework in play determines the meaning attached to globalization.

Realists, for example, do not think much of globalization because of the importance they attach to the state and national interests. To them, globalization is basically a product of "positional competition" by states, in their efforts to gain advantage in non-military sectors. For some developing nation analysts, globalization is a form of esternization and colonization that can be traced back several centuries. They perceive it in terms of the domination of the non-industrial world by industrialized countries. The market-orientated liberals, on the other hand, have defined globalization primarily in terms of the contemporary movement of capital, investment, and other economic interactions, thereby equating it with economic interdependence. They sometimes regard globalization as the hidden force behind economic cooperation, financial markets, and free trade rules. Thus, the establishment of the World Trade Organization in the mid-1990s was a major development in global governance. Hurrell and Woods summed up the liberal perspective, in which globalization is a "process of increasing interdependence and global enmeshment which occurs as money, people, images, values, and ideas flow ever more swiftly and smoothly across national boundaries."[39] The "flow" of people across state borders has to be qualified, as most developed countries have restricted the entry of developing world peoples. For constructivists, globalization is a part of the global structure that constitutes the identities and interests of international actors and is, in turn, constituted by the interactions of these actors.

In this chapter, the term "globalization" is used to describe the intensity and breadth of interactions within the political, technological, economic, social, and cultural domains, most of which are derived from Western, and especially capitalist, values and practices. Due to improvements in information technology, globalization partly refers to the processes through which social, political, and economic relations can be conducted instantaneously throughout the world and may sometimes elude state attempts at restriction. In a globalized world, political, cultural, economic, and social events tend to become more interconnected. The emphasis is on the size, depth, and speed of interactions.[40]

Globalization implies universalization, harmonization, and homogeneity, which ultimately means that the values, institutions, interests, and norms of some peoples and societies have to be sacrificed. To the extent that globalization implies the promotion of values and standards derived from the West, it inevitably poses a threat to the existence of non-Western traditions and institutions. The threat that globalization poses to developing world peoples is not only more severe but also of a different type from that which it presents to those of the developed, global north.

While some liberals have suggested that globalization has eclipsed the state both within its territory and internationally, realists argue that globalization has in fact been created and maintained by states. As Ian Clark has observed, globalization could be seen as a symptom of "wider political and economic policies" and as "the product of specific state policy choices."[41] There is no doubt that globalization has had some effects on state behaviour. Rapid changes in the technology of transport and communications have made it necessary for policy-makers to devise new ways of responding to both domestic and global problems. In this sense, globalization is a restructuring process that cannot be ignored by policy-makers. However, states, especially the great powers, still determine the environment in which other international actors operate. For example, it was the developed countries that organized financial rescue plans for Indonesia, South Korea, and Thailand in 1997. It is partly for this reason that some have argued that globalization is directed by states' policies.

Explaining how globalization relates to global governance requires a reiteration of my earlier discussion of sovereignty. Sovereignty not only defines the identities and capabilities of groups in world politics, but also limits the ability of outsiders to interfere in domestic affairs. Thus, sovereignty determines agency or the capacity for independent action in world politics. In this sense, sovereignty and self-determination are interrelated. Self-determination provides a theory to explain when state boundaries are legitimate and when they are not, thus implying guidelines to use for deciding whether they should be honoured or not. The pursuit of self-determination legitimizes sovereignty. As with sovereignty, what self-determination involves has changed over time. A monarch could, literally, claim that his military capacities presented a *fait accompli* without worrying too much about whether he had the right to rule; he was, materially, self-determining. The French and American revolutions challenged this position and spread the notion that sovereignty ought to be popular. Then, the twentieth century produced two competing norms regarding "who" the "self" is in self-determination, each norm embodied in an international treaty. The Treaty of Versailles promoted ethnic self-determination and thereby legitimated sovereignty based on the nationalist norm. However, later international treaties, including the charters of the United Nations and the Organization of African Unity, promoted state self-determination, thereby legitimating sovereignty based largely on the territorial norm. What these conceptions shared was the idea that a group ought to be able to determine its own future, and that sovereignty was necessary to enable true autonomy.

With globalization, the interpretation of sovereignty and state capacity for independent action in world politics has been affected by two factors. Firstly, values which are associated with the West have been universalized and depoliticized. This has made possible the second factor, namely the change in international norms relating to development trajectories. There are no longer alternative paths to successful development. Modernization theory, discarded decades earlier, has made a comeback. Societies are arrayed on a single line: successful, civic, progressive, and Western at one end; failed, ethnic, primitive, and non-Western at the other. This has delegitimized political life outside the West, making intervention in non-Western states acceptable.

Globalization has prompted observers to claim that the Earth has become a global village. However, if the Earth is a global village, it is one where only some inhabitants retain their traditions, cultures, rituals, and symbols. Western-derived rules and standards have constructed the socalled global village. The interests and values of non-Westerners are largely ignored, except as tourist attractions. The "global" values which are trumpeted under the banner of globalization were not arrived at through reflection and consensus in international society. They are the norms, symbols, and standards that have been promoted by the powerful Western countries, largely for their own benefit. Non-state actors, and especially NGOs, concerned with numerous problems such as human rights abuses, poverty, environmental degradation, and weapons of mass destruction have facilitated the promotion of Western values in the developing world.

It is no wonder that, as the forces for harmonization and universalization grow, non-Western peoples and their communities are striving to preserve control over local identities, symbols, and values. Thus localization, nationalism, and ethnic and religious revivalism have assumed significance partly because of the threat which universalization and harmonization pose to different cultures, standards, and interests. These defensive reactions by non-Westerners to some aspects of globalization do not suggest that their identities and interests have always remained stagnant. They merely signal that the globalizing processes involved are too enormous and happen too fast. Indeed, it is partly through the speed of its challenge to diversity and identity that globalization constitutes a threat to the security of developing world peoples. It is perhaps for this reason that UN Deputy Secretary-General Louise Fréchette has argued that globalization brings uncertainties in which "there are losers as well as winners." She touched on the nerve of globalization's contradictions when she observed that "globalization confronts us with the challenge of reconciling the imperatives of global markets with the socio-economic needs of the world's people; and of realising its full potential while minimizing the threat of new divisions in our world, of backlash and recourse to the damaging 'isms' . . . populism, nationalism, ethnic chauvinism, fanaticism, and terrorism."[43]

The non-Western peoples and communities view globalization as a cause of alienation; they feel apathetic, detached, socially dislocated, powerless, and normless in the face of globalization. They are apathetic because they see themselves as outsiders in the global village. They also feel that the globalization processes have cast them aside. Alienation undermines what has been described as human security.[44] In this instance, it results from the differences in power, opportunities, and advantages between the Western and non-Western societies.

Recent attempts to assert "Asian values" are partly a reaction to globalization. There is no consensus among the people of Asia as to what constitutes "Asian values," but it is a label with which some political leaders seek to legitimize certain forms of internal political order. Political leaders who seek to maintain authoritarianism and contain the opposition within their societies have exploited "Asian values." These leaders may be believed by sections of the population, especially when they argue that their goal is to preserve Asian traditions in the face of the globalization juggernaut. Similarly, Islamic resurgence can be explained partly in terms of efforts by some Muslim groups to prevent the total erosion of their cultures. Occasionally, radical groups have used the cover of this resurgence to engage in political violence. For example, the establishment of the Hezbollah in Lebanon's Bekaa Valley by Iranian zealots in the early 1980s, was partly based on the fact that the Shia Muslims in Lebanon were treated as second-class citizens, both economically and politically. But, Hezbollah was funded by the Iranian regime as part of its efforts to promote its own brand of Islam and to reshape the Middle Eastern regional order. The result was insecurity for foreigners in Lebanon, and hostage seizures.

However, it is not only non-Western peoples that fear the impact of globalization on their interests. French government officials have expressed serious concerns about the relationship between free trade and culture, particularly with regard to trade in audio-visual products. France was among several European countries that criticized aspects of the 1993 GATT agreement because of its potential impact on French culture and identity. Canadians have struggled with the potential of imported books and periodicals to edge out Canadian content, and have experimented with laws that establish excise tax or minimum quotas for Canadian content. And many of the most powerful Western countries, the engines behind globalization, re-enact the same confrontation domestically with immigrants. Even with the enormous power asymmetry intact, some local French, Americans, Germans, and Australians, for example, fret publicly over the "threat" that immigrants supposedly pose to their culture. Nevertheless, the West as a whole celebrates globalization.

The United Nations and the future of global governance

Globalization and global governance will go on with or without the United Nations. Global governance has so far reflected mainly the interests of Western societies, but the United Nations has the potential to make it truly global. It has the potentiality to ensure that the ideas, norms, and rules which underpin global governance reflect the diversity of values and interests in the world. The United Nations needs to work out its programmes in such a way that racial, gender, cultural, and economic inequalities are taken into account wherever possible. Deputy Secretary-General Fréchette has emphasized three broad imperatives for the United Nations: legitimacy, instruments and institutions, and effectiveness.

These are very important factors, but they are more complex than they first appear. This is because the United Nations means different things to various groups. In the remaining part of this chapter, I will briefly look at how realists, liberals, and constructivists view the legitimacy of the United Nations, and I will suggest finally that UN "managers" need to reinterpret the Charter consistently.

The United Nations appears to straddle the borderline between realism and liberalism, and it has lasted this long partly because it has been perceived by both realists and liberals to be in each of their own interests. Realists care about the legitimacy of the United Nations, but for them this legitimacy is derived from the United Nations serving as an instrument of state interests. A United Nations without the potentiality to serve as a device through which states use their power to pursue national interests has little legitimacy for the realists. There is no doubt that sections of the United Nations, especially the Security Council, serve as a platform for power politics.[45] What generally concerns developing world states is that most of the power within the United Nations is held by Western countries, which dominate the international system politically, economically, technologically, and militarily. Western countries also have the means to promote their values and norms more effectively than the non-Western states. That is why Samuel Huntington has argued: "The West in effect is using international institutions, military power, and economic resources to run the world in ways that will maintain Western predominance, protect Western interests, and promote Western political and economic values."[46] Other realist scholars have made similar claims in relation to the Western states' control of the United Nations and other international organizations. For example, John Mearsheimer has argued: "The most powerful states in the system create and shape institutions so that they can maintain their share of world power, or even increase it."[47] If the United Nations is to remain acceptable to the majority of people around the world, it has to erase the perception that it serves as a mechanism through which the values of powerful states are imposed on weaker ones.

If realists have been mainly interested in the exercising of power and the pursuit of national interests, liberals have been interested in the United Nations' universalist and progressive character. Liberals believe that the United Nations has put power politics in check and facilitated the collective management of global public goods. From some liberal perspectives, the United Nations derives legitimacy from its inclusiveness and its potential to bring about human progress. As Ramesh Thakur has argued: "The greatest strength of the United Nations is that it is the only universal forum for international cooperation and management. It must continue to play a central role in establishing a normative order which strikes a balance between the competing demands of equity and political reality."[48]

On the issues of democratization and participation, some liberals have argued that the United Nations has neglected non-state actors for too long. Hence the increasing calls for the United Nations to involve the "global civil society" more deeply in global governance. There is no doubt that a good number of NGOs have achieved phenomenal success in specific issue areas. However, agreeing on a mechanism for their participation with the United Nations in global governance is likely to raise difficult questions. NGOs have the capacity to do a great deal, but they have no obligation to do anything. Voluntary organizations are not accountable, even in theory, to those whom they serve. The United Nations requires great ingenuity to pursue democratization without compromising the effectiveness and universal acceptability of its actions.

For constructivists, the legitimacy of the United Nations is derived largely from its constitutive and transformative character. The United Nations is both a product, and producer, of ideas, norms, and state interests and identities. The world's leading constructivist in the international relations discipline, John Ruggie, is a senior adviser to the United Nations Secretary-General. Ruggie has said his transition from academia to the UN "went surprisingly smoothly because it quickly became apparent that creative leadership in international organization is social constructivism in action." The United Nations has been an agent of transformation. It has generated numerous ideas on such issues as development, the environment, human rights, women's rights, and peace-keeping. In this respect, the United Nations has become a very important norm-setting organization. As the interests, preferences, and identities of Member States are neither fixed nor exogenously given, the United Nations has participated, however marginally, in influencing the way they are defined and redefined.

However, there is a perception in the developing world that the United Nations' transformative power has been harnessed by the West and works to the detriment of non-Western interests. Some of these criticisms came out at the 1993 UN conference on human rights in Vienna, where China and developing countries described the universalization of human rights as a conspiracy by Western governments to pressure non-Western states to change their identities and political and economic systems. However, the Vienna Declaration and Programme of Action achieved a classic compromise by stating that human rights are universal, indivisible, interdependent, and interrelated, while also recognising "the significance of national and regional particularities and various historical, cultural, and religious backgrounds." The Vienna Declaration underscored the clash of two principles—universalism and relativism. Western countries and NGOs from both the north and the south supported the universalist perspective, while non-Western states took the relativist line. The conference also underlined the imperative for the United Nations to devise a formula through which its ideas and norms in the future will reflect the diversity of the global village.

The exigencies of global governance in this millennium require the United Nations to rethink its norms, structures, procedures, and practices. If the United Nations were to make a difference to global governance, it would need to address more seriously the imperative for democratization in its agencies, taking account of growing demands for transparency and popular participation. Greater openness cannot be achieved without creative efforts to recast sovereignty. Thakur has argued in the introduction of this volume that the "partial erosion of the . . . principle of national sovereignty is rooted today in the reality of global interdependence," but there is a general perception that this "erosion" is too slow and too minimal. For example, in discharging their responsibilities in the human rights area, UN secretaries-general have often been constrained by the UN Charter, especially Article 2 (7) which prohibits intervention "in matters which are essentially within the domestic jurisdiction of any state." This part of the Charter has previously been interpreted in a manner by which it has indirectly shielded dictators from international scrutiny of their human rights records. However, in his address to the General Assembly in September 1999, Kofi Annan said, "nothing in the Charter precludes a recognition that there are rights beyond borders."[50] This line of rethinking should be stretched further. With the rapid changes brought about by globalization, what was "essentially" within the domestic jurisdiction of states in 1945 may not remain so in this millennium. Therefore, it is incumbent upon UN "managers" to reinterpret the Charter to reflect the new global realities. It would be a travesty if the UN Charter were to serve as a hindrance to the evolution of state sovereignty. The imperative is to reinterpret the Charter consistently.

Notes

1. I am deeply indebted to Sue Downie, Kanishka Jayasuriya, and John Mugambwa for useful comments on earlier drafts of this paper.
2. Commission on Global Governance, *Our Global Neighbourhood* (Oxford: Oxford University Press, 1995): 2.
3. For the purposes of this chapter, the terms "global politics" and "international politic" are used interchangeably.
4. K. Jayasuriya, "Globalization, law and the transformation of sovereignty: The emergence of global regulatory governance," *Indiana Journal of Global Legal Studies*, 6/2, (1999): 425–55.
5. Commission on Global Governance, *op. cit.,* 4.
6. Other theories such as feminism, critical social theory, and the international society approach would powerfully illuminate some aspects of global governance, but space

does not allow me to explain them here. However, I will refer to them in the chapter when necessary.
7. S. M. Walt, "International Relations: One World, Many Theories," *Foreign Policy* 110 (1998): 44.
8. M. Mastanduno, "Preserving the unipolar moment: Realist theories and us grand strategy after the cold war," *International Security.* 21/4 (1997): 49–88.
9. K. N. Waltz, *Theory of International Politics* (Reading, MA: Addison-Wesley, 1979).
10. M. Mastanduno and E. B. Kapstein, "Realism and state strategies after the Cold War," in Kapstein and Mastanduno (eds.), *Unipolar Politics: Realism and State Strategies After the Cold War.* (New York: Columbia University Press, 1999).
11. M. Doyle, *Ways of War and Peace* (New York: W. W. Norton, 1997).
12. *Ibid.*: 210.
13. *Ibid.*: 211.
14. *Ibid.*: 211.
15. C. Reus-Smit, *The Moral Purpose of the State* (Princeton: Princeton University Press, 1999); J. G. Ruggie, *Constructing the World Polity* (London: Routledge, 1998); A. Wendt, *Social Theory of International Politics* (Cambridge: Cambridge University Press, 1999).
16. Commission on Global Governance, *Op. cit.*: 69.
17. *Ibid.*: 7.
18. *Ibid.*: 81.
19. G. Evans, "Cooperative security and intrastate conflict," *Foreign Policy* 96 (1994): 9.
20. B. Boutros-Ghali, *An Agenda for Peace.* 2nd ed (New York: United Nations 1995): 44.
21. A. Roberts, *Humanitarian Action in War*, Adelphi Paper No. 305 (London: Oxford University Press, for International Institute of Strategic Studies, 1996).
22. L. Gordenker and T. G. Weiss, "Pluralizing global governance: Analytical approaches and dimensions," in L. Gordenker and T. G. Weiss (eds.), *NGOs, the UN and Global Governance* (Boulder: Lynne Rienner, 1996): 17.
23. Some passages in this paragraph are taken from the final report of the governance workshop, which was prepared by Professor John Groom.
24. T. J. Biersteker and C. Weber (eds.), *State Sovereignty as Social Construct* (Cambridge: Cambridge University Press, 1996): 21.
25. A. James, "Sovereignty: Ground rule or gibberish?" *Review of International Studies* 10/1 (1984): 12.
26. N. L. Wallace-Bruce, *Claims to Statehood in International Law* (New York: Carlton Press, 1994): 58.
27. H. J. Morgenthau, *Politics Among Nations: The Struggle for Power and Peace* (New York: Knopf, 1967): 299.
28. J. Bodin and J. H. Franklin, *On Sovereignty* (Cambridge: Cambridge University Press, 1992): 1.
29. A. B. Murphy, "The sovereign state as a political-territorial ideal: Historical and contemporary considerations," in Biersteker and Weber, *State Sovereignty* (see note 24, above): 85
30. F. H. Hinsley, *Sovereignty* (Cambridge: Cambridge University Press, 1986): 26.
31. C. Reus-Smit, *The Moral Purpose of the State* (Princeton: Princeton University Press, 1999): 87–121.
32. Cited in Doyle, *Ways of War and Peace* (see note 11, above).
33. R. B. J. Walker, "Sovereignty, identity and community: Reflections on the horizons of contemporary political practice," in R. B. J. Walker and S. H. Mendlovitz (eds.), *Contending Sovereignties: Redefining Political Community*, (Boulder: Lynne Rienner, 1990): 159 and 171.

34. S. D. Krasner, "Compromising Westphalia," *International Security* 20/3, (1996): 115.
35. S. D. Krasner, *Sovereignty: Organized Hypocrisy* (Princeton: Princeton University Press, 1999).
36. T. J. Biersteker and C. Weber (eds.), *Sovereignty as Social Construct* (Cambridge: Cambridge University Press, 1996): 11.
37. A. Wendt, "Constructing international politics," *International Security* 20/1 (1995): 71–81.
38. J. A. Scholte, "The Globalization of World Politics," in S. Smith and J. Baylis (eds.) *The Globalization of World Politics* (Oxford: Oxford University Press, 1997): 14.
39. A. Hurrell and N. Woods, "Globalisation and Inequality," *Millennium* 24/3 (1995): 447.
40. S. M. Makinda, "Globalisation as a policy outcome," *Current Affairs Bulletin* 74/6: 4–10.
41. I. Clark, *Globalisation and Fragmentation* (Oxford: Oxford University Press, 1997).
42. S. M. Makinda, "The United Nations and State Sovereignty: Mechanism for Managing International Security," *Australian Journal of Political Science* 33/1 (1998): 101–15.
43. Speech of the Deputy Secretary-General, UN University, 21 January 2000.
44. R. Thakur, "From national to human security," in S. Harris and A. Mack (eds.), *Asia–Pacific Security: The Economics-Politics Nexus* (St. Leonards, Sydney: Allen & Unwin, 1997).
45. The United Nations is so big and differentiated that generalizations about its activities are bound to be inaccurate.
46. S. P. Huntington, "The clash of civilizations?" *Foreign Affairs* 72/3 (1993): 40.
47. J. J. Mearsheimer, "The False Promise of International Institutions," *International Security* 19/3 (1994–95): 13.
48. R. Thakur, "UN peacekeeping in a new world disorder," in R. Thakur and C. A. Thayer, (eds), *A Crisis of Expectations* (Boulder: Westview Press, 1995): 21–2.
49. J. G. Ruggie, *Constructing the World Polity* (London: Routledge, 1998): xii.
50. United Nations Press Release, 1999.

10
Democracy and regression

Sakuntala Kadirgamar-Rajasingham

A global trend towards democracy

Amartya Sen had no difficulty in determining that the most significant development of the twentieth century was the rise of democracy. According to Sen, democracy has come to be recognized both as a universal value—an intrinsic good in its own right—and as the pre-eminently acceptable form of governance.[1] Even distinctly undemocratic governments claim either to be "democratic"—North Korea is known as the "Democratic Peoples' Republic of Korea"—or they claim to strive for democracy, assuring both the international community and their own peoples that democracy will be "installed" when the conditions are "most appropriate." This is the frequent claim of the Burmese military, which issues periodic declarations that it is merely a caretaker government seeking a transition to democracy—when the country is deemed to be "ripe" for democracy.

Democracy has become a dominant belief in the contemporary world, paralleled at least partially with the demise of historic ideological rivalries. Absolute monarchies have been dispensed with and have been replaced by parliaments, republics, and constitutional monarchies. The defeat of Nazism and fascism, and the general decline of mass mobilization models, have been contributing forces. De-colonization introduced many new entrants into the "democracy club" from Asia, Africa, and the Caribbean. Authoritarian and military regimes in Europe (Greece, Spain, and

Portugal) were replaced in the 1970s by democratically elected governments, as were military regimes in Central America and Latin America. Many of the authoritarian regimes in Asia (Taiwan, the Philippines, Thailand, Korea, and Indonesia) have been replaced by democratically elected governments. The 1980s and 1990s were characterized by the fall of the Berlin wall, which discredited communism as a competing ideology. The dismantling of the Soviet Union created a further rush of democratic states, with the newly independent republics opting to choose their governments through popular ballot.

In 1900 there were no countries in the world that had governments elected on the basis of universal enfranchisement through competitive multi-party elections. Today there are 120 governments elected on this basis—the highest number of democracies ever, and a gain of three over the last year.[2]

Recognizing the challenges facing emerging democracies

The trend towards "democracy," the increase in the mass of people living under some form of democratic rule, certainly helps to reinforce the optimistic belief in the pre-eminence of democracy. But, as we have seen the waxing and waning of other powerful beliefs and political systems, can we be as confident that democracy is here to stay? One may well ask: does the march of history demonstrate that democracy will be the defining feature of the world order? Will it last forever?

Besides the questions of consolidation and institutionalization of democracy, other challenges relate to the performance of democracy on several fronts. Will governments elected on the basis of democracy ensure a better (meaning economically prosperous and politically peaceful and stable) world? Will democratic governments be less corrupt, more compassionate, less likely to go to war with each other or against their own citizens? Can the benefits of democracy be enjoyed evenly both within and between states? In this new world order, income inequalities within and between states are ever increasing, and poverty and illiteracy limit the full exercise of political rights and freedoms. Will this impact negatively on the practice of democracy?

Will the trend towards democratization have an impact on international relations? Will it contribute to greater stability in the world order, a reduction in conflicts and inequalities? Will democracy—which advocates political and economic freedom and rights—protect the individual in the face of globalization? How will the integrity and accountability of national democratic governments be maintained in the face of globalization? Does democracy necessarily create national stability, prosperity, and economic growth? Are all countries undertaking the transition to democracy likely to consolidate their democracies, or will some, or many of them, simply stagnate in a state of limbo? Or will some of them even regress and slide back to authoritarianism (with feudal or militant nationalists at the helm) or military dictatorships?

Can the international community assist countries effectively in the move towards democratization and in the consolidation of democracy? How can countries with weak institutions and disadvantageous historical legacies be better prepared for democracy? What are the emerging challenges for this rapidly democratizing world in the twenty-first century? If the trend towards democratization is reversed, how will the international order, with its integrated capital and labour markets and trade flows, respond to the aftershocks of a wave of democratic regression? Will there be a spate of wars to reinstall democracy, or will national insurrections be encouraged to topple governments by international supporters of democracy?

Challenges facing established democracies

Established and well-consolidated democracies face challenges of a different type from those faced by emerging democracies. Voter apathy and a drift away from active political participation may undermine the system, leaving government vulnerable to capture by single-agenda groups or other conservative and intolerant forces. Established Western democracies that have embraced globalization and free trade are less enthusiastic supporters of the free movement of labour. As most recently demonstrated by developments in Austria, many Western democracies have strong and enlarging constituencies of illiberal groups who mobilize against immigrants and around symbols of protective nationalism. The impact of this trend on consolidated democracies must be addressed.

This is surely the most appropriate historical moment and the best forum at which we should ask ourselves: what is the performance and the promise of the proliferation of democracy? Hard questions should be asked, and historical records should be reviewed with a dose of realism, if we are to learn anything from the times in which we live.

What is democracy?

Too many people (especially those in government) view democracy as the equivalent of majority rule. Indeed, it is this minimalist view of democracy, stressing the absolute sovereignty of the majority, which is expressed through elections. Many governments resent the scrutiny of their post-election performance in the protection of political and economic rights, the rule of law, or in the delivery of public goods. They see it as unwarranted interference. Holding on to the principle of the absolute sovereignty of the people has led to a centralization of power and authority, and the exclusion of political, religious, ethnic, and racial minorities. This in turn has led large segments of alienated people to resort to protest outside the "majoritarian/democratic" framework, losing faith in democracy as they know it. Elected governments in Peru, Zimbabwe, and Malaysia, to name but a few, have claimed to represent the will of the majority and have eroded the powers of many political institutions, such as the courts, and the rights of many other sectors, including ethnic and religious minorities.

The greatest fallacies that underpin popular notions of democracy include the notions that intemperate majority rule is democratic, that elections alone guarantee a democracy, and that the holding of elections is the equivalent of securing democracy. Democracy is more than majority rule. Democracy is a complex phenomenon. It is a process (for constituting a government, through elections based on a range of possible electoral formulae); it includes institutions of representation based on law (parliaments, presidencies, and unitary and federal systems of government) and a unique set of values (guaranteeing freedom and equality). Integral to the concept of democracy is the concept of freedom. Democracy is seen as the only political system guaranteeing human freedom. This includes civic, political, economic, social, and cultural freedoms. This freedom is guaranteed on the basis of equality—for men and women, for members of all ethnic and religious groups, and for advocates of diverse political views—without distinction.

It is not unexpected that there should be varied conceptions and misconceptions of democracy. It took the United Nations more than 50 years to acknowledge explicitly that the links between the principles enshrined in the Universal Declaration of Human Rights and the founding principles of a democratic society were indissoluble.[3] And it took the United Nations more than 50 years to acknowledge explicitly that democracy, development, and respect for all human rights and fundamental freedoms are interdependent, and that the right to full participation so firmly upheld in all UN resolutions, and in international law and instruments, is really democracy by another name.

Democracy is the only political system that guarantees, as a matter of principle, a range of political, civic, social, cultural, and economic rights and freedoms. Historically, these rights and freedoms have not been secured by any other political system.[4] For 50 years, the United Nations felt unable to publicly marry respect for national sovereignty with the rights of the citizens it seeks to protect through universal human rights standards. It did so indirectly through a normative framework packaging together the UN Charter, the Universal Declaration of Human Rights, and the Declaration on the Granting of Independence to Colonial Countries and Peoples, to constitute a type of UN Bill of Democratic Rights and Duties. This was given further expression through international covenants and conventions guaranteeing political, civic, social, cultural, and economic rights. We have indeed come a long way from those cautious times.

The protection of human rights and freedoms on the basis of equality is integral to democracy. The notion that human rights and freedoms include political, civic, cultural, social, and economic rights, and that they are indivisible, is also integral to democratic freedom. Democracy—"liberal democracy"—is the only political system that can protect and promote human rights. This perhaps should form the basis of our shared understanding of democratic ideals.

Although 120 countries (or two-thirds of the world's countries) have achieved democratic rule through elections, only 85 countries (44 percent) were classified as free, providing their citizens with a broad range of civil liberties and political rights that come close to the democratic ideals.[5]

This perhaps reinforces the view that elections *per se* do not guarantee freedom in the political and economic realm. Elections are a necessary condition for democracy. They are not, however, a sufficient condition for democracy and for political, civic, social, and economic freedom. One of the many challenges in the new millennium will be to broaden and deepen the advance of human freedom through democracy. This requires preserving and improving the democratic freedoms in "free" countries in the face of new social, political, and economic challenges. It requires enabling democratic freedoms to take root in the 48 countries that are "not free" and improving the quality and extent of freedom in the 59 countries that enjoy partial freedom; this may be the most visible challenge. Promotion and support of democracy must go beyond the support of democratic freedom as an ideal and provide practical assistance that will help communities to realize and experience democratic freedom in their daily lives.

Complacency and apathy are as great a challenge to democracy, because freedom can be lost by neglect as much as it can be taken away by force. In advanced/mature democracies, the challenges that undermine the political system include public apathy, low voter turnouts, and a decline in participation in political parties. There is a growing view that national governments simply do not matter in the same way in the face of globalization. Governments have less control over the economy, provide fewer services to the community, cease to be the largest employer, and appear to be less able to guarantee the security and welfare of the community. In partly free democracies, where there is a commitment to democracy, governments may be vulnerable to ongoing civil wars, domination by hegemonic institutions and social forces, pervasive violence, and corruption.

Models of democracy

The century-long move towards democracy has yielded a diverse array of democratic practices and institutions. There is no consensus on a single universal model of democracy. There are several types or forms of democratic governments, and the "best" choice of government, or the best practice of democracy in the final analysis, is only the "most appropriate" one that works best in the context of a given country.

Democratic choices include presidential as well as parliamentary systems, and governments chosen on the basis of direct representation, proportional representation, or a mix of the two. There are unitary, federal, and confederational political systems based on written and unwritten constitutions. Legal systems are equally varied, and include common-law-based and civil-code-based systems. Political party structures vary in democratic countries and are based on unipolar, bipolar, and multipolar party systems. Democracies have activist judiciaries with wide powers of constitutional review and interpretation, and judiciaries that have a more restricted role in judicial review. Some democracies set thresholds for parliamentary representation, permitting absolute majorities in some cases or qualified majorities in others.

While political outcomes cannot be predicted with the certainty of weather forecasts, it is possible to anticipate the broad implications of institutional choices. However, it is the mix and combination of institutional choices that are most significant. It is not the presidential system or parliamentary system that are in themselves the critical determinant. For instance, a presidential system in a unitary state, with a non-activist judiciary and a legislature chosen on the basis of "first past the post" elections, will clearly operate differently from a presidential system in a federal or confederational political system, with elections based on proportional representation.

The choice of political systems is vital for the effective transition to and consolidation of democracy. Yet there are no "rules of thumb" that can be applied to such choices. What turns out, with the benefit of hindsight, to be "best practice" in country A may have inimical results in country B. Poor institutional choices or practices are often the foundations for the unravelling of a democratic government (as demonstrated in the tragic case of Sri Lanka). This is often the most vital arena in which newly democratizing countries require assistance—to understand the need to provide for transitional arrangements to come out of a political morass such as a civil war, prolonged military dictatorship, or communist domination; to anticipate the potential implications of longer-term choices; and to establish the processes needed to draw in the support of critical segments of the community and follow through on reforms.

Beyond trends—understanding the reality and facing the challenges of democracy

Resilience and pervasiveness of authoritarian institutions and practices

While there has been a surge in the number of countries that have held elections, not all of these countries have gone beyond that first democratic impulse. In many countries, the governments that were installed by that first election have not been able to dismantle all of the authoritarian institutions of the past, and in some instances authoritarians have simply recast themselves, regrouping in order to contest elections and re-enter the new political paradigm.

Several countries that were part of the "third wave" of democracy have not gone beyond the gains of their first elections. Elections have not always led to the election of democrats, and newly-elected governments have often been made up of old authoritarians, who deliver their messages of authoritarianism and control through a new idiom. For instance, the communist party remains significant in many post-communist countries, such as Belarus, and elections in many post-communist countries simply brought in old autocrats reconstituted as elected democrats, such as recently in Croatia. Many countries find it difficult to put their authoritarian pasts (or institutions) behind them completely, and these institutions, such as the military in Pakistan, merely wait in the wings for democracy to unravel and provide them with the opportunity to intervene in the political process. Even more disturbing is the tendency in many multi-ethnic states for electoral democracy to lead to the marginalization and complete exclusion of minority religious or ethnic groups, sowing the seeds of further political instability.

Democratic consolidation is not inevitable

The collapse of authoritarian regimes does not necessarily or inevitably lead to democracy or democratic consolidation, any more than the holding of elections leads to democracy. A consolidated democracy is only one among the many possible outcomes of the collapse of an authoritarian regime. Even if democracy is established through an election, it may not necessarily be consolidated. Under certain conditions, democratic institutions may systematically generate outcomes that cause some politically important forces to opt for authoritarianism. For instance, weak parliaments that are unable to deal effectively with poverty and underdevelopment or ethnic and religious conflicts may give way to ultra-nationalist leaders, or military control (directly or indirectly), or oligarchic control of major political institutions.

A transition to democracy must be distinguished from a consolidation of democracy. Often, authoritarian regimes give way to democratization without a pervasive democratic culture, and democratic institutions may be uneven and incomplete. Important elements vital for a democracy, such as freedom of the press and rights of assembly, may be badly impaired or missing, or democratic institutions may be spread unevenly across the country, present in some regions and extremely weak or non-existent in others. Representative institutions may be so ineffectual that the chief executive makes all-important decisions. This tendency has been reflected in countries such as Argentina, Peru, Brazil, and Bolivia. In many cases, communism was replaced through elections by ultra-nationalist authoritarianism.

The need to develop realistic expectations of democracy

Democracies are not homogeneous and can be graded and distinguished.[6] Doing so may develop realistic expectations of the potential and performance of these systems. The strengths of democracies vary. Democracies range from the well-consolidated democratic regimes (Norway, Sweden, and Denmark) to "semi-democratic" and "low quality" democracies.[8] They include democracies with hegemonic party systems,[9] and pseudo-democracies[10] that have formally democratic institutions but where the political behaviour of their leadership reveals authoritarian tendencies. There are also totalitarian regimes that repress all forms of autonomous structures and processes but claim, nevertheless, to be committed to democracy and to securing the rights of their people. The lowest common denominator that all these regimes rely on is the resort to periodic elections to constitute their national legislatures. Looking behind the façade may help make the initial determination of what is likely to prevail, and what will not.

Democratic elections usher in regimes that can be seen to fall into one of three categories: stable, partially stable, and unstable. Democracy does not always guarantee regime stability, and while it opens up many possibilities for wider participation and inclusion, it may also create political uncertainties in the short term. Democratic elections may provide a stable regime whose institutionalization, and level and breadth of popular legitimacy, make it highly likely to persist. Democratic elections may also install a partially stable regime that is neither fully secure nor in danger of imminent collapse. The institutions of a partially stable regime may, over time, acquire some measure of depth, flexibility, and value, but not enough to ensure secure passage through severe challenges. Democratic elections may also install an unstable regime, which is highly vulnerable to breakdown or overthrow in periods of uncertainty and stress.

Not all democratic transitions will consolidate. Some will, others may stagnate, and yet others may regress. However, there are factors besides the laws of time and nature that may explain these events, and this does have implications for a world that has come to accept democracy as the only game in town.

As a matter of policy, it is important to assess the starting point from which the process of democratization began, by analyzing the process of democratic transition and consolidation. This process of assessment helps to identify the flaws of weak democracies, anticipate reversals, and provide strategic assistance and measures to stem the tide—where possible.

The recent waves of democratization have been from post-colonial states—such as Nigeria and Indonesia—from post-communist Eastern Europe—areas such as Poland, the Czech Republic, Slovakia, and Hungary—from the Soviet Union and its former Republics—for example, Georgia, Belarus, and Ukraine—from military dictatorships in Central and Latin America, and from Asian authoritarianism (Taiwan, Korea, Thailand, and Indonesia). While they may have ridden a common wave to democracy through elections, they have done so—to stretch the metaphor somewhat—on different surfboards, and they will surely experience the ride differently.

The probability of these states managing the transition to democracy is affected by the unique political experiences and legacies of each state. The impact of communism, imperialism, or militarization on a country, the degree of political democratization that had begun to emerge prior to the transition, the degree of market reforms that were undertaken in the given state, and the extent to which external factors are available to support the transition, are all factors that determine whether a transition to democracy may eventually lead to a consolidation of democracy.[11]

Some countries undertake the transitions with relatively homogeneous populations (Hungary), whereas others undertake the transitions with open ethnic or political antagonisms that undermine both the state and the fledgling democracy, as is the case in Nigeria and Russia. Many of these countries had fragile or no political institutions that could support a transition to, and eventual consolidation of, democracy. Many are challenged with managing an overloaded agenda for transformation. This includes reconciling divisive ethnic and national rivalries and fending off threats from oligarchies and vested interests, such as the military or communist party. Besides coping with a lack of democratic leadership and lack of supportive democratic institutions (such as a free media, political parties, an independent judiciary, and a well-organized or supportive civil society), they are faced with the challenge of managing a transition to democracy with a fragmented polity and an institutional deficit. The events in the Balkans and in Russia have laid bare the fragility of the transition process in countries dealing with these problems. Comparisons can be drawn to the process in India, which embarked on institutionalizing the state and democratic government after independence while coping with the human devastation caused by partition. India, though weakened by religious and ethnic conflicts, had strong democratic political leadership and state institutions that could see it through the process—features that many of the post-communist countries appear to lack.

All this points to the fact that an assessment of the viability of a democratic transition to consolidate itself may depend on a cluster of factors that include historical experiences of a country, its prevailing political, social, and economic realities, the structure of the social forces in operation, the political, social, and economic institutions that are adopted during the transition and thereafter, and political leadership, among others. It is a complex mixture.

Democratic consolidation, at its very minimum, requires two electoral cycles to establish a tentative pattern of alternating power. Even so, a democracy may not be secure after a period of ten years, any more than a marriage is safe from the passing of "the seven-year itch." Patience is vital in working with, as well as in assessing, the process of democratization. Consolidation is rarely a linear movement that follows a neat upward trajectory.

Providing support for emerging democracies

Support for emerging democracies and countries in transition must be strategic and sustained. It is necessary to understand that support must be structured around the unique conditions and political, social, and economic realities that define the context and situation of the country in question. Any assistance must be based on an assessment of the country's situation and the strength and capacities of its national actors, and must be in tune with the country's priorities and national agenda for reform. Half measures are as useless and perhaps more destructive than no assistance at all. Democracy support must be committed for a realistic period of time, balancing the need to prevent permanent dependencies with the dangers of pulling out support before a satisfactory degree of consolidation has taken place.

Assessing democracy

A critical contribution to strengthening democracy can come from national as well as international efforts to audit the performance of democracy on the ground—to determine how responsive a given political system is, and what degree of political egalitarianism it supports. These are critical elements that engender democratic legitimacy. This will take us beyond the trends, to an understanding of the practice of democracy on the ground. Quantitative standards (frequency of elections, votes cast, legislative seats secured) are often used to describe whether a country has a democratically elected government. Clearly this quantitative approach must be supplemented by a comprehensive, qualitative analysis and assessment of the nature of legal and political institutions and processes, the historical and political context in which the institutions are rooted and from which they continue to evolve, and the societal impact of these institutions.

A "democratic audit" or "democracy assessment" to review a country's "state of democracy" is a useful prerequisite before a declaration is made that any given country is a democratic country, or that it is a country in danger of regressing from democracy. Such an audit would ideally require the complex appraisal of the country's performance, along a comprehensive set of indices.[12] It would also require "hearing the voices" of the people who live within those systems—their views, perceptions, and expectations of their political system. A comprehensive assessment of the state of democracy within a country has the added advantage of shifting the eye of scrutiny away from the deficiencies of the existing regime, to demand analysis of more fundamental and systemic issues. The most useful feature of such an exercise is that it may provide an impetus for many countries, including "established democracies," to reappraise their own institutions and performance in the light of these indicators.

Popular control of government through elections is most commonly identified as the critical indicator of democratic government. However, it is vital to assess the degree or extent of popular control by probing the reach of the electoral process, its inclusiveness, its built-in protections to preserve fairness in electoral competition, and its independence from the government of the day. The integrity and impartiality of the electoral system—how governmental outcomes actually reflect the choices made through the electoral process, how much effective choice the system offers citizens, as well as how it treats its citizens—are critical factors.

But popular control of government in a democracy goes beyond elections. A government must be "open and accountable" to public opinion and to its constituencies. Governments must remain politically accountable for their policies to parliament or the legislature, legally accountable to the courts for its conduct and execution of policies, and financially accountable, both to the courts and parliament, for the handling of public resources. This accountability is integral to the democratic process and should remain an important issue after elections have occurred.

Popular control of government can be exercised only where citizens have secured political and civil rights or liberties that include the right or freedom to dissent. In addition, it requires effective institutions (such as the press and courts) through which citizens can air their dissenting views individually or through organized groups and associations. Along with free citizens, independent societal groups are also critical to the functioning of an effective democracy, and these groups too require legal protection and political space within an effective democracy. The degree of representativeness of the media, access to the media by different social groups, the ability of the media to operate as a balanced forum for informed political debate, support for basic democratic principles from the traditions and culture of society, people's confidence in the ability of the political system to solve the main problems confronting society and their own ability to influence it—these are all explanatory factors that reveal the state and dynamics of democracy.

Democracy audits/assessments have to be periodic to make a meaningful contribution to our understanding of whether there is a trend towards democratization, whether this is leading to democratic consolidation or merely a series of elections around the globe, and whether there is also a trend towards regression. It will also provide a better appreciation of national fault-lines—whether countries deliver more effectively on electoral accountability than on post-electoral accountability, whether countries provide legal recognition of political rights that are in effect unenforceable due to social or economic constraints, and whether social and economic inequalities skew effective political participation.

Democracy and regression

Democracy is vulnerable to challenges both from outside and within the system. It can be undermined by democratic leadership or by its mass base. It is vulnerable to a sudden collapse as well as an insidious and incremental erosion of institutions and practices over a period of time. Democracies can be brought down by political events and actors (such as a change in government through elections and its replacement by illiberal political leadership) and by coups, and it can be undermined by economic failures and social factors (such as social unrest stemming from inequalities, divisive ethnic and religious conflicts, and failures in nation-building).

The most visible sign of "regression from democracy" is the usurpation of political power from an elected government by non-elected leaders. Military coups—armed insurrections against an elected government—clearly fall into this genre. However, while the international community was unequivocal in its condemnation of the military coups in Pakistan and the Ivory Coast, the local populations, including civil-society organizations, seemed to view these developments differently. Clearly, the coups did not support a movement towards democracy, but neither were they viewed as particularly regressive, since the regimes they replaced no longer enjoyed widespread legitimacy; they were riddled with corruption, violence, and systemic failures. Sadly, the institutional alternatives to replace these corrupt and inefficient regimes were also lacking. Weak political parties organized along ethnic lines and based on feudal privilege have not contributed to the development of a political culture that supports democracy. The military remained, in these and similar societies, the only coherent and stable institution. The erosion of democracy by democratic actors may lead to an undermining of popular belief in democracy as a system of government that can effectively deliver public goods and that is capable of renewal and self-correction.

"Democratic actors" from within the system can also undermine democracy. The decision of a regime not to hold an election and thus to further perpetuate itself in power, or the continued use of exceptional powers such as emergency rules that suspend ordinary parliamentary procedures and the civil liberties of individuals and political actors, marks a regression. In addition, a democratically elected leader's decision to violate constitutional requirements forbidding re-election would also undermine the democratic system. This creates a paradox, because the electorate is free (in theory) to reject the unconstitutional bid for an additional term in office. In reality, however, the choice is often couched in terms of effective political leadership versus a cumbersome constitutional impediment. Peru may soon be faced with the choice of re-electing an authoritarian president, one who seeks an additional term despite a constitutional prohibition on his running for re-election. Likewise, in Venezuela the democratic device of a "referendum" was used to constrain institutions that could exercise countervailing power over the presidency.

Democracy cannot survive without popular support for its institutions. Yet, paradoxically, an over-politicized electorate can also undermine the effectiveness of the regime by bringing continuous pressure to bear on its representatives. In the context of ethnically divided societies, popular pressures can undermine elite negotiations to accommodate ethnic diversity and bring down vulnerable coalition governments. Pressures on elected representatives may induce them to adopt populist and illiberal policies that undermine the democratic consensus. An over-centralized party leadership, and the complete absence of political opposition at the parliamentary level, may lead to an unresponsive and isolated political leadership, creating greater incentives for extra-parliamentary struggles that will eventually undermine democracy.

Not all regression takes place in one fell swoop. In as much as there is movement towards democracy, there may be movements away from democracy—a backsliding that does not quite deserve the epitaph of "regression," but is nevertheless a move away from democracy and may require intermediate responses. There is often a build-up over time that includes populist rhetoric, or (in the case of multi-ethnic societies) ultra-nationalist and exclusionary rhetoric accompanied by discriminatory or centralizing legislation or acts of violence that set the stage for more drastic forms of control of the political system.

These movements can be detected only if the international obsession with elections and the formal aspects of constituting a democratically elected government give way to more painstaking analysis of national situations. This analysis must surely review the legal framework that regulates political competition (constitutions, electoral laws, citizenship laws, equality provisions and access to the courts), the social and economic conditions and opportunities for major political actors, the expectations of major political actors and groups, and their perceptions of how well (in terms of proportionality) and effectively (in terms of powers) they are represented in the political structure. It is necessary to assess both the nature and content of pre-election commitments made and post-election performance in fulfilling these promises. However, these are sensitive activities that many governments resent as a violation of their sovereignty.

Building sustainable democracy—coping with the impact of sudden and unexpected events

The catalysts that activate a transition to democracy or democratic regression can come in varied forms. There is a tendency to see catalysts that support democratization as positive events and catalysts that cause a slide to regression as negative events, although the events themselves may be of the same genre.

The death of a leader (as in the cases of Nigeria and Croatia) or a sudden regime collapse (as in Indonesia) may create a positive incentive for democratization. It may create the opportunity for an election and for post-election support in a country committed to making a transition to democracy. Failure to assist in a timely and sustained way may lead to an opportunity irretrievably lost. In Indonesia and Nigeria, such opportunities were indeed created. However, the untimely death of a leader in an unconsolidated democracy may yield negative results. In this respect, transitions to democracy are most vulnerable to leadership changes, and it is important to build and reinforce multiple levels of democratic leadership to support the process.

Unexpected electoral victories may also derail the system. The unanticipated electoral victory of the Islamic party in Algeria caused the army to declare the elections void, drove the Islamic groups underground, and created a spiral of violence. It discredited the military and has confounded the prospects of democratic transition.

Even natural events such as hurricanes and earthquakes can derail all national efforts to build up a sustainable economy, and leave a transitional democracy extremely vulnerable. To cope with such natural events, governments often resort to emergency powers that quickly become institutionalized.

Economic crashes have had the unusual effect of derailing authoritarianism in Indonesia; but, on the other hand, the economic turbulence in Russia has left its Duma weakened, and has created a growing nostalgia for the certainties and security of the communist regime.

Although civil wars and coups are frequently categorized as sudden and unexpected events, many of them, in reality, could be anticipated, with the only uncertainty being the exact date and time. Analysts had long commented on the erosion of public confidence in the regime of Nawaz Shariff that stemmed from his own violation of democratic norms, his control of the judiciary, the rise in corruption and ethnic and political violence, and the economic failures associated with his democratically elected regime. The military coup in Pakistan was not seen as a shock, although it could not have succeeded without the element of surprise. Similarly, the genocide in Rwanda was preceded by a series of political events that increased the predictability of this tragedy. Likewise, the civil war in Bosnia, and later in Kosovo, followed a steady erosion of minority rights, heightened militant nationalism, and a general breakdown in ethnic accommodation.

Democratization and globalization

In as much as there is a trend towards democratization, there is also a growing trend towards economic integration and liberalization. The integration of capital markets and the free flow of trade and private investments is now a feature of our world. The process has been greatly assisted by revolutionary advances in communications that have broken down barriers to the accessing of information and communication. There have been several distinctive developments that are outcomes of globalization and that have affected the nature and role of the state, both in relation to markets and its own citizens.

Globalization is viewed as the zenith of economic freedom. Globalization has encouraged direct foreign investment, created economies of scale, and rationalized labour markets. It promotes economic freedom through an "efficiency-centred" model of development, as opposed to a "people-centred" model of freedom as development. Many countries have experienced diminished control of their economies as a result of these trends. National governments have lost control of their currencies, and the security and welfare of labour has been threatened by an ever-increasing search for global efficiency. Weaker economies that have been required to restructure in order to become more competitive have had to follow policy prescriptions meted out by international financial institutions that have not received the support of national legislatures. Paradoxically, while the trend towards democratization is increasing, there is also erosion at the supranational level of the democratic values of transparency and accountability, especially as they relate to macroeconomic policies.

The internet revolution is viewed as a positive feature of globalization, breaking down the monopolistic controls over information that many governments have acquired. However, many still depend on traditional instruments of communications and the mass media for information. Globalization has increased the divide, creating income inequalities both within and between countries, because not all communities have access to these opportunities.

Globalization has also contributed to monopolistic control over the dissemination of information by large conglomerates. This monopolistic control is being used to advance and promote capitalism and the market rather than the human values necessary for long-term stability. There is no inevitable correlation between economic freedom and political freedom. There is, apparently, no obvious or automatic link between macroeconomic development and broad-based human development. Some countries are more effective than others in converting the income from their GDP and GNP into broad-based human development and increasing the quality of life for all their citizens. This reinforces the view that, while competitive market economies and economic freedom may create the necessary conditions in which democracy can take root and advance, they are not sufficient conditions.[13]

In the short term, globalization has led to frustration and despair among peoples who are rendered uncompetitive in the globalized world. With unemployment and income inequalities rising, so are the prospects for violence and instability. There are realistic fears that communities that are uncompetitive in this new paradigm will retreat into exclusive nationalisms that may find violent expression.

How has democracy been promoted?

Democracy has been advanced through a range of advocacy programs and support programs.[14] Democracy support has come in different forms, with the use of both negative sanctions and positive incentives by the promoters of democracy. Originally, democracy promotion was seen as a Western enterprise, with the former colonial powers (especially the United Kingdom) and the United States taking the lead. Multilateral agencies and international organizations have also contributed to this enterprise. Democracy has been introduced to countries by assistance or sometimes by force, tied to bilateral and multilateral aid packages that provide governments with incentives to reform their legislation and practices. Democracy support has included training programmes, technical assistance, and even funds for infrastructure development—for example, to optimize the workings of the courts and human rights commissions, and to strengthen national legislatures.

Historical model of force

The historical record on democracy promotion is mixed. The value of democracy and, eventually, democratic institutions was introduced to much of Asia and Africa by colonial governments that clearly did not practice what they preached. In many cases, however, colonial governments introduced democratic values (universal franchise, elimination of caste, and gender equality) that were resisted by conservative local elites. They also introduced democratic institutions and electoral systems that were carbon copies of their own political systems, were often inappropriate to their subject territories, and that unravelled shortly thereafter.

The democracy that was thrust after the Second World War onto the defeated Germany and Japan did not appear to have a supportive democratic culture or any local institutions or traditions that could assist in the transition. Yet, democracy has prevailed over time in these countries. International efforts in supporting post-war reconstruction were intense and unstinting, with the emphasis on integrating these countries politically and economically into the international order. More recently, efforts to bring democracy and freedom to the Balkans have included the use of bombs, trade sanctions, and other punitive measures, with mixed or dubious results.

While the forcible export of democracy does stand out as a historical prototype, it may not be the one that yields the best results. Democracy can be advanced most realistically if there is significant national support for it. That support may come from the government, or from national groups in opposition to the government that represent significant and effective social groups within the country.

Democracy support

Strengthening networks of national actors

Democracy is an intergenerational affair. It is a long-term project and requires the support of a variety of actors and institutions. It requires the support of its political leaders and political parties, the judicial system, bureaucracy, media, civil society actors, and, most of all, its citizens. Consequently, the promotion of democracy will require the promotion of these various actors and institutions. This crucial group needs to think about the concept of democracy and be empowered to act to support democracy. They will do so only if they see their personal interests tied to democracy. If major social groups (ethnic or religious minorities, political parties, and social classes) are excluded, they will be disinclined to appreciate the intrinsic value of democracy and will not have any incentive to support it.

Providing comparative information on models and systems

Knowledge of comparative models and systems, the practical operation of these systems, and their implications is always useful to national actors. In many instances, democracy actors are trained or supported in isolation. For instance, political parties are trained in the workings of democratic political parties, and journalists are trained to operate a free media. There is a need for greater cross-training and less role differentiation of democracy actors.

Encouraging review and renewal of institutions

Democratic systems need to be reviewed and renewed periodically. "Appropriate institutions" must be appropriate for the national circumstances, reflecting the changing needs and realities of the community, and, at a practical level, they must be affordable, enforceable, and comprehensible to the local community. Countries such as Lebanon and Nigeria based their representative political institutions on census records that were hopelessly outdated and irrelevant to the existing realities. Consequently, these institutions faced fierce challenges from their constituents.

Integrating democracy into the lives of citizens through education

Democracy promotion efforts should focus on educating people about democracy and integrating democracy as an aspect of their daily lives. This requires a significant and long-term investment in people—in critical education and in human development—ensuring that they make their political and economic choices from a threshold where their basic needs are met. It goes beyond civic education programmes targeting electoral cycles. Democracy promotion has grown to be a thriving industry, with a great deal of money and training being put into institutional development. Yet structural adjustment policies call for the reduction of public spending on education; cuts in jobs create angry, dissatisfied ex-workers, while parallel calls are being made for the mobilizing of an engaged citizenry.

Who can advance democracy effectively?

External actors (such as colonial powers, dominant superpowers, or medium powers) have promoted democracy by force, and also by more benign means, such as linking democracy-related reforms to conditionality clauses for aid or trade concessions. Multilateral agencies such as the World Bank and the United Nations have also supported democracy programmes through good governance programmes, and through providing technical assistance, training, and infrastructure development aid. International foundations[15] and other international organizations[16] have also provided national actors with assistance that has included help with the design of political institutions, electoral systems, and election management bodies, the provision of options for more inclusive forms of political representation, and the management of conflict through democratic institutions and processes.

Internal efforts are crucial, and powerful agents of democratization are "bringing" democracy to their countries even in the face of conservative resistance. The commitment of Nelson Mandela to democracy remains a powerful example of such a leadership paradigm. In Indonesia, it was the relentless demands of citizens—students no less—that pushed and pressed for *democrasi* and *reformisi*. The process has also required and even depended on the active support of political parties, civil society groups and associations, and the media.

Support for democracy requires a practical approach, working with national partners and assisting them to make for themselves the choices most appropriate for their particular situation. National partners should not be limited to governments but to a broader range of political actors, both within and outside government. National partnerships should represent the political as well as demographic face of the country. This support may include providing them with options and choices on political institutions and systems that can create an effective national government. It may include comparative experiences, strategies, and options, to be used by national actors to overcome social, ethnic, and religious divisions and consolidate nation-building strategies.

Democracy promotion and support are long-term challenges and are most effectively served by the sustained support of multiple actors (national as well as international, governmental as well as non-governmental groups) over time. Democracy is best promoted when it is integrated into national educational programmes and media policies and strategies. Democracy must be achieved through the promotion of civil society, and through initiatives targeted specifically at political actors and institutions, such as national parliaments and political parties

Challenges for democracy in the twenty-first century

The major challenges in the twenty-first century will include ensuring that national governments will remain relevant and accountable to their constituencies, and deliver basic goods and services, in a world dominated by corporations, capital markets, and free trade. The supra-state does not have a form as yet; it remains unregulated, unaccountable, and its obligations are not clearly defined. It is vital that the democratic freedoms of the individual, and of communities, are protected, and that development include human development as opposed to commercial development alone.

Major problems of governance in the twenty-first century will be within democracy, making it more difficult to handle as it is wrapped in a mantle of legitimacy. Democracy in the twenty-first century must cope with the pressures of race and ethnicity, of religious fundamentalism, and of technology, capitalism, and the anomie and social dislocation created by global society. How to consolidate democracy in ethnically and culturally divided states and prevent the rise of illiberal democracies will remain a key challenge.

Communities have high expectations of democratic government. The technologies of registering dissatisfaction, as well as the technologies for violent and destabilizing protest, are more readily available today than in the past. Governments are increasingly challenged by secessionist wars that have ballooned from unmet community needs, and there is a rising demand from subnational groups for democracy *vis-à-vis* dominant national groups. While globalization and integration takes place at one level, there is an increasing demand for fragmentation into micro-units at another level.

Policy proposals to support the consolidation of democracy

Focus on developing appropriate institutions and processes at an appropriate pace

Support for democracy must be firmly rooted in the national context and linked to national needs, capabilities, and agendas. Democracy supporters do a disservice to all if they overload the agenda in post-conflict situations (with demands for speedy elections, and hastily conceived peace treaties or electoral pacts) or pull out of the process too early.

Developing democracy for and within subnational groups

Democracy has too often been viewed as an issue of and for governments. While democracy is a relationship between the state and the individual, it is also a relationship between social groups *vis-à-vis* the state and *vis-à-vis* each other. In many countries, democratic politics have failed to accommodate the relevance of nationalism as an organizing basis for democratic government. While nationalism can become divisive and exclusive, it can also be a legitimate organizing principle for communities. The suppression of nationalism has led to prolonged conflicts in many cases, whereas the recognition of nationalism—through political arrangements for regional autonomy, an effective bill of rights, or political representation in national legislatures—defuses the intensity of nationalism as a sole principle of political mobilization. However, nationalism poses other challenges. Few nationalist groups have considered issues of internal democracy or their own democratic relations with other national groups. If nationalism is another cry for democracy for the group, it is qualitatively different to nationalism based on the exclusivity of the group. The former offers greater prospects for democratic stability.

Consensus building as a democratic value

There is no doubt that developing a democratic consensus on institutions, processes, the distribution of resources, and on non-material issues such as identity and recognition is an exhausting, time-consuming, and resource-draining endeavour. In the case of ethnically and religiously divided societies it is even more so. Nevertheless, the process of such consensus-building has value in itself irrespective of its outcomes, and is at the heart of the democratic struggle.

The role of new technologies in developing appropriate democratic institutions and processes

The power of the media could be used to develop support for democratic norms, among both citizens and political leadership. If some of the energies used to develop insatiable appetites for consumerism are used instead to promote democratic freedom as a value, a political culture more supportive of democracy is likely to develop over time.

The ever-increasing use of the internet and other means of communication can be used in deepening the democratic process. Institution-building and nation-building could perhaps develop at a different pace if we effectively harness these new technologies to support the process.

Integrating emerging democracies into international networks and partnerships

Democracy support does not only require financial and material support. Integrating emerging democracies into international relationships and partnerships may also integrate the country more fully into the informal democracy club and provide it with additional support. The wish to join the European Union has had a positive effect on the transition processes of many emerging democracies in Eastern Europe and, for instance, in Turkey. Membership in the European Union requires a standard of compliance with democratic norms, and there are many positive incentives for membership.

Supporting democracy: challenges for the United Nations

The United Nations has come a long way by linking its fundamental Charter and covenants to democracy. It continues to have to deal with governmental resistance to efforts to maintain democratic accountability, which are viewed by these governments as unwarranted interference. Yet it is the United Nations that is eventually called upon to intervene when political failures lead to humanitarian crises. This in itself creates greater leverage for the United Nations to demand more accountable and responsive government at the national level.

The United Nations has a wide and deep field presence, and has access to governments and non-governmental organizations. By widening its mandate to include issues of assistance in the transition from post-conflict situations, in governance, and in public sector reform, it is well placed to work on supporting national democratization efforts. Clearly, the United Nations should make strategic partnerships with organizations that have expertise in these areas, and should play an important role in coordinating democracy support, to ensure that a coherent and consistent national programme of democracy support is developed, as opposed to ad hoc democracy projects that do not contribute to a larger endeavour.

For the United Nations to be able to support democracy globally, it too must be supported by global democrats and would-be democrats. This would require financial as well as moral support for the programmes undertaken by the United Nations, as well as a willingness to accept reviews of national policies that support or undermine democracy without rejecting such reviews as challenges to national sovereignty. In the final analysis, securing this support may be the ultimate challenge.

Notes

1. Amartya Sen, "Democracy as a universal value," Keynote address at the Global Conference on Democracy, New Delhi, February 1999, p. 4.
2. Freedom House, *Freedom in the World: The Annual Survey of Political Rights and Civil Liberties 1999–2000* (New York: Freedom House, 2000).
3. The UN Human Rights Commission adopted Resolution no. 57, "Promotion of the right to democracy," on 27 April 1999.
4. These include: the rights to freedom of opinion and expression; freedom of thought, conscience, and religion; the right to of peaceful assembly and association; the right to freedom to seek, receive, and impart any idea through any media; the right to the rule of law, legal protection, and the independence of the judiciary; the rights to universal and equal suffrage; free voting in periodic free elections; the right to political participation and equal opportunity for all citizens to be political actors; transparent and accountable government institutions; the right to equal access to public services in one's own country.
5. Fifty-nine countries (31 percent of the world's total) are classified as "partly free" and 48 countries (or 25 percent of the world's total) are considered to be "not Free." See Freedom House, *Freedom in the World* (see note 2, above).
6. Philippe C. Schmitter and Terry Lynn Karl, "What democracy is . . . and is not," in Larry Diamond and Marc F. Plattner, *The Global Resurgence of Democracy*, 2nd ed. (Baltimore: Johns Hopkins University Press, 1996).
7. In "semi-democratic" countries, the effective power of elected officials is very limited and/or political party competition is restricted, or the fairness and freedom of the process is compromised (e.g., Singapore, Malaysia, Senegal, Mexico, and Turkey).
8. Low-quality democracies include low intensity democracies, poor democracies, and delegative democracies. These are cases where there are fair and competitive elections, authentic power for elected officials, freedom of press and expression, and independent organizations and media, but where there is nevertheless a lack of accountability, responsiveness, institutional balance, and effectiveness between elections. This is the case with the unconsolidated democracies of the "third wave" (such as Argentina and Brazil) and longer-functioning systems such as India and Venezuela that have entered into a period of decay and stress. See Schmitter and Karl, "What democracy is . . . ," (see note 6, above).
9. Such as is the case in Malaysia and Mexico.
10. Pseudo-democracies are less institutionalized, more coercive, personalized, and unstable, for example; Kenya, Cameroon, Gabon, and most of Central America in the 1970s.
11. See Alexander J. Motyl's introduction to *Nations in Transit* (New York: Freedom House, 1997) cited in Allen Lynch, *Nations in Transit: The Year in Context* (New York: Freedom House, 1999–2000).
12. David Beetham, "Key principles and indices for a democratic audit," in David Beetham (ed.), *Defining and Measuring democracy* (London: Sage, 1994): 25–43.
13. See UNDP, *Human Development Report 1999* (Oxford: Oxford University Press, 1999).
14. See T. Carothers, *Aiding Democracy Abroad: The Learning Curve* (Washington, DC: Carnegie Endowment for Peace, 1999).
15. For example, National Endowment for Democracy (NED), National Democratic institute (NDI), Westminster Foundation, etc.
16. International Institute for Democracy and Electoral Assistance (International IDEA).

11
Civil society and global governance

Michael Edwards

> We have entered a new era of ever-greater partnership, and there are few limits to what civil society can achieve . . . it is clear that there is a new diplomacy where NGOs, international organizations, and governments can come together to pursue their objectives.
>
> Kofi Annan, UN Secretary-General, 7 May 1999

> In all its forms, civil society is probably the largest single factor in development, if not in its monetary contribution then certainly in its human contribution and its experience and history.
>
> James Wolfensohn, World Bank President, 21 January 1999

Ten years ago, there was little talk of civil society[1] in the corridors of power. Now, the walls reverberate with at least the rhetoric of partnership, participation, and the role of citizens' groups in promoting sustainable development. Though poorly understood and imperfectly applied in practice, concepts like "new diplomacy," "soft power," and "complex multilateralism" place civil society at the centre of international policy debates and global problem-solving.[2] This radical change in international relations bodes well for our common future, but it is also a highly contested debate in which questions abound and answers are in short supply. In reality, "civil society" is an arena, not a thing, and, although it is often seen as the key to future progressive politics, this arena contains different and conflicting interests and agendas.³ For their part, global institutions are still the prisoners of a state-based system of international negotiation and find it exceptionally difficult to open up to non-state participation at any meaningful level.

We may dream of a "global community" but we do not yet live in one; too often, "global governance" means a system in which only the strong are represented and only the weak are punished. Resolving these deficiencies will be an immensely complex task for governments, intergovernmental organizations, business, and civil society to undertake together over the coming years. In this chapter, I pose three questions: why has civil society risen so quickly up the international agenda, what dilemmas lie ahead, and what should the United Nations be doing to reconcile the demands of the different actors who will shape the regimes of the twenty-first century?

The rise and rise of civil society

Changing ideas about international development

There are at least three reasons for the resurgence of civil society in the international arena. The first concerns changing ideas about international development. In recent years, there has been a significant move away from what was known as the "Washington consensus"—the belief that market liberalization and Western-style democracy offered a universal blueprint for growth and the reduction of poverty across the world. Central to the emerging "post-Washington consensus" are a number of ideas that place civil society at the heart of the development policy debate. The first of these ideas is that a strong social and institutional infrastructure is crucial to growth and development; "social capital"—a rich weave of social networks, norms, and civic institutions—is just as important in these areas as other forms of capital. Second, more pluralistic forms of governance and decision-making are seen to be more effective in developing a social consensus about structural changes in the economy and other key reforms; shared ownership of the development agenda is seen as the key to its sustainability. Third, public, private, and civic roles are being reconceptualized and reshaped, in both economics and social policy; the best route to problem-solving lies through partnerships and alliances between these different actors. Fourth, international institutions require stronger public and political constituencies to support them; otherwise they will continue to lose legitimacy, with potentially fatal consequences.

Civil society is central to all these ideas, and to their successful application. Although the empirical evidence for some of the underlying assumptions involved is incomplete, there is already a consensus among the donor community that a "strong civil society" is crucial to successful development performance. Civil society has entered the mainstream of international development discourse as a topic of central concern.

New conceptions of governance

Picking up on some of these ideas as they apply outside the domestic arena, the second major shift concerns a quiet revolution in conceptions of international relations. When Kofi Annan talks of "new diplomacy," he is echoing a common perception that the characteristics of global governance—the rules, norms, and institutions that govern public and private behaviour across national boundaries—are changing in new and important ways.[4] As economic and cultural globalization proceeds, the state's monopoly over governance is challenged by the increasing influence of both profit-making and non-profit private actors.[5] Corporations and private capital flows react very quickly to the opportunities provided by an increasingly integrated global market. By contrast, the response of states and civil society is necessarily slow, fragmented, and messy, because of the demands of democracy and the need to negotiate among so many different interests. In theory, civil society can be a counterweight to the expanding influence of markets and the declining power of states, but in practice there are few formal structures through which this countervailing authority might be expressed, especially at the global level. Transnational non-governmental organization (NGO) networks abound, but there is no world government to speak of and few global citizens to constitute a "global civil society" in the deeper meaning of that term. The result is a growing democratic deficit in the processes of global governance.

Despite these difficulties, it is already clear that governance in the new millennium is unlikely to mean a single framework of international law applied through a unified global authority. It is more likely to involve a multi-layered process of interaction between different forms of authority (states, citizens, and markets) and different forms of regulation (laws, conventions, and social norms), working together to pursue common goals, resolve disputes, and negotiate new trade-offs between conflicting interests. The early stages of this model of governance, described as "global public policy" by some[6] and "multi-track diplomacy" by others,[7] can already be discerned in global environmental regimes, such as the Montreal protocol, and in international, cross-sector campaigns over landmines, debt, child labour, and other high-profile issues. Civic groups play a key role in all these experiments: over 15,000 transnational civic networks are already active on the global stage, 90 percent of which have been formed during the last 30 years.[8] This form of governance is messy and unpredictable, but it will ultimately be more effective—by giving ordinary citizens a bigger say in the questions that dominate world politics and a greater stake in the solutions.

Currently, civil-society involvement in global regimes tends to operate through networks of interest groups (especially NGOs), rather than through formal representative structures.[9] This raises important questions about civic groups and their future role, especially issues of structure, governance, and accountability that may erode their legitimacy as social actors in the emerging global order. As I will show below in this chapter, it is precisely in this area that commentators are raising increasingly critical questions. However, the role of civil society is certain to grow as global governance becomes more pluralistic and less confined to state-based systems that are defined according to territorial sovereignty.

"It's good for business"

In addition to these conceptual arguments, United Nations agencies and international financial institutions have become more interested in civil society, and more open to working with civic groups, for a simpler and more commercial reason—it is "good for business." International institutions have found that operational partnerships and a broader policy dialogue contribute to more efficient project implementation and a lower rate of failure, a better public image, and more political support, especially among key shareholder governments in North America and Western Europe, and research and policy development which is more informed and less constrained by internal orthodoxy. Given these tangible benefits, it would be difficult for any international agency to retreat from the trend towards greater civic engagement. The practical and political costs would be too high.

This positive assessment is a comparatively recent phenomenon. Prior to 1980, there was little structured contact between civic groups and multilateral institutions, and almost no formal non-state involvement in global regimes. Toward the middle of the 1980s, such contacts became more frequent and more organized, including the consolidation of NGO advisory or consultative bodies for the specialized agencies of the UN system, the formation of the NGO Working Group on the World Bank in 1984, and some early global campaigning efforts around debt, structural adjustment, and popular participation.[10] Global civic organizing increased at a much faster rate after the end of the Cold War, with the number of international NGOs quadrupling to over 20,000 in less than two decades, and other civic actors (such as international labour union federations and networks of professional associations) beginning to take a higher profile.[11] Successive UN conferences on gender, population, the environment, social development, and habitation provided a vehicle for these emerging civic alliances to test out their skills, and both the United Nations and the World Bank began to form strategic partnerships with key NGOs in ventures such as the Global Alliance for Forest Conservation and Sustainable Use and the World Commission on Dams. The assumption underlying these partnerships is that "global civil society" can broaden democratic practice by creating additional channels for popular participation, accountability, consultation, and debate, thus improving the quality of governance and promoting agreements that will last. The World Bank, the United Nations Development Programme (UNDP), and many bilateral aid agencies have embarked on a systematic effort to increase their understanding of civil society and its role in these contexts, and to enhance their capacity to engage effectively with civic groups at both the national level—through planning processes such as the World Bank's Comprehensive Development Framework—and the international level.

However, towards the end of the 1990s critical questions began to be raised about this phenomenon from inside the international institutions, especially about the role of intermediary (advocacy) NGOs as a subset of civic actors. Having portrayed civil society in earlier times as something of a "magic bullet" for state and market failure, it is not surprising that attention is now turning to the failings (actual or perceived) of civil society itself. It is increasingly common to hear senior agency staff, academics, and journalists echo the complaints of some governments (especially in the Southern hemisphere) that NGOs are self-selected, unaccountable, and poorly rooted in society, thereby questioning their legitimacy as participants in global debates. It is not that the principle of civic engagement is being questioned; more that the practice of civic engagement may be distorted in favour of organizations with greater resources and more access to decision-makers in capital cities, perhaps marginalizing grassroots constituencies in the process. Current trends in the UN system illustrate this ambiguity of commitment: there have been strong declarations from the Secretary-General and others about the importance of civic engagement, accompanied by increasing attempts to formalize—some would say restrict—access by NGOs to the formal machinery of debate and decision-making, especially in New York.[12] At the turn of the millennium, therefore, there are forces acting both for and against the deepening of civil-society involvement in global regimes. The dilemmas created by this situation provide a useful agenda for dialogue and action-planning among civic groups and intergovernmental organizations over the coming years.

From rhetoric to reality: The dilemmas of non-state involvement in global governance.

As a result of the political openings of the last decade, civic groups increasingly feel that they have the *right* to participate in global governance. Much less attention has been paid to their *obligations* in pursuing this role responsibly, or to concrete ways in which these rights might be expressed in the conduct of international institutions and the governance of global regimes. This is sensitive and difficult ground for both governments and civil society. There are at least four areas of tension.

Legitimacy, accountability, and representation

The first set of issues—and by far the most contentious—concerns legitimacy and accountability; who speaks for whom in an NGO alliance or network, and how are differences resolved when participants vary in strength and resources? Who enjoys the benefits and suffers the costs of what the movement achieves, especially at the grassroots level? Whose voice is heard, and which interests are ignored, when differences are filtered out in order to communicate a simple message in a global campaign? In particular, how are grassroots voices mediated by institutions of different kinds—networks and their members, northern NGOs and southern NGOs, southern NGOs and community groups, and so on down the line?

In the mid-1990s, North American NGOs claimed to represent a southern consensus against the replenishment of the International Development Association (IDA), the soft loan arm of the World Bank, on the grounds that social and environmental safeguards were too weak. In contrast, southern NGOs (mainly from Africa) insisted that the IDA go ahead regardless of the weakness of these safeguards, because foreign aid was desperately needed even if its terms were imperfect.[13] The "banana wars" of 1998–99 provide a more recent example of this problem, where NGOs supporting small-scale banana producers in Central America and the Caribbean found themselves on opposite sides of a landmark dispute before the World Trade Organization. On some issues (like debt or landmines), there is a solid south–north consensus in favor of a unified lobbying position. However, in other areas (especially trade and labour rights and the environment), there is no such consensus, since people and their civic representatives may have conflicting short-term interests in different parts of the world. As globalization proceeds, these areas will become the centrepiece of the international system's response, so it is vital that NGO networks develop a more sophisticated way of addressing differences of opinion within civil society in different localities and regions.

Very few networks have mechanisms in place to resolve such differences democratically.[14]

In cases like these, discussions often focus on the thorny issue of representation, though there are really two questions that are being asked: first, is representation the only route to NGO legitimacy in global governance? Second, how "representative" must an organization be in order to qualify for a seat at the negotiating table? These questions are often conflated, with results that make sensible discussion of policy options impossible.

Legitimacy is generally understood as the right to be and do something in society, a sense that an organization is lawful, admissible, and justified in its chosen course of action; but there are different ways in which these things can be validated. Legitimacy in membership bodies is claimed through the normal democratic processes of elections and formal sanctions that ensure that an agency is representative of, and accountable to, its constituents. Trade unions and some NGO federations fall into this category, though whether these processes operate effectively and democratically is another matter. Agreeing on some minimum standards in this regard is an important part of the agenda for the future. A small number of intermediary NGOs also have a membership base of this kind (Amnesty International is a good example), but most do not, and very few international NGO networks have democratic systems of governance or accountability. This creates obvious problems in claiming legitimacy through representation; these problems are exacerbated by the financial gains that come from serving as a trusted intermediary for donors who want to fund NGO advocacy, but who cannot make grants directly to every participant. This sets up an unhealthy dynamic, since NGOs in Washington, London, or Brussels have a vested interest in maintaining the role of intermediary rather than encouraging NGOs, especially those based in the south, to represent themselves directly. The financial implications of losing this precious status are one reason why criticisms of legitimacy touch off such a fierce reaction among northern NGOs; this is one of the rawest of NGO nerves.

In their defence, intermediary NGOs do not need democratic ways of sustaining their legitimacy, since their legitimacy is defined by legal compliance, effective supervision by their trustees, and recognition by other legitimate bodies that they have valuable knowledge and skills to bring to the debate. Since global governance is inevitably going to be a combination of formal and informal political processes, it is perfectly possible for NGOs to be legitimate but not representative participants in global debates, so long as they are clear on the implications of the different ways in which legitimacy is claimed. No one expects Oxfam, for example, to be perfectly representative of developing world opinion; only that its proposals on debt and other issues should be solidly rooted in research and experience and sensitive to the views and aspirations of its developing world partners. However, even if Oxfam conforms to these conditions (which is a challenge in itself), this gives them no formal rights to participate in global decision-making, since this is an area in which legitimacy must be claimed through representation. Non-membership bodies may have the right to a voice, but not to a vote. In this sense, the best representative of civil society is a democratically elected government, complemented by the checks and balances provided by non-state membership bodies (such as labour unions) and pressure groups of different kinds. The resulting mix will be very messy, but it is standard practice in national politics and looks set to shape the emergence of more democratic regimes at the global level too. The world will never be perfectly democratic, but it can be increasingly pluralist, and if that pluralism allows all interests to be represented and debated then a better set of decisions will emerge over time.

It is no accident that questions about legitimacy are being raised at a time when NGOs have started to gain real influence on the international stage. In that sense they are victims of their own success. Neither is there any shortage of hypocrisy among the critics, especially when it appears that NGOs are being singled out in contrast to businesses (and even many governments) that are even less accountable than they are. Nevertheless, the criticisms are real, and must be addressed if NGOs are to exploit the political space that has opened up in the post–Cold War world. At minimum, that means no more unsubstantiated claims to "represent the people" and more concerted and creative efforts to change the balance of power in global civic alliances. This will always be difficult but, when different routes to legitimacy are confused, the issues are impossible to resolve in any sensible way.

NGOs: From the local to the global

Globalization requires both governments and NGOs to link different levels of their activity together—local, national, regional, and global. For governments this challenge is somewhat more straightforward, since they have a chain of intergovernmental structures like the United Nations through which debate and decision-making can be linked, at least in theory. The situation is much more challenging for NGOs, since there are no parallel structures to facilitate supranational civic participation, and no civic representation in intergovernmental bodies.

All around the world, governments, NGOs, and businesses are already experimenting with "dialogic politics" at the local level, sharing in planning and decision-making to generate a better and more sustainable set of outcomes. These experiments are the local building blocks of future global governance. By laying a strong foundation for negotiations over labour standards, environmental pollution, and human rights, they offer the potential to connect ordinary citizens to global regimes. But this can only work if local structures are connected to more democratic structures at higher levels of the world system, helping to ensure that sacrifices made in one locality are not exploited by less scrupulous parties elsewhere. Recent tripartite agreements on child labour in Bangladeshi garment factories are a sign of the future in this respect, with NGOs, government, and business striking mutually advantageous local bargains within a framework of global minimum standards set out in the provisions of International Labor Organization Conventions dealing with child labour. Other regimes could follow this example by embedding local agreements in a nested system of authorities that balance necessary flexibility with a core of universal principles. Getting things right at the base of the system is much more important than introducing new global institutions that are divorced from their local roots—an exercise akin to building castles in the sky. Until such linkages become the norm, NGOs will continue to struggle to make connections between their work at the local and global levels.

These problems are not helped by a tendency among some NGOs to focus on global advocacy to the exclusion of the national-level processes of state-society relations that underpin the ability of any country to pursue progressive goals in an integrated economy. There is always a temptation to "leap-frog" the national arena and go directly to Washington or Brussels, where it is often easier to gain access to senior officials and achieve a response. This is understandable, but in the long term it is a serious mistake. It increases the influence of multilateral institutions over national development and erodes the process of domestic coalition-building that is essential to the development of pro-poor policy reform. In addition, the constant appearance of NGOs in international fora, combined with the dominance of NGO voices from the north, reinforces the suspicion among developing world governments that these are not genuine global alliances but yet another example of the rich world's monopoly over global debates. The NGOs concerned may see themselves as defending the interests of the poor, but it is still outsiders—not the government's own constituents—who are deciding the agenda. Most of these attacks are self-serving, but the asymmetry of NGO networks makes such criticisms inevitable. For example, only 251 of the 1,550 NGOs associated with the UN Department of Public Information come from the south, and the ratio of NGOs in consultative status with ECOSOC is even lower.[15]

Addressing this problem requires a different way of building NGO alliances, with more emphasis on horizontal relationships among equals, stronger links between local, national, and global action, and a more democratic way of deciding on strategies and messages. Jubilee 2000 (though a relatively easy case because of the absence of any south–north NGO fault-line) provides some good examples of these innovations. In Uganda, for example, a network of local NGOs has developed a dialogue with their own government on the options for debt relief, supported with technical assistance from northern NGOs like Oxfam. The results of this dialogue were then incorporated into the international debt campaign. Research has shown that NGO networks can achieve their policy goals, build capacity among NGOs in the south, *and* preserve accountability to grassroots constituents, if they consciously plan to do so from the outset and are prepared to trade off some element of speed and convenience in order to negotiate a more democratic set of outcomes.[16] Sadly, relatively few northern NGOs seem willing to follow this approach, though, to their credit, NGOs such as Oxfam and ActionAid have started to reorient some of their resources in this direction—as with the Uganda Debt Network, cited above. Perhaps the costs seem too high, in terms of profile lost and decision-making made more complex. As we shall see, governments can help NGOs to deal with these costs and encourage them to make the transition to alliances which are less dominated by voices from the north.

From campaign slogans to constituencies for change

One of the consequences of globalization is that traditional answers to social and economic questions become redundant, or at least that the questions become more complex and the answers more uncertain. The theoretical underpinnings of pro- and anti-free-trade positions, for example, are highly contested. We cannot know in advance whether one course of action will be better than another, whatever the theory predicts. But this is a far from theoretical question; what if the NGOs who protested so loudly in Seattle turn out to be wrong in their assumptions about the future benefits that flow from different trading strategies? Returning to the issue of accountability, who pays the price? Not the NGOs themselves, but the farmers in the developing world, who will be suffering the consequences for generations. Of course, the same strictures apply to pro-free-traders too, but NGOs cannot use this as a defence. All protagonists must face up to the same question: in an uncertain world, what does it mean to advocate responsibly for a predetermined position?

Humility would be a start, which is a challenge in itself to organizations used to occupying the moral high ground. More investment in research and learning is also crucial, so that the alternatives that NGOs are lobbying for can be properly grounded, tested, and critiqued. NGOs are adept at saying "no, this is wrong," but not so good at saying "yes, here is a viable alternative." Yet, a politics of pure opposition is unlikely to contribute very much to the regimes of the future. One of the consequences of this dilemma is likely to be a switch from "conversion" strategies, the traditional NGO view of advocacy, to "engagement" strategies, which aim to support a process of dialogue rather than simply lobbying for a fixed set of outcomes. This will take NGOs further into territory that may seem obvious ground—building public constituencies for policy reform—but which has thus far been largely absent from their agenda.

A strong constituency in the industrialized world is a prerequisite for the success of more equitable global regimes, new forms of governance, and the sacrifices required to alter global patterns of consumption and trade. Codes of conduct to govern multinational corporations, for example, are of little use unless they are backed by large-scale consumer pressure to enforce them. Although governments and businesses can play an important role in building these constituencies, the major responsibility is likely to fall to NGOs, since it is they who have the public trust and international connections to talk plainly and convincingly about global justice. NGOs have always talked of the need to build constituencies, but have focused on problems in the developing world instead of lifestyle change at home, playing on the idea that "your five dollars will make the difference." It rarely does, and what would make a difference (mass-based public protest against Western indifference, for example) is never given sufficient attention. Many NGOs have cut back their public education budgets in recent years (seeing this as an overhead instead of a core activity), while government spending is only slowly resurfacing after the insularity of the Thatcher/Reagan years. A deeper engagement in constituency-building does not mean abandoning campaigns or surrendering the power of protest. But it does mean a better balance between traditional forms of NGO advocacy, and slower, longer-term work on the causes of injustice. To support this shift, NGOs will need to develop a range of new skills and competencies in public communications, and work with academics, think tanks, trade unions, and others who can help them to develop and articulate more nuanced positions on issues like trade and labour markets, adapted to different country contexts.

Ways forward: What role for the United Nations?

Civil society involvement in global governance cannot be legislated into existence or imposed from above. Nevertheless, the United Nations has a crucial role to play in nurturing this historic shift, both as "midwife" and as "host," making sure that its own structures and mechanisms are open to participation and serve as role models for the rest of the international community. This is far from the case at present. Since many of the questions laid out in this chapter concern dilemmas of governance and accountability, the United Nations, as the body charged with negotiating and monitoring global standards, has a special responsibility to lead in this field. In its role as "midwife," there are plenty of avenues for action.

First, civic groups, governments, and businesses need a "safe space" in which to exchange ideas about the practicalities of global governance, and about the implications for the different actors involved ("safe" meaning a forum free from the accusations and counter-accusations that often dominate the dialogue). A large amount of thinking and research is going on about new experiments in global public policy, but it is fragmented and poorly disseminated, especially among civic groups themselves. The United Nations is generally a more trusted convenor than the international financial institutions or the World Trade Organization, and is well placed to host substantive discussions of this kind in the run-up to the Millennium General Assembly. As far as possible, such discussions should be based on careful analysis of innovative practice (like the Commission on Sustainable Development), not discussions of general principles. Civic groups need more support (and less uninformed criticism) in developing concrete new approaches to governance, accountability, and communications in global networks.

Second, the United Nations can help to support concrete innovations in global civil society in three crucial areas:

- Levelling the playing field for civic involvement, so as to encourage participation by the broadest possible range of organizations, especially from the south. This will mean additional support for southern groups to develop new capacities and skills and to travel to global fora (perhaps as members of national delegations), restrictions on the number of northern groups at the negotiating table (by country, region, and sector), and decentralized mechanisms that relocate the centre of gravity away from New York and Washington.
- A greater degree of structure and order to the "rules of the game" that govern civic involvement in global debates, without imposing bureaucratic rules from the top down, since that would damage the creativity and spontaneity that characterize the best of global citizen action. Codes of conduct set and policed by NGOs themselves provide a useful way forward here. The "Guidelines for NGO participation in the CSD Steering Committee" provide a good example, setting high standards for transparency, accountability, representation, and behaviour that result in sanctions if NGOs fail to observe them. APEC's "legitimacy determinants" are another example—a way of selecting NGOs on the basis of the degree of "helpful knowledge" they bring to the discussions. At

CIVIL SOCIETY AND GLOBAL GOVERNANCE   217

present, these rules vary widely and unnecessarily, given that most intergovernmental organizations face common dilemmas. There are other ways of clarifying the rights and responsibilities of access and participation, such as an independent ombudsperson to arbitrate in disputes between civic groups and intergovernmental organizations, or between NGOs in a network who may feel aggrieved. Humanitarian relief agencies, for example, look set to introduce such a mechanism voluntarily, after a period of intensive debate.[17] However, such formal mechanisms may not be welcomed very widely, and may be of limited use in practice: the World Bank's Inspection Panel has had relatively little success in institutionalizing accountability, though it is certainly an advance on what went before.

- A voice, not a vote, for civic groups in global governance. NGOs must recognize that there are justifiable limits to their participation in decision-making, set by their (mostly) non-representative character and the legitimacy of democratically elected governments. The key to civil society involvement lies through a structured voice in global debates, not through a formal vote in the Security Council. The challenge will be to structure this voice in ways that promote a genuine sense of equality and democracy in global civil society itself.

Third, the United Nations can play an important role in promoting greater rigour in the debate, in place of the anecdotes, prejudice, and confusion that currently predominate. This applies especially to the vexed questions of legitimacy and representation, where general statements are often applied across the board to radically different types of organization, forms of participation, issues, and requirements. This obscures the discussion of practical alternatives, and renders governments and intergovernmental organizations vulnerable to the charge that they are using the difficulties of practice to frustrate progress on points of principle. A number of critical test cases will arise in the near future that can be used to experiment more creatively with the principles laid out above, especially the Millennium General Assembly in 2000 and the follow-up conferences to Beijing, Copenhagen, and Rio de Janeiro. The United Nations must lead this process.

Conclusion

Whatever the remaining problems of legitimacy and accountability, of structure and relationships, one thing is certain: at the aggregate level, the increasing involvement of civil society in global policy debates in the last ten years has been a significant force for good. The landmines campaign,

Jubilee 2000, the women's and environmental movements, and many others have secured real advances for people on the margins of global progress. NGOs are rarely angelic in their behaviour, but generally speaking they are on the side of the angels, and the world is a better place for them.

At the start of a new century, civil society and intergovernmental organizations have reached an historic moment in their relationship with each other. The old antagonisms have largely disappeared, to be replaced by a more complex picture in which there are no easy answers and few issues that generate an immediate consensus. Greater openness to civic involvement in global regimes brings increased responsibilities to play that role effectively, sensitively, and in ways which genuinely give voice to the poor. This is a challenge to all civic groups, and to all governments, without whose active support it will be impossible to consolidate the gains of the recent past. For their part, intergovernmental organizations must be supportive of civic efforts to grapple with this new agenda, and committed to meeting their side of the bargain in opening the regimes of the future to global citizen action.

Notes

1. Civil society is a contentious term with no common or consensus definition. The definition I prefer is as follows: "Civil society is the arena in which people come together to advance the interests they hold in common, not for profit or political power, but because they care enough about something to take collective action. It includes all networks and associations between family and state, except firms."
2. M. Edwards, *Future Positive: International Cooperation in the 21st Century* (London: Earthscan, and Sterling: Stylus, 1999).
3. J. Scholte, *Global Civil Society: Changing the World?* (University of Warwick: Department of Politics and International Studies, 1999).
4. K. Annan, "The quiet revolution," *Global Governance* 4, (1998): 123–38.
5. D. Archibugi and D. Held, *Cosmopolitan Democracy* (Cambridge: Polity Press, 1995); J. Rosenau and E. Cziempel (eds.), *Governance Without Government: Order and Change in World Politics* (Cambridge: Cambridge University Press, 1992).
6. W. Reinicke, *Global Public Policy: Governing Without Government* (Washington, DC: Brookings Institution, 1998); and I. Kaul et al. (eds.), *Global Public Goods: International Cooperation in the 21st Century* (Oxford: Oxford University Press, 1999).
7. J. Smith et al. (eds.), *Transnational Social Movements and Global Politics: Solidarity Beyond the State* (Syracuse: Syracuse University Press, 1998); P. Waterman, *Globalization, Social Movements and the New Internationalism* (London: Mansell, 1998).
8. M. Edwards, D. Hulme, and T. Wallace, "NGOs in a Global Future: Marrying Local Delivery to Worldwide Leverage," *Public Administration and Development* (1999): 19, 117–36; R. O'Brien et al., *Challenging Global Governance: Social Movements and Multilateral Economic Institutions* (Cambridge: Cambridge University Press, 1998).
9. R. Higgott and A. Bieler (eds.), *Non-State Actors and Authority in the Global System* (London: Routledge, 1999); M. Keck and K. Sikkink, *Activists beyond Borders: Trans-*

national Advocacy Networks In International Politics (Ithaca: Cornell University Press, 1998).
10. T. Weiss and L. Gordenker, *NGOs, the UN and Global Governance* (Boulder; Lynne Rienner, 1996); P. Willetts, *The Conscience of the World: The influence of NGOs in the UN System* (London: Hurst and Co., 1996); J. Fox and L. D. Brown (eds.), *The Struggle for Accountability: The World Bank, NGOs and Grassroots Movements* (Cambridge, MA: MIT Press, 1998).
11. C. Runyan, "Action on the Front Lines," *World Watch* (November/December, 1999).
12. J. Rosenau, "The adaptation of the UN to a turbulent world," in R. Thakur (ed.), *Past Imperfect, Future Uncertain: The UN at Fifty* (London: Macmillan, 1998); United Nations, Arrangements and practices for the Interaction of NGOs in all activities of the UN system: Report of the Secretary-General, UN Doc. A/53/150, 1998; J. Paul, *NGO Access at the United Nations* (New York: Global Policy Forum, 1999).
13. S. Cleary, "The World Bank and NGOs," in P. Willetts, *The Conscience of the World* (see note 10, above); P. Nelson, "Internationalising economic and environmental policy: transnational NGO networks and the World Bank's expanding influence," *Millennium* 25/3 (1996).
14. J. Covey, "Accountability and effectiveness in NGO policy alliances," in M. Edwards and D. Hulme (eds.), *Beyond the Magic Bullet: NGO Performance and Accountability in the post Cold–War World*. (London: Earthscan, and West Hartford: Kumarian Press, 1995).
15. K. Kendig, *Civil Society, Global Governance and the United Nations* (Tokyo: United Nations University, 1999).
16. M. Edwards and J. Gaventa (eds.), *Global Citizen Action* (Boulder and London: Lynne Rienner, 2000); Fox and Brown (eds.), *The Struggle for Accountability* (see Note 10, above); Covey, "Accountability and effectiveness in NGO policy alliances," (see Note 14, above).
17. J. Mitchell and D. Doane, "An ombudsman for humanitarian assistance?" *Disasters* 23/2 (1999).

12
The United Nations and human rights

David Forsythe

> We enter the new millennium with an international code of human rights that is one of the great accomplishments of the twentieth century . . .
>
> [W]e insist on the responsibility of governments to uphold human rights regardless of their political, economic, social, or cultural systems and notwithstanding their economic and social situation . . .
>
> Respect for human rights, as proclaimed in the international instruments, is central to our mandate. If we lose sight of this fundamental truth, all else will fail.
>
> UN Secretary-General's Annual Report, 1999, paragraphs 257, 275, 276

This chapter address three questions: what is the place of human rights in general in the United Nations' activities at the start of the new millennium, what is the relationship between human rights and globalization, and what are the most important challenges confronting the United Nations in its human rights programmes? Most of the chapter deals with this third question.

In line with the Secretary-General's observation, this chapter argues that human rights are absolutely central to everything that the United Nations does, although many states do not act in line with this logic. The chapter then argues that globalization has been broadly misunderstood as only a purely economic process, whereas it should be seen as a multidimensional process in which human rights play a central role. Finally, I will argue that the United Nations should build on the past fifty years, which represent a legal and diplomatic revolution in favour of human rights, by pushing for certain progressive changes.

In the final analysis, the United Nations has the requisite experience and comparative advantages to continue to be an important catalyst in helping to achieve more of the promise of a better world offered by universal human rights.

The United Nations and human rights

It is easy to forget how the discourse on human rights has altered the culture of international relations since 1945. Secretary-General Kofi Annan, in his 1999 annual report to the United Nations General Assembly, remarked that the development of universal human rights was one of the great achievements of the twentieth century. That view is duplicated by other distinguished observers and is likely to endure over time.[1] Remarkable changes have occurred in the theory and practice of personal rights in the last fifty years.[2]

Secretary-General Annan also noted that, unless human rights was kept front and centre in all UN programmes, the United Nations would fail in a most fundamental sense. This also is a sound view. Everything that the United Nations undertakes is to be ultimately measured against the protection of personal rights defined under international law. The UN seeks not a value-free peace and security, much less a peaceful order imposed by the likes of Saddam Hussein, but peace and security based on human rights. This is evident in UN objectives in places such as Bosnia, Kosovo, El Salvador, Mozambique, Cambodia, and Namibia. Moreover, the organization seeks not just any type of development, but sustainable development reflecting the centrality of the person. This is evident in recent changes at least in the theory of the UN Development Programme, while certain development (and relief) agencies, such as UNICEF, have also become more rights-orientated. Furthermore, the United Nations pursues ecological protection compatible with the recognized rights of the person. One can see this change, for example, in the fact that the UN refugee office, the (UNHCR), now contains an environmental unit. Protecting human rights is not a marginal add-on, a sop to warm-hearted and fuzzy-headed political liberals, but a central purpose of the United Nations that relates to realistic security and economic (and other) basic concerns.

Given the extensive range of universal human rights already recognized by the international community, it is crucial that more be done to secure their implementation—to move the law on the books into the realm of living law. This does not preclude the development of new standards as threats to human dignity emerge. But without new and sustained efforts to apply what has already been established, the existing norms will become discredited. The most pressing general issue now for the United Nations and human rights is primarily that of implementation.

Globalization

The question of the effect of globalization on the implementation of human rights is sometimes posed, as if globalization were only an economic process and one that controlled the fate of other concerns. In this essentially post-communist world, Marx would be pleased with this understanding of globalization.

Although there is a trend to think of globalization as if it were a strictly and narrowly economic process—a matter of buying and selling goods and services on a planetary, or at least massively international, basis—this trend reflects misunderstanding. It is more accurate to think of globalization as a rope consisting of several intertwined threads: military, social (human rights and ethics), ecological, and economic. All four threads are produced by the global principles of science and technology that affect communication, transportation, weaponry, and production.

If economics is becoming more and more global, so is the matter of ethics and human rights. In fact, the globalization of human rights preceded the most recent round of globalization of economics (the latter being reflected in the meta-mergers of business enterprises in the 1990s, in an effort to maximize the economies of scale). But human rights were globalized in the first half-decade after World War II, when the UN Charter, the Universal Declaration of Human Rights, and the Nuremberg Tribunal (and to a lesser extent its companion in Tokyo) began to make an impact on international relations. Unlike the previous turn of the century, when an increase in international economic activity was *not* accompanied by an increase in references to human rights in an international context, the present turn of the century into the new millennium has been quite different.

The globalization of human rights was based on two concerns in 1945, neither of which was narrowly economic. World War II produced the related beliefs that massive slaughter could no longer be tolerated on ethical grounds (as if World War I had not made the point sufficiently), and that national authoritarianism and repression were too dangerous as a political or security issue to treat as a domestic matter of absolutely sovereign states. Hence we saw the birth of the global human rights movement, based on a combination of ethics and security concerns.[4]

In other words, a fundamental and indeed primary meaning of globalization is that human rights standards have been denationalized and transformed into an international, global, planetary subject. A similar argument can be made about ecology and security. Clearly, globalization is not just about economics.

Even when globalization is considered to be an economic process, one cannot realistically and intelligently ignore its inherent social and political implications. As a result of economic globalization, unemployment may be increased in some places. Democratic governments may lose control of the development process. Exploitation of workers may occur. Personal privacy and other aspects of human dignity may be adversely affected. This was one meaning of the debacle of the World Trade Organization (WTO) meeting in Seattle during late 1999. Various parties, both inside and outside the formal meeting, registered their view that a narrow economic focus was inadequate for the construction of a just international society; one needed to pay more attention to such things as democratic decision-making, labour rights, and ecological protection.

One would have thought that a half-century of experience with the World Bank would have been sufficient to show the pitfalls of pursuing human welfare on a narrowly economic basis, as if the World Bank could promote "development" and not be a social and political organization as well as an economic one. Just as the World Bank has had to create an environmental unit and move, however haltingly, towards consideration of broad standards of good governance,[5] so the WTO will have to broaden its focus and develop linkages with social, humanitarian, and human rights concerns. Humans are more than producers and consumers.

Economic, social, and political globalization cannot be considered in isolation from each other. As far as the UN era is concerned, first came military globalization through opposition to war, then social globalization through the establishment of global human rights and humanitarian standards, then growing awareness of ecological oneness; and now comes economic globalization. Our daily discourse has the historical process exactly backwards. Economics, at least in its contemporary form, is something of a recent characteristic to this trend. This is not to deny the importance of economic concerns, or that economic globalization may cause both positive and negative effects, such as the process of material and moral integration of persons and nations, at dizzying new speeds.

As should become clear in the following section, the question is not so much one of how international economics affect human rights, but of how global economic, security, and ecological concerns can be integrated with a central and fundamental concern with global human rights as a means to human dignity.

Key challenges in the short and middle term

Integration of human rights and economic concerns

It follows from the above that one of the major challenges to the United Nations in the new millennium is to better integrate human rights and economic concerns. This first major challenge manifests several dimensions. (The order in which the challenges are listed is neither entirely arbitrary nor exactly scientific.)

The international financial institutions (IFIs), above all the World Bank and the International Monetary Fund, need to be brought into the human rights movement. The World Bank is moving erratically but inexorably towards the use of "political conditionality" and broad standards of "good governance" in an effort to advance capitalistic development with a human face. Its self-critical comments about its performance in Indonesia, and its misguided efforts to turn a blind eye toward corruption and repression, are some of the latest confirmations of this trend. The same trend is evident in the Inter-American Development Bank. These and other IFIs need to follow the example of the European Development Bank and systematically integrate human rights considerations into their loan policies. The toughest nut to crack will be the IMF, which, much more than the World Bank, resists efforts to broaden its perspectives so as to include limited but explicit human rights concerns. (The IMF claims not to be a development agency in the first place, but rather a technical monetary agency.)

The alternative, to consider the IFIs as beyond the reach of human rights expectations, is to repeat the mistakes of the past. When the United Nations was trying to facilitate the consolidation of liberal democracy in El Salvador in the late 1980s and early 1990s, which required significant governmental spending for land reform and other measures to integrate the former rebel parties into mainstream Salvadoran society, the Bank and the Fund (together known fondly as "the Bunk") were pressing austerity measures on the government. This was detrimental to the main thrust of the human rights and security efforts undertaken by the rest of the international community.[6]

It is said that the Bank and the Fund have to be true to their original charters, which preclude consideration of political factors. But practice can lead to customary law that effectively amends treaties. Voting in various international organizations has been changed over time through practice. The Bank first argued against, but now accepts, an ecological dimension. Or, the Bank first said ecology was politics, and now the Bank says ecology is appropriately linked to sustainable economics. Likewise, the Bank is clearly, if inconsistently, instituting at least certain human rights considerations into its loan policies.

Given the importance of the resources at the disposal of the Bank and the Fund, they should not be allowed to subsidize gross violators of internationally recognized human rights. This the Bank recognized when it held up a loan to Croatia, after Zagreb refused to turn over certain indicted suspects to the International Criminal Tribunal for the former Yugoslavia. Similarly encouraging is the addition of the Bank to the UN Inter-Agency Standing Commission, headed by the UN Office for the Coordination of Humanitarian Assistance, designed to coordinate the UN humanitarian response on the ground in "man-made" (and natural) disasters. It has been recognized on all sides that the Bank needs to be a part of post-conflict, democratic development efforts in coordination with humanitarian and human rights agencies. Humanitarian relief should be, and increasingly is, linked to democratic development; hence the role of the Bank.

Transnational corporations (TNCs) also need to be brought into the human rights movement. As important as the Bank and the Fund are, not to mention regional development banks and bilateral official development assistance, transnational private investment dwarfs public development assistance by a factor of almost ten. In the legal systems of national liberal democracies, private corporations are not allowed to discriminate against persons or groups, or to otherwise violate human rights. It should also be the case in international society, similarly organized according to principles of liberalism.[7]

This matter is a legal thicket, primarily because public international law has traditionally regulated public, not private, authorities. Legal duties under the international law of human rights are borne primarily by states and intergovernmental organizations, not by private corporations. Legally speaking, matters may be changing through various court cases rather than through new treaty principles.

In the meantime, there is much that can be done. The United States government facilitated an agreement among private parties to deal with labour exploitation in the transnational, but mostly American-based, apparel industry. (Most of the most affluent TNCs are incorporated in only two states, the United States and Japan.) That is to say that the US government mediated an agreement between various apparel companies on the one hand and consumer groups on the other, designed to ameliorate abuse of workers rights around the globe. A principal feature of the agreement is inspection of production facilities and public reporting by a recognized, private, and independent human rights agency. Prominent companies, and even major American universities with lines of sports clothing, have signed on to the agreement. Likewise, the German government facilitated a private agreement to deal with child labour in the making of rugs in places like South Asia. The World Bank has a programme to pay families to keep children in school, and thus out of sweatshops and other processes employing child labour. Beyond the Bank, the United Nations can play similar intermediary roles.

There are many ways in which TNCs can be persuaded that a reputation for responsible business—for pursuit of profit with attention to relevant human rights standards—can be an asset in the eyes of the buying public. TNCs do not like to be faced with the prospect of consumer boycotts and other negative actions because of labour exploitation and other violations of human rights. It did not help the reputation of the Springfield Rifle Company to be convicted of illegally selling arms to South Africa under apartheid in violation of international and US law. And it would not help other weapons suppliers to be exposed for selling light arms, particularly in contemporary trouble spots of the world. The policies of not only the World Bank but also UNICEF and the ILO show that the United Nations can and should be involved in these efforts of monitoring, reporting, and mediating. Some TNCs have turned to UN agencies such as the UNDP for help in implementing socially beneficial projects in local communities where the TNCs do business. The notion of social responsibility, which includes attention to human rights, is not foreign to many businesses.

There needs to be an improved UN–TNC partnership for the advancement of certain human rights. Practice shows that international law is no barrier to many practical measures.

Socio-economic rights need to be given more serious attention. Socio-economic rights have always been the step-child or relatively ignored part of the International Bill of Rights. Civil and political rights have received the lion's share of attention—mostly because of the emphasis of Western states and Western-based private human rights organizations. But Mary Robinson, the second UN High Commissioner for Human Rights, is correct to try to make increased attention to socio-economic rights one of the hallmarks of her tenure, and of the UN's human rights work in the new millennium.

The point of human rights is to produce a life with human dignity and/or social justice, and it is perfectly clear that socio-economic subsistence rights are part of the very foundation of such a life.[8] If persons are unable to purchase adequate food, clothing, shelter, or health care through productive labour in private markets, the just society will put policies in place that assist in achieving those goods and services, at least on a temporary or exceptional basis. Socio-economic human rights standards seek to advance such developments. Persons want not only to have their civil and political rights respected, but also to have their social security protected.[9]

It cannot be persuasively argued that starvation or malnutrition, or lack of access to available medical science, is just a risk of life to be endured depending on race, nationality, or economic class, any more than lack of opportunity to vote or access to legal counsel can be considered just a risk of life to be endured. The society that allows mass starvation is just as complicit as the society that allows mass murder. The society that allows adequate health care or basic education to be based on ability to pay cannot be considered a just society supportive of human rights. Sins of omission are just as damaging as sins of commission. If I watch you die from starvation or inadequate medical care, while having the ability to help you, I am just as morally responsible for your death as I would be if I had actually killed you.[10]

It is perfectly reasonable to be concerned about cultures of dependency, in which individuals do not assert themselves because of the expectation that public authorities will provide for them. It is also reasonable to be concerned about the negative aspects of bureaucratic regulation and control. Nevertheless, some nations that take socio-economic rights relatively seriously, such as the Netherlands, have compiled a quite remarkable record concerning national economic growth, not to mention individual assertiveness and responsibility. There is obviously nothing inherent in the social democracies of Western Europe that prevents them from being among the most wealthy and stable countries of the world. One can strike a reasonable balance between individual freedom, economic prosperity, and socio-economic subsistence rights. It happens every day of the year in numerous countries.

At the risk of being politically incorrect, I would also argue that the poorer countries of the global south should tone down their expectations about financial support for socio-economic rights from the wealthy countries of the global north, at least until they get their own houses in order as regards this question. Far too many poorer countries (like Zimbabwe of late, unfortunately) spend far too much on dubious weapons acquisitions and military adventures and far too little on the socio-economic rights of their own citizens. Some of the countries in Africa being ravaged by the AIDS epidemic are the very same countries that are spending vast amounts of time, energy, and money in transnational armed conflicts that detract from both economic growth and adequate health care.

Based on changes in both the global north and global south, UN agencies like the World Health Organization, the World Food Program, and UNICEF should be given more support for their rights-based approach to socio-economic programming. The UN Human Rights Commission should be more balanced in its approach to supervising the International Bill of Rights, giving more attention to socio-economic rights.

The role of the United States

Given that the new millennium is characterized by a one-superpower world, one has to face the fact that a number of policy-makers in the United States believe either in absolute state sovereignty, unilateral foreign policy, or neo-isolationism. This situation mandates for the United Nations a difficult and no doubt long-term effort to make US foreign policy more cosmopolitan. Human rights issues are at the center of this tension between the United States and the United Nations.

As explained elsewhere, the American elite and general population consider themselves an exceptionally good people that stand, above all else, for personal freedom, with a mission to teach the rest of the world about the American way of life.[11] The US Constitution and its Bill of Rights symbolize this national self-image. Hence, moral lessons flow from the United States to others, not the other way around. The United States has great difficulty in accepting that international law and organization should take precedence over strictly American standards and procedures.

Thus, the United States refuses to accept that its adherence to the International Covenant on Civil and Political Rights should require any changes in US laws, or be the legal basis for any judicial action in US courts. It also refuses to ratify the International Covenant on Economic, Social, and Cultural Rights, or the Inter-American Convention on Human Rights. Likewise, the United States refuses to accept the projected International Criminal Court, given the possibility that it might assert jurisdiction over US personnel who may be linked to the subjects of genocide, war crimes, and crimes against humanity (and perhaps crimes against peace).

The United States will assert a broad competence for international law and organization when the United States is in the majority, or is part of dominant opinion, or possesses a veto, and thus is not likely to become a target of authoritative international action. Hence it was in favour of the creation of ad hoc criminal courts for the former Yugoslavia and also Rwanda, but not of the standing criminal court that might find itself with jurisdiction over US personnel.[12] From 1945 on, the United States has consistently rejected a supranational international law of human rights, whether regional or global, that would lead to supranational review of the US relevant record. This is in striking contrast to its democratic allies in Western Europe, all of which have accepted the supranational authority of the European Court of Human rights, and 15 of whom have accepted the supranational authority of the European Court of Justice, connected to the European Union, which can also make human rights judgments—as it did early in the year 2000, on the subject of gender equality in the German army.

When it comes to evaluation of the US record on human rights, dominant American opinion is supportive of an absolutist conception of state sovereignty for itself, however much it might be prepared to make significant in-roads on claims to sovereignty by others. This policy orientation is very much bound up in the American self-image or self-proclaimed identity. For a balanced, progressive, and cosmopolitan approach to international human rights, this American self-image and absolutist defence of self-sovereignty needs to be challenged. After all, its European allies in NATO are liberal democracies, but the European Court of Human Rights is hardly withering away because of a lack of cases involving these (and other) states. Indeed, exactly the reverse is happening, as the Court has had to revise its procedures to accommodate its heavy case-load. It is clear that American society could likewise profit from authoritative international review, regardless of the positive contributions to human rights made by US law and its court system.[13]

It also follows from the above that the United States should frequently be fond of unilateral rather than multilateral diplomacy. In fact, part of the US political spectrum is clinically paranoid about action through the United Nations, seeing in the United Nations—quite irrationally, given the US veto in the Security Council and their prominent position elsewhere—a threat to US security, freedoms, and independence. Simply put, there is a bias against the United Nations in a number of policy-making circles in Washington.

All states reserve the right to take unilateral action in matters of the highest importance, a view reflected in Article 51 of the Charter and the recognition of an inherent and unilateral right of action for self-defence. Moreover, it can be fairly stated that the United States prefers to act with the approval of the UN Security Council or other source of collective approval and cooperation, as demonstrated by its search for multilateral and indeed UN approval for its policies in the Persian Gulf in 1990–91, Bosnia 1992–95, Haiti 1994, Somalia 1992, and so on. Still further, some of its actions outside the UN Security Council, such as in Kosovo and Serbia in 1999, can be reasonably defended, even if reasonable people still disagree on the wisdom of that course of action. In any event, US action in Kosovo and Serbia in 1999 remained multilateral in the context of NATO.[14]

Still, the United States, as the most powerful state in world affairs in the 1990s, has consistently opposed strengthening the United Nations' capacity for decisive multilateral action. This is not just a question of international peace and security, but also of the capacity for humanitarian intervention and direct international enforcement of human rights. Washington has opposed a standing rapid reaction military force under the control of either the Secretary-General or Security Council. It has opposed any drastic upgrading of the United Nations' independent capacity for intelligence-gathering and analysis. And it has opposed any creation of UN coercive power apart from US control or veto in other ways. Worse still, the United States even blocked UN deployment of multilateral forces in the Great Lakes region of Africa in the mid-1990s when other states were prepared to play the role on the ground that the United States would not. The unfortunate truth is that, after ten years of a one-superpower world, we still find the United Nations woefully weak in a reliable capacity to really enforce human rights protection. The main reason for this lies in US fears about truly effective multilateral action on the part of the United Nations. The United States does not want to see the rise of any countervailing power. President Clinton was disingenuous in going to the United Nations and saying that the organization should do more to stop genocides, because the United States had made it impossible for the United Nations to act in places like Rwanda and the Democratic Republic of the Congo.

United States assertions of a right to reduce its legally obligatory payments to the United Nations, regardless of what the UN Charter or General Assembly might say, is indicative of a dangerous and irresponsible unilateralism in US policy-making, not made any more palatable by its origins in the lunatic fringe of congressional Republicans rather than in the White House or State Department. The much-praised agreement between the executive and legislative branches that allowed the release of US funds to the United Nations in late 1999 contained numerous diktats in which Washington unilaterally imposed conditions on the United Nations, in clear violation of Charter provisions. Also indicative of a continuing strong strain of unilateralism is the widespread view in Washington that US military personnel should not serve under UN command. Such service is normal for all others but not for the United States. When the totally independent US command in Somalia took decisions leading to a debacle in central Mogadishu in October 1993, the highest levels of the US government tried to shift the blame to UN officials.

The US penchant for periodic unilateralism and bias against the United Nations remains a problem for global human rights protection, as it does for other dimensions of UN activity.

Much has been written about isolationism in American diplomatic history, and there has been considerable talk about neo-isolationism in contemporary American society. The situation is complex. Presidential candidates in both major parties are clearly internationalists of either liberal or conservative persuasion, or more likely some mixture of the two. And most of the public is clearly not supportive of more radical forms of isolationism such as withdrawal from the United Nations or the construction of a "fortress America" built on the blatant nativism and protectionism, as recommended by marginal public figures like Patrick Buchanan.

But American society is clearly not in active messianic mode, as it was in the 1898 Spanish–American War, forced on a reluctant Spain so that the United States could "liberate," at least eventually, the Philippines and Cuba, and incidentally acquire some dependencies in the process. Where attention to human rights abroad entails considerable cost, especially in terms of military action resulting in the loss of American lives, American society is ultra-cautious. United States interventions in Lebanon under Reagan and in Somalia under Clinton, and congressional wariness about interventions in Haiti and Bosnia under Clinton, all suggest definite reservations about loss of American lives in pursuit of objectives other than traditional conceptions of US vital national interests. This is not altogether a bad thing. Prudence in expending human lives is normally a virtue. Moreover, some evidence suggests that the American public was prepared to pay a relatively high cost to expel Iraqi forces from Kuwait in 1991, and might, given effective presidential leadership, have supported the dispatch of US ground troops to fight in Kosovo in the spring of 1999.

The fundamental point is that American society is, most of the time, disengaged from the daily management of international affairs. Thus, if Washington policy-makers try to run foreign policy on the cheap, and slash most forms of spending for foreign affairs (the military budget excepted), the American public will defer.[15] The United States remains a large, powerful, self-centred nation. In the 1990s it replaced an internationally orientated president with one whose interest in international affairs was sporadic at best, until the waning days of his administration and his belated concern about his place in world history. American society also coughed up a Republican-controlled Congress whose leadership sometimes boasted of not owning passports and not seeing the merits of international travel. Of course, this was the same polity that fashioned NAFTA, joined the WTO, and agreed to expand NATO membership. The issue was not one of simple isolationism but of the persistent and responsible management of international affairs—because those affairs were not just international but transnational or intermestic, impinging deeply on supposedly local concerns. That everyone's backyard had been increasingly internationalized was more obvious in the smaller and weaker countries of the world than in the United States.

The leadership of the United Nations, made up of both the international Secretariat and key Member States, needed to face the challenge of dealing with a single superpower that was still parochial in many ways. The United States frequently defended its turf with claims to absolute sovereignty, was periodically suspicious of the compromises entailed in true multilateral diplomacy, and as a society was detached from daily aspects of international relations. United States foreign policy was sometimes deeply problematic for the United Nations, and the organization would require diplomatic skill and patience in trying to moderate some of these policies over time. United Nations human rights programmes were negatively affected by these US characteristics, as were other parts of the organization.

The role of the UN Security Council

The UN Security Council (UNSC), having been creative in expanding the concept of international peace and security so as to compensate for the absence of an accepted doctrine of humanitarian intervention to protect human rights in places like Bosnia, Somalia, and Haiti, should take care that a blizzard of paper solutions in New York does not exceed the realistic capacity to protect *sur place*. Given that the United States and certain other states on the Council are reluctant to incur costs for the rights of others, care must be taken that the Council adopt appropriate policies when faced with egregious violations of human rights. Unfortunately, the Council seems to be making the same mistakes again, in places like Sierra Leone, in 2000.

Starting with the subject of Iraqi Kurds in the spring of 1991, and building on the complex cases of Rhodesia in the 1960s and South Africa in the 1970s, the UNSC began to invoke Chapter VII of the Charter to deal with matters that were traditionally considered to be internal or domestic by focusing on the international repercussions of repression and malfeasance, essentially inside states. This same logic was applied to Haiti and Somalia. Areas of the former Yugoslavia presented more complex issues. Whatever the judgments about the nature of conflicts in the former Yugoslavia, the UNSC progressively adopted many legally binding decisions, many of them pertaining to the human rights of persons caught up in some type of armed conflict, disorder, or "complex emergency," in the 1990s.

At times, the members of the UNSC refused to authorize the amount of force recommended by the Secretary-General as needed for the attainment of objectives. At other times the Council authorized objectives, such as the creation of safe havens for non-combatants, without adequate provision for their defence. At other times, UN field commanders, special representatives, or even the Secretary-General himself refused to authorize the use of force even though such authorization was available in principle. The result, as sometimes admitted by UN reports themselves *ex post facto*, was a discrediting of the United Nations when attempting to protect human rights, not to mention a failure to protect the rights, including the right to life, of persons in the affected areas.[16]

The UNSC seemed to believe that tough talk in New York would intimidate some quite ruthless political and military leaders in places like Serbia, the Serb Republic in Bosnia, Somalia, and elsewhere. As might have been expected, these warriors without honour[17] continued their systematic murder, rape, torture, and lesser abuses, mostly of civilians. The United Nations never realized at the time the extent of evil on the other side, and thus never chose the appropriately robust actions to counteract it. Journalistic usage notwithstanding, peace-keeping is not enforcement or direct protection. One cannot keep a peace which reflects human rights when peace has not yet been made, and when the parties involved carry out mayhem without respect for the most elementary standards of human decency.

This record mandates caution in the future regarding UNSC recourse to the language of Chapter VII, and subsequent language in demanding some important change in the behaviour of fighting parties. The unfortunate reality is that if the UNSC really believes that physical coercion, or at least the credible threat of coercion, might be necessary to stop violations of human rights, it is going to have to contract out this task to states that are willing and able, but with proper supervision from some UN unit—whether it be the Council, a subcommittee of the Council, or an office in the Secretariat. Paper threats will not suffice. The United Nations is still not prepared for genuinely supranational enforcement action. Once again, this is as much a human rights and humanitarian issue as a security issue.

Merging human rights, humanitarian, and refugee affairs

The United Nations needs to consider effectively merging human rights, humanitarian action, and refugee affairs into one meta-regime, as far as action on the ground is concerned. Existing legal and diplomatic "boxes" for categorizing events and victims do not work very well, although they could be resurrected in the event of criminal judicial proceedings.

Given the decentralized way in which decisions are normally reached concerning what is "peace" or "war," and what is "international" or "internal" armed conflict, it has been clear for some time that it is only with great difficulty that the international community can reach a consensus as to the legal status of a particular situation involving serious conflict or unrest. That being so, it is frequently not clear whether some part of international humanitarian law applies, or whether the international law of human rights in peacetime should be legally controlling.

Likewise, it is clear that many persons can find themselves in dire straits and without the benefit of a normal relationship with the government of the state in which they normally reside, without meeting the legal qualifications of a conventional refugee. One might be an internally displaced person, a returnee, or a person fleeing war or instability. One might not therefore be a person with a well-founded fear of individual and provable persecution but may have crossed an international border because of not being able to rely on a "normal" relationship with one's government.

In the scrum of international relations, various actors try to protect and assist persons who find themselves in dire straits, because of "man-made" events, without much attention to legal categories about situations and victims. The UNHCR or UNICEF may become the lead UN agency for provision of relief to needy civilians on the ground, without paying much attention to the matter of who is technically a refugee and who is not, or whether relief goes to civilians other than needy mothers and young children. The International Committee of the Red Cross, which is not a UN or public agency, may share roles with UN actors without paying much attention as to whether one is dealing with national unrest, an internal armed conflict of a Protocol II type or a Common Article 3 type, a traditional international war situation or a Protocol I situation, or a so-called complex emergency.[18] Thus, these and other agencies dealing with international humanitarian protection and relief—the protection of certain human rights in armed conflict and human displacement—have drawn up codes of conduct that transcend legal arguments about situations and victims. They are working on quantifying what is required to meet international standards for adequate relief across various situations, including natural disasters.

This trend should be encouraged through the facilitation of the UN Office for the Coordination of Humanitarian Affairs (OCHA). It might not be totally naive to think that OCHA, under capable leadership, might eventually assume the relief functions now spread across the UNHCR, UNICEF, and the WFP, leaving those agencies free to work in the area of diplomatic-legal protection for various types of displaced persons, needy mothers, and children. The Red Cross agencies could continue as independent partners in relief, with the ICRC having specialized roles concerning prisoners of war and so on. The great alphabet soup of NGOs would also continue as vital partners of UN humanitarian schemes.

It does not matter much whether the revised UN scheme is called the "human dignity regime" or something else. The central point would still be to enhance the protection of and assistance to persons who are in need because of political events. This would be done through improved coordination and a clear sharing of tasks, on the basis of agreed-upon standards. An essential part of the change would be a careful study of the comparative advantage that each major relief agency brings to the table. There would need to be a careful consideration of improved funding; these activities should not be run on unpredictable shoestring budgets. In the event of criminal justice proceedings at either the international or national level, suspects could still be prosecuted under international humanitarian law or the international law for human rights in peacetime, according to the precedents of various tribunals. Existing treaties would not have to be revised or erased, and nothing would be lost from the criminal justice tradition that has already emerged. But, currently, there is a disconnection between all of the legal categories devised for situations and victims of political unrest and human displacement, and the reality of international protection and assistance efforts *sur place*. That disconnection needs to be remedied.

The fate of civilians in armed conflict

One of the great problems in the new millennium is the fate of civilians in armed conflict and related or similar situations. It is not easy for the United Nations to take long-term action to improve their situation, because basic standards are set in treaties of international humanitarian law negotiated outside the United Nations; the ICRC, a private agency whose governance body is made up only of Swiss citizens, has played an important role in the development and supervision of this law since the middle of the nineteenth century.

The United Nations, perhaps through the Secretary-General, the General Assembly, or the Human Rights Commission, could at least call on states to file reports with the Swiss government, the depository of international/humanitarian law, or the ICRC, or the Red Cross and Red Crescent Conference, concerning the teaching of humanitarian law to their military personnel. As weak as reporting requirements are under the international law of human rights in peace, at least they exist and require some national agency to compile the material and send it to the United Nations. There is no such reporting requirement under the Geneva Conventions and Protocols. There should be. Until that defect is remedied, the United Nations could encourage the practice of voluntary reporting. That would at least allow some states to see what others are doing, while putting subtle pressure on states to take the existing standards on protecting and assisting civilians seriously. The Red Cross and Red Crescent Conference, which meets, in principle, every four years, collects some information on this subject, but the process generates little pressure on states to take the dissemination of international humanitarian law seriously.

Similarly, the United Nations should call on states to discuss the funding of activities that take place under the 1949 Geneva Conventions and 1977 Protocols. Currently, states are able to profess their commitment to the humanitarian standards found within one or more of these instruments, but pay not one centime for the protection and assistance activities that transpire. The same situation exists, for the most part, regarding forced displacement, since the UNHCR operates mostly on voluntary contributions from states. States should be asked to place their money where their diplomatic mouth is. If they get the public relations benefit that comes from accepting the law, they should make a payment for its application, perhaps according to an equitable formula. The meagre funding of humanitarian activities (and also human rights activities) should be remedied. Funding patterns for the regular UN budget indicate that human rights and humanitarian affairs are still considered by states to be marginal rather than central activities of the United Nations. The organization can at least encourage a dialogue on this subject, while continuing with its new coordinated appeals by OCHA for voluntary contributions to UN relief actions.

Criminal actions against human rights violators

The United Nations, having stumbled into the creation of ad hoc criminal courts as a short-term public relations manoeuvre, and then having pushed for the creation of a standing International Criminal Court, has no option now but to see the latter matter through to a successful conclusion; but the organization should beware of judicial romanticism and of falling into the trap of expecting courts to be more effective and have greater impact than the facts warrant.

The UNSC, not wanting to authorize decisive intervention into the Bosnian affair in 1993 because of anticipated costs, fell back to the creation of an ad hoc criminal court in order to give the impression that it was doing something about atrocities. Having done so once, the Council did so again about a year later, for essentially the same reasons, in Rwanda. From this ignominious beginning evolved a widespread push for criminal justice and an end to impunity for egregious violations of human rights and humanitarian law. In 1998, a diplomatic conference overwhelmingly approved a statute for a new International Criminal Court, to be loosely associated with the United Nations.

The fact that only a handful of states had ratified the ICC statute by early 2000 indicates a need for careful review of the Rome diplomatic conference. Broad evidence strongly suggests that there is no single, preferred, best approach to responding to past gross violations of human rights and humanitarian law.[19] South Africa and El Salvador, among others, have moved toward an end to bloodshed and the stabilization of liberal democracy by avoiding criminal prosecution which focuses on the past, in favour of qualified amnesty and national reconciliation that looks toward the future. Other parties had tried a variety of measures, including doing nothing, holding national trials, supporting national or international truth commissions, barring violators from public office, and so on.

In some situations there is a clear conflict between peace and justice, between making political compromises to end violence and trying to punish gross violators. The new ICC was created on the basis of complementarity, which means that the Court—once the necessary ratifications have been obtained—will become active only if the relevant national authority fails to carry out a proper investigation and, if warranted, prosecute. Various safeguards are built into the statute to restrain the independent prosecutor from bringing specious charges against a state. Still, the prosecutor, and the special panel of judges to whom the prosecutor must report, will be faced with the exercise of an essentially political judgment in some situations. Would a future prosecutor and judicial panel seek to overturn national decisions in favour of amnesty, national reconciliation, and/or a truth commission, in lieu of criminal justice? Would a future prosecutor second-guess a future Nelson Mandela on the wisdom of avoiding criminal justice relating to past political struggle?

Moreover, in future situations similar to that of the Great Lakes region of Africa in the 1990s, it should be clear that regional hostility in these instances is so great that a few court cases, whether national or international, are not going to stem the tide of calculated brutality. The extent of hatred in these situations is beyond judicial resolution.

Nevertheless, having come this far towards international criminal justice, the United Nations should urge that the two ad hoc courts be melded into the new ICC, and that all states sign and ratify the statute. Existing international courts have certainly made some specific contributions to enhanced protection of human rights and humanitarian standards. The new Court should be given a chance to prove its worth, including proving that it knows when to defer to national decisions that bypass punishment for the sake of a relatively just if imperfect peace. Most liberal democratic states support the new Court, including Canada, Italy, Britain, and France. These are states that have practical experience in putting their soldiers in harm's way in complicated foreign situations. Therefore, United States opposition to the Court should be seen for what it is—an exercise in romantic nationalism that bears little relation to the adequate safeguards against abuse built into the statute.

Changing attitudes in the long term

Finally, in this brief list of major challenges in the short and medium term, the United Nations should recognize that, for many human rights and humanitarian problems, there is no substitute for patient diplomacy, diplomacy that educates across generations,[20] over the long haul. There is plenty of evidence to suggest that progressive ideas do make a difference over time.[21] In the past we have seen the end of foot binding, colonialism, slavery (mostly), European Stalinism, South African apartheid, and so on. In recent years we have seen greatly increased attention to women's rights, the rights of the child, racial discrimination, liberal democracy, and so forth.

In a final analysis, the United Nations, being an intergovernmental organization, can only do what its members, especially the most powerful members, allow to be done. Thus, there is no avoiding the need to educate states about the desirability of increased protection of human rights and humanitarian standards.

Whatever the politics of the moment allow by way of immediate protective action, whether by humanitarian intervention or creation of criminal courts, for example, there will always be a need for conferences on racism and xenophobia, on women's equality, on freedom for sexual preference among consenting adults, and on any number of other human rights subjects that generate controversy in various parts of the world.

Conclusion

Despite its weaknesses, the UN system will remain heavily engaged in human rights developments in the coming years. This is not just because of the current Secretary-General's obvious interest in the subject, or the fact that he is now supplemented by a highly committed UN High Commissioner for Human Rights.[22] The United Nations has universal membership, established human rights commissions and agencies, specialized bodies with considerable experience, and, quite frequently, a good reputation for serious work. Moreover, human rights is now increasingly accepted as a legitimate and regular part of international relations. There are now more liberal democracies in the world, and states aspiring to be liberal democracies, than at any other time in world history. All of this bodes well for the United Nations and human rights.

It is true that some regional arrangements, mostly in Europe, provide more reliable international protection of civil and political rights than does the United Nations. It is true that some human rights NGOs have more dynamic reputations than some UN agencies. It is true that state foreign policies can sometimes give UN human rights proceedings the unmistakable odour of national ideology or self-interest. Some of these weaknesses and distortions can be at least somewhat counterbalanced by giving fuller UN participation to human rights NGOs, creating a forum where business responsibility can be discussed and advanced, interjecting human rights more deeply into the relatively new Council on Sustainable

Development, endorsing the new International Criminal Court, and improving coordination among human rights and humanitarian actors, so as to maximize impact.[23]

We will never run out of human rights issues and problems. And, while we cannot be asked to predict the unpredictable, it is clear that the future will bring increasingly complex problems of individual privacy (the internet, for example) and biomedical-science (such as cloning). It is likely that these developments will necessitate still more global human rights standards. Yet an increase in standards without a corresponding increase in effective implementation measures leaves the glass less than half-full.

On the basis of progress made during the past fifty years, it does seem that global human rights issues hold out the promise of proving "as important as the great revolutions of the preceding centuries," despite the persistent problems and perplexities involved.[24] The United Nations is likely to continue to be at the centre of all this, as it has been since 1945.

Notes

1. Michael Ignatieff, *The Warrior's Honor: Ethnic War and the Modern Conscience* (New York: Metropolitan, 1997).
2. From the vast literature on the subject, see Jack Donnelly, *Universal Human Rights in Theory and Practice* (Ithaca: Cornell University Press, 1989); and David P. Forsythe, "The United Nations and human rights at 50," *Global Governance* 1/3 (1995): 297–318.
3. Jan Herman Burgers traces the evolution of the human rights discourse in international relations in "The road to San Francisco: The revival of the human rights idea in the twentieth century," *Human Rights Quarterly* 14/4 (1992): 447–77. He shows that the international moralism from the middle of the nineteenth century on did not translate into international human rights claims until 1945. It has often been noted that the world was relatively connected, economically speaking, before the First World War, and that the world did not regain that same degree of economic connectedness until recently. The earlier phase of economic connectedness was not accompanied by an increase in references to international human rights.
4. See David P. Forsythe, *Human Rights in International Relations* (Cambridge: Cambridge University Press, 2000). It is important to recall that human rights language was written into drafts of the UN Charter long before the Nazi death camps were liberated and publicized in the spring of 1945.
5. David Gillies, "Human rights, governance, and democracy: The World Bank's problem frontiers," *Netherlands Quarterly of Human Rights* 1/1 (1993): 3–24; David P. Forsythe, "The United Nations, human rights, and development," *Human Rights Quarterly* 19/2 (1997); 334–49.
6. See David P. Forsythe, "The United Nations, democracy, and the Americas," in Tom J. Farer (ed.), *Beyond Sovereignty: Collectively Defending Democracy in the Americas* (Baltimore: Johns Hopkins University Press, 1996): 107–31.
7. See Forsythe, *Human Rights in International Relations* (see note 4, above): chapter 8.

8. The best theoretical argument along these lines is to be found in Henry Shue, *Basic Rights: Subsistence, Affluence, and US Foreign Policy,* 2nd ed. (Princeton: Princeton University Press, 1996).
9. Francis Fukuyama, in his influential book, *The End of History and the Last Man* (New York: Free Press, 1992), does not give sufficient attention to this point when arguing that the liberal argument in favour of civil and political rights is the ultimate argument for justifying the exercise of political power.
10. See Peter Siner, *Practical Ethics* (Cambridge: Cambridge University Press, 1993).
11. For a classic but more positive slant on American ideology, see Samuel P. Huntington, "American ideals versus American institutions," *Political Science Quarterly* 97/1 (1982). For a highly negative view of American ideology, see Michael Hunt, *Ideology and US Foreign Policy* (New Haven: Yale University Press, 1987). See also David P. Forsythe, *American Exceptionalism and Global Human Rights,* Distinguished Lecture Series (Lincoln: University of Nebraska, 1998).
12. Ironically, when the United States took military action in 1999 in the former Yugoslavia, it placed itself under the jurisdiction of the International Criminal Tribunal for the former Yugoslavia, whose staff made a study of possible US and NATO war crimes. However, the Chief Prosecutor of the ICTFY, however, a Swiss national, tried to distance herself from that study.
13. See Forsythe, *Human Rights in International Relations* (see note 4, above): chapters 5 and 6. See also David P. Forsythe (ed.), *Human Rights and Comparative Foreign Policy* (Tokyo: United Nations University Press, 2000). What is needed is more meetings like the one that occurred in the Security Council in early 2000, in which Jesse Helms articulated his view of US legal supremacy, which was then challenged by certain other members of the Council.
14. The Secretary-General was right that US and NATO action in modern Yugoslavia in 1999 undermined the authority of the Security Council. The United States was faced with a difficult choice. If it took the Kosovo question to the Council and met a Russian and/or Chinese veto, it would have been less able to take action to stop Serbian persecution of Albanian Kosovars. This would have made its foreign policy a prisoner of Russian and Chinese views, something that would not go down well in American domestic politics. Its decision to engage in de facto humanitarian intervention via NATO picked up support from parts of the United Nations; for example, through comments by Mrs Sadako Ogata, head of the UNHCR. See further the postscript in Forsythe (ed.), *Human Rights and Comparative Foreign Policy* (see note 13, above).
15. For a brief review of the decline in US spending for foreign affairs, see Joshua Muravchik, "Affording foreign policy," *Foreign Affairs* 75/2 (1996): 8–13. See also Edward Luttwak, "Where are the great powers?" *Foreign Affairs* 73/4 (1994), 23–29.
16. UN reports about its roles at Srebrenica and in Rwanda were available from the UN homepage on the internet.
17. The phrase is Ignatieff's, (see note 1, above).
18. I am making reference here to types of armed conflict as foreseen in contemporary international humanitarian law, based on the 1949 Geneva Conventions and Additional Protocols I and II of 1977.
19. Martha Minow, *Between Vengeance and Forgiveness: Facing History after Genocide and Mass Violence* (Boston: Beacon Press, 1998).
20. For an analysis of traditional UN human rights diplomacy as, essentially, exercises in political education over time, see David P. Forsythe, "The United Nations and human rights 1945–1985," *Political Science Quarterly* 100/3 (1989), 249–269.
21. In general see Paul Gordon Lauren, *The Evolution of Universal Human Rights: Visions Seen* (Philadelphia: University of Pennsylvania Press, 1998).

22. See Andrew Clapham, "Mainstreaming human rights at the United Nations," in *Collected Courses of the Academy of European Law*, vol. VII, book 2 (The Hague: Kluwer, 1999): 159–234. A revised version, taking into account developments during the tenure of the second High Commissioner, is forthcoming.
23. See Chadwick F. Alger (ed.), *The Future of the United Nations System: Potential for the Twenty-first Century* (Tokyo: United Nations University Press, 1998), especially chapters 6, 8, and 9.
24. Editorial, *International Herald Tribune*, 9 December 1999, p. 8.

13

Gender and international society: Law and policy

Christine Chinkin

Major trends and policy implications

In many ways the twentieth century was the century of women. Through legal reform at the national level, the century witnessed the growing inclusion of women within public life exemplified by the development of universal suffrage in most states.[1] In many states, other examples of the enhanced legal status of women included changes to property and inheritance laws and reformed family and labour laws. At the international level, three broad trends relevant to the theme of governance can be identified. The first was the formal articulation of the norm of non-discrimination on the grounds of gender, which was included among the purposes of the United Nations Charter[2] and in the International Bill of Rights.[3] Commitment to the advancement of women was backed institutionally by the creation, in 1946, of the Commission on the Status of Women within the United Nations, and was furthered by the adoption by the General Assembly of the Convention on the Elimination of All Forms of Discrimination against Women (CEDAW, or the Women's Convention) in 1979.[4] The Convention contains the fullest catalogue of equality rights for women ever to be agreed upon by states, and, as of March 2000, has 165 states parties. Articles 7 and 8 of the Women's Convention emphasize the location of women within the public sphere. Article 7 considers the position of women in national public life. States commit themselves to undertaking appropriate measures to eliminate discrimination against women in the political and public life of the country, particularly with respect to the right to vote, to participate in policy-making, to hold public office, and to participate in non-governmental organizations.[5] Article 8 looks to the position of women in the international arena; states undertake to ensure women the opportunity to represent their governments at the international level and to participate in the work of international organizations.[6]

The second trend was the inclusion of women within the discourse, and to some extent the practice, of development.[7] The third trend came to the forefront at the end of the century with the shift from perceiving women's economic and social disempowerment as an issue for development policy to the affirmation of women's legal entitlements through the recognition of women's rights as human rights. This assertion was historically made at the World Conference on Human Rights in Vienna in 1993[8] and was reiterated in the Beijing Platform for Action agreed upon at the Fourth World Conference on Women in 1995.[9]

The concept of women's rights as human rights has become a significant issue in international human rights law at the beginning of the twenty-first century. It is based upon an understanding of equality that goes beyond *de jure* equality, as prescribed by the norm of non-discrimination, to ensure that, throughout their lives, women receive the same choices, respect, and integrity, and the same understanding of human dignity, as are accorded to men. A good definition is the following:

Gender equality means an equal visibility, empowerment, and participation of both sexes in all spheres of public and private life. Gender equality is the opposite of gender inequality, not of gender difference, and aims to promote the full participation of women and men in society.[10]

Gender equality thus encompasses women's empowerment through participation in *all* spheres of life. It also involves accountability for the violation of women's human rights, and state and individual responsibility for gender-specific violations of human rights law such as violence against women, whether committed by state or non-state actors and whether committed in armed conflict or non-conflict situations. It seeks to ensure the full legal and civic status of women across the spectrum of public and private activity in matters such as ownership of property, access to credit, freedom of movement, rights before, during, and after marriage, and equal pay for equal work. The assertion of women's rights as human rights moves matters of concern to women away from the discourse of "needs" to that of entitlement, as humans, to the full panoply of human rights.[11]

At all stages, these developments have been engineered through the instrumentality of women themselves.[12] Since before the twentieth century, women have organized nationally and internationally for their own advancement and autonomy (as well as being significant players in other social movements such as those against slavery and for peace).[13] Women have made effective use of methods such as networking, campaigning, and alliance-building to bring their concerns to governments and intergovernmental organizations, often in the face of strong resistance.

However, a description of these positive trends is misleading without full recognition of the reality that the twentieth century has also seen a continuation of the subordination and domination of women, and, in many instances, denial of their humanity. The international legal and policy framework has been developed in ways which are positive for the advancement of women, but abuses of women continue worldwide. These include the legal, political, social, and economic subordination of women, often under domestic laws; the widespread commission of violence against women by state and non-state actors; the insistence that traditional and religious practices and laws that are harmful to women should prevail over guarantees of women's human rights; and the increase in the phenomenon of the feminization of poverty.[14]

Women also remain largely excluded from political life and national and international decision-making and policy-making.[15] Universal adult suffrage has not yet been achieved.[16] The much-heralded wave of democratization[17] has not been accompanied by gendered democratization. Indeed, one of the consequences of the political and economic restructuring in Eastern Europe has been a marked decrease in the number of women in national legislatures.[18] It appears that, as legislatures gain increased importance and reflect more accurately the distribution of power and wealth within a community, the number of women within them decreases. The Committee on the Elimination of Discrimination against women has commented:

In all nations, the most significant factors inhibiting women's ability to participate in public life have been the cultural framework of values and religious beliefs, the lack of services, and men's failure to share the tasks associated with the organization of the household and with the care and raising of children. In all nations, cultural traditions and religious beliefs have played a part in confining women to the private spheres of activity and excluding them from active participation in public life.[19]

Where women are included within international and national legislative and administrative institutions, they have typically been confined to bodies concerned with "women's issues" such as health, education, and welfare, rather than in those dealing with "hard" issues such as the economy and security.[20] There is considerable debate about whether women have different priorities or make decisions differently from men, and whether predominantly male representatives effectively take issues that are of concern to women into account.[21] Whatever the conclusion on these matters, under-representation of half the world's population is incompatible with good governance. The silencing of women's voices and the invisibility of women's contributions and experiences militate against transparency and comprehensive decision-making. Indeed, "the concept of democracy will have real and dynamic meaning and lasting effect only when political decision-making is shared by women and men and takes equal account of the interests of both."[22]

The impact of globalization

Globalization has impacted upon gender relations in complex and contradictory ways. The centralization of power within the sovereign state that has been fragmented by globalization was not predicated upon, nor necessarily supportive of, equality between women and men. The power structures of the nation state have been organized around patriarchal assumptions that have granted to men monopoly over power, authority, and wealth. A number of structures have been erected to achieve this imbalance that have disguised its inequity by making it appear to be natural and universal; for example, constructions of citizenship that concentrated upon civic duty (for example, payment of taxes, military service, public office) from which women were excluded through the public/private dichotomy and the subordination of women within the family.[23] At the same time, the role of men in the public sphere has been supported by divisions between productive and unproductive (or reproductive) work, presenting women's work as lacking in any economic value.[24] Emphasis upon the normative impact of the public/private divide has been legitimately criticized for universalizing a Western model of social ordering.[25] While the fluidity of any demarcation between public and private spheres should be acknowledged, the undervaluing of women's contributions and the primary responsibilities of women within the family have impeded their advancement across many, if not all, societies. The opening up of new spaces by the apparent weakening of the nation state creates the possibility of undermining the traditional gender hierarchies and devising new bases for gender relations.

On the other hand, the reality that the state is no longer the sole institution that can define identity has denied women the space to assert their own claims to gendered self-determination. Power has become fragmented through the emergence of internal/external groups (sub-state national groups/supra-state religious bodies) who demand loyalties from their members and present their claims internationally through their collectivities, often to the detriment of individuals, most notably women. In many instances the position and role of women within the group is itself a defining feature of the collectivity. This is especially true of those who define themselves through religious or cultural norms. It must be remembered that the state has been the locus of the protection (as well as the denial) of human rights, and its inability to defend human rights in the face of particularized claims has worked against the empowerment of women. Furthermore, the outbreaks of armed conflict arising from ethnic tensions and nationalist claims have been accompanied by widespread and extreme forms of gendered violence, including genocide,[26] where women have been targeted and subject to forms of abuse as a way of undermining the cohesion and strength of the collectivity.

Another aspect is the dispersal of power through what have been identified as the non-democratic forces of "globalization from above"—corporate enterprises, markets, and movements of capital.[27] These have weakened the effective decision-making and policy-making powers of the state, notably in economic and labour policies. Governments are unwilling to assert the rights of their workers in cases where to do so would discourage investment. Consequences such as social exclusion, unemployment or low-paid employment, and weakening of trade union organizations have had gendered dimensions. "Economic systems which value profits often do so at the expense of female labour." Women are seen, and hence favoured, as a passive, compliant, temporary workforce that will accept low wages without demanding human and labor rights. The traditional gendered division of labour (the location of women in employment to which they are regarded as inherently suited; for example, the caring profession or textiles industry) has been furthered through the addition of new locations and forms of work (such as service industry, tourism, work in free trade and export process zones). What remains constant is the low economic value accorded to work performed primarily by women—often migrants—in circumstances where exploitation, often poor and unsafe working conditions, and total lack of job security are common. Human rights violations can be a part of this scene; directly, through prohibitions on labour organizations, and indirectly, through further abuses that have occurred where women have claimed the right to organize or to be free from sexual harassment.

The impact of economic reconstruction—through structural adjustment programmes—upon human rights has attracted the attention of the United Nations human rights bodies.[29] This too has a gendered impact and has contributed to the feminization of poverty.

Globalization may have dire consequences for human rights generally and women's human rights particularly, in terms of eroding civil, political, economic, social, and cultural rights in the name of development and macro-level economic restructuring and stability. In the countries of the south, structural adjustment programmes have led to increased impoverishment, particularly amongst women, displacement, and internal strife resulting from the political instabilities caused by devaluing national currencies, increasing debt and dependence on foreign direct investment.[30]

"Astonishingly large numbers" of women are migrating across international borders to engage in unregulated and poorly paid employment, including domestic work.[31] Migrant workers in positions of powerlessness and dependency are exposed to acute risks of physical or psychological violence and often to theft of their economic gains. Impoverished women are also especially vulnerable to being tricked or coerced into being trafficked, to sexual violence and exploitation. The Special Rapporteur on violence against women has noted the increase in the number of trafficked women as a result of the economic crisis in East Asia, and the linkages between economic transition in East Europe and the increase in trafficking and forced prostitution of women.[32] This has been exacerbated by a number of trends. Social exclusion, loss of previously accepted benefits (for example, affordable childcare and maternity leave) and personal insecurity aggravated by dislocation and unemployment—coupled with the greater mobility of persons that has been facilitated by increased ease of communications and the opening of certain borders—have all contributed to this increase. Economic liberalization has encouraged organized transnational crime in sex and pornography—in persons and goods. Free-market imperatives have inhibited restrictions on the sale of pornography and erotica, thus reinforcing and working alongside the trade in persons.

One of the most insidious recent international developments has been the creation of a perception of the market, and free movement of capital, as being natural and inevitable, making any challenge to this basic assumption difficult. At the Beijing conference on women there was no alternative voice offered in opposition to the benefits of market policies; the goal was to ensure women's participation in, and access to, the dominant structures of the market, not to question the underlying assumptions of these structures or consider alternative models.[33] Another adverse consequence is that the market has "distorted" priorities, placing an emphasis on the pursuit of global profits rather than gender equality or human rights.

However, despite the enormous potential for abuse, it is an oversimplification to assume that the consequences of globalization have been exclusively detrimental to women, or that they have been the same in all locations. There have also been benefits. For example, global pursuit of profit has enhanced paid employment opportunities for women where previously they had not existed. While these may be exploitative, they have nevertheless facilitated a new degree of economic independence for many women and lessened their subordination within the family; for example, by freeing them from early marriage or pregnancy. This in turn provides the necessary public space for women to assert their own agency and generates the self-esteem that comes from such independence. Families (especially children) also benefit from women's earnings. Migration also enhances women's freedom of movement and opens up choices. The solution to the abuses discussed above is not to reduce women's mobility (as has been done in some cases) or employment opportunities, but to work for compliance with human rights standards within the opportunities offered by globalization, and to ensure accountability for any failure to do so.

The global social movement of human rights has become an irresistible force, bringing the language and beliefs of human rights to all parts of the globe and into all aspects of social, political, and economic life, and exposing the falseness of the public/private divide. Affirmation of the universality of legal norms prohibiting discrimination on the grounds of gender have provided women with a set of international standards to use against adverse national or local codes. The technological and communications revolutions have added new dimensions to women's long-standing organizational methods. In a manifestation of the concept of "globalization from below," groups working for the recognition of women's human rights have furthered their skills and strengths in campaigning and communicating globally. Instantaneous communications have facilitated the formation of alliances and coalitions, lessened isolation for women in remote or secluded areas, allowed for rapid mobilization over issues, and coordinated support on a global basis. But, again, there are also concerns that women's strategic organization is formulated and centred in the north while primarily targeted at the south. Electronic means of communication have heightened the gap between those that have such access and those that do not. There is a danger that international NGOs operate to their own agendas and to the detriment of grassroots organizations.

Another area where revolutionary technologies have had particular consequences for gender relations is that of reproductive technology. Again, the picture is mixed. On the one hand, this has allowed women (especially economically affluent women) greater freedom and choice with respect to reproduction; on the other, it has created innumerable health problems for women who are not given adequate attention by state agencies or the medical establishment. Women's health conditions—especially gynecological ones—that could be relieved with little expenditure are frequently overlooked or remain untreated through cultural taboos. Other problems arise when technologies are used alongside state policies with respect to women's fertility; for example, reproductive technology that allows predetermination and selection of the gender of a child alongside a national "one-child" policy or a policy demanding sons for the continuation of a national struggle. "Modern technology has been the means of liberation and choice for many women, but for others it has resulted in death and exploitation."[34]

Key challenges in the short and medium terms

Unlike other topics, gender policy covers the totality of international laws and relations, including those relating to good governance, democracy, and human rights. Therefore, this section cannot focus upon a single, or limited, number of issues, but tries to identify some of the key challenges that exist to reformulating gender relations in ways that would enhance women's empowerment. They are interlocking and require conceptual rethinking, political will, leadership, reallocation of resources, and commitment not just to the rhetoric of women's empowerment but to the social restructuring that would lead to its genuine achievement.

The short- and medium-term challenges are not to evolve new legal norms with respect to the position of women. The legal framework is largely in place. The key challenges are twofold: to reconceptualize concepts around the empowerment of women, and to encourage states to uphold undertakings with which they are under a legal obligation to comply. In the longer term, the challenge is to rethink basic concepts and ideas of societal advancement, rather than simply repeating the masculine model and assuming that it will endure.

The key challenges include:

- Developing the understanding that gender-based inequality is socially constructed and rests upon stereotyped assumptions about the role and position of women, not upon biological difference. This construction includes "the historically unequal power relations between men and women which have led to domination over and discrimination against women by men."[35] Since inequality in gender relations is not natural, such relations can be reconstructed so as to achieve equality.
- Recognizing diversity among women and the cross-cutting exclusionary impact of diverse forms of discrimination—for example, discrimination based upon ethnicity, class, sexuality, religion, age, disability, and race—on women.
- Achieving greater participation by women in all areas of public and private life, at all levels of policy- and decision-making. While increasing women's numerical participation is important, it is not sufficient. It

must be accompanied by an inclusive understanding of citizenship and participatory democracy that encompasses women's lives and women's contributions to society, and would thereby enhance women's sense of identity and belonging.
- Identifying the reasons for women's exclusion from political life and the obstacles to women's effective participation in national and local decision- and policy-making bodies, and taking positive measures to redress this imbalance.[36] In sum, "it is the Government's fundamental responsibility to encourage these initiatives to lead and guide public opinion and change attitudes that discriminate against women or discourage women's involvement in political and public life."[37]
- Reimagining concepts such as security, peace, conflict, reconstruction, dispute resolution, and governance to take account of women's experiences and women's actual and potential contributions to them, and to ensure women's participation within them. To ensure that all those involved as decision- and policy-makers, or as active participants, understand and are committed to such approaches.
- Overcoming the threats presented by religious fundamentalism to the realization of women's dignity and self-determination, while supporting the enhancement of women's rights within women's own religious contexts.
- Gaining acceptance of a rights-based approach to women's advancement; asserting that women's rights are an issue of human rights, not a "women's problem," nor a failure of development policies, nor a matter of welfare.
- Achieving universal ratification of the CEDAW and the withdrawal of reservations to the Convention that are incompatible with its objects and purposes.
- Enhancing state responsibility to comply with women's human rights. One instrument with the potential to do this is the Optional Protocol to CEDAW.[38] Accordingly, it is important that it is brought into force and, once in force, that appropriate actions are initiated to make it a dynamic and vibrant instrument.
- Enhancing individual responsibility for gender-based crimes against humanity and war crimes. To this end it is important that the ad hoc war crimes tribunals for the former Yugoslavia and Rwanda continue to indict gender-specific crimes and develop the jurisprudence around such offences.[39] The relevant provisions in the Statute for an International Criminal Court must be supported by unambiguous definitions of gender-related crimes and Rules of Procedure and Evidence.[40]
- Developing thinking on the matter of corporate responsibility for compliance with human rights standards and addressing entrenched gender relations.[41]

GENDER AND INTERNATIONAL SOCIETY   251

- Giving full effect to both the Nairobi Forward-Looking Strategies and the Beijing Declaration and Platform for Action.
- Promoting the integration and indivisibility of all human rights and the importance of economic and social rights for women; enhancing measures for their assessment, evaluation, and enforceability through the use of methodology that asserts multi-layered obligations to protect, respect, and fulfill all human rights.
- Giving effect to the international legal norms at the national level in acknowledgment of local particularities; developing institutions at the local, national, regional, and international levels that can effectively ensure implementation of the applicable norms.
- Enhancing women's economic independence through labour law reforms with respect to equal pay and the combating of sexual harassment in the workplace; providing affordable access to training and education to enhance women's employment choices and to counteract the gendered division of labour; allowing women to hold legal title to property, including through inheritance, and to access credit facilities.
- Eliminating and punishing gender-based violence, whether committed by state agencies or non-state actors, in public or in private.[42]
- Recognizing that certain traditional practices and assumptions deny women's bodily integrity—and even their right to life—and taking legal and social steps aimed at their eradication.
- Giving effect to women's reproductive rights and reproductive and sexual health, as understood within the Programme of Action of the United Nations International Conference on Population and Development.[43]
- Enhancing the education opportunities for girls and women. Lack of education and illiteracy are integrated with all other issues in that education has been urged as the single most effective step for the advancement of women. Factors that deny education opportunities for females—be they social, cultural, or economic—must be tackled as a priority.
- Convincing states of the seriousness of women's human rights as an ethical imperative, but also as a basis for sound governance and international peace, security, and development. Gender apartheid is comparable to racial apartheid, and states should combine to bring the full range of tools to bear against it, as they did to defeat the apartheid regime.

Despite the length of this list of key challenges, they can be reduced to one single, simple proposition: to make the legal trends that have emerged throughout the last century to enhance women's empowerment effective. Nevertheless, while law and legal reform are important, they are inadequate on their own to achieve societal transformation. The key challenge is laid down in CEDAW, Article 5, which states:

States shall take all appropriate measures:

(*a*) To modify the social and cultural patterns of conduct of men and women, with a view to achieving the elimination of prejudices and customary and all other practices which are based on the idea of the inferiority or the superiority of either of the sexes or on stereotyped roles for men and women.

How national governments and the international community might more broadly address the questions

Since the Third World Conference on Women, held in Nairobi in 1985, the strategy of gender mainstreaming in all social interactions has been promoted. This was reiterated at both the Vienna Conference on Human Rights in 1993[44] and the Fourth World Conference on Women in Beijing in 1995. Two definitions of mainstreaming are as follows:

Mainstreaming involves placing an issue within the pre-existing institutional, academic, and discursive framework. It is the opposite of marginalization and, as such, is an appropriate way to characterize the objective of gender-perspective integration . . . Gender mainstreaming is thus the process of bringing an awareness of the status of women into the public arena.[45]

Gender mainstreaming is the (re)organization, improvement, development, and evaluation of policy processes, so that a gender equality perspective is incorporated in all policies at all levels and at all stages, by the actors involved in policymaking.[46]

Mainstreaming thus concerns relations between women and men. The use of gender as a defining category, rather than a focus only upon women, emphasizes that gender is not an isolated issue, but one that interacts with other policy issues such as economic development, environmental, social, and welfare matters, law-making and law compliance, and enforcement. It is not a static process but an evolving one that is open to changing parameters as needs change. Gender mainstreaming must therefore be incorporated within legally binding instruments (a good example is the inclusion of gender throughout the 1998 Rome Statute of the International Criminal Court), within resolutions of the organs of the United Nations, including the Security Council, and within the practices and policies of the organs, specialized agencies (including the international financial institutions), and programmes of the United Nations and regional and national bodies. It should thus be integrated into technical assistance projects by all agencies that offer such services, and into the implementation of programmes across all activities; for example, with respect to judicial or law enforcement, personnel training, peace-keeping activities, and societal reconstruction after conflict. Coordination between the various service providers is required. However, "top-down" imposition of gender mainstreaming from international institutions will not be effective to change societal constructs of gender roles. Consultation and participation with those involved at the operational level, as well as with local and regional communities, is essential.

The concept of gender mainstreaming also shifts the focus from "pleading for women" to an identification of different needs within the community and the formulation of policies and strategies that address those needs. It allows policy formulation to take account of difference without undermining the assumption of legal equality between women and men. It requires an active approach that overturns and replaces existing practices; it cannot be achieved by default.

The emphasis on gender rather than on women does not, however, remove the need or desirability for women-specific programmes or projects. These may remain necessary to redress particular instances of past discrimination, or long-term, systemic discrimination. Gender mainstreaming should not be allowed to obscure the objective of gender equality. What mainstreaming does require is an integrated and holistic approach to planning, policy-making, and implementation that includes targets and methods for evaluation, and that involves all people at all levels. It must be recognized that this is a long-term commitment that requires ongoing monitoring, evaluation, and adaptation according to local contexts and conditions.

Another strategy is to adopt a rights-based approach that places the conceptualization and implementation of policies and programmes in the context of an overarching question: how do these policies support the realization of all human rights?[47] A rights-based approach focuses upon legal entitlement rather than needs or social desirability, placing the role of law at the centre of the discourse. This includes the need for legal institutions, affordable and real access to justice, and independent judiciary and law enforcement agents. It emphasizes individuals as rights-holders with corresponding duties. Gender mainstreaming can be incorporated into a rights-based approach and this provides an important moral basis for women's claims that is hard to refute.[48] A rights-based approach also provides a set of unifying standards, a common reference point for setting objectives and assessing outcomes.[49]

A third strategy, which can also be combined with elements of the two preceding strategies, is to focus upon poverty reduction. In the late 1990s, development banks such as the World Bank[50] and the Asian Development Bank[51] have adopted poverty reduction strategies as their overarching objectives. Denial of human rights—including discrimination—is both a cause and a consequence of poverty. Trends show that discrimination against certain groups, such as women, racial, or ethnic minorities, or indigenous persons, goes hand in hand with poverty within those groups. In many instances, such people suffer double (or multiple) exclusion; that is, discrimination on the basis of their category and the further discrimination that flows from their poverty. While discrimination is an intrinsic wrong that must be redressed, further work is needed on understanding the nexus between discrimination and poverty and the different ways in which groups that are discriminated against experience poverty. For example, the feminization of poverty is not simply about the numbers of women who are poor, but also encompasses understanding of the gendered ways in which women fall into poverty and its consequences for them. Ways in which women become impoverished include widowhood, lack of paid employment (or low-paid irregular employment, or employment in the informal sector) and thus no pension entitlement, domestic violence causing departure from the family home, and legal restrictions on the ownership of property. The experience of poverty is also gendered, as can be seen in the differential impact upon women of economic restructuring. Increases in the price of food, declines in real family incomes, and reductions in health and social services all directly impact upon women's role as the principal homemakers.[52] The Beijing Platform for Action states that "the empowerment of women is a critical factor in the eradication of poverty."[53] Human rights provide a tool for that empowerment, creating linkages between strategies aimed at poverty reduction, human rights, and gender mainstreaming.

Again, however, the picture is complex. Subordination of women and denial of their rights may exist quite apart from poverty, in states such as Saudi Arabia and Kuwait. It has also been shown that, in some instances, alleviating poverty will not necessarily prevent subordination of women and, indeed, can lead to a greater emphasis on women's societal roles and less autonomy.[54] In any strategy, it is important to consider the local context and tailor one's approach accordingly.

What comparative advantage might the United Nations have in working with the international community in addressing the challenges?

The United Nations is the body through which international instruments for the advancement of women's rights have been negotiated. It has the mandate for the continuation of this policy into the next stages. It has the available institutional structures and machinery, including bodies with specialist expertise in human rights, women's human rights, and gender issues. These include the Commission on the Status of Women, the Division for the Advancement of Women, the Committee on the Elimination of Discrimination against Women, the UN Development Fund for Women (UNIFEM), and the International Research and Training Institute for the Advancement of Women (INSTRAW). It has taken important steps with respect to documenting the global situation of women through the collection and collation of gender-disaggregated data and their analysis. Commitment to enhancing the rights of women has been expressed by the Secretary-General. Specialist agencies and other bodies have taken steps towards incorporating gender issues into their programmes and are beginning to develop useful experience across the totality of international affairs.

However, while women's advancement has long been an objective of the United Nations, progress, even with respect to gender balance within its own institutions, has been painfully slow. Emphases upon state sovereignty and equitable geographic representation have impeded the selection of women in key positions, although there is some progress. Functional compartmentalization within the organization risks constant reinvention of the wheel through the pursuit of common policies by different agencies. Too often, real progress rests upon the energy and expertise of a committed individual in the appropriate position. The United Nations draws upon a vast array of technical, legal, professional, and operational experts, consultants, and service providers. It is important that such people are aware of the importance of gender issues and are capable of incorporating them into their work. Experts in gender should be sought out across all areas of the organization's work, and people should not be re-employed simply because they have previously been used. There is need for greater overall coordination and direction in target-setting and allocation of resources and responsibilities.

Potential for partnerships among states, international organizations, commercial organizations, and civil-society actors in addressing the challenges

Throughout the twentieth century, women have organized and campaigned for political and economic rights at the grass-roots, national, and international levels. The advancements that have occurred have been gained largely through such civil-society action. Most recently, the assertion of women's rights as human rights at the 1993 Vienna conference on human rights, the adoption of the United Nations Declaration on the

Elimination of Violence against Women, the adoption for ratification of the Optional Protocol to CEDAW, and the inclusion of gendered crimes in the Rome Statute for the International Criminal Court have been achieved through the efforts of women's NGOs.

The women's movement has thus shown itself willing and able to use the arenas of the United Nations for the furthering of women's empowerment. What is now needed is to give effect to the policies and initiatives that have been accepted, through partnerships. These should be established at all levels—between international institutions and international civil society (including the corporate sector), between national governments and national civil society, and within local communities, with adequate communication channels accessible between and across all levels. Information and ideas must travel and be shared both horizontally and vertically.

Genuine partnership is also needed between women in the north and women in the south, between international NGOs (often dominated by the north) and national and grassroots NGOs. Civil society can too easily replicate the "top-down" tendencies of international institutions and national elites, to the detriment of local empowerment.

However, the most vital area of partnership is between women and men throughout society, with acknowledgment of the need to remove social, economic, and political imbalances in society. Changed gender relations must be worked out between women and men, and men must share in the responsibility for doing this. Too often, meetings, conferences, and planning sessions where gender relations are considered are attended predominantly by women. Such shared responsibility applies throughout societal and economic structures, including within the family, with respect to such issues as the division of paid and unpaid work, and child-raising. Government policies that are directed towards facilitating this (through, for example, flexible working hours, tax regimes, and broader understandings of the family) must be worked out between governments and civil society. The United Nations, too, can take a lead by introducing such practices within is own workforce.

The element of surprise, unpredictability, and potential critical developments

The twentieth century repeatedly demonstrated the fragility of gains in women's advancement. Gender relations are fluid and subject to constant negotiation within the family, the workforce, and the community. Inequality persists regardless of a state's prevailing political ideology. The reality of women's subordination remains constant. Advancement in women's interests is susceptible to being lost through political, economic, and societal changes, both those that are deemed generally progressive and those that are destructive. On many occasions, for example, women have participated in national self-determination movements, but the social reconstruction that has followed upon national liberation has not included guarantees of women's human rights.

Transition to democracy and market economies in Eastern Europe resulted in lowered participation in public office for women and loss of a range of economic rights. More generally, economic downturn within a state has a particularly harsh impact upon women; for example, through high unemployment or the introduction of austerity measures and structural adjustment programmes. Continued stereotypes of men as the primary breadwinners with family responsibilities lessen women's employment security, even in the face of statistical evidence of households headed by women. Reconstruction after conflict often focuses on the need to find employment for men who were formerly in military or paramilitary units, rather than on the continuation of female employment.

The international community has become involved in peace-building and reconstruction; for example, in Bosnia, Kosovo, and East Timor. In each of these territories, there are immense problems of unemployment, social disintegration, insecurity, and physical destruction. It is important that gender-specific aspects of these issues are recognized and that local women are consulted, can participate, and are integrated at all stages of reconstruction, especially with respect to capacity-building for self-government. Exceptionally, gender is included in the Security Council mandate for East Timor.[55] To be effective, the inclusion of women must not be limited to "international humanitarian law, human rights, and refugees issues" but must be taken as an overriding requirement, and must be accompanied by an effort to ensure expertise in gender perspectives and commitment on the ground. Otherwise the exclusion of women from public and political life is unlikely to be addressed.

Armed conflicts (whether internal or international) have repeatedly caused women to be targeted for attack by opposing forces, and to be subject to policies within their own community that place the interests of the collectivity above those of women (for example, the importance that is attached to reproduction to ensure the continuation of the group; and the promotion of the "family" as a sub-unit of the state that is to be protected as such, combined with the presentation of women's roles as being restricted to within that family). Control of government by religious or other extremists that introduce a form of sexual terrorism also leads to substantial reversals of women's advancement.

In the context of gender, international society, and policy the priority is not so much preparing for elements of surprise and unpredictability as realizing the consistent ease with which women's advancement is subordinated to other international, national, and subnational imperatives. Focused commitment to advancement by those with the authority and in the position to make it happen is needed at all times.

Notes

1. In 1893, New Zealand became the first country to accord women the right to vote.
2. Charter of the United Nations, Articles 1 (3), 55, 56.
3. The Universal Declaration of Human Rights, GA Res. 217A, 10 December 1948, Article 2; International Covenant on Economic, Social and Cultural Rights, 16 December 1966, 993 UNTS 3, Articles 2 (2), 3; International Covenant on Civil and Political Rights, 16 December 1966, 993 UNTS 171, Articles 2, 26.
4. 18 December 1979, 1249 UNTS 13.
5. Article 7 builds upon the Universal Declaration of Human Rights, Article 2, the International Covenant on Civil and Political Rights, Article 25, and the United Nations Convention on the Political Rights of Women, 20 December 1952, 193 UNTS 135, which asserts the right of women to vote and hold political office.
6. Article 8 builds upon the Charter of the United Nations, article 8.
7. See H. Pietilä and J. Vickers, with foreword by Gertrude Mongella, *Making Women Matter: The Role of the United Nations* (London and Atlantic Heights, NJ: Zed Books, 1994).
8. "The human rights of women and of the girl-child are an inalienable, integral and indivisible part of universal human rights" (Vienna Declaration and Programme for Action, 1993, UN Doc. A/Conf.157/23, 12 July 1993, I, para.18).
9. Beijing Declaration and Platform for Action, UN Doc. A/Conf.177/20, 17 October 1995, para. 213.
10. Council of Europe, *Gender Mainstreaming* (Strasbourg: Council of Europe, 1998).
11. See H. Charlesworth, "What are women's human rights?" in R. Cook (ed.), *Human Rights of Women: National and International Perspectives* (Philadelphia: University of Pennsylvania Press, 1994): 58.
12. For a history of women's human rights see A. Fraser, "Becoming human: The origins and development of women's human rights," *Human Rights Quarterly* 21 (1999): 853.
13. J. Connors, "NGOs and the human rights of women at the United Nations," in P. Willetts (ed.), *The Conscience of the World: The Influence of Non-governmental Organizations in the United Nations System* (London, Hurst, 1996): 147.
14. See H. Charlesworth and C. Chinkin, *The Boundaries of International Law: A Feminist Analysis* (Manchester: Manchester University Press, 2000), chapter 1, 'Women and the International Legal System.'
15. See United Nations, *Women in Politics and Decision-Making in the Late Twentieth Century: A United Nations Study* (1992); United Nations, *The World's Women 1995: Trends and Statistics* (1995).
16. There remain restrictions on women's voting rights in some states, for example Kuwait, Saudi Arabia, Qatar, Oman, the United Emirates, Equatorial Guinea, and Surinam. Women also suffer indirect discrimination regarding their ability to exercise the right to vote in some instances. For example, in Bhutan, only one member of a household is allowed to vote, which effectively bars women from exercising their right to vote.
17. T. Franck, "The emerging right to democratic governance," *American Journal of International Law* 86 (1992): 46.

18. For up-to-date figures on women's representation in national parliaments, see the website of the Inter-Parliamentary Union: <http://www.ipu.org/wmn-e/world.htm>. In May 2000 the world average is approximately 13 percent
19. Committee on the Elimination of Discrimination against Women, General Recommendation 23, *Political and Public Life*, 13 January 1997, para. 10.
20. V. Randall, *Women and Politics: An International Perspective* (Basingstoke: Macmillan, 1987).
21. See A. Phillips, *Engendering Democracy* (Cambridge: Polity Press, 1991).
22. Committee on the Elimination of Discrimination against Women, General Recommendation 23, para. 14.
23. On the public/private dichotomy, see C. Pateman, "Feminist Critiques of the public/private dichotomy," in S. Benn and G. Gaus, *Public and Private in Social Life* (London: Croom Helm, and New York: St Martin's Press, 1983): 285; M. Thornton (ed.), *Public and Private Feminist Legal Debates* (1995).
24. M. Waring, *Counting for Nothing: What Men Value and What Women are Worth* 2nd ed. (New York: University of Toronto, 1999).
25. For example, see the views expressed throughout the essays in M. Alexander and C. Mohanty (eds.), *Feminist Genealogies, Colonial Legacies, Democratic Futures* (New York: Routledge, 1997).
26. *Prosecutor v. Jean-Paul Akayesu*, Judgment of 2 September 1998, ICTR-96-4-T.
27. R. Krut, with K. Howard, E. Howard, and H. Gleckman, *Globalisation and Civil Society: NGO Influence in International Decision-Making* (Geneva: UNRISD, 1997).
28. Preliminary Report submitted by the Special Rapporteur on violence against women, its causes and consequences, Ms Radhika Coomaraswamy, UN Doc. E/CN.4/1995/42, 1995, para. 55.
29. Effects of structural adjustment policies on the full enjoyment of human rights, report by the independent expert, Mr Fantu Cheru, submitted in accordance with Commission decisions 1998/102 and 1997/103, UN Doc. E/CN.4/1999/50, 24 February 1999.
30. Report of the Special Rapporteur on violence against women, its causes and consequences, Ms Radhika Coomaraswamy, on trafficking in women, migration and violence against women, submitted in accordance with Commission on Human Rights resolution 1997/44, UN Doc. E/CN.4/2000/68, 29 February 2000, para. 59.
31. Human rights of migrants, Report of the Special Rapporteur, Ms. Gabriela Rodríguez Pizarro, submitted pursuant to Commission on Human Rights Resolution 1999/44, UN Doc. E/CN.4/2000/82, 6 January 2000, para. 59.
32. Report of the Special Rapporteur on violence against women, its causes and consequences, Ms Radhika Coomaraswamy, on the Mission to Poland on the issue of trafficking and the forced prostitution of Women (24 May—1 June 1996), UN Doc. E/CN.4/1997/Add. 1, 1996.
33. D. Otto, "Holding up half the sky, but for whose benefit? A critical analysis of the fourth World Conference on Women," *Australian Feminist law Journal* 6 (1966): 7.
34. Preliminary Report submitted by the Special Rapporteur on Violence against Women, para 57.
35. Beijing Declaration and Platform for Action, para. 118.
36. The Convention on the Elimination of All Forms of Discrimination against Women (CEDAW), Article 4, provides for the adoption of "temporary special measures" to accelerate de facto equality between women and men.
37. Committee on the Elimination of Discrimination against Women, General recommendation 23, para. 28.
38. The Optional Protocol to the Convention on the Elimination of All Forms of Discrimination against Women was adopted by GA Res. 54/4, 15 October 1999. It provides for

individual complaints of violation to be made to the Committee on the Elimination of Discrimination against Women and an enquiry procedure.
39. See for example, *Prosecutor v. Delalic and others*, Judgment of 16 November 1998, IT-96-21-T; *Prosecutor v Anto Furundzija*, judgment of 10 December 1998, IT-95-17/1-PT; *Prosecutor v. Jean-Paul Akayesu* (see note 26, above).
40. Statute for an International Criminal Court, UN Doc. A/Conf.183/9. Rome, 17 July 1998. The Statute has provisions on gender prosecution as a crime against humanity, crimes of enslavement, forced pregnancy, and rape, and requires there to be judges with gender expertise at the Court.
41. See S. Rees and S. Wright, *Human Rights Corporate Responsibility* (2000).
42. In accordance with the United Nations Declaration on the Elimination of Violence against Women, GA Res. 48/104, 20 December 1993.
43. Cairo, UN Doc. A/Conf.171/13, 18 October 1994, especially Chapter IV, Gender Equality, Equity and Empowerment of Women.
44. Vienna Declaration and Programme for Action, I, para. 18; Beijing Declaration and Platform for Action, para. 221.
45. Report of the Secretary-General, The question of integrating the human rights of women throughout the United Nations system, UN Doc. E/CN.4/1998/49.
46. Council of Europe, *Gender Mainstreaming* (Strasbourg: Council of Europe, 1998).
47. S. Goonesekere, "A rights-based approach to realizing gender equality," in *A Rights-Based Approach to Women's Empowerment and Advancement and Gender Equality*, FAO Headquarters, Report of workshop held at FAO Headquarters, 5–7 October 1998, (Rome: FAO, 1998).
48. For a good example of such an approach see Human Rights Committee, General Comment no. 28, Equality of Rights between Men and Women, Article 3, CCPR/C/21/Rev.1/Add.10, 29 March 2000. The General Comment provides a gendered analysis of the individual articles of the International Covenant on Civil and Political Rights.
49. Goonesekere, A right-based approach" (see note 47, above).
50. For the World Bank Poverty Reduction Strategy, see <http://www.worldbank.org/poverty/strategies/keydocs.htm>.
51. For the Asian Development Bank Poverty Reduction Strategy, see <http://www.adb.org/Poverty/adb_gl00.htm>.
52. Economic, Social and Cultural Rights, Effects of Structural Adjustment Programmes on the Full Enjoyment of Human Rights, UN Doc. E/CN.4/1999/50, 24 February 1999, para 85.
53. Beijing Declaration and Platform for Action, para. 49.
54. E.g., "From a gender perspective one might wonder what poverty targeting will offer the high birth-order girl child in a landed rural household in Northern India which may not be very poor but in which such a child may be very much at risk." C. Jackson, "Rescuing Gender from the Poverty Trap," *World Development* 24 (1996): 489.
55. Security Council Res. 1272, 25 October 1999, establishing the United Nations Transitional Administration in East Timor (UNTAET), "underlines the importance of including in UNTAET personnel with appropriate training in international humanitarian, human rights and refugee law, including child and gender-related provisions, negotiation and communication skills, cultural awareness and civilian–military coordination."

14
Decentralized governance for human development

G. Shabbir Cheema and Mounir Tabet

Decentralized governance can play an essential role in promoting and sustaining human development at the local and subnational level if properly planned and carefully implemented. Many countries in the world are beginning to acknowledge the importance of the role of local government, NGOs, and firms in meeting the developmental challenges at the local and national level, as is reflected in a global trend of increased political and fiscal decentralization.

This chapter introduces the concepts of human development and decentralized governance and establishes the relationship between them. It examines the global trends in political and fiscal decentralization. It then briefly examines the motives behind decentralization and some of its inherent dangers, and describes five recent experiences in decentralization. The findings of original, as yet unpublished, research consisting of nine case studies are presented, and five hypotheses defining the relationship between decentralized governance and the enabling environment, participation, partnerships, initiative and leadership, and capacity-building are examined. Evidence for the hypotheses is provided and lessons are drawn in conclusion.

Human development, good governance and decentralization: A conceptual entry point

Decentralized governance, carefully planned, effectively implemented, and appropriately managed, can lead to significant improvement in the welfare of people at the local level, the cumulative effect of which can lead to enhanced human development.

The United National Development Programme defines human development as "pro-people, pro-jobs, and pro-nature. It gives the highest priority to poverty reduction, productive employment, social integration, and environmental regeneration." Human development is development that not only generates economic growth but also distributes its benefits equitably, that regenerates the environment rather than destroys it, and that empowers people rather than marginalizes them. It gives priority to the poor, enlarging their choices and opportunities and providing for their participation in decisions affecting their lives. It also means "protection of the life opportunities of future generations . . . and . . . the natural systems on which all life depends" (UNDP, 1996).

Human development and good governance are indivisible. Governance is defined as the set of values, policies, and institutions by which a society manages its economic, political, and social affairs through interactions among the government, civil society, and the private sector. It is the way a society makes and implements decisions, achieving mutual understanding, agreement, and action. It comprises the mechanisms and processes for citizens and groups to articulate their interests, mediate their differences, and exercise their legal rights and obligations. Its rules, institutions, and practices set limits and provide incentives for individuals, organizations, and firms.

The core characteristics of governance—including participation, partnerships, the rule of law, transparency, accountability, responsiveness, subsidiarity, consensus orientation, equity, sustainability, effectiveness, and efficiency—are clearly interrelated and mutually reinforcing, and cannot stand alone. For example, accessible information means more transparency, broader participation, and more effective decision-making. Broad participation contributes both to the exchange of information needed for effective decision-making and for the legitimacy of those decisions. Legitimacy, in turn, means effective implementation and encourages further participation. And responsive institutions must be transparent and must function according to the rule of law if they are to be equitable.

These core characteristics represent an ideal. Through broad-based consensus-building processes, societies need to develop their own visions of good governance and aim to define which of its core features are most important to them and what the best balance between the state, the market, and society is for them. The challenge for all societies is to create a system of governance that promotes, supports, and sustains human development to realize the highest potential of everyone and the well-being of all, thus eliminating poverty and all other forms of exclusion.

Decentralized governance

As part of the overall governance system of any society, decentralized governance offers important opportunities for enhanced human development. However, if it is improperly planned or poorly implemented, decentralized governance can also be a challenge that may easily frustrate local efforts to enhance human development.

Organizationally, decentralized governance refers to the restructuring or reorganization of authority so that there is a system of co-responsibility between institutions of governance at the central, regional, and local levels according to the principle of subsidiarity, thus increasing the overall quality and effectiveness of the system of governance while increasing the authority and capacities of institutions at the subnational levels.

Conceptually, decentralization relates to the role of, and the relationship between, central and subnational institutions, whether they are public, private, or civic. Improved governance will require not only strengthened central and local governments but also the involvement of other actors from civil society organizations and the private sector in partnerships with government at all levels. Building capacity in all three domains of governance—state, civil society, and the private sector—is crucial for sustaining human development. Civil society organizations, for example, are increasingly seen as effective mechanisms for targeting disadvantaged groups, and the private sector is now more often seen as a natural partner for governments seeking innovative ways and means of improving service quality and delivery. The role of the government becomes that of a facilitator, a catalytic force for enabling the innovative sharing of responsibilities and creating enabling environments for the effectiveness of people and partners in pursuing their legitimate objectives. Within this context, civil society and the private sector become key partners of national and subnational governments in the transition towards improved forms of local governance through decentralization. Generally speaking, there are four major forms of public sector decentralization arrangements that are often included in discussions of decentralization. These include:

Political decentralization

This normally refers to situations where political power and authority have been decentralized to subnational levels. The most obvious manifestations of this type of decentralization are elected and empowered subnational forms of government ranging from village councils to state-level bodies. The creation of these elected bodies is best undertaken as a result of an overall strategic developmental vision. It usually involves reviews of legal frameworks and could include constitutional reforms. Devolution is considered a form of political decentralization.

Devolution
Devolution refers to the transfer of responsibility, decision-making, resources, and revenue generation to a local level of public authority that is autonomous and independent from the devolving authority. Units that are devolved are usually recognized as independent legal entities (such as municipal corporations) and are ideally (although not necessarily) elected.

Administrative decentralization

Administrative decentralization aims at transferring decision-making authority, resources, and responsibilities for the delivery of a select number of public services from the central government to other, lower levels of government, agencies, and field offices of central government line agencies. This transfer is of two basic types, with different implications as regards accountability for resource mobilization and management, and for service delivery. It is the accountability factor that differentiates the major types of administrative decentralization.

Deconcentration
Deconcentration transfers authority and responsibility from one level of the central government to another, e.g., by setting up branch offices of central agencies and ministries while maintaining the same hierarchical level of accountability from the local units and branches to the central government ministry or agency which has been decentralized.

Delegation
Delegation redistributes authority and responsibility to local units of government or specialized agencies that are not necessarily branches or local offices of the delegating authority. While some transfer of accountability to the subnational units to which power is being delegated takes place,

accountability is still principally vertical and to the delegating central unit.

Fiscal decentralization

Cutting across all other forms of decentralization, some level of resource reallocation is made to allow local government to function properly. Decentralizing responsibilities, authority, and accountability without assignment of adequate levels of resources to the decentralized units does not work. Arrangements for resource allocation are usually negotiated between local and central authorities and depend on several factors including concerns for interregional equity, availability of central and local resources, and local fiscal management capacity.

Divestment or market decentralization

This form of transfer of government responsibilities and authority is done in favour of non-public entities where planning and administrative responsibility or other public functions are transferred from government to voluntary, private, or non-governmental institutions with clear benefits to and involvement of the public. This often involves contracting out partial service provision or administration functions, deregulation, or full privatization. This kind of decentralization is typically undertaken for services that had been monopolies of the central government and, ideally, are earmarked for divestment to local entities where the benefits are accruing to the local population.

Decentralization is seen as a more effective means than central government for delivery of services to the local population. Proximity to the demand base for a service renders response more effective and promotes a more rational use of resources. This proximity also allows for closer monitoring by the beneficiary population of projects intended to serve them, and has been shown to reduce costs in some cases.

Decentralization is also seen as promoting equity between subnational regions and within regions. Governmental transfers favouring poorer regions enhance equity between regions and enhance service delivery, and the resulting improved access contributes to increased equity within regions.

Decentralization, of course, is not a panacea for all ills and is not without its challenges. One of the more commonly expressed concerns about decentralization is that it could merely strengthen the heavy hand of local elites. When this happens, the prospects for poverty reduction and human development are undoubtedly dimmed.

Also, decentralization sometimes translates into the dumping of responsibilities onto lower levels of government—commonly labelled "load-shedding"—without allocating sufficient resources or strengthening local capacity to undertake these responsibilities. Moreover, participation without resources is not likely to have a lasting impact on human development. Many poor people in developing countries are trapped in areas that are economically backward and resource-scarce. Conferring greater local decision-making powers on them might not do a great deal to enhance their welfare if they are not able to finance their developmental needs.

Worsening regional inequalities are also an undesirable outcome of badly planned decentralization. Left to their own devices, richer regions are likely to develop faster than poor ones. Typically, a system of matching grants, intended by central government to motivate local government to raise funds, exacerbates the problem of regional disparities, where richer regions can raise more local funds and poor regions are unable to meet their basic needs. Without dampening incentives to mobilize local resources, a system of resource transfers that includes equalization grants is often needed to narrow disparities.

Decentralization can also weaken national unity and increase the separatist sentiments of geographically based ethnic groups.

Improving human development and strengthening democracy through decentralization is a long-term process. It takes careful planning and patient implementation. It is ideally guided by a clear, long-term vision that is formulated in a participatory manner. It requires clearly articulated goals, and strengthened capacities at the local and central levels to attain them. It also requires resources and a great deal of coordination. It involves the people through a variety of participatory mechanisms and introduces new forms of accountability. An effective and empowering decentralized governance is not an overnight process.

Global changes and decentralized governance

Profound and transformational global trends have arisen in the past two decades that have made an unprecedented impact on democratic developments in developing and developed countries alike. Many societies are re-examining the role of the state in the provision of services that enhance the welfare of the citizen, in response to the emergence of many recent trends. These trends include the globalization of trade, finance, and environmental concerns and the restricted flow of capital, goods, and human resources, and are underscoring the importance of developing a new concept of public goods, especially transborder public goods. They also include a revolution in communication and information technology and increased access to information and knowledge, which the state cannot control and which are broadening the horizons of political awareness. Spurred by remarkable improvements in education standards and a more active civil society, an increasing number of societies have responded to these trends by widening the democratic space and making more efficient use of their human resources. Sixty-one percent of countries in the world had some form of democratic government in 1998 compared to only 28 percent in 1974 (World Bank, 1999).

These transformations have also changed the focus on public policy at the national level. While more attention is being given to global issues and to those national concerns arising out of globalization, governments are realizing that development at the local level can no longer be efficiently and effectively addressed by central administrations alone. Local governments, non-governmental organizations (NGOs), and the private sector are increasingly being recognized as important development partners at the local level. National government policies are changing to reflect this new reality. An increasing number of countries are devolving political, administrative, fiscal, and economic powers to subnational levels. In 1998, some 95 per cent of democracies had some form of elected subnational government. Out of 75 developing and transitional countries with populations greater than 5 million, all but 12 claim to have embarked on some form of transfer of political power to local units of government (World Bank, 1999).

In the immediate post-colonial era, governments argued against decentralization and built strong central governments in the name of nation-building and national unity. In the late 1990s, the governments of many developing countries are using decentralization as a means to promote political stability. Delegating part of the central authority to local government is empowering to ethnic groups and geographic areas that had hitherto felt that they were outside the decision-making process. Decentralization is also seen as promoting an orderly, consensus-oriented way of sorting out differences and negotiating developmental rights. South Africa, Uganda, and Ethiopia, as well as Bosnia and Herzegovina, have all experimented with decentralization as a mechanism for enhanced political stability.

Governments are decentralizing to increase direct popular participation in decision-making. Authoritarian regimes in the past have failed to deliver the economic, political, and social means for enhanced well-being of the populations of many countries. Decentralization is seen as a tool to widen the circle of participation and make more effective use of local human resources.

The structure of central government spending in the post-colonial era was such that major expenditures were made on defence and large public works, leaving very little for social spending, which has a greater potential for decentralization. As spending on social issues increases, governments are seeing more opportunities to decentralize some areas of basic health, primary education, water supply, and similar services.

As pointed out earlier, the trend toward decentralization is on the rise. Table 14.1 shows the current state of political decentralization in many countries. The table reflects a great appeal for, and wide application of, political decentralization across the world. Out of the 106 countries listed in the table, close to 90 percent conducted local-level elections in 1999 alone. Many more have conducted similar elections in previous years and others may be intending to undertake them in the future. The 1999 elections alone will have created 1,621 jurisdictions at the intermediate level and a staggering 478,000 jurisdictions at the local level. In terms of widening the base of electoral democracy, these figures are quite telling: this large number of elected representatives to legislative and executive bodies at the local level means that there is not only a wider representation of the population in decision-making but also a wider chance for local needs to be addressed and met. It also means increased opportunities for more effective participation in decision-making and closer scrutiny of government performance. This is a pattern that is spreading across the world.

As was observed earlier, one of the major areas of concern for decentralized governance is the availability of resources. While funds may be available from local sources in the form of taxes and fees, most countries still rely heavily on intergovernmental transfers to finance local expenditures. Table 14.2 shows the recent trends in decentralized expenditures and revenues. Subnational expenditures, a percentage of total public expenditure, in 1997 varied from 55.6 percent to 2.6 percent, with more than 56 percent of the 57 countries shown spending at least one-quarter of their total public expenditures at the local level. This is an improvement over the 1990 figures, which showed only 45 percent of these countries spending more than a quarter of their total public expenditures locally.

On the revenue side, the trend shows a decrease of 1 percent in revenue generated locally as a percentage of total revenues. This is an average for all 57 countries shown. It includes a strong downward trend associated with ex-socialist countries reflecting the serious fiscal constraints they experienced in the 1990s. If these countries are excluded, the trend reveals a steady increase of 7 percent in revenues generated locally. The table also shows that 28 percent of the countries examined generated more than one-fifth of their resources locally; China leads the group, with 51.4 percent of total tax revenues generated locally.

Table 14.1 Political Decentralization in selected countries, 1999

Country	Subnational elections		No. of elected subnational tiers	No. of jurisdictions	
	Intermediate	Local		Intermediate	Local
Albania	No	Yes	1	—	374
Algeria	No	No	0	48	1,552
Argentina	Yes	Yes	2	24	1,617
Armenia	No	Yes	1	—	931
Australia	Yes	Yes	2	8	900
Austria	Yes	Yes	2	9	2,353
Bangladesh	No	Yes	1	—	4,642
Belarus	No	No	0	—	179
Belgium	Yes	Yes	2	10	589
Benin	No	No	0	—	77
Bolivia	No	Yes	1	9	312
Bosnia and Herzegovina	Yes	Yes	3	2	137
Botswana	No	Yes	1	—	17
Brazil	Yes	Yes	2	28	5,581
Bulgaria	No	Yes	1	—	294
Burkina Faso	Yes	Yes	2	45	250
Cameroon	No	Yes	1	—	336
Canada	Yes	Yes	2	12	4,507
Central African Republic	No	Yes	1	—	174
Chile	No	Yes	1	—	340
Colombia	Yes	Yes	2	33	1,068
Costa Rica	No	No	0	—	496
Côte d'Ivoire	No	Yes	1	50	196
Croatia	Yes	Yes	2	21	543
Cuba	Yes	Yes	2	15	169
Czech Republic	No	Yes	1	—	5,768
Denmark	Yes	Yes	2	16	275
Dominican Republic	No	Yes	1	—	90
Ecuador	Yes	Yes	2	21	1,079
Egypt, Arab Rep.	No	No	0	—	199
El Salvador	No	Yes	1	—	262
Eritria	No	Yes	1	6	—
Estonia	No	Yes	1	—	254
Ethiopia	Yes	Yes	2	11	910
Finland	No	Yes	1		455

continues

Table 14.1 continued

Country	Subnational elections		No. of elected subnational tiers	No. of jurisdictions	
	Intermediate	Local		Intermediate	Local
France	Yes	Yes	3	22	36,559
Georgia	No	Yes	1	—	4,000
Germany	Yes	Yes	3	16	16,121
Ghana	No	Yes	1	—	110
Greece	Yes	Yes	2	13	5,922
Guatemala	No	Yes	1	—	324
Guinea	No	Yes	1	—	33
Haiti	No	Yes	1	—	133
Honduras	No	Yes	1	—	293
Hungary	Yes	Yes	2	20	3,153
India	Yes	Yes	2	32	237,687
Iran, Islamic Rep.	No	Yes	1	—	720
Ireland	Yes	Yes	3	8	80
Israel	No	Yes	1		273
Italy	Yes	Yes	3	20	8,104
Japan	Yes	Yes	2	47	3,233
Jordan	Yes	Yes	1		669
Kazakhstan	No	No	0	16	303
Latvia	No	Yes	1	33	566
Libya	No	Yes	1		1,500
Lithuania	No	Yes	1	10	56
Madagascar	No	Yes	1		1,391
Malaysia	No	No	0	13	143
Mali	No	Yes	1		279
Mexico	Yes	Yes	2	32	2,418
Moldova	No	Yes	1	3	35
Morocco	No	Yes	1	65	1,547
Mozambique	Yes	Yes	2	10	33
Nepal	Yes	Yes	2	75	4,053
Netherlands	Yes	Yes	2	12	572
New Zealand	Yes	Yes	3	12	155
Nicaragua	No	Yes	1	—	143
Niger	No	No	0	32	150
Nigeria	Yes	Yes	2	31	589
Norway	No	Yes	1	—	435
Pakistan	No	No	0	4	5,195
Papua New Guinea	No	Yes	1	—	284

continues

Table 14.1 continued

Country	Subnational elections		No. of elected subnational tiers	No. of jurisdictions	
	Intermediate	Local		Intermediate	Local
Paraguay	Yes	Yes	2	17	212
Peru	No	Yes	1	—	1,808
Philippines	Yes	Yes	2	76	1,541
Poland	Yes	Yes	3	16	2,489
Portugal	No	Yes	2	—	275
Romania	No	Yes	1	41	2,948
Russian Federation	Yes	Yes	3	90	2,000
Rwanda	No	No	0	—	143
Senegal	No	No	0	10	99
Sierra Leone	No	Yes	1	—	204
Slovak Republic	No	Yes	1	—	2,834
Slovenia	No	Yes	1	—	192
South Africa	Yes	Yes	2	9	840
Spain	Yes	Yes	3	17	8,082
Sri Lanka	No	Yes	1	9	238
Sudan	No	Yes	1	—	615
Sweden	Yes	Yes	2	24	286
Switzerland	Yes	Yes	2	26	3,000
Syrian Arab Republic	No	Yes	1	—	300
Tajikistan	No	No	0	3	41
Tanzania	No	Yes	1	—	101
Thailand	No	Yes	1	—	149
Togo	No	Yes	1	—	30
Tunisia	No	Yes	1	—	257
Turkey	No	Yes	1	80	2,801
Uganda	Yes	Yes	2	58	1,040
Ukraine	No	Yes	1	27	619
United Kingdom	Yes	Yes	1	135	319
United States	Yes	Yes	3	51	70,500
Uruguay	No	Yes	1	—	19
Uzbekistan	No	No	0	14	281
Venezuela	Yes	Yes	2	24	330
Zambia	No	Yes	1	—	72
Zimbabwe	No	Yes	1	—	80

Source: Adapted from World Bank, 1999.

Table 14.2 Extent of fiscal decentralization in selected countries, 1990–1997

	Share of subnational government (%)			
	In total public expenditures		In total tax revenue	
Country	1990	1997	1990	1997
Albania	—	24.9	—	0.9
Argentina	46.3	43.9	38.2	41.1
Armenia	—	5.1	—	3.3
Australia	50.9	47.9	2.0	22.7
Austria	31.9	32.2	21.7	20.7
Belarus	30.6	32.5	29.4	23.7
Belgium	11.9	11.8	4.5	5.4
Bolivia	17.7	36.3	15.1	19.1
Botswana	7.9	3.8	0.1	0.6
Brazil	35.3	36.5	30.9	31.3
Bulgaria	18.9	15.7	22.4	11.8
Canada	58.7	49.4	49.5	43.5
Chile	7.2	8.5	6.4	7.0
China	—	55.6	—	51.4
Costa Rica	3.0	2.8	2.3	2.3
Croatia	—	12.1	—	7.5
Czech Republic	—	21.3	—	12.3
Denmark	54.8	54.5	31.1	31.5
Dominican Republic	1.6	2.6	0.5	0.2
Estonia	34.8	22.4	26.5	14.2
Ethiopia	1.5	—	1.6	—
Finland	46.5	41.2	25.9	27.6
France	18.7	18.6	9.7	10.8
Germany	40.2	37.8	28.9	28.8
Guatemala	10.1	10.3	1.3	1.7
Hungary	20.6	23.7	7.6	8.9
India	51.1	53.3	33.8	36.1
Indonesia	13.1	14.8	2.9	2.9
Iran, Islamic Rep.	4.9	—	8.4	—
Ireland	27.9	30.7	2.5	2.4
Israel	12.7	15.1	6.9	6.2
Italy	22.8	25.4	3.6	6.5
Japan	—	—	37.8	—
Kenya	4.4	3.5	2.2	1.9
Latvia	—	25.8	—	15.8
Lithuana	30.4	22.6	14.4	16.2

continues

Table 14.2 continued

	Share of subnational government (%)			
	In total public expenditures		In total tax revenue	
Country	1990	1997	1990	1997
Malaysia	20.2	19.1	3.7	2.4
Mexico	17.8	26.1	19	20.6
Netherlands	29.0	26.1	3.4	4.1
New Zealand	9.3	10.8	6.9	6.3
Nicaragua	3.5	9.6	2.5	8.3
Norway	36.7	37.4	20.9	19.6
Paraguay	1.9	2.6	0.8	2.0
Peru	9.8	24.4	1.2	2.1
Philippines	6.5	—	4.0	—
Poland	—	22.0	21.3	9.6
Portugal	8.7	11.6	3.6	5.9
Romania	15.4	13.3	12.8	9.2
Russian Federation	—	37.6	—	40.0
South Africa	20.7	49.8	5.5	5.3
Spain	34.3	35.0	13.3	13.8
Sweden	39.8	36.2	28.2	31.4
Switzerland	51.2	49.3	37.0	35.5
Thailand	7.5	9.6	4.4	5.5
United Kingdom	29.0	27.0	5.9	3.6
United States	42.0	46.5	33.8	32.9
Zimbabwe	13.5	—	3.4	—

Source: World Bank, 1999.

These figures clearly show that an increasing financial role is being played at the local level on both the revenue and expenditures sides of the equation, in recognition of the importance of local government in the development process.

Five recent experiences in decentralized governance

The global trends described above have resulted in an array of successes and failures in decentralizing governance across the world. Often a clear and realistic objective for decentralizing responsibilities and services is not sufficiently well articulated, nor are the milestones expected in the process well defined. This makes it difficult to judge successes and failures in decentralization accurately. Additionally, documenting decentralization experiences is a recent endeavour, and more empirical evidence is required to draw definitive lessons on what makes decentralized governance work. Nevertheless, some experiences are indicative, and five comprehensive approaches are described below.

In India widening popular participation in decision-making is creating new opportunities and challenges. Thanks to two amendments to India's constitution in 1992, local governments are now elected and strengthened. In 1999, a little under 238,000 local councils were elected across the country. They are made up of 3 million elected representatives, one-third of whom are women, and 660,000 of whom are from the hitherto marginalized scheduled castes. These reforms have the potential to bring about radical changes in power relations throughout the country. Now India's system of governance is being built slowly from the bottom up—based on direct democracy—instead of being spread from the top down. In many locations, people are making tangible progress in taking control of their lives. Civil society organizations are actively joining with local government to promote change. At the village level, people are conducting "social audits" of government funds to ensure accountability and transparency. *Gram Sabha*, or village assemblies, are more frequently contesting corruption and abuses of power. Local governments are mobilizing new tax revenues and initiating their own development projects, which are identified and elaborated using participatory methods of consultation. This system is, of course, not without its challenges. Greater democracy at the local level is threatening old, entrenched relations of power, and in some cases local elites may gain strength as a result of elections. The management of this system is undoubtedly a monumental task and will require intensive coordination efforts and resources.

In Ghana local needs are integrated in national plans through district-level planning and increasing resource allocation. The experience of Ghana illustrates a case in which substantial progress has been made, but in which challenges remain. The reforms have devolved significant authority to local districts. Within the guidelines provided by the National Development Planning Commission, districts now have considerable autonomy to decide their own development needs and priorities. The districts in Ghana also have more control over resources. They can raise some of their own revenues and negotiate directly with external donors for additional resources. In addition, 5 percent of the national budget is allocated to them—based partly on need—specifically for development purposes, with one-fifth of this amount earmarked for poverty-reduction activities. This innovation underscores the general point that devolution of responsibilities has to be accompanied by devolution of resources.

Despite some success, the Ghana experience could benefit from increased and strengthened participation in the local development planning process. Higher participation will broaden ownership of the development plans and therefore increase their chances of success, and will also strengthen accountability. The experience shows that democracy needs to be deepened to consolidate the process of devolution.

In Uganda capacity-building at the local level constitutes the next important step in implementing the most comprehensive of all African Decentralization programmes. The new constitution adopted in 1995 calls for the devolution of responsibilities and power to local government. The Local Government Act of 1997 clearly spells out that local councils are granted the power to raise revenues and initiate their own development projects. Local councillors were elected in 1998 at various levels of government.

Fiscal decentralization has accompanied the decentralization of responsibilities. Sub-counties are now allowed to retain about two-thirds of the revenue collected in their areas. However, overall resources remain meagre. A 1996 Auditor General's report also indicates that a significant portion of funds is diverted away from development purposes. Local elites still exercise considerable influence in determining how funds are utilized.

Another challenge is the management of the local councils. Once a village council elects a council executive, for example, this body often takes over the role of the council itself. Council meetings then become infrequent. Many local leaders are held back by illiteracy, lack of knowledge of government procedures, and lack of awareness of their rights. Often they become embroiled in settling community disputes rather than focusing on development. Encouragingly, community participation is high. Issues are openly and democratically discussed. This results in strong commitment to clinics, schools, roads, and other services and investments, which the local people participate in selecting and planning. Additionally, accountability is highly valued. The procedure for transferring funds from the district to the village is as transparent as possible. Instead of relying on a traditional system of financial audit, there is more reliance on the "public audit," where the costs and use of funds are widely known in the community.

In Nepal participation in district-level planning is proving to be the key to success in local development. Past experience in Nepal, as elsewhere, shows that centrally designed, administered, and managed programmes, such as the Integrated Rural Development Programmes, do not have much impact on local development. By contrast, those programmes implemented with the close involvement of beneficiaries—even when they incur higher costs for delivery of services—tend to be more successful. Often, these programmes rely on strong and effective local government institutions to coordinate the implementation of multiple interventions.

The Government of Nepal has been actively carrying out decentralization since the early 1980s, but it has only been in the 1990s that these efforts have been successfully married to concerted efforts to build participatory institutions at the local level. The real breakthrough came in the early 1990s with the reinstatement of a multi-party system and the passage of a number of new governance laws. Consequently, local bodies have gained increased authority and responsibility and have been empowered to collect more taxes and strengthen their administrative capacities. District development committees were created and supported. Their role in the planning process became fundamental. Villagers are encouraged to join community organizations in order to identify their needs and the resources available primarily inside their villages, such as the savings mobilized by group schemes, but also from outside, such as from the district, the central government or external donors. As a result substantial funds were granted to village development committees. A Participatory District Development Programme has helped empower committees in 20 districts to undertake participatory planning processes and design district development plans, which have addressed pressing local needs such as job creation, women's empowerment, and environmental management. So far, the decentralization effort seems successful: during the fiscal year 1998/99, more than 60 percent of the district plans reviewed by the planning commission have been approved and funded.

Self organization in Yemen was shown to prepare the ground for effective decentralized governance. Yemen, newly united and still relatively poor, faced formidable challenges in the 1990s, including the need to continue uniting the north and south of the country, periodic internal military conflicts, the return of 800,000 workers owing to the 1991 Gulf War, and high population growth. Despite these problems, it has been moving aggressively ahead to address one of its major developmental challenges—poverty. Decentralized governance, with an increased role for civil society, is being considered as a means to target poverty.

Yemen has considerable experience with decentralized development, dating back to its local development associations of the late 1960s. These groups were able to mobilize most of their resources from local communities to build schools and health clinics. Regional development initiatives, piloted in five governorates, emphasize foster community self-reliance in addition to providing micro-credit or technical assistance. This involves thorough discussions with participants at the start of the project in order to mobilize their support for building organizations at three different levels: small micro-credit groups of three to five households, community associations of about a dozen micro-credit groups, and area development schemes formed by several community associations. Because the approach stresses the beneficiaries' self-organization, it can take considerable time to show results, but ultimately communities learn to take control of their own local development and come together on a large scale to influence decision-making at the regional level.

Yemen still has many challenges to meet if it is to make effective use of decentralized governance as a means to combat poverty and enhance human development. It is currently reviewing a decentralization law that will lay down a legal framework for strengthening local governments. It is looking for lessons from its pilot activities and is keenly aware of the financial responsibilities that need to be decentralized in order to reap the full developmental benefits of decentralized governance.

These examples point to the opportunities that decentralized governance makes available. They also show the complexity of the process and the inherent dangers if proper planning and implementation are not carried out.

The complex relationship between decentralized governance and human development

In addition to the above five examples, the following section describes the findings of an original research effort undertaken by the Management Development and Governance Division (MDGD) of the UNDP's Bureau for Development Policy (BDP). MDGD/BDP recently sponsored a series of case studies examining the impact of participation on local governance in nine developing countries. The research was conducted by national research institutions in Brazil, Honduras, India, Jordan, Pakistan, the Philippines, Poland, Uganda, and South Africa, with the assistance of the Massachusetts Institute of Technology (MIT). An outline for the research was agreed upon during a meeting of all the researchers in January 1998. The papers were required to introduce the national governance context of each of the countries being studied, describe the local success case, analyse the reasons for its success, and draw policy lessons. Although the national governance context and its implications were not sufficiently explored, the studies clearly pointed to a number of reasons behind success in decentralized governance at the local level. The following brief review of these studies reveals the importance of the challenge that developing countries will face as they become increasingly involved in initiating, promoting, and implementing decentralization programmes and initiatives.

The case studies ranged from simple forms of decentralization to more complex devolution of authority. They all involved some form of partnership that promoted participation. The national decentralization frameworks that guided most of the initiatives studied aim at addressing enhanced and more equitable service delivery. Some were sector-specific, while others were broader and more general. Table 14.3 summarizes the objectives, sectors, implementing agencies, and partnerships of the cases studied. (The nine cases and their synthesis are being published by UNDP in 2000; the cases can be found on the website <http://magnet.und.org/> under the decentralized governance programme.)

In the context of these studies and for the purposes of this chapter, five hypotheses are being put forward with regard to the factors that have contributed to the success of the cases. Each hypothesis is justified and evidence is introduced to demonstrate the relationship between the good governance principle being explored and the local success case.

1 Enabling environment

An enabling environment at the national level can promote and sustain decentralized governance. Proper government policies and institutional structures facilitate the effectiveness of decentralized governance in the delivery of services in favour of human development.

1	Laws are necessary but not sufficient
2	Decentralization and privatization of strategies are contingent on: (a) democratic organizational structures; (b) clear distribution of duties, obligations, and rights under a legitimate framework; (c) complementary and compatible interests, roles, rights, and obligations
3	Local leadership is critical
4	Civil society is essential
5	Outside involvement should be prudent
6	A whole system approach contributes to effective harmonizing of policy and practice among the multiple levels and can be used to reconcile different interests and priorities
7	Celebration of success helps sustain mobilization of resources and efforts

Figure 14.1 Decentralization and good governance

Table 14.3 Sustainable human development objectives in the case studies

Country	Sector	Objective	Implementing agency	Partners
Brazil	Municipal health	Enhanced access to basic health services	Local councils through municipal health councils	Ministry of health and local health services suppliers
Honduras	Municipal planning	Improved overall municipal planning	Local council and in particular the Mayor	The Central government
India	Local Panchayats	Improved service delivery	Local Panchayats	CBOs and the private sector
Jordan	Education	More effective management of education at the local level	District education directors and school principals	Ministry of Education
Pakistan	Squatter settlements normalization	Reduction in illegal squatting and improved conditions in squatter settlements	Specialized agency for squatter settlements	Central Government and the private sector
Philippines	Village health services	Enhanced access to local health services and reduced maternity risks	Local government	CBOs
Poland	Private partnerships	Enhanced municipal services to attract investments and job creation	Local government	Private sector and central government
Uganda	Privatization of market services	Improve market services	Local government	Private sector and a vendors' association
Uganda	Local tax collections	Enhanced local tax collection	Local government	Private sector
South Africa	Participatory budget preparation	Enhanced local tax collection	Local government	CBOs

Source: UNDP, 1999

Almost all of the cases had the benefit of an enabling environment. But that environment alone was not enough; neither was the source of the initiative that created or strengthened it the most important. Equally important were constitutional and legislative frameworks supported by central government policies, with clear objectives of the decentralization initiative. Some local initiatives were critical to the successful change they brought about. Many additional factors needed to be present for decentralization to be effective.

In all of the cases discussed, the improved performance occurred in at least partial response to efforts by some level of government to change the environment under which local governments and community groups worked. While in most cases the enabling environment emerged from broad policies and pronouncements at the central level, focus on a specific sector and local policies were key factors in bringing about the desired change. The Brazil case, for instance, focused on health, Pakistan on housing, Jordan on education, while in Honduras, India, and South Africa the effort was more general. For varying reasons decentralization brought about genuine devolved autonomy in cases such as Brazil, while in other cases, such as Jordan, the effort can more accurately be described as deconcentration.

While in Brazil a broader national decentralization initiative, embodied in constitutional and legal reform, was initiated at the central level, a proactive role for the local government of Belo Horizonte allowed it to register notable success in implementing the decentralization of basic health services through the Brazilian Unified Health System (SUS). By focusing its objective on widening access to basic health services through developing its own policies of transparent and inclusive partnerships, and by engaging in a serious dialogue with the central government, the local council of Belo Horizonte created the enabling environment it needed to reach its objectives.

By contrast, it was the central government's decision to decentralize some of the responsibilities for educational services that allowed Jordan's directors of education at the governorate level to take advantage of this enabling environment and strengthen the decision-making power of school principals. Enhanced access to basic education at the local level and more effective management of the education system is, in this case, a direct result of a central government initiative, albeit one of deconcentration and not devolution.

Broad decentralization reforms have been in the background for all of the other successful cases studied. In Honduras, national decentralization laws and reform programmes have been under way since 1990. India amended its constitution in 1994 to strengthen the role of municipal governments and created state-level finance commissions to develop rules and procedures for implementing the reforms. The Philippines has developed one of the most comprehensive decentralized government systems in Asia since the passage of the Local Government Code in 1991. Uganda also began a major decentralization initiative in 1993, greatly strengthened by the pro-decentralization 1995 constitution and the 1997 Local Government Act.

In order to support the decentralization process and enhance service delivery, many countries strengthen existing structures at the central and/or local levels or create new institutional mechanisms. In some cases, such as Brazil and South Africa, these mechanisms were essentially initiated at the national level. In other cases, such as Honduras and India, they emerged primarily from lower tiers. In some cases the mechanisms were highly formal, in others primarily consultative. In all cases, these mechanisms broadened the decision-making and/or managerial base, sometimes through community participation, at other times through even broader partnership coalitions.

In Sinuapa, Honduras, the case studied revealed a substantial increase in service delivery as a result of the creation of the innovative Municipal Development Council (CODEM) by the mayor. In a clear attempt to engender broader involvement in municipal decision-making and project implementation, Sinuapa's CODEM included members of NGOs, community-based organizations (CBOs), and the private sector. It also became an effective institution that played a direct and fundamental role in identifying priorities, contributing to the planning process, and getting involved in monitoring implementation, thereby substantially enhancing effective service delivery.

The innovation in the case of Pakistan is actually the reincarnation of an ineffective existing institution. The Sindh Katchi Abadis Authority (SKAA), a provincial government agency with a mandate to expedite the process of regularization and improvement of squatter settlements by granting squatters leases on the land they occupy, had been involved in an ineffective arrangement where the local government councils acted as implementing agencies to SKAA-funded activities. When SKAA realized that processing and approving squatter lease applications was too slow, it created a new arrangement whereby it took direct responsibility for the process, simplified procedures, and set up lease camps in the targeted settlements. By doing so, SKAA reduced costs significantly and dramatically improved the delivery of its service. It delivered the proper lease agreements and enhanced the living conditions of an increasingly satisfied settlement community.

Some type of institutional innovation was involved in the successful activities of most of the other cases studied. The municipalities in Jordan created a sector-specific body, the Committees of Educational Develop-

> 1 Decentralization can contribute to service delivery improvement and impact.
> 2 Centralized bureaucratic procedures are less likely to succeed in the delivery of local services at the neighborhood and settlement levels.
> 3 Local bureaucracy can be more effective/efficient than the central bureaucracy in service delivery.
> 4 Quality and quantity depend on interaction between stakeholders, especially local government and civil society.
> 5 Private sector generally has a positive role but must be integrated in a prudent manner.
> 6 System-wide synergy contributes to exceptional performance and achievement of results.

Figure 14.2 Service delivery and institutional structures

ment, which have played substantial roles in coordinating the different actors involved in planning, implementing, and evaluating the educational process. In Poland, there were a number of local institutional innovations, such as the Bilgoraj Regional Development Agency, which provides loan guarantees and helps to support fledgling businesses. The Uganda case involved the creation of a coordination mechanism to run a local market.

While the case studies are clearly focused on local successes, they are all examined against a background of national decentralization reform initiatives. Due to the specific focus on participation in the case studies, the full legal, financial, and administrative institutional and policy changes that provide the context for the studies are not examined in detail. But the good governance implications of these cases are well documented, and they are summarized in Table 14.4.

2 *Participation*

Decentralized governance is effectively strengthened and rendered more accountable when participation is encouraged, facilitated, and institutionalized. Communities, neighbourhoods, and individuals can play a crucial role in ensuring that local government responds to their needs by participating in the planning and implementation of activities and projects affecting their lives. This eventually affects the level of human development they maintain.

DECENTRALIZED GOVERNANCE FOR HUMAN DEVELOPMENT 283

Table 14.4 Good governance principles in the case studies

County	Sector	Participation	Partnership	Transparency	Equity
Brazil	Municipal health	Open community-level forums with management.	Some public, limited private good CBOs	Public reporting of expenditures	Improved delivery of affordable public services
Honduras	Municipal planning	Open participation of civil society at the municipal level	Partnership potential with all sectors	Public reporting and accountability is strong	Increased equity through local participation
India	Local Panchayats	Active public leadership in participative approach	Opportunity for partnerships is open	Public reporting and accountability is provided for	Equity only occurs where Panchayat leadership is exercised
Jordan	Education	The Local Parental Council and the Committees of Educational Development	Limited collaboration between public education and that offered by NGOs and private institutions	Funding is centrally controlled and allocated with limited expenditure authority at the local level.	Generally felt that remote and less fortunate areas are not prioritized
Pakistan	Squatter settlements normalization	Squatter settlement participation in planning, improving and managing their own services	Government in partnership with NGO Training Institute and squatter community CBO	Community plans and implements many of its own improvements	Leasing of public land to qualified squatter communities who chose to participate
Philippines	Village health services	Local village health committees planning, education and implementation	Local Government Units partnerships with local health committees	Committees focus on leveraging wise use of available resources	Primary health care in the hands of local people

continues

Table 14.4 continued

County	Sector	Participation	Partnership	Transparency	Equity
Poland	Municipal associations	Municipalities, represented by their mayors, negotiate agreements.	Municipalities' horizontal co-operation with central government vertical co-operation	Public reporting and accountability for use of funds	Same quality of service goes to all municipality members and the households in them
Poland	Private partnerships	Local participation in planning new services	Tax incentives, public investment, and spatial planning in partnership with private enterprise	Public accounting for revenues and expenditures	Increased tax revenues from new business applied to social services and housing for the poor
Uganda	Privatization of market services	Market vendors' association sub-committees open to 18,000 vendors	Partnership with government contracted management firm	Increased revenues reapplied to municipal services	Market services improved for the millions who use the market
South Africa	Participatory budget preparation	Community-based stakeholder participation	No partnership involved	Open participation in budget preparation	Aimed at through system of local tax collection

More effective participation of civil society and the private sector in local development processes that are managed by local governments is often cited as one of the more important reasons for success in decentralization initiatives. In all of the cases studied, participation has played a significant role. These range from consultation on education issues (Jordan) to involvement in decision-making (Brazil and Honduras) and actual implementation of community projects (India).

In the Honduras case, all the communities in the municipality of Sinuapa have organized neighbourhood associations. These coordinate their plans and activities among themselves and with municipal authorities through CODEM, the coordinating municipal-level body mentioned above. The communities, through their associations, directly submit proposals to CODEM for prioritization and financing. Plans submitted to CODEM are supported by communities not only through their involvement in decision-making, but also through the launching of specific projects. The distribution of municipal resources is based on these annual plans, which are discussed jointly between neighbourhood associations and CODEM.

The India case, involving the rural local government, Jamunia Tank Gram Panchayat, particularly focuses on community-level participation. In this case, efforts were made to involve local residents in a wide variety of activities from which they had formerly been excluded or in which

1 Participation is more efficient when institutionalized.
2 Civil society is essential.
3 Local authorities gain legitimacy and strength by involving civic participation and interaction between local government and population fosters mutual trust and culture of cooperation.
4 Role of local leadership is critical because a change agent—close to the people—helps in the introduction of new programmes.
5 Decentralization facilitates involvement of the community in decision-making.
6 Community organizing is an important preparatory step for participation.
7 Effective commitment to participation and organized movement bring positive results.
8 Participation of stakeholders facilitates holistic approach.

Figure 14.3 Participation

they had been only marginally involved. In the building of low-cost latrines, for example, residents were involved in site selection, in the preparation of a list of beneficiaries that consciously included as many people as possible, and in estimating the actual cost of the latrines. This resulted in cost savings and delivery of a service that was community-owned, better maintained, and suited to local needs.

Other instances of community participation included both labour and financial contributions by residents to the construction of a village drainage system, raising funds within the community for a teacher's salary, volunteering to teach illiterate adults, and organizing a house-to-house campaign to encourage women to attend literacy classes. The active involvement of the community in the planning and development of village projects has developed a sense of unity among those involved, strengthened their capacity and skills in negotiating with higher levels of authority, and increased their confidence in managing local affairs.

The Philippines local government cases, where civil society is very strong, are also impressive cases of local participation. For example, the Balilihan Country Action Program (BCAP) used *puroks* (neighbourhood associations) extensively. The BCAP has encompassed seven sectoral concerns: health and sanitation, agricultural development, education, livelihood and environmental protection, peace and order, infrastructure, and youth and sports development. The BCAP has also supported income-generating projects, such as livestock dispersal, with interest-free loans provided by the municipal government. Neighbourhood volunteers have worked in each of the seven sectoral programmes. Prominent members of the community have donated small plots of land for neighbourhood kiosks, which are used as feeding centres for malnourished children in the neighbourhoods as well as for keeping neighbourhood records, statistics, and maps, and as places where the neighbourhood associations meet.

Local participation is a nascent concept in Poland, but it is emerging as an increasingly important factor. Participation has taken different forms and the degree of citizens' involvement has varied across the various municipalities. The municipality of Tarnovo, for instance, formed citizen committees, which have played an important role in the financing and implementation of municipal infrastructure projects. Local residents have provided substantial financial contributions to a host of investment projects, including gas lines (41 percent), development of the telephone network (77 percent), and water supply systems (48 percent). The municipal budget and subsidies from the central government covered the balance of the investment requirements. In Bilgoraj, about ten voluntary local committees are involved in the development of infrastructure, including water supply and sewerage systems, street lighting, and road construction.

Community participation was an integral part of the local decentralization innovations in all of the other countries. In the Brazil case, some community participation was inherent in Belo Horizonte's use of the health care committees discussed earlier, and community activism was encouraged by the committees. In both cases in Jordan, there was some level of local participation in the educational development committees. SKAA in Pakistan delegated selected decision-making authority to the community, and the community monitors the work of contractors. In the case of Jinja in Uganda, the market vendors' association was a major player in the partnership examined below, and they encouraged participation in making decisions about the market.

3 Partnerships

Forging equitable and mutually beneficial partnerships at the local level can strengthen decentralized governance and can increase the potential resources available to local government, which can then be put at the service of human development.

Many of the institutional and participatory reforms discussed above have involved some degree of broadening of the set of actors involved in service planning, financing, and/or delivery. In a few cases, various types of partnership, often between the public and private sectors, are seen as a key element of good performance. Some of these partnerships are informal arrangements that mutually benefit the partners, while others are partnerships that are formalized through contractual and legal arrangements. It is the basic principle of equity that makes partnerships effective. The characteristics that make partnerships effective include a clear role for each of the partners, well-established accountability mechanisms, absence of a patronizing attitude from the stronger partner, and effective mechanisms for conflict resolution when needed.

Jordan's educational system reforms in Ma'n and Irbid involved a three-way dynamic interaction of institutional actors at central and local levels. The Ministry of Education played a vital role in implementing a more decentralized process of decision-making and capacity-building through delegation of authority, upgrading of the performance of the Ministry staff, curriculum modernization, and interactions with the local community. Local parent councils and Committees of Educational Development have substantial roles in organizing citizens' participation in planning, implementing, and evaluating the educational process. Moreover, the involvement of several parties in providing complementary and supplementary educational services has also been crucial to the successful decentralization of the sector. These parties include the private sector, which has provided high-quality services, and NGOs, which have provided educational services to the poor and to individuals with special needs. Other civic and religious organizations, including churches, mosques, and the UNRWA, have also participated in the provision of educational services. This large number of partners involved in a range of formal and informal partnerships makes managing the process and the partners quite a challenge, bringing to light the importance of equity in partnerships.

Among the cases studied, the Jinja market in Uganda is both the most innovative and most formal of the partnerships observed. When the Jinja Central Market was under the control of the Jinja municipality, it was managed and administered through the municipal departments of public health, law enforcement, and the treasury. Poor and inefficient revenue collection, high recurrent expenditures, unsanitary conditions, and poor security plagued the market at that time. The relationship between vendors and local authorities was often acrimonious: municipal authorities were taxed highly without maintaining the market, while vendors were permanently in arrears on payment.

With the passage of a decentralization act in 1993, the Jinja Central Division (JCD) took over the administration of the Jinja Central Market. JCD then decided to transfer the responsibility for revenue collection from local authorities to a private entity. GOKAS, a private management firm, was selected through competitive bidding by a tendering board consisting of members of the local council and the community. The resulting arrangement emphasizes co-management of the market by a broader coalition of stakeholders, including the municipality, JCD, GOKAS, and the vendors through their vendors' association. Under this arrangement, delineation of responsibilities was clearly specified from the outset. The municipality sets service delivery standards, while JCD is responsible for ensuring that revenues (which have greatly increased) are collected and that selected services, such as garbage removal, are provided. GOKAS manages the collection of dues and provides and maintains key services, including water, electricity, and sanitation. Finally, the vendors are responsible for security in the market premises and settlement of inter-vendor disputes.

Some elements of partnership have been important in most of the other countries under review. The Belo Horizonte case involved both public and private health care providers, although there have been some conflicts, as well as complementary roles for the municipal, state, and central governments. SKAA in Pakistan collaborates with NGOs and local private contractors in various ways, as noted above, most notably with the Orangi Pilot Project NGO. The Philippines cases also involved strong partnerships between NGOs and formal government structures.

4 Initiative and leadership

The initiative and leadership of local actors, including local government leaders as well as civil society leaders or private-sector actors can be a determinant catalyst that can transform communities and bring about the necessary change to render decentralized governance more effective and better oriented toward human development.

Most of the cases studied were successful because of the initiative taken by some person or group willing to do things differently. The enabling environment discussed earlier is clearly important, but unless some strategically placed actor is willing to take the initiative to implement new possibilities creatively, there is no guarantee that the provisions of new laws and regulations will be implemented. Such initiative may come from the centre, but in many of the cases studied it came from a local actor such as a mayor or an NGO.

In the case of Honduras, the role of the mayor of Sinuapa as a consensus-builder between communities and the local government and as a mediator with departmental, national, or international assistance bodies has been an important element. A previous mayor initiated open council meetings to consult with both urban communities and rural villages and to help them identify problems and to establish priorities for the council work plan. When funding for these proposals was not available at the local level, the mayor diligently sought external funding from international agencies and the central government. The new mayor, a member of the CODEM and of the same party as the previous mayor, is continuing and expanding the process of consultations.

In the Indian case, a relatively informal coalition of local actors, led by a dynamic local NGO, put pressure on the Department of Public Health

---

1. Role of local leadership is critical.
2. Celebration of success helps sustain mobilization of resources and efforts.
3. NGOs/CBOs should guide and not substitute the community.
4. In some instances advocacy that targets the local leadesrhip and citizens can lead to effective participation.
5. A change agent—close to the people—helps in the introduction of new programmes.

Figure 14.4 Initiative and leadership

and Engineering (PHE) to improve the performance of local projects. These collective efforts among villagers, the Sarpanch, and the NGO compelled PHE officials to inspect the project and, subsequently, to initiate a dialogue among the contractor, villagers, and officials. The villagers demanded suspension of a partial payment to the contractor to ensure that remedial measures on the inferior work would be provided. The Sarpanch utilized this opportunity to leverage additional benefits for the community by demanding that the PHE officials install a hand pump in the village.

In the case of the Philippines, NGOs and community groups have taken the critical initiative to bring about the successful reforms in service provision. The implementation of primary health care (PHC) service delivery in Surigao City through women's clubs was initiated by a motivated midwife from the city's health office. The midwife, along with Barangay health workers, organized mothers in neighbourhoods and trained them in nutrition education, responsible parenthood, and sanitation. This enabled them to assist in the delivery of PHC services, including immunization, family planning, nutrition education, the national tuberculosis programme, and an anti-diarrhoea project. The PHC has also been running a weekly programme to promote health awareness, and the women's clubs have collaborated with a programme formed by their husbands and various youth groups. The primary health care project in Irosin was initiated by an NGO called LIKAS (*Likas para sa Kalusugan ng Sambayanan,* or Caring for the Health of the People), and in Balilihan the mayor initiated the effort.

Leadership has also been cited as important in most of the other cases under review. In Brazil, community leaders worked together to ensure that the new health committee system would work properly in Belo Horizonte. The reform-minded Minister of Education in Jordan pushed forward with some decentralization efforts that were radical in the context of that country. In Pakistan, there was a change in leadership of SKAA. The new director-general was heavily influenced by the Orangi pilot project, an internationally known shelter innovation in Karachi, and he was further motivated by the cessation of funds from the provincial government. Enlightened and energetic local leadership is portrayed as extremely important in all of the successful municipalities in Poland.

Thus, some catalyst—in the form of strong leadership, NGO initiative, a crisis that threatens the viability of the local institution—is often a critically important factor in stimulating successful reform. It is important to keep in mind, however, that decentralization policy-makers and practitioners should be concerned less with the catalysts themselves and more with the replicable actions that the catalysts took to bring about productive change.

5 Operationalizing reforms: Routine procedures, finance, and capacity-building

Innovation and change in routine procedures, focus on capacity, and sufficient financial resources are essential for building more effective decentralized governance.

In addition to the enabling environment, an adequate level of resources is often cited as an important factor for successful decentralization. This includes transfers from the central government and locally raised resources. The case studies address the issue of financing as a background to the participation theme and show how participation strengthens local government's capacity and resolve to secure higher levels of resources. They also show the important role that local participation can have in curtailing expenditures as a result of close vigilance and cost savings through volunteerism.

Capacity-building is also shown to play an important role. The most interesting form of capacity-building is shown, in these cases, to be that of enhancing the capabilities of the local population to play its participatory role effectively and thereby to enforce strong accountability requirements. Local governments responded to these requirements by becoming more innovative and more effective in service delivery, and also by becoming more transparent and by promoting and supporting new types of partnership with NGOs, CBOs, and the private sector. These partnerships often needed to be guided by clear principles to work equitably and effectively. This process of widening participation in decision-making has rendered these local governments more credible.

Not all of the case studies under consideration here deal in detail with the mechanics underlying the decentralization reform process. It is clear from most of them, however, that the development of effective routine procedures, adequate sources of finance, and appropriate capacity-building programmes is important in order to operationalize and sustain the benefits of decentralization initiatives. Some of these have arisen already, but this section provides a brief integrated summary of some of the key points.

Most of the cases involved innovations in routine operating procedures that brought in new actors, increased transparency, and created incentives for better performance, in some cases simplifying complex bureaucratic procedures. In the Brazil, Jordan, and Philippines cases, standards for sector-specific services were developed and new ways of delivery experimented with. Procedural innovations were also made in the multi-sector approaches undertaken in Honduras and India. SKAA in Pakistan completely changed the way it approached its core business of squatter upgrading, allowing bureaucrats more flexibility in the ways they met their responsibilities. The Polish municipalities changed their procedures and mechanisms for developing infrastructure and interacting with the private sector, and the South African local government developed new mechanisms and incentives to improve revenue collection. The Uganda case focused on the innovative partnership arrangement for managing the Jinja market, but the procedures developed to implement and sustain this arrangement were equally important.

The majority of the cases also involved innovations in financing that brought either new resources from higher levels or cost-sharing among various partners. Service-specific decentralization in Brazil and Jordan brought both new resources and cost-sharing among partners. In Honduras and India, local resource mobilization was enhanced and additional resources from higher levels of government were tapped. SKAA in Pakistan was forced to raise revenue from its activities and to become financially independent when the resources provided by the central government were cut. The primary health care innovations in the Philippines have been financed from various sources, including the municipality's share of the internal revenue, appropriations from sectoral departments, contributions from neighbourhood members, and revenues from income-generating projects. The Polish cases all involved substantial local cost recovery and mobilization of capital from the private sector. In South Africa, local communities dramatically increased contributions to finance local service delivery. Finally, in Uganda, the partnership approach to managing the Jinja market led to substantial increases in market fee yields.

In all of the cases examined here, there has been some type of technical assistance, training, and/or capacity-building on the demand side and sometimes on the supply side. In the Brazil case, educational programmes were developed to stimulate community interest and participation in the health service reforms. Similar efforts were also required in the Honduras and India cases to ensure fuller involvement of residents unaccustomed to—or uninterested in—working closely with the local governments. The Orangi Pilot Project was heavily involved in training in the SKAA case in Pakistan, and NGOs were also key players in community awareness-raising activities, as well as managerial and leadership training in the Philippines cases. In Ivory Park in South Africa, the local authority made substantial efforts to inform and communicate with citizens, and there were also educational campaigns financed by the central government.

Conclusion and summary of the main lessons

While the global trends clearly show that more and more countries are opting to decentralize services, responsibilities, decision-making, and resources to the local level, more empirical evidence is required to elucidate exactly what makes decentralization work and why. The implications of such trends on national governance systems are still to be explored, but the Indian example of 3 million elected local government councillors points to a trend of expanding democratic space with rising developmental opportunities and challenges. Other examples show that a gradual approach is preferred by some countries.

The case studies sponsored by MDGD focused on local governance and did not sufficiently explore the linkages with and implications on the national governance systems. The principles of good governance briefly described above guided most of the case studies. When viewed in conjunction with the sector-specific and more general objectives of each of the decentralization initiatives that serve as background to the cases, it becomes obvious that the relationship between human development and good governance at the local level is indeed very complex.

Addressing health, education, sustainable livelihood, and job creations, as well as a myriad of other developmental goods of the human development type while maintaining good governance principles at the local level is a challenge to be kept in mind by governments that are now involved in, or are considering, decentralization as a means to achieve sustainable human development objectives. Indeed, this is one of the reasons why sometimes the term "decentralized governance" is preferred over "decentralization." The latter implies a one-way action undertaken by the entity that is decentralizing, while the former implies governance at the local level, including that which is decentralized from and that which is generated locally. Decentralized governance also implies the application of the good governance principles mentioned above.

While the linkages between national governance and local governance systems and their mutual influences will continue to be studied and documented, the following lessons can be drawn with regard to local successes in decentralized governance:

1 The broader enabling environment for decentralization, including government policies and attitudes about local governments, is typically important for reform, but the degree of significance varies.
2 Carefully crafted new institutional structures that go beyond the common "business-as-usual" approach and alleviate the resistance of existing institutions to change can play an important role in supporting decentralization.

3 Enhanced community and neighbourhood participation, if appropriately structured and implemented, is often crucial in improving successful local government activities.
4 Appropriately designed partnerships among different interested parties can lead to major improvements in the way local governments do business.
5 Decentralization is normally thought of as a central government undertaking, but motivated actors from various levels of government and society can play a crucial role in initiating and/or energizing decentralization and local government reforms.
6 Decentralization reform programmes need to integrate key components of local governance and service delivery systems rather than focus on single dimensions.
7 Certain vital support components are required to operationalize and sustain decentralization reforms. Basic operating procedures consistent with the objectives of reforms are required. This often involves simplifying and consolidating status-quo bureaucratic procedures, improving their transparency, allowing greater flexibility, and developing incentives for good performance. Although access to funds is no guarantee of good performance, mobilizing adequate sources of revenue is another key concern. This often involves some sort of partnership among levels of government, NGOs, and/or private firms, and a degree of local contribution seems to "connect" people to local activities. Finally, it is necessary to provide appropriate technical assistance, training, capacity-building, and information. This refers not only to the supply side—that is, making local providers more technically proficient in performing their functions through training and standards—but also cultivation of the demand side. In situations where democracy is evolving and people are not used to expecting much from local governments, higher levels of government and NGOs may have to educate local people about their rights and responsibilities as local government constituents.
8 Decentralization is often seen as a goal or an output but, in fact, successful decentralization is a process—of gradually and strategically building capacity and trust.
9 Decentralization can help to achieve Sustainable Human Development (SHD) goals, but this is a long-term process.
10 All the actors involved in decentralization—from communities to local governments to central governments to international donors—can learn from experiences to date.

The cases considered here provide some lessons that can be used to improve performance in the future. Central governments need to understand the potential importance of setting a national climate conducive to good governance and of supporting lower levels of government and civil society as they move forward with reform. Local governments must realize that they can independently take some important actions to improve governance and local government performance—they do not have to stand by idly until the centre moves forward. NGOs and citizens should see that they need not wait for the public sector to act—there may be steps they can take to pressure the government to move forward with reforms. All actors should recognize that they must work together in creative and mutually supportive ways to make local governments more effective.

Further reading

Al-Kayed, Zuhair, Mohammed Ta'amneh, Awni Halseh, and Mutaz Assaf, 1999. *Extending educational access through deconcentration of services in Jordan*. Amman: Jordan Institute of Public Administration (JPA) and UNDP.

Avila, Oscar, and Leticia Salomon, 1999. *Decentralization and citizen participation in Honduras*. Tegucigalpa: Centro de Documentación de Honduras (CEDOH) and UNDP.

Birungi, Harriet, Betty Kwagala, Nansozi Muwanga, Tobias Onweng, and Eirik Jarl Trondsen, 1999. *What makes markets tick? Local service delivery in Uganda*. Kampala: Makerere Institute of Social Research and UNDP.

Cheema, G. Shabbir, and Dennis Rondinelli, 1983. *Decentralization and Development*. Sage Publications.

Datta, Chandann, 1999. *Facilitating local participation in rural Panchayats in India*. New Delhi: Society for Participatory Research in Asia and UNDP

Ghaus-Pasha, Aisha, 1999. *Squatter settlement transformation through decentralized participation in Pakistan*. Karachi: Social Policy Development Centre and UNDP

Gorzelak, Grzegorz, Richard Woodward, Bohdan Jalowiecki, Wojciech Dziemianowicz, Wojciech Roszkowski, and Tomasz Zarcycki, 1999. Releasing local private enterprise through municipal strategies in Poland. Warsaw: University of Warsaw, Centre for Social and Economic Research (CASE), European Institute for Regional and Local Development and UNDP.

Humphries, Richard, Steven Friedman, Paul Thulare, and Tebogo Mafakoana, 1999. *Decentralizing services delivery through participation in South Africa*. Johannesburg: Centre for Policy Studies and UNDP.

Somarriba, Mercês, Edite Novais da Mata Machado, and Telma Maria Concalves Menicucci, 1999. *Universalising health care access through popular participation in Brazil*. Belo Horizonte: Governance School of Minas Gerais and UNDP

Tapales, Proserpina Domingo, 1999. *Expanding basic health service delivery through partnerships with the of the people in the Philippines*. Quezon City: Local Government Centre, University of the Philippines and UNDP.

UNDP, 1993. *The Human Development Report 1993*. New York: UNDP.

UNDP, 1996. Human Development Report 1996. New York: UNDP.

World Bank, 1999. *World Development Report 1999/2000*. Washington, DC: World Bank.

15

Governing global public goods in a multi-actor world: The role of the United Nations

Inge Kaul

There is considerable debate today about "managing globalization." At times, the discussion is heated and tumultuous, as we saw in Seattle at the 1999 meeting of the World Trade Organization. Yet even there, consensus began to emerge. It was recognized that fairness must be an ingredient of a viable free trade system. The Asian financial crisis of the late 1990s led to a similar conclusion. It helped strengthen political support for a more equitable burden-sharing of the costs of crises among borrowers and lenders. More than that, the crisis probably persuaded even the remaining sceptics that in order to function efficiently, markets need to be institutionally embedded. They need property rights, rule of law, norms—in short, a certain amount of predictability to minimize risks that cannot be priced. Hence, added stress is now being placed on such policy measures as proper banking regulation and supervision. It is increasingly seen as inefficient—and unfair—for the costs of lax regulation in one country to be borne by others. The same view is being taken on pollution spillovers, on the careless handling of outbreaks of contagious diseases, and on allowing human deprivation, such as poverty or human rights violations, to push streams of asylum-seekers and illegal migrants across borders. It is increasingly being realized that growing inequity—economic, social, and cultural—can also entail significant negative externalities. Large gaps in income and wealth can contribute to frustration and despair that may translate into terrorism, crime, and violence, seriously straining the global political fabric.

All this constitutes a call for greater balance between "private" and "public"—between the activities of private actors, whether individual states, corporations, or individuals and their local communities, and the public, the *other* states, corporations, people, and communities. It is a call for individual actors to assume more responsibility for the consequences of their actions, notably the negative consequences and those actions from which others will suffer. It is a call for an enhanced provision of global public goods.

This chapter examines the role of the United Nations in ensuring an enhanced provision of global public goods (GPGs). The chapter is organized in three main parts. The first section takes a more detailed look at today's major policy concerns through the lens of global public goods. The second section examines some of the challenges involved in providing GPGs. And, against this background, the third section explores how the United Nations could help the international community to better manage—and govern—the provision of GPGs. It outlines six policy options to strengthen the United Nations' role for this purpose.

The overall conclusion is that there is an urgent need for a custodian of GPG concerns. Today, GPG concerns are typically addressed one by one, and often managed in a technocratic way, by representatives of the executive branches of government and other sector specialists. Political governance of global issues and balances is sorely lacking. The United Nations could help fill that vacuum. However, in order to do so it would have to undergo a major transformation. It would have to turn from an intergovernmental technocratic organization into an intergovernmental parliamentary body.

Today's policy concern, seen through the lens of global public goods

Definitions

How do we define public goods in general, and GPGs in particular?[1] Public goods are best understood by looking at their counterpart, private goods. Private goods are typically traded in markets. Buyers and sellers meet through the price mechanism. If they agree on a price, the ownership or use of the good (or service) can be transferred. Thus, private goods tend to be excludable. They have clearly identified owners, and they tend to be rival. For example, others cannot enjoy a piece of cake, once it has been consumed.

Public goods have just the opposite qualities. They are non-excludable and non-rival in consumption. An example is a street sign. It will not wear out, even if large numbers of people are looking at it; and it would be extremely difficult, costly, and highly inefficient to limit its use to only one or a few persons, and to try to prevent others from looking at it too. A traffic light or clean air are further examples.

This poses immediately the question of who provides public goods. Once they exist, they are there for all to enjoy. So, for private actors, it is often the most rational strategy to let others work to provide public goods, and then seek to enjoy these goods without contributing to their production. This is, indeed, a dilemma that public goods face. Without some sort of collective-action mechanism they risk being under-provided. Conversely, without collective action, public "bads"—such as pollution, noise, risky bank lending, and so on—would be over-provided.

Global public goods are public goods whose benefits reach across borders, generations, and population groups. They form part of the broader group of international public goods which include, as another subgroup, regional public goods.

To make the notion of a global public good more concrete, consider, for example, the eradication of smallpox. Once accomplished, the whole of humanity benefits—people in all parts of the globe, present and future generations, rich and poor. Similarly, if the international community were to succeed in ensuring peace, everyone would be able to enjoy it. Much the same holds true for well-functioning international markets. And averting the risk of global climate change would secure intergenerational as well as geographically widespread benefits, although people in various parts of the world might benefit in different ways. Similarly, international regimes such as those for civil aviation, postal services, and telecommunications, or those recognizing a document such as a passport, all have significant properties of "global publicness."

Traditional global public goods

Global public goods are nothing new. The natural commons, such as the atmosphere, the ozone shield, and the high seas, predate even human activity. And agreements, such as those on the free access of nations to the high seas, date back to the seventeenth century. They began to proliferate as international economic activity intensified in the nineteenth and early twentieth centuries—shipping, telecommunication, civil aviation, and the delivery of mail. If they are multilateral in nature and global in scope, these agreements themselves have a global-public-good character. They establish international orders, rules, and regulations, whose benefits, once they exist, tend to be available to all.

This traditional class of GPG includes two types of issues: matters that are external to countries, such as the natural commons, and relations between countries, so-called "at-the-border" issues such as trade tariffs, capital controls, and military security. Together, these two types of traditional GPG constitute what are conventionally known as "foreign affairs." They continue to be important, probably more so than ever before, because international economic activity is growing and new challenges, such as the internet, are arising.

A new class of global public goods

Yet, the global challenges that figure most prominently on today's policy agendas represent a new, quite different class of global public goods. They are not "over there"; they cut across borders and call for behind-the-border policy convergence, increasing harmonization of national public policy. They concern public goods—such as clean air, health, financial stability, market efficiency, and knowledge management—which can no longer be produced through domestic action alone, or goods—such as human rights and equity—which can no longer be under-provided behind the shield of national borders. Put differently, they concern global policy outcomes that require joint, cross-border policy harmonization and actual change on the ground, not just agreements.

Several factors are behind this new type of global public goods. Among them is the increasing openness of countries, which facilitates the spread of global "bads" such as "social dumping," competitive devaluation, and risky consumer behaviour (such as cigarette smoking). Another is the growing number of global systemic risks, which require more respect for thresholds of sustainability, such as volatility risks inherent in international financial markets, the risk of global climate change, or the political risks arising from explosive global inequity. A third factor is the growing strength of non-state actors, such as the private sector, civil society, and notably, transnational corporations. Both these actor groups have stepped up the pressure on governments to adhere to common policy norms, from basic human rights to technical standards.

It may be useful to examine more closely the link between this new class of GPGs, which we call here "global policy outcomes," and the natural human-made commons, identified in table 15.1.

The global natural commons (the first category listed in table 15.1) have for a long time been perceived as "free" goods, until it became clear that many of them suffer from serious overuse. This brought the issue of environmental sustainability on to the international policy agenda. Environmental sustainability now figures among the global policy outcomes to be achieved. Put differently, we are not concerned about the natural global commons as such, but about making their use sustainable.

Table 15.1 Global concerns as global public goods: A selective typology

Class and type of global good	Benefits		Nature of the supply or use problem	Corresponding global bad
	Nonexcludable[1]	Nonrival[2]		
1. Natural global commons				
Ozone layer	Yes	No	Overuse	Depletion and increased radiation
Atmosphere (climate)	Yes	No	Overuse	Risk of global warming
2. Human-made global commons				
Universal norms and principles (such as universal human rights)	Partly	Yes	Underuse (repression)	Human abuse and injury
Knowledge	Partly	Yes	Underuse (lack of access)	Inequality
Internet (infrastructure)	Partly	Yes	Underuse (entry barriers)	Exclusion and disparity (between information rich and information poor)
3. Global conditions				
Peace	Yes	Yes	Undersupply	War and conflict
Health	Yes	Yes	Undersupply	Disease
Financial stability	Partly	Yes	Undersupply	Financial crisis
Free trade	Partly	Yes	Undersupply	Fragmented markets
Freedom from poverty[3]	No	No	Undersupply	Civil strife, crime and violence
Environmental sustainability[3]	Yes	Yes	Undersupply	Unbalanced ecosystems
Equity and justice[3]	Partly	Yes	Undersupply	Social tensions and conflict

Source: Inge Kaul, "Global public goods: Concepts, policies and strategies," in Inge Kaul, Isabelle Grunberg, and Marc A. Stern (eds.), *Global Public Goods: International Cooperation in the 21st Century* (New York: Oxford University Press, 1999).

Note: This typology includes primarily issues that are the subject of the case studies in this volume. In addition, it refers only to final global public goods and bads, not to intermediate ones such as global regimes and institutions.

[1] Here, non-excludable means that it is difficult for anyone to avoid bearing the costs of the bad.
[2] Here, non-rival means that one person's being affected by a bad—such as a disease—does not reduce the extent to which others are affected.
[3] The demand for these goods emerges to the extent that the overuse of natural global commons or the underuse of human-made global commons assumes alarming proportions.

A similar point can be made in respect of the human-made global commons. As indicated in table 15.1, their provision problem is just the opposite; that is, under-use. Certainly, these GPGs interest us in some ways in their own right; otherwise they would probably not have been created. Yet, they also figure on the international agenda, because in some countries these GPGs, such as universal human rights, are still so seriously underused or curtailed that the resultant ill effects spill across borders, in the form of political conflict, intolerable genocide, shameful poverty, illegal migration, and so on. Thus, the human-made commons turns back into a policy concern that needs active management—they slip into the third category of GPGs shown in the table, the new class of GPGs. In a way, this fact tells us that some human-made commons, such as some of the universal human rights, are not yet truly commons. Those that are, such as the ban on slavery, have a clearer external, "untouchable" quality. They form a firm part of our normative environment.

Clearly, the new class of GPGs is often not just additional to the more traditional ones. It also poses more complex management challenges. In addition to agreements between countries, these GPGs require concrete developmental change at the national level; and often not just change that governments are primarily responsible for, but change that also involves the public at large.

Most of these changes have been in the making for decades. Maybe we have been so preoccupied with the globalization of private activity and market forces that the basically quite obvious need for a matching globalization of public goods has escaped our attention. Also, it has been only recently that the accumulating effects of the current under-provision of these goods has made itself felt more acutely. But now that policy analysts, political leaders, and the general public are becoming more aware of this new class of global public goods, what do we know about the process of producing them? And what could be the United Nations' role in ensuring an enhanced provision of GPGs, notably that of the new type of GPGs?

Providing global public goods: Some of the challenges involved

The "standard" collective-action problems

Most public goods, whether the scope of their benefits—or costs—is local, national, regional, or global, tend to have provision problems. Public goods tend to suffer from under-supply if there is no collective-action mechanism. The reason is their publicness: the fact that, once they exist, they are available for all. So, it is often the best and most rational strategy for individual actors to let others step forward and make the effort; and when the good exists, simply to enjoy it, free of charge. This problem is known as "free-riding." But the need for collective action that many public goods pose also gives rise to other problems, such as the "prisoner's dilemma," which stems from information problems and uncertainty.

At the national level, the state is often brought in to help individual, private actors to overcome such collective-action problems—through the promulgation of laws, the setting of standards and taxation, or the direct provision of certain goods and services. Internationally, nation states tend to behave like private actors: they pursue their own respective national (private) self-interest. But as the mounting volume of international agreements demonstrates, international cooperation can nevertheless succeed. Collective-action problems among states have been thoroughly investigated and, by now, we know quite well the factors that foster international cooperation. Among them are, for example: certainty—about the nature of the problem and possible solutions; good economics—clear net benefits; fairness—if not in the short term, then at least, in the medium and longer term; credible agreements—clear "carrots and sticks" for compliance and non-compliance, and so on.[2]

These considerations also promote international cooperation around the new type of GPGs. But the new class of goods also raises new issues.

Additional public policy challenges

Many of the new GPGs do not fit well into the existing system of public policy-making. They suffer from three key weaknesses, or gaps.

The jurisdictional gap

This gap refers to the discrepancy between the global nature of today's major policy challenges and the still predominantly national scope and focus of policy-making. There are several dimensions to this problem. One is that in many, if not most, countries, there still exists a rather sharp divide between "domestic" and "foreign" affairs.[3] Foreign affairs is being treated like a separate sector, typically consisting of external political relations with other countries and some trade and defence matters. Moreover, foreign affairs is typically handled by the executive branch of government, notably the conventional diplomatic corps. Their focus is often on defence, keeping problems out of the country and safeguarding external security, or on promoting national interests in a competitive way.

Increasingly, foreign embassies are also staffed with representatives of other sector ministries, covering issues such as the environment, human rights, finance, drugs, or terrorism. That change reflects a first adjustment to the new GPGs. It may help to bring a stronger sense of interdependence into international relations; but it does not change the predominantly technocratic management of international relations.

Another dimension of the jurisdictional gap is that parliamentarians, the legislative branch of government, are conspicuously absent from international negotiations and cooperation.[4] They often come into contact with international agreements only when these agreements have been finalized and need to be translated into national law. Agreements that have no treaty character may not be seen at all by parliamentarians. And, if parliamentarians join national delegations to international meetings, they participate more as observers than as full members. As a result, they have little involvement in international affairs, and the focus of their work is essentially domestic. Also, one cannot take it for granted that in pursuing domestic concerns policy-makers will always consider the possible externalities—cross-border spillovers—of national actions. That practice is still rare. At best, it exists to some degree in the environment area.

As a result, the systematic combination of national and international action that today's major policy issues require often does not occur. While many GPGs require a bottom-up provision process, the control of the corresponding bads can often be carried out in a top-down manner, at the international level. Take the example of financial crises; to build financial stability, many countries would have to change and create requisite national capacity. Achieving this goal is complex and time-consuming. Putting in place an international bail-out arrangement can be done more easily. The same applies to reducing poverty, which cannot simply be done "overnight," and may, in addition, sometimes face political opposition in the country in which it exists, or lack political support in possible donor countries. Tighter border controls to protect a richer nation against some of the unwanted effects of illegal immigration or other consequences of the persistence of poverty will often be a more plausible solution—albeit not necessarily an effective or efficient one.[5]

Similarly, while there is constant talk about budgetary constraints, governments always seem to find the resources to address the effects of crises—financial, environmental, social, political, and military.

Hence, we find at present a certain preoccupation with controlling bads. Some reasons for this are understandable. Compared to the provision of goods, controlling bads is often a more evident and, in terms of time and resources, more limited activity. But the control of bads often does not lead us towards the desired goods. For example, providing a financial rescue package to a country may not necessarily help in enhancing its banking regulations and supervision or improving its accountancy practices. Or, trying to assist rising numbers of unemployed may not necessarily do much for stimulating the world economy and restoring global growth.

National coping strategies or international emergency arrangements are important and necessary, but not sufficient for remedying the current under-provision of so many GPGs.

The participation and incentive gaps

As we saw before, the provision of GPGs is often a multi-actor process. Because of their legislative powers, governments often come into play. But many goods depend on contributions from all actors. Many, such as the issue of a stable global climate, even concern future generations.

Yet, international cooperation is still primarily an intergovernmental process. Other actors, notably civil-society organizations (CSOs), are trying hard to come into the process. This participation gap also affects other actors. Developing countries are often underrepresented in international gatherings. And so, of course, are the voices of future generations.

The result is that the international policy agenda often reflects only the concerns of the more strongly represented actors, and ignores those of the poor and other marginalized groups. The fact that the benefits of certain goods are public does not necessarily mean that all actors value them equally. The priority they attach to certain goods, private and public, may vary, depending on their specific living conditions—stage of development, socio-cultural and political context, and so on.

And although goods are public, and hence non-excludable, they may not be accessible for all. This may sound paradoxical. But consider, for example, the internet. It has strong qualities of a GPG. Yet, poor people may not be able to afford a computer or the fee for the internet service provider. Or, malaria may not be a top concern for rich people in northern, industrial countries, but it is for many people in developing countries; and a malaria-free world would be a GPG.

The meeting of the World Trade Organization in Seattle in late 1999 provided another important lesson. A multilateral free trade regime qualifies as a GPG. But free trade in a highly unequal world may re-inforce inequality and lead to "winner-take-all" situations. Because of the intergovernmental, technocratic, and "exclusive" nature of trade negotiations, it took this issue a long time to enter the debate fully. And, in Seattle, it was finally heard, because of massive CSO rallies and street demonstrations.[6] All of this demonstrates that lack of participation can distort political agendas, weaken the legitimacy of forums and seriously impede collective action.

Lack of adequate opportunities and mechanisms for participation is itself a disincentive to participate, and is therefore closely linked to the third public policy weakness to be examined here, the incentive gap.

International cooperation today is broader in scope than the cooperation required by traditional GPGs. As noted above, it has moved from between-country and at-the-border issues to issues of behind-the-border policy convergence and joint production of actual developmental change. This makes the operational (implementation) side of international agreements more important. And, because of the systemic risks we are facing, international cooperation also calls for attention to clearly defined targets (e.g., pollution limits) and dates.

Yet, the implementation of international agreements all too often relies, still, only on the aid modality.[7] Other, more effective and efficient incentive mechanisms are sorely lacking. Some are under discussion. For example, the Clean Development Mechanism, recommended under the Kyoto Protocol on climate change, constitutes a first step towards a more market-based mechanism for trading global environmental services. The same holds true for the incremental-cost approach adopted by the Global Environment Facility (GEF).

Effective incentives are especially important in a world of such extreme diversity as ours. They are needed in order to motivate actors, who may have different policy preferences, to find common ground and to act jointly on certain urgent issues.

Thus, important aspects of the current public policy-making institutions are out of synch with today's policy issues and hence in need of reform, nationally and internationally. What role could the United Nations play in encouraging such reform and in assisting the international community to better manage the provision of GPGs?

The United Nations' role in provisioning global public goods

It is puzzling that, at a time when interdependence is increasing and the globalization of private activity and public policy becomes more urgent, the United Nations seems to be in crisis. Is it therefore even appropriate to ask what future role there is for it in managing GPGs?

The United Nations' present "crisis"

International economic activity has increased during the past decades, especially if we take into account not only intended but also unintended activities; that is, externalities of national activities. Consequently, international cooperation in many areas has gained in importance and is, in many instances, requiring a highly professional, technical approach. This requirement has led to a growing differentiation in international cooperation; that is, to the emergence of a growing number of specialized forums—for telecommunications, transport, law, health, agriculture, and environmental issues, for example. Consider how many facilities and mechanisms have emerged concerning the latter issue area.

The result of these trends has been an "out-migration" of issues from the United Nations. Issues that previously figured on the agenda of, for example, the Economic and Social Council (ECOSOC) are now being handled in more specialized fora—for example the GEF, the WTO, or the World Bank. In addition, some types of cooperation have become so well established—e.g. those in the area of civil aviation—that they progress without serious political conflict, and therefore without attracting much attention.

The United Nations' present "crisis" is, in large measure, a consequence of its success—of progress in multilateral cooperation. And it is a reflection of today's multi-actor world and the horizontal de-concentration of power that it entails. Many issues are now being simply handled by other, more specialized actors. But again, it is not a crisis to avert the over-burdening of international, intergovernmental fora with issues that other actors are better suited to address. Rather, it is a sign of efficiency—of saving in terms of transaction costs.

The question can be phrased in a more pointed way: what, if anything, could the United Nations do in terms of managing GPGs that other organizations, including the specialized agencies of the UN system, could not do as well or better?

Possible elements of a UN role: Putting GPGs into focus

The following list is not exhaustive. It just illustrates some first steps and the types of activities that could be appropriate for the United Nations to take in order to assist the international community in better managing the provision of GPGs.

Enhancing the understanding of GPGs: the United Nations as manager of a global GPG knowledge bank

The time has come to take the concept of public goods, and notably GPGs, out of the rarified circle of select economists and international relations specialists and bring it directly to the general public. After all, GPGs are the goods of the global public sphere.

The United Nations itself constitutes a GPG: an intermediate GPG required to produce such final GPGs as peace and security or global justice and balanced development. The same holds true for the specialized agencies of the UN system. The World Health Organization (WHO) is an intermediate good for the production of global health; the United Nations

Environmental Programme (UNEP) or the GEF are goods that feed into the production of environmental sustainability. So who, if not the United Nations, would be most concerned about clarifying the concept of GPGs and creating enhanced awareness of them?

In order to make the concept actionable and a cornerstone of future international cooperation, more than just a few additional academic studies or public relations campaigns are needed. The goal should be to create a global knowledge bank on GPG-related issues. A major task of such a facility could be to store information on issues that are critical to fostering international cooperation. Examples are: the likely costs of continuing the under-provision of particular GPGs and their distribution between different population groups and countries; the nature of various GPGs and existing knowledge about their production technology; the geographical and social distribution of the likely net benefits that an enhanced provision of certain goods might yield; the actors involved in producing certain goods; and the nature of the collective-action problems that certain goods pose, and what they might require in terms of negotiating processes.

Such a GPG-focused knowledge bank would considerably enhance the transparency of international negotiations and cooperation. In particular, it would be of valuable assistance to smaller countries whose delegations are increasingly strained by the growing number of issues that figure on the international political agenda. The bank would also help national policy-makers to be better connected with international policy dialogues, and would go a long way toward overcoming the present "domestic-foreign" divide.

Such a knowledge bank would be a joint endeavour of the United Nations and the various UN system agencies. Efforts towards constructing such an arrangement are emerging in various places. The WHO's FluNet and WHONET are steps in this direction, as are the United Nations Development Programme's (UNDP) NetAid and the World Bank's Global Development Network (GDN). Also, as the experience with these networks and websites illustrates, a GPG knowledge bank should not just be an intergovernmental endeavour but would need to be systematically linked with all concerned actors—academia, politicians, global advocates, business, media, grassroots activists, and so on.

Today, one would be hard-pressed to find the GPG concept in any UN document or report; and it would be similarly difficult to find UN analyses that assess—and seek to improve—cooperation processes from a GPG perspective. The GPG notion, and hence the insight into the organization's own functioning, is one of the best-kept secrets in the United Nations. Changing this is a prerequisite of further reform and a revitalized role for the United Nations.

Spotting under-provision: The need for a new Global Trusteeship Council

One wonders why millions perish from malaria, but billions in research and development dollars are lavished on less lethal diseases; or why unequal access to the internet is not yet receiving more policy attention. And why are we not as yet more concerned about the under-utilization of existing knowledge, commercial and otherwise? Why is there not more anxiety over the effects of lead poisoning on the health of children in the world's mega-cities? Are we waiting for the next mass demonstrations, the next catastrophe?

Surely, information on all these issues is available; and many reports have issued warnings. Yet, these alerts seem to be unable to grab the full attention of policy-makers. Obviously, some stronger whistle-blowing is needed. It could be appropriate for the United Nations, notably the Secretary-General, to take on this role. A council of eminent, independent personalities—a new Global Trusteeship Council—could assist the Secretary-General in this task of acting as a custodian of sustainable, or "steady-course" development.

It could be part of the council's mandate to look out for emerging crisis situations but also to bear in mind the question of "whose GPGs?" and to help ensure that the international development agenda is just and fairly balanced. A report of the Global Trusteeship Council's observations could be annually submitted by the Secretary-General to the UN General Assembly, with requests for action, if needed, by the Security Council, ECOSOC, or the specialized agencies.

Promoting participatory policy-making: the United Nations as a multi-actor venue

The Global Trusteeship Council will help promote a more comprehensive and just agenda for international cooperation. Yet it is no substitute to affording all population groups a fair chance to be represented in the global policy dialogue, express their own concerns, and propose policy options. Participation in decision-making is crucial to fostering ownership of policy change and to participation in its implementation; and the provision of GPGs depends on just and fair—legitimate—decision-making. It also depends on linking national-, regional-, and global-level actions more systematically.

From an intergovernmental viewpoint, the United Nations is one of the world's most participatory multilateral organizations. It has achieved considerable progress in collaborating with CSOs and, most recently, with private businesses. Yet, the involvement of non-state actors has often developed in an ad hoc manner and in response to pressure. In order to foster these new relationships more systematically and create examples that others might emulate, it would be important for the United Nations to rigorously assess the experiences gained to date and encourage broad-based consultations on how to organize tripartism in the future.

A vast set of issues would need to be clarified in this respect. Chief among them is the question of whether the United Nations is to be an intergovernmental body that seeks to be more open to consultations with other actors, or whether it should become a genuinely tripartite body—a joint gathering of representatives of states, business, and civil society. One option does not exclude the other. The United Nations could be a venue for both types of gatherings—for intergovernmental meetings (with provisions for systematic consultation with the other two major actor groups) and for tripartite meetings (in which all actors would meet as full participants). Each of these options poses different organizational challenges. Obviously, the world is beginning to sense the need for joint tripartite forums. The "Davos Forum," organized by the World Economic Forum, is an expression of this fact. It constitutes a pragmatic response to what is as yet an uncertain, and often not even fully recognized, requirement. Similarly, a growing number of loosely knit tripartite global public policy partnerships are emerging, centred around a number of quite varied issues, ranging from malaria control to combating corruption and establishing "good policy" principles for the construction of dams.[8] But will such loose arrangements suffice in future? Or, is there a need to institutionalize such arrangements more firmly?

The issue of a new tripartism between governments, business, and civil society, emphasizes the need for horizontal coordination between actor groups. The vertical dimension concerns the linkages between various regional institutions—notably the regional economic blocs—and global multilateralism. As global public bads become more pervasive, regional bodies—such as the EU, OAU, OAS, and ASEAN—will play a larger role in forging consensus on policy responses and, more importantly, in promoting effective implementation of international agreements. The United Nations can play a central role in bringing regional bodies into the global policy debate—both to help build knowledge and consensus on problems and possible solutions and as key partners in implementing global policies.

At present, the various regional bodies are largely disconnected from the global policy debate. The Secretary-General can begin a new process of revitalizing those bodies in preparation for a future where they serve as reliable partners of the United Nations in the management of GPGs. This could help create synergies between the different provision levels and also encourage a more systematic approach to subsidiarity.

Meetings are costly, and large meetings even more so. So, they should be used sparingly and with a clear purpose in mind. The purpose of the expansion of meetings suggested here would be to enhance developmental effectiveness and efficiency. Enhanced openness and transparency of UN meetings will strengthen their legitimacy; and strengthened political support, or "buy-in," will encourage follow-up. Problems might be addressed more promptly, rather than only after they have led to costly emergencies.

Finding a "home" for all GPG issues: The need to complement sector-based with issue-focused organizations

When the United Nations was founded, the prevailing notion of development was not only one of national development but one of national economies being composed of sectors such as education, health, industry, agriculture, and transport. National development was largely seen as the sum total of sector development, and global development as the sum total of national development. By now we have realized that cross-cutting issues also matter, e.g., those of equity, including gender equity, and sustainability. Moreover, many problems that, at first sight, may appear to be a sector-specific concern, such as the control of contagious diseases, in effect also pertain to a host of other sector issues, such as budgetary matters, policies of employment and poverty reduction, education, and cultural norms. Hence, the development of sectors as such is often not enough. Sector efforts must be focused on the issue at hand. They must be in line, as discussed before, with the production technology by which a particular public good is created.

The present organization of the UN system still follows primarily traditional sector lines. Yet, present policy challenges often require a strong issue—or product—focus. They call for the production of specific global public goods and services, often involving a multitude of actors at various levels, contributing inputs from a multitude of sectors. Again, UN Member States have reacted to these new challenges in a flexible manner. More and more issue-specific mechanisms have been created, as discussed above. For example, besides UNEP, which represents the environment in a general way, there now exists a host of issue-specific environment fora concerned with such issues as biodiversity, desertification, forests, the ozone shield, water, and so on.

While the development of an issue focus has progressed in some areas, it is still lacking in others. The area of "social development" is a case in point. One reason for this shortfall could be that social issues are still being perceived as primarily domestic issues. There is a pervading notion that all that is required internationally in this field is for governments to share national experiences and concerns in a general and noncommittal way. As a result, for example, meetings of the UN Commission for Social Development cover issues ranging from poverty reduction to employment, social security, and social integration. They rarely lead to specific, credible commitments. Many long-standing objectives, including, for example, that of basic education for all, remain unmet. Certainly, it is important for a body such as the Commission to consider in a comprehensive way how people fare in the development process. Yet, cooperation agreements need to be forged on a more issue-specific basis. The field of "social development" is certainly among those areas that would need to be further divided into more negotiable, "biteable" sub-issues, and in which a proper "home," or negotiating forum, would have to be found for each sub-item to move it forward in a more targeted and decisive manner.

Clearly, if we had a global trusteeship council, such stalemates in negotiations might have already been detected and brought to the fore. In the absence of such a Council, who would want to "blow the whistle?" The countries who under-invested in social development? Those who may have to foot the bill if they point out the problem? As the present situation once again demonstrates, GPGs, including those of global equity and cohesiveness, suffer without a mechanism for collective action.

One of the United Nations' roles in the future should thus be to spot issues that require international negotiation and cooperation, and, once political consensus exists, to actually tackle them and help find the "ready" issues in the right specialized forum to negotiate concrete, operational cooperation agreements. Just as it has so successfully done in the past, the United Nations should help create cooperation mechanisms; short-term or longer-term ones, depending on the requirements of the situation. The more pro-actively it helps move issues through the "cooperation chain," the freer will be its vision—and its agendas—for new, emerging concerns.

Addressing cross-cutting concerns: The United Nations' proper role

The foregoing suggestion raises the question of whether such further differentiation of international cooperation will lead to a further thinning of the United Nations' agenda, and thus to further marginalization of the organization. It might, indeed, shift some items, notably from the agenda of ECOSOC or the General Assembly. But these would be very detailed, technical issues, that probably ought not to figure in the first place. A less crowded agenda of the main UN bodies would create room for the consideration of new concerns, which no other institution would be as well suited to address as the United Nations. These are the broad issues of where the world as a whole is headed, in terms of growth, stability, justice, sustainability, and peace; these are the types of issues that the Secretary-General, based on the report of the Global Trusteeship Council, would be expected to bring to the world's attention.

In fact, one could envision the future United Nations as the governance centre of the UN system and its growing number of specialized agencies, programmes, and mechanisms. In order to explain this role more fully, it is useful first to examine the proposal for a changed composition of Member State delegations to the United Nations.

Changing the composition of Member State delegations: The United Nations as an interparliamentary body

International cooperation, whether at the level of consultation, negotiation, or operational activities, is currently primarily in the hands of the executive branches of government. Parliamentarians are largely absent from these processes. Thus, at present, public policy-making in its true sense happens essentially only at the level, and within the confines, of the state. International cooperation, and hence globalization, is a technocratically-managed process. This creates serious discrepancies between national policy needs and international action, between international agreements and incentives for national-level follow-up.

In order to reduce these discrepancies and create closer links between all levels of development, it would be important to have a venue in which representatives of national parliaments could meet—for example, the chairs of various parliamentary committees—to discuss international cooperation perspectives and needs. Possibly, the United Nations' main bodies could be transformed to serve as such a venue. This would mean drawing the main members of the delegations to the United Nations not from the executive branches of government, but from the legislative ones. The chief delegates would not be bureaucrats or technocrats but national legislators. Their decisions and agreements could be passed on for implementation, either to the national level, to regional bodies, or to the specialized UN or UN system entities.

The specialized UN system bodies could probably continue to be staffed by representatives of the executive side of government (in addition, of course, to representatives of other, non-state actor groups). Or alternatively, representatives of the concerned parliamentary committees could participate also in these meetings in a more systemic way than before.

A UN General Assembly composed of national parliamentarians would be the right forum for offering a more integrated, political perspective on world trends and providing the political oversight of international cooperation so sorely lacking now.

Conclusion

This chapter has addressed three main issues: the GPG nature of today's major policy challenges; some of the key challenges entailed in the provision of GPGs; and possible elements of a role that the United Nations could play in order to assist the international community to enhance the availability of GPGs and move the world out of the present web of crises in which it seems to be caught.

The discussion has shown that we are facing a new class of GPGs, which we have called "global policy outcomes." The emergence and growing importance of these goods requires that international cooperation move from dealing just with "between" or "at-the-border" issues to also managing a growing number of issues of "behind-the-border" convergence in national public policy. This challenge is still a rather unfamiliar one; and, most importantly, it does not fit easily into the conventional patterns of public policy-making. In fact, from the viewpoint of the new class of GPGs, public policy-making is beset by three major weaknesses: a jurisdictional, a participation, and an incentive gap. All three impede international cooperation and cause under-provision of GPGs. One of the most serious obstacles is linked to the jurisdictional gap: the divide between "foreign" and "domestic" affairs, that is still strong in most countries, and that keeps parliamentarians, the legislative side of government, largely out of international cooperation—and, consequently, keeps international cooperation out of policy-making.

This chapter recommends, in particular, six steps through which the United Nations could assist the international community in better managing the provision of GPGs. All six steps imply a major reform of the United Nations. However, while each one of them is more or less self-contained and could be taken separately, the first five would stand a better chance of success and be more meaningful if the last would be implemented as a matter of priority; the proposal to transform the United Nations from an intergovernmental, executive body into an intergovernmental, legislative—an interparliamentary—body.

Having witnessed the terrible devastation caused by the two world wars, the political leaders in the 1940s had the vision to recognize that many concerns, notably those of freedom from want and fear, are global, and that it may at times be detrimental to allow national borders to cut through their globality. But in some respects, the United Nations was born before its time. Many states, which are—and will continue to be—crucial as policy-making entities, had yet to be created. Now that this task is accomplished, the international community faces the daunting challenge of how to combine the existence of nation states with the globality of so many policy concerns. It will again require tremendous leadership and vision to resolve this challenge. A way forward could be to firmly and unwaveringly respect the external sovereignty of countries—the security of their borders. But that does not—and ought not—prevent national policy-makers from using their policy-making sovereignty more flexibly—not just nationally but, when it is best for the issue under consideration, also regionally and globally.

Notes

1. The discussion in this section draws on Inge Kaul, Isabelle Grunberg, and Marc A. Stern (eds.), *Global Public Goods: International Cooperation in the 21st Century* (New York: Oxford University Press, 1999). The interested reader may also consult Richard Cornes and Todd Sandler, *The Theory of Externalities, Public Goods, and Club Goods*, 2nd ed. (Cambridge: Cambridge University Press, 1996); Todd Sandler, *Global Challenges* (Cambridge: Cambridge University Press, 1997); and Todd Sandler "Intergenerational public goods: Strategies, efficiency and institutions," in Inge Kaul et al. (eds.), *op. cit.*
2. For more detailed discussions on the "dos" and "don'ts" of international cooperation, see, for example, Robert Axelrod, *The Evolution of Cooperation* (New York: Basic Books, 1984); Robert O. Keohane, *After Hegemony: Cooperation and Discord in the World Political Economy* (Princeton: Princeton University Press, 1984); Stephen D. Krasner (ed.), *International Regimes* (Ithaca: Cornell University Press, 1983); Lisa L. Martin, "Interests, Power, and Multilateralism," *International Organization* 46/4: 1992): 765–92; and Kenneth A. Oye (ed.), *Cooperation Under Anarchy* (Princeton: Princeton University Press, 1986).
3. An interesting survey of "foreign affairs," based on a collection of case studies covering industrial as well as developing countries, is presented in Brian Hocking, *Foreign Ministries: Change and Adaptation* (New York: St Martins Press, 1999).
4. The information on this point comes from a survey of delegations of UN Member States to selected meetings and conferences. See Erik Eldhagen, "Agenda, arena, and actors in the new diplomacy," Mimeo, Office of Development Studies, United Nations Development Programme, New York, 1999.
5. For overview analyses of the production function of various GPGs, see in particular Todd Sandler, *Global Challenges*, (see note 1, above), and Rajshri Jayaraman and Ravi Kanbur, "International public goods and the case for foreign aid," in Inge Kaul et al. (eds.), *Global Public Goods* (see note 1, above). The differences in strategy that often exist between "controlling bads" and "producing goods," have, in particular, been identified in Inge Kaul, "Global public goods: Concepts, policies and strategies," in Inge Kaul et al. (eds.), *Global Public Goods* (see note 1, above). More detailed discussions on the provision of selected GPGs, ranging from market efficiency and financial stability, to equity, health, knowledge, culture, and the environment, as well as peace and security, see the case studies contained in Inge Kaul et al. (eds.), *Global Public Goods* (see note 1, above).
6. For reports on CSO initiatives linked to the December 1999 WTO meeting in Seattle, see, for example, Guy de Jonquières and Frances Williams, "Collapse: A goal beyond reach," *Financial Times*, 6 December 1999. As these reports show, the CSOs from developing countries had different concerns from those that brought industrial-nation CSOs to Seattle. Southern CSOs were, among others, concerned about further marginalization of their countries, while Northern CSOs, including trade unions, feared that free trade would lead to a reversal in their countries' standards in areas such as wage levels and environ-

mental norms, or, as regards child labour, would violate their human rights ideals. The shared element of their concerns was that "free trade" and "market efficiency" cannot be the sole principles by which we organize our lives.
7. An interesting attempt at analyzing the use of aid resources for non-aid purposes, notably purposes that serve "global housekeeping" goals such as the protection of the ozone shield or other global environment objectives, is presented in Kunibert Raffer, "ODA and global public goods: A trend analysis of past and present spending patterns," Background Paper, Office of Development Studies, United Nations Development Programme, New York, 1999.
8. Wolfgang H. Reinicke, "The other world wide web: Global public policy networks," *Foreign Policy* (Winter 1999–2000): 42–57, presents an overview of the growing trend towards global public policy partnerships.

Contributors

G. Shabbir Cheema is Director of the Management Development and Governance Division, Bureau for Development Policy, United Nations Development Programme.

Christine Chinkin is Professor of International Law, London School of Economics and Political Science.

Michael Edwards is Director of Governance and Civil Society in the Ford Foundation's Peace and Social Justice Programme, and former Senior Civil Society Specialist at the World Bank.

David Forsythe is Charles J. Mach Distinguished Professor of Political Science, University of Nebraska–Lincoln.

Brian Job is Professor of International Relations, Institute of International Relations, University of British Columbia.

Sakuntala Kadirgamar-Rajasingham is a Senior Executive at the International Institute for Democracy and Electoral Assistance (International IDEA).

Inge Kaul is Director of the Office of Development Studies, Bureau for Development Policy, at the United Nations Development Programme.

Elisabeth Sköns is Project Leader (Military Expenditure and Arms Production), Stockholm International Peace Research Institute (SIPRI).

Trevor Findlay is Executive Director of the Verification Research, Training, and Information Centre (VERTIC), London.

Samuel Makinda is Head of the School of Politics and International Studies, Murdoch University, Perth, Western Australia.

David M. Malone is President of the International Peace Academy in New York, and was formerly a Canadian Foreign Service Officer.

Edward Newman is an Academic Programme Associate in the Peace and Governance Programme of the United Nations University.

Chantal de Jonge Oudraat is an Associate at the Carnegie Endowment for International Peace, Washington, DC.

Paul Stares is Director of Studies at the Japan Center for International Exchange.

Mounir Tabet is Technical Advisor, Management Development and Governance Division, Bureau for Development Policy, United Nations Development Programme.

Ramesh Thakur is Vice-Rector for Peace and Governance, United Nations University.

The opinions expressed in this book do not necessarily reflect the views of the institutions with which the authors are affiliated.

Index

A

AALCC. *See* Asian-African Legal Consultative Committee
ABM. *See* Anti-Ballistic-Missile Treaty
Absolutist conception of state sovereignty, 229
Accountability
 in non-state involvement, 210-212
ACDA. *See* United States Arms Control and Disarmament Agency
ActionAid, 214
Actors. *See* Civil-society actors; Multi-actor world
Administrative decentralization, 264-265
 by deconcentration, 264
 by delegation, 264-265
Advocacy groups. *See* Non-governmental organizations (NGOs)
Agenda for Peace, An, 31-32
Agenda 2000, 137
Agents of intervention, 59-63
Alignments
 as an organizational arrangement, 112
Alliances
 as an organizational arrangement, 112
 and regional security developments, 14, 108-130
Amnesty International, 211
Annan, Kofi, 9, 28, 31-32, 44, 51, 168, 179, 205, 207, 220-221
 Clinton Administration attacks on, 34-35
Anti-Ballistic-Missile (ABM) Treaty, 134, 137
ANZUS. *See* Australia-New Zealand-United States Security Treaty
APEC forum, 117, 216
Appropriate democratic institutions and processes
 developing at an appropriate pace, 201-202
 role of new technologies in developing, 202
ARF. *See* ASEAN Regional Forum
Armed conflict. *See* Conflicts
Arms control. *See* Nuclear arms control process
Arms production
 countries leading in, 93
 need for transparency in, 104
Arms transfers
 challenges of, 99-104

determinants of, 91-94
economic aspects of, 96-99
future of, 89-90
impact of globalization on, 94-96
trends in, 13-14, 82, 84-88
ASEAN. *See* Association of South-East Asian Nations
ASEAN Regional Forum (ARF), 118, 120, 124, 126
Asian-African Legal Consultative Committee (AALCC), 122
Asian Development Bank, 253-254
Assessing democracy, 191-193
Association of South-East Asian Nations (ASEAN), 116, 118, 124-126
Association of South-East Asian States, 120
Austinic juristic theory, 170
Australia Group, 140
Australia-New Zealand-United States Security Treaty (ANZUS), 120
Authoritarian institutions and practices
resilience and pervasiveness of, 188
Axworthy, Lloyd, 22

B

Baker, Jim, 36
BDP. *See* Bureau for Development Policy
Beijing Platform for Action, 17, 243, 247, 251
BICC. *See* Bonn International Centre for Conversion
Biersteker, Thomas, 168
Bin Laden, Osama, 25, 54
Biological weapons
outlook for the new millennium, 139
Biological Weapons Convention (BWC), 14, 132, 139
verification of, 142
Black Sea Economic Cooperation (BSEC), 122
Bodin, Jean, 169
Bonn International Centre for Conversion (BICC), 97-98
Boutros-Ghali, Boutros, 24, 31, 167-168
Robert Dole's attacks on, 36
Bradley, Bill, 36
BSEC. *See* Black Sea Economic Cooperation

Buchanan, Patrick, 231
Bureau for Development Policy (BDP), 277
Management Development and Governance Division, 277
Bureaucrats
national, working alongside international civil servants, 1
Burgers, Jan Herman, 239
Bush, George, 36, 142, 167
Business dimensions to civil society, 208-209
BWC. *See* Biological Weapons Convention

C

CACEU. *See* Central African Customs and Economic Union
Canadian Human Security Initiative, 41, 43
Canberra Commission, 137-138
Capacity-building
operationalizing reforms for decentralized governance, 291-292
Caribbean Community, 119
Carnegie Corporation, 28
Carter, Jimmy, 30
Case studies, 273-292
good governance principles in, 283-284
sustainable human development objectives in, 279
CBOs. *See* Community-based organizations
CD. *See* Conference on Disarmament
CEDAW. *See* Commission on the Elimination of All Forms of Discrimination against Women
Central African Customs and Economic Union (CACEU), 119
Challenges
facing democracy, 183-184, 201-203
facing the Security Council, 34-40
in gender relations, 249-252
in human rights, 224-238
of human security in a system of states, 129-130
in intervention, 13, 46-76
in military expenditure and arms transfers, 99-104

of the new millennium, 4-6
of providing global public goods, 301-305
for the UN supporting emerging democracies, 203
of verification, 143-144
of weapons of mass destruction, 141-148
Changing attitudes
constituencies for, 212-214
towards long-term human rights, 237-238
Changing composition
of Member State delegations, 312
Charter of the United Nations, 2, 26, 156, 185, 222
Chapter VI of, 108
Chapter VII of, 24, 33, 52-53, 68, 233
Chapter VIII of, 56, 71, 108, 110
continual reinterpretations of, 177
difficulties of Member States in living up to, 26
promoting state self-determination, 174
purposes of, 114, 242
US violations of, 230
Cheema, G. Shabbir, 17-18, 261-295, 317
Chemical weapons
outlook for the new millennium, 138
Chemical Weapons Convention (CWC), 14, 132, 138-139
reinterpretation of, 142
Chinkin, Christine, 17, 242-260, 317
CIS. *See* Commonwealth of Independent States
Citizens
fate of in armed conflict, 235-236
Civil servants
international, working alongside national bureaucrats, 1
Civil society
business dimensions to, 208-209
defining, 218
and global governance, 16-17, 205-219
involvement in global regimes, 209
NGOs as key elements of, 147
rise of, 206-209
role of UN regarding involvement in global government, 215-217
Civil-society actors
partnerships among in addressing gender relations, 255-256

Civil-society organizations (CSOs), 304
Clark, Ian, 173
Clean Development Mechanism, 305
Climate Change Convention, 147
Clinton, Bill, 150, 230-231
"CNN effect," 27
COE. *See* Council of Europe
Coercive actions
UN role in building support for, 64-65
Cold War
collective defense arrangements underpinning, 108
conflicts fueled by, 37
era following, 9, 14, 77-80, 125, 152
state-centric interpretation of sovereignty underlying, 171-172
US winning of, 142
Collective-action problems, 301-302
Collective defense
multilateral regional arrangements for, 111-112, 114
Collective security
multilateral regional arrangements for, 112, 114
Collective security institution
as an organizational arrangement, 112
Commercial organizations
partnerships among in addressing gender relations, 255-256
Commission on the Elimination of All Forms of Discrimination against Women (CEDAW), 242, 244, 250, 252
Optional Protocol to, 255
Commission on Global Governance, 150, 163, 167-168
Commission on the Status of Women, 242, 255
Commission on Sustainable Development (CSD), 216
Commonwealth of Independent States (CIS), 26, 121
Commonwealth Secretariat, 122
Community. *See* International community; Interpretive community
Community-based organizations (CBOs), 281
Compliance lacuna, 144
Composition of Member State delegations changing, 312

Comprehensive Development Framework, 209
Comprehensive Test Ban Treaty (CTBT), 14, 132-133, 137
　mishandling of ratification of, 142-143
　Provisional Technical Secretariat for, 141
Comprehensive Test Ban Treaty Organization (CTBTO), 148
Concert
　as an organizational arrangement, 112, 114
Conference on Disarmament (CD), 137-138
Conference on Security and Cooperation in Europe (CSCE). See Organization for Security and Cooperation in Europe (OSCE)
Conflicts
　addressed by Security Council (UNSC), 23-27
　fate of citizens in, 78, 235-236
　fueled by the Cold War, 37
　racial and ethnic, 154
Congressional Research Service (CRS), 84
Consensus building
　as a democratic value, 202
Consolidation of democracy
　policy proposals to support, 201-203
Constituencies for change, 212-214
Constructivism
　in global politics, 165-166, 169-170
Control. See Nuclear arms control process
Conventional weapons
　leading suppliers of major, 86
　volume of imports of major, 85
Cooperative security
　multilateral regional arrangements for, 113-115
Coping with the impact of sudden and unexpected events, 195-196
Council for Security Cooperation in the Asia-Pacific (CSCAP) region, 118, 125
Council of Europe (COE), 117, 121
Council on Sustainable Development, 238-239
Criminal actions
　against violators of human rights, 236-237
CRS. See Congressional Research Service

CSCAP. See Council for Security Cooperation in the Asia-Pacific region
CSCE. See Organization for Security and Cooperation in Europe (OSCE)
CSD. See Commission on Sustainable Development
CSOs. See Civil-society organizations
CTBT. See Comprehensive Test Ban Treaty
CTBTO. See Comprehensive Test Ban Treaty Organization
CWC. See Chemical Weapons Convention
"Cyber warfare," 153

D

Debt relief, 10-11
Decentralization
　administrative, 264-265
　fiscal, 265, 269-271
　market, 265-266
　political, 264, 269-271
Decentralized governance
　complex relationship with human development, 277-292
　enabling environment for, 278, 280-284
　forms of, 263-266
　global changes and, 266-273
　good, 278
　for human development, 17-18, 261-295
　initiative and leadership in, 289-290
　operationalizing reforms for, 291-292
　participation in, 282, 285-287
　partnerships for, 287-288
　recent experiences with, 273-277
Declaration on the Granting of Independence to Colonial Countries and Peoples, 186
Deconcentration, 264
Delegation, 264-265
Delivery systems
　outlook for the new millennium, 139-140
Demobilization
　social costs of, 98
Democracies
　challenges facing emerging, 183-184
　challenges facing established, 184
　low-quality, 204

"multi-track," 207
  providing support for emerging, 191
Democracy
  agents promoting effectively, 200-201
  assessing, 191-193
  building sustainable, 195-196
  challenges in the twenty-first century, 201-203
  claims to, 182
  defining, 184-187
  developing for and within subnational groups, 202
  global trend towards, 182-184
  models of, 187
  need to develop realistic expectations of, 189-191
  policy proposals to support the consolidation of, 201-203
  promotion of, 198-200
  regressions from, 16, 182-204
  understanding the reality of, 188-191
"Democracy audit," 192
Democracy support, 199-200
  encouraging review and renewal of institutions, 199
  integrating democracy into the lives of citizens through education, 199-200
  providing comparative information on models and systems, 199
  strengthening networks of national actors, 199
Democratic consolidation
  not inevitable, 188-189
Democratic institutions and processes
  development of appropriate, 201-202
Democratic value
  consensus building as, 202
Democratization
  and globalization, 196-197
  of knowledge, 3
Department of Peacekeeping Operations
  Lessons Learned Unit, 101
Determinants
  of military expenditure and arms transfers, 90-94
Development. *See also* Human development
  of appropriate democratic institutions and processes, 201-202
  changing ideas about international, 206-207

Devolution, 264
Dialogue organizations, 113, 115
Diplomacy, 165
  revolutionary change in, 5
Disarmament
  new partnerships in, 146-147
  reviving the role of the UN regarding, 144-146
District development committees, 276
District-level planning, 274-275
Divestment, 265-266
Division for the Advancement of Women, 255
Dole, Robert, 36

E

EAPC. *See* Euro-Atlantic Partnership Council
ECOMOG. *See* Military Observer Group
Economic aspects
  of military expenditure and arms transfers, 96-99
Economic Community of West African States (ECOWAS), 24, 60-61, 117, 119
Economic insecurity, 154
  integrating with human rights, 224-227
Economic sanctions, 69, 71
ECOSOC. *See* UN Economic and Social Council
ECOWAS. *See* Economic Community of West African States
Edwards, Michael, 16-17, 205-219, 317
Emerging democracies
  challenges facing, 183-184
  integrating into international networks and partnerships, 203
  providing support for, 191
Environmental degradation, 154
EO. *See* Executive Outcomes
Epidemiological threats, 155
Established democracies
  challenges facing, 184
Ethnic conflict, 154
Euro-Atlantic Partnership Council (EAPC), 121
European Court of Human Rights, 228-229
European Court of Justice, 228

European Development Bank, 224
European Union (EU), 117, 121, 228
Evans, Gareth, 167
Executive Office of the Secretary-General
  Strategic Planning Unit, 3
Executive Outcomes (EO), 61
Expectations of democracy
  need to develop realistic, 189-191

F

Federation of the World Red Cross and
  Red Crescent Societies, 27, 235
Finance. *See also* International financial
  institutions (IFIs)
  operationalizing reforms for
    decentralized governance, 291-292
Findlay, Trevor, 14-15, 131-149, 317
Fiscal decentralization, 265
  extent of in selected countries, 272-273
Fissile Material (Cut-Off) Treaty (FMT),
  137, 142
FluNet, 307
FMT. *See* Fissile Material (Cut-Off) Treaty
Forsythe, David, 17, 220-241, 317
Fourth World Conference on Women, 243,
  252. *See also* Beijing Platform for
  Action
Fowler, Roger, 22
Fréchette, Louise, 3, 175-176
Future
  military expenditure and arms transfers,
    89-90
  the UN and global governance, 176-179

G

GATT agreement, 176
GCC. *See* Gulf Cooperation Council
GDN. *See* Global Development Network
GEF. *See* Global Environment Facility
Gender relations
  challenges in, 228, 249-252
  impact of globalization on, 245-249
  law and policy, 17, 242-260
  trends in, 242-245
General Assembly, 29, 53, 56, 70

Geneva Conventions, 57-58, 72-73, 235
Global Alliance for Forest Conservation
  and Sustainable Use, 209
Global changes
  and decentralized governance, 266-273
Global concerns
  as global public goods, 300
Global Development Network (GDN), 307
Global Environment Facility (GEF), 305
Global governance
  civil society and, 16-17, 205-219
  dilemmas of non-state involvement in,
    210-215
  globalization and, 172-176
  and the interpretive community, 166-168
  of public goods in a multi-actor world,
    18, 296-315
  recasting, 15-16, 163-181
  role of UN regarding civil society
    involvement in, 215-217
  sovereignty and, 168-172
  theoretical context of, 164-166
  the UN and the future of, 176-179
Global non-governmental organizations,
  212-214
Global public goods (GPGs)
  addressing cross-cutting concerns in,
    311-312
  defining, 297-298
  enhancing understanding of, 306-307
  finding a "home" for all issues
    concerning, 310-311
  global concerns as, 300
  new class of, 299-301
  policy concerns for, 297-301
  public policy challenges of providing,
    301-305
  putting into focus, 306-312
  "standard" collective-action problems
    with, 301-302
  traditional, 298-299
  UN managing a knowledge bank on,
    306-307
  UN role in provisioning, 18, 305-312
Global trend towards democracy, 182-184
Global Trusteeship Council, 312
  need for a new, 308
Globalization, 9
  contradictions within, 175
  defining, 148
  democratization and, 196-197

effects on weapons of mass destruction, 140-141
and global governance, 172-176
impact on gender relations, 245-249
impact on human rights, 222-223
impact on human security agendas, 153-155
impact on military expenditure and arms transfers, 94-96
impact on national security agendas, 152-153
impact on security, 152-155
Good governance
decentralization and, 278
defining, 163
principles illustrated in the case studies, 283-284
Gorbachev, Mikhail, 131, 167
Goulding, Marrack, 24
Governance, 163-315
changing context of, 8-12
civil society and global, 16-17, 205-219
decentralized, for human development, 17-18, 261-295
defining, 7-8, 163
global, of public goods in a multi-actor world, 18, 296-315
new conceptions in, 7-8, 207-208
in the new millennium, 7-18
principles of good, 283-284
recasting global, 15-16, 163-181
Governments. *See* International governmental organizations (IGOs); National governments; Non-governmental organizations; Regional-level arrangements; States
GPGs. *See* Global public goods
Gram Sabha, 274
Gregorian, Vargan, 28
Gulf Cooperation Council (GCC), 122

H

Hammarskjöld, Dag, 32
Helsinki Accords, 116
Henry L. Stimson Centre, 143
Hinsley, F. H., 169-170
Hobbes, Thomas, 169
Holbrooke, Richard, 35-36

Human development
complex relationship with decentralized governance, 277-292
conceptual entry point for, 262-263
decentralized governance for, 17-18, 261-295
sustainable objectives for, 279
Human rights
challenges of, 224-238
changing long-term attitudes, 237-238
criminal actions against violators of, 236-237
enumerated, 204
impact of globalization on, 222-223
integrating economic concerns with, 224-227
knowledge basic to, 3
merging with humanitarian action and refugee affairs, 233-235
role of the Security Council in, 232-233
role of the United States in, 228-232
the UN and, 17, 220-241
Human security
impact of globalization on agendas for, 153-155
in a system of states, 129-130
Humanitarian action
merging with human rights, 233-235
Humanitarian intervention
new doctrine of, 55-59
Huntington, Samuel, 177

I

ICBL. *See* International Campaign to Ban Landmines
ICC. *See* International Criminal Court
ICRC. *See* International Committee of the Red Cross (ICRC)
IDA. *See* International Development Association
IGAD. *See* Intergovernmental Authority on Development
IGOs. *See* International governmental organizations
ILO. *See* International Labor Organization
IMF. *See* International Monetary Fund
Improvisation within the Security Council of the 1990s, 12-13, 21-45

326 INDEX

Incentive gap in public policy challenges, 304-305
Inconsistencies in the Security Council of the 1990s, 12-13, 21-45
Indian Ocean Council (IOC), 120
Indispensability of the Security Council of the 1990s, 12-13, 21-45
INF. *See* Intermediate-range Nuclear Forces Agreement
Initiative in decentralized governance, 289-290
Institutional developments within the Security Council, 30-33
Institutional structures. *See also* Authoritarian institutions and practices; Democracies; Democratic institutions and processes; Organizations
service delivery and, 282
INSTRAW. *See* International Research and Training Institute for the Advancement of Women
Instruments of intervention, 63-66
Integrated security community
as an organizational arrangement, 113, 115
Integrating emerging democracies into international networks and partnerships, 203
Inter-American Convention on Human Rights, 228
Inter-American Development Bank, 224
Interest groups. *See* Non-governmental organizations (NGOs)
Intergovernmental Authority on Development (IGAD), 117, 120
Intermediate-range Nuclear Forces (INF) Agreement, 134, 139
International affairs
Eurocentrism in, 1
International Atomic Energy Agency (IAEA), 133, 136-137, 141, 148
International Bill of Rights, 226-227, 242
International Campaign to Ban Landmines (ICBL), 147
International civil servants
working alongside national bureaucrats, 1
International Committee of the Red Cross (ICRC), 17, 27, 234-235

International community
addressing gender questions, 252-254
working with the UN, 254-255
International Court of Justice, 53, 137
International Covenant on Civil and Political Rights, 228
International Covenant on Economic, Social, and Cultural Rights, 228
International Criminal Court (ICC), 12, 23, 32, 144, 147, 164, 236-237, 239, 250, 255
International Criminal Tribunals, 32, 57, 68, 73, 225
International development
changing ideas about, 206-207
International Development Association (IDA), 210
International financial institutions (IFIs), 224. *See also individual institutions*
International governmental organizations (IGOs), 8, 163
International Labor Organization (ILO), 213, 226
International Legal Commission, 67
International Monetary Fund (IMF), 99, 224-225
bringing into the human rights movement, 224
version of "good governance," 163
International networks and partnerships
integrating emerging democracies into, 203
International non-governmental organizations, 16
International Peace Academy (IPA), 28
International relations
bipolar model of, 8
International Research and Training Institute for the Advancement of Women (INSTRAW), 255
International society. *See also* Interpretive community
law and policy, 17, 242-260
Internet revolution, 197
Interpretive communities
global governance and, 166-168
Interregional organizations
involved in peace-keeping and peace-related activities, 119-123
Intervention
agents of, 59-63

defining, 46
  instruments of, 63-66
  legal framework for, 52-55
  new doctrine of humanitarian, 55-59
  role of the UN in, 66-68
  trends and challenges in, 13, 46-76
Involvement. *See* Non-state involvement
IOC. *See* Indian Ocean Council
IPA. *See* International Peace Academy
Iran-Iraq war
  attempts to resolve, 21

J

Jackson, Jesse, 55
James, Alan, 169
Job, Brian, 14, 108-130, 317
"Jubilee 2000" movement, 10, 218
Jurisdictional gap
  in public policy challenges, 302-304

K

Kadirgamar-Rajasingham, Sakuntala, 16, 182-204, 317
Kaldor, Mary, 95
Kaul, Inge, 18, 296-315, 317
KFOR (United Nations Force in Kosovo), 28
Khripunov, Igor., 134
Krasner, Stephen, 171
Kühne, Winrich, 56-57
Kyoto Protocol, 164, 305

L

Landmine Convention
  model of, 146-147
Landmine Monitor, 147
LAS. *See* League of Arab States
Laski, Harold, 170
Lavrov, Sergey, 37
Law and gender in international society, 17, 242-260
Leadership, 289
  in decentralized governance, 289-290

responsibility of the United States, 142
League of Arab States (LAS), 123
League of Nations, 2
"Leakage." *See* "Nuclear leakage"
Legal framework for intervention, 52-55
  new doctrine of humanitarian, 55-59
Legitimacy of non-state involvement, 210-212
Lessons Learned Unit, 101
Leviathan, 169
Liberalism in global politics, 165, 169-170
Local councils, 274-275
Local non-governmental organizations, 212-214
Locke, John, 170

M

Major conventional weapons
  leading suppliers of, 86
  volume of imports of, 85
Makinda, Samuel, 15-16, 163-181, 317
Malone, David M., 12-13, 21-45, 317
Management Development and Governance Division (MDGD), 277
Market decentralization, 265-266
Marx, Karl, 222
Mass destruction. *See* Weapons of mass destruction
MDGD. *See* Management Development and Governance Division
Mearsheimer, John, 177
Member States
  changing composition of delegations from, 312
  difficulties in living up to the Charter of the United Nations, 26
  preserving prerogatives of, 129
  reporting required from, 103
  smaller, 39
Middle Powers Initiative, 137
Military expenditure
  challenges of, 99-104
  determinants of, 90-91
  economic aspects of, 96-99
  future of, 89-90
  impact of globalization on, 94-96
  as a percentage of GDP, 87-88
  regional, 83
  trends in, 13-14, 79-83

UN reporting instrument on, 103-104
world, 81-82
Military force
   need for increased transparency in, 102-103
   uses of authorized by Security Council, 50
Military Observer Group (ECOMOG), 59-60
Military Professional Resources Incorporated (MPRI), 61
Military Staff Committee, 59, 67
Millennium conference, 3-4. *See also* New millennium
Millennium General Assembly, 216-217
Missile Technology Control Regime (MTCR), 139
MNCs. *See* Multinational corporations
Modernization theory, 174
Mollander, Anders, 25
MPRI. *See* Military Professional Resources Incorporated
MTCR. *See* Missile Technology Control Regime
Multi-actor world
   governing global public goods in, 18, 296-315
   UN within, 308-310
Multilateral Agreement on Investments, 11
Multilateral regional arrangements, 111-130
   for collective defense, 111, 114
   for collective security, 114
   for cooperative security, 114-115
   forms of multilateral security management, 111-113
   in the post-Cold War era, 115-118
Multilateral security management
   forms of, 111-113
Multinational corporations (MNCs), 164
Murphy, Alexander, 169

N

NAFTA, 231
Nairobi Forward-Looking Strategies, 251
NAM. *See* Non-Aligned Movement
National governments
   addressing gender questions, 252-254
National security. *See* Security

National security agendas. *See also* Subnational groups
   impact of globalization on, 152-153
NATO. *See* North Atlantic Treaty Organization
NetAid, 307
New Agenda Coalition, 137
New millennium
   confronting the challenge of, 4-6
   weapons outlook for, 132-140
New technologies
   role in developing appropriate democratic institutions and processes, 202
"New world order," 167
Newman, Edward, 7-18, 317
NGOs. *See* Non-governmental organizations
Non-Aligned Movement (NAM), 22
Non-governmental organizations (NGOs), 8, 163-164. *See also individual NGOs*
   increased access for, 32-33, 147, 178
   international, 16
   from the local to the global, 212-214
   problems with, 248
   questions about legitimacy of, 209-212
   role in "global civil society," 166
   transnational networks of, 207
Non-proliferation
   new partnerships in, 146-147
   reviving the role of the UN regarding, 144-146
Non-Proliferation Treaty (NPT), 14, 133, 137-138, 142
Non-state involvement
   dilemma in global governance, 210-215
"Non-traditional" security challenges, 15, 150-159
North Atlantic Council, 69
North Atlantic Treaty Organization (NATO), 26, 109, 122
   bombing China's Belgrade embassy, 36
   composition of, 229, 231
   debate over air strikes in Kosovo and Serbia, 47, 51, 110-111, 134
   redefining its Strategic Concept, 116
   as a regional organization, 56, 127
NPT. *See* Non-Proliferation Treaty
Nuclear arms control process
   rejuvenating, 142-143

"Nuclear leakage"
  tackling Russian, 143
Nuclear Non-Proliferation Treaty, 132
Nuclear Proliferation Data Exploitation
  Centre, 145
Nuclear Suppliers Group, 140
Nuclear weapons
  outlook for the new millennium, 133-138
Nuclear weapons states (NWS), 133-138, 140, 147
Nuremberg Tribunal, 222
NWS. *See* Nuclear weapons states

O

OAS. *See* Organization of American States
OAU. *See* Organization of African Unity
OCHA. *See* UN Office for the Coordination of Humanitarian Assistance (OCHA)
OIC. *See* Organization of the Islamic Conference
Organization for Security and Cooperation in Europe (OSCE), 26, 103, 116-117, 121, 125
Organization for the Prohibition of Biological Weapons (OPBW), 139, 148
Organization for the Prohibition of Chemical Weapons (OPCW), 138, 141, 148
Organization of African Unity (OAU), 26, 38, 116-117, 119, 126
  charter of promoting state self-determination, 174
Organization of American States (OAS), 25, 116-117, 119, 126
Organization of the Islamic Conference (OIC), 123
Organizational arrangements, 111-130
  alignment, 112
  alliance, 112
  collective security institution, 112
  concert, 112, 114
  security community, 113, 115
  security dialogue organizations, 113, 115
  strategic partnership, 112

Organizations. *See also individual organizations*
  involved in peace-keeping and peace-related activities, 119-123
  partnerships among international in addressing gender relations, 255-256
Otunnu, Olara, 28
Oudraat, Chantal de Jonge, 13, 46-76, 317
Oxfam, 211-212, 214

P

P5. *See* Permanent Five
Paine, Thomas, 170
Participation, 285
  in decentralized governance, 282, 285-287
  and incentive gaps, 304-305
Participatory policy-making
  promoting, 308-310
Partnership for Peace (PFP), 116, 121
Partnerships, 8
  in addressing gender relations, 255-256
  for decentralized governance, 287-288
  in disarmament, 146-147
  of emerging democracies, 203
Peace and security
  maintaining in the post-Cold War era, 118-124
  role of regional security developments in UN's promotion of, 14, 108-130
"Peace dividend," 95
Peace-keeping activities
  budget estimates of organizations involved in, 126
  limitations on, 108-109
  organizations involved in, 119-123
Peace-keeping operations (PKOs), 23, 42, 127, 164
  in Sierra Leone, 34
Peace of Westphalia, 170
Peace-related activities
  budget estimates of organizations involved in, 126
  organizations involved in, 119-123
  at the regional level, 124-126

Peaceful Nuclear Explosions Treaty (PNET), 142
Peck, Connie, 126
Pérez de Cuéllar, Javier, 21, 31, 167
Permanent Five (P5)
  members of the Security Council, 21-23, 32, 142
  resentments among, 39
Pervasiveness of authoritarian institutions and practices, 188
PFP. *See* Partnership for Peace
PKOs. *See* Peace-keeping operations
Pluralistic security community
  as an organizational arrangement, 113, 115
PNET. *See* Peaceful Nuclear Explosions Treaty
Policy and gender in international society, 17, 242-260
Policy-making
  promoting participatory, 308-310
Policy proposals
  to support the consolidation of democracy, 201-203
Political decentralization, 264
  devolution, 264
  in selected countries, 269-271
Post-Cold War era
  maintaining peace and security in, 118-124
  multilateral regional arrangements in, 115-118
Poverty-reduction activities, 274-275
Promotion of democracy, 198-200
  agents of, 200-201
  by force, 198-199
Public goods, global
  global concerns as, 300
  transnational management of, 18
  UN role in governing, 18, 296-315
Public policy challenges
  incentive gap, 304-305
  jurisdictional gap, 302-304
  "standard" collective-action problems, 301-302

R

Racial conflict, 154
Reagan, Ronald, 131, 231
Realism in global politics, 165, 169, 172-173
Red Cross and Red Crescent Conference, 235
Reforms
  operationalizing for decentralized governance, 291-292
Refugee affairs
  merging with human rights, 233-235
Regional-level arrangements
  peace-related activities at, 124-126
  and the UN, 126-129
Regional military expenditure
  estimates of, 83
Regional organizations
  involved in peace-keeping and peace-related activities, 119-123
Regional security. *See also* Multilateral regional arrangements
  arrangements in the post-Cold War era, 115-118
  developments in the UN's role promoting peace and stability, 14, 108-130
Regressions from democracy, 16, 182-204
Reporting instrument on military expenditure
  UN as, 103-104
Representation in non-state involvement, 210-212
Resilience of authoritarian institutions and practices, 188
Responses to weapons of mass destruction, 141-148
Reus-Smit, C., 170
Rio Group, 119
Roberts, Adam, 168
Robinson, Mary, 29, 226
"Rogue states"
  threat from, 152
Routine procedures
  operationalizing reforms for decentralized governance, 291-292
Ruggie, John, 178
Russian "nuclear leakage"
  tackling, 143

S

SADC. *See* Southern African Development Community
Sanctions imposed by the Security Council, 48-49
Sankoh, Foday, 55, 67
Scholte, Jan Aart, 172
SDI. *See* Strategic Defense Initiative
Second World War, 1-2, 222
Secretary-General, 3-4. *See also individual Secretaries-General*
　Executive Office of, 3-4
　Millennium Assembly report, 4
Secretary-General's Special Representatives (SRSGs), 31
Secularization
　of knowledge, 3
Security, 21-159. *See also* Human security; Regional security
　changing context of, 8-12
　defining, 7
　impact of globalization on, 152-155
　in the new millennium, 7-18
　new thinking in, 7-8
Security challenges
　addressing, 155-157
　"new" and "non-traditional," 15, 150-159
　role of the UN regarding, 158-159
Security community
　as an organizational arrangement, 113, 115
Security Council (UNSC)
　challenges facing, 34-40
　conflicts addressed by, 23-27
　considerations driving decision-making by, 27-30
　cumulative impact of decisions made by, 33-34
　decisions made by, 23-34
　evolving dynamics within, 41
　institutional developments within, 30-33
　interventions by, 13
　Non-Aligned Movement within, 22
　Permanent Five members of, 21-23, 32, 142
　role in human rights, 232-233
　Russia's performance within, 37-38
　in the 1990s, 12-13, 21-45
　sanctions imposed by, 48-49
　uses of military force authorized by, 50
Security dialogue organizations
　as organizational arrangements, 113, 115
Security management
　forms of multilateral, 112-113
Self organization, 276
Service delivery
　and institutional structures, 282
SHD. *See* Sustainable human development
Shearer, David, 61-62
SIPRI. *See* Stockholm International Peace Research Institute data
Sköns, Elisabeth, 13-14, 77-101, 317
Society. *See* Civil society; International society
Southern African Development Community (SADC), 117, 120
Sovereignty
　defining, 167-1670
　and global governance, 168-172
SRSGs. *See* Secretary-General's Special Representatives
Stability
　role of regional security developments in UN's promotion of, 14, 108-130
Stares, Paul, 15, 150-159, 318
START I agreement, 134, 139
START II agreement, 134-135
START III agreement, 134
State-centrism
　predominating in non-proliferation and disarmament fields, 146-147
States. *See also* Member States
　human security in a system of, 129-130
　partnerships among in addressing gender relations, 255-256
Stimson Centre, 143
Stockholm International Peace Research Institute (SIPRI) data, 81-89, 93, 103
Strategic Concept of NATO
　redefining, 116
Strategic Defense Initiative (SDI), 134
Strategic partnership
　as an organizational arrangement, 112
Strategic Planning Unit, 3
Subnational groups
　developing democracy for and within, 202

Subregional organizations
  involved in peace-keeping and peace-related activities, 119-123
Sudden events
  coping with the impact of, 195-196
Support for emerging democracies
  challenges for the UN, 203
Supporting emerging democracies, 191
Supranational authorities, 228
Supreme Allied Commander in Europe (SACEUR), 69
Sur, Serge, 57
Surprise in gender gains, 256-258
Sustainable democracy
  building, 195-196
Sustainable human development (SHD)
  in the case studies, 279

T

Tabet, Mounir, 17-18, 261-295, 318
TCNs. *See* "Troop-Contributing Nations"
Technologies. *See* New technologies
Thakur, Ramesh, 1-6, 177, 318
Third World Conference on Women, 252
Threshold Test Ban Treaty (TTBT), 142
TNCs. *See* Transnational corporations
Tokyo Forum, 137
Transnational corporations (TNCs), 225-226
Transnational NGO networks, 207
Transparency in arms production
  need for, 104, 143
Transparency in military matters
  need for increased, 102-103
Treaty of Versailles, 174
Trends
  in arms transfers, 13-14, 82, 84-88
  in gender, 242-245
  global, towards democracy, 182-184
  going beyond, 188-191
  in intervention, 13, 46-76
  in military expenditure, 13-14, 79-83
Trilateral Initiative, 136
"Troop-Contributing Nations" (TCNs), 30, 44
TTBT. *See* Threshold Test Ban Treaty

U

Uganda Debt Network, 214
UN Blue Helmets, 128
UN Department of Public Information, 213
UN Development Fund for Women (UNIFEM), 255
UN Disarmament Commission (UNDC), 146
UN Disarmament Fellowship Programme, 145
UN Economic and Social Council (ECOSOC), 32, 306, 308, 311
UN Human Rights Commission, 204
UN Institute for Disarmament Research (UNIDIR), 145-146
UN Inter-Agency Standing Commission, 225
UN Monitoring, Verification, and Inspections Commission (UNMOVIC), 136
UN Office for the Coordination of Humanitarian Assistance (OCHA), 225, 234, 236
UN Register on Conventional Arms, 104
UN Special Commission (UNSCOM), 136
UNDC. *See* UN Disarmament Commission
UNDP. *See* United Nations Development Programme
UNEP. *See* United Nations Environmental Programme
Unexpected events
  coping with the impact of, 195-196
UNHCR. *See* United Nations High Commission for Refugees
UNICEF, 17, 221, 226, 234
UNIFEM. *See* UN Development Fund for Women
United Nations (UN), 1-2. *See also* Charter of the United Nations; Department of Peacekeeping Operations; General Assembly; Member States; Military Staff Committee; Secretary-General; Security Council
  as an interparliamentary body, 312
  challenges supporting emerging democracies, 203
  and the future of global governance, 176-179
  and human rights, 17, 220-241

"managers" of, 177, 179
managing a global GPG knowledge bank, 306-307
as a multi-actor venue, 308-310
perceptions of its acceptability, 177-178
present "crisis" in, 305-306
relations with the United States, 34
renaissance within, 109
reporting instrument on military expenditure, 103-104
reviving its role regarding weapons of mass destruction, 144-146
role in governing global public goods, 18, 296-315
role in interventions, 66-68
role of regional security developments in its promotion of peace and stability, 14, 108-130
role regarding civil society involvement in global government, 215-217
role regarding security challenges, 158-159
as a trusted convenor, 216
working with the international community, 254-255
United Nations Declaration on the Elimination of Violence against Women, 255-256
United Nations Development Programme (UNDP), 209, 226, 262
Bureau for Development Policy, 277
NetAid, 307
United Nations Environmental Programme (UNEP), 306-307, 310
United Nations High Commission for Human Rights, 29, 226-227, 238
United Nations High Commission for Refugees (UNHCR), 17, 27, 221, 234, 236
United Nations Institute for Training and Research (UNITAR), 145
United Nations International Conference on Population and Development, 251
United Nations Relief and Works Agency for Palestine Refugees in the Near East (UNRWA), 27
United Nations University (UNU)
millennium conference at, 3-4
mission and roles of, 2-3, 145

United States
Constitution and Bill of Rights, 228
leadership responsibility of, 142
relations with the UN, 34
role in human rights, 228-232
United States Arms Control and Disarmament Agency (ACDA), 84
"Uniting for Peace" resolution, 56
Universal Declaration of Human Rights, 185, 222
Unpredictability
in gender gains, 256-258
UNSC. *See* Security Council
Urquhart, Brian, 59
US-Japan defense agreement, 116, 124

V

Védrine, Hubert, 36
Verification challenge, 143-144
Versailles Conference, 171
Vienna Conference on Human Rights, 252, 255
Vienna Congress, 171
Vienna Declaration and Programme of Action, 178
Village assemblies, 274
Village development committees, 276
Violators of human rights
criminal action against, 236-237

W

Walker, Rob, 170
Walt, Stephen, 165
Warsaw Pact
dissolution of, 80, 109, 116
Wassenaar Arrangement, 140
Weapons delivery systems
outlook for the new millennium, 139-140
Weapons of mass destruction (WMD), 14-15, 131-149. *See also* Arms production; Conventional weapons
challenges and responses, 141-148
effects of globalization on, 140-141
growing access to, 153

INDEX

leading suppliers of major, 86
outlook for the new millennium, 132-140
reviving the role of the UN regarding, 144-146
Weber, Cynthia, 168
Wendt, Alexander, 172
Western European Union (WEU), 117, 121
Western institutions
  dominance in "global civil society," 166-167
Westphalian sovereignty, 170-171
WFP. *See* World Food Programme
WMD. *See* Weapons of mass destruction
Wolfensohn, James, 205
Women's Convention. *See* Commission on the Elimination of All Forms of Discrimination against Women
Working Group on the World Bank, 208
World Bank, 224-226
  bringing into the human rights movement, 224, 253-254
  Comprehensive Development Framework, 209
  forming partnerships with key NGOs, 209
  Global Development Network, 307
  Inspection Panel, 217
  International Development Association, 210
  version of "good governance," 163, 223
World Commission on Dams, 209
World Conference on Human Rights, 17, 243
World Court, 32
World Food Programme (WFP), 17, 227, 234
World Health Organization (WHO), 227, 306-307
  FluNet, 307
World military expenditure, 81-82, 105
World Trade Organization (WTO), 164, 173, 210, 231, 296
  alliances forged to frustrate, 5
  demonstrations challenging, 11, 223, 304, 314
World War II. *See* Second World War
WTO. *See* World Trade Organization

Y

Yeltsin, Boris, 38

Z

Zangger Committee, 140